DATE DUE		

Federalism in Canada and Australia: The Early Years

EDITED BY

BRUCE W. HODGINS
DON WRIGHT
W. H. HEICK

321.020971
F31
108869
Mar. 1979

Canadian Cataloguing in Publication Data

Main entry under title:

Federalism in Canada and Australia

Includes index.
ISBN 0-88920-061-0

1. Federal government - Canada - History -
Addresses, essays, lectures.   2. Federal government
- Australia - History - Addresses, essays,
lectures.   3. Canada - Politics and government -
Addresses, essays, lectures.   4. Australia -
Politics and government - Addresses, essays,
lectures.   I. Hodgins, Bruce W., 1931-
II. Wright, Don I.   III. Heick, W. H., 1930-

JL27.F43   321'.02'0971   C78-001441-3

Copyright © 1978
Wilfrid Laurier University Press
Waterloo, Ontario, Canada
N2L 3C5

Preface

This volume grew out of a desire on the part of the editors and some of the other contributors to see the history and politics of our two sister societies compared with one another rather than, as is traditional, with that of the United Kingdom and the United States. Some of us were particularly interested in promoting more contact and exchange among Canadian and Australian scholars who were investigating various features of the two societies. Because some of us were individually involved in aspects of federalist studies, an examination of the early evolution of federalism in what once were the two sister dominions seemed quite an appropriate area in which to begin comparisons.

The project was initiated by Bruce Hodgins when in 1970 he spent two terms as an honorary fellow of the history department of the Australian National University in Canberra. Close ties were then established among Don Wright, Ron Norris, the Reverend John Eddy and himself. We agreed that no single historian in either country then had the knowledge, inclination or wit to write a comprehensive comparative history of early federalism in the two societies. Even an introductory study would have to be a multiauthor effort, and most of the individual chapters would have to deal with an historical aspect of only one of the two federations. Comparisons would flow implicitly from the overall collection and explicitly from the Introduction and Epilogue. Bruce Hodgins returned to Australia for a month over Christmas-New Years, 1973-74, to facilitate final Australian and joint arrangements.

Meanwhile, we were putting together the Canadian part of the team. Three of the Canadians, Welf Heick, Ken Pryke and Bruce Hodgins, had all studied British Empire history, with a "dominion" emphasis, under the late W. B. Hamilton of Duke University's Commonwealth Studies Center. Tom Tanner was unique among the group in that he was a Canadian, teaching in Canada, who had obtained his doctorate in Australia on an Australian topic. Elwood Jones, Brian Young, Peter Toner, Donald Swainson and Rob Edwards had all been actively engaged in research connected with the regional aspects of the immediate pre- or post-Confederation years.

Coordination halfway around the world, even among friends, was not easy. Delays and frustrations were, perhaps unavoidable. Finally, we were able to assemble and edit the collection which is here presented by the editors, with thanks to all the other contributors.

Chapter One, "The Plans of Mice and Men," attempts a comparative overview of the planning and evolution of Canadian federalism from about 1864 to 1880 and of Australian federalism from about 1897 to 1914. In the notes for that chapter are explicit references to the other chapters of the volume, where matters being discussed only briefly in the Introduction are considered in greater depth. The chapters in the Canadian section examine the background and changes wrought in early Canadian federalism, generally relating the regional perspective to the national scene but ending with a study of the operation of federalism from the centre during the five years, 1873-78, when the Liberal prime ministership of Alexander Mackenzie interrupted the long Conservative reign of Sir John A. Macdonald. The chapters in the Australian section look at early federalism in that country more from the continental perspective, as befits its greater territorial social homogeneity, although there is a chapter on New South Wales before union and one examining the conflict among three states over the resources of an area, the Murray River valley, a conflict only resolved by major central intervention.

We should like to thank the many persons and institutions that made this volume possible. Individual authors would have their own lengthy lists. The Canada Council assisted Bruce Hodgins with three grants for research assistance and made his essential second trip to Australia possible. A generous grant from Trent University and assistance from the Australian National University Press facilitated publication. Thelma Chuter typed and retyped much of the manuscript and dispatched scores of letters and packets around Canada and across the Pacific. Archivists and librarians throughout the two societies were always cheerful and most helpful.

Bruce W. Hodgins
Don Wright
Welf H. Heick

July 1978

Contributors

Editor: Bruce W. Hodgins
Professor of History
Trent University

Coeditors: Don I. Wright
Senior Lecturer in History
University of Newcastle

Welf H. Heick
Professor of History
Wilfrid Laurier University

Other Contributors: J. J. Eddy, *S.J.*
Senior Fellow in History
Research School of Social Sciences
Australian National University

Robert C. Edwards
Statistics Canada

Elwood H. Jones
Associate Professor of History
Trent University

Ronald Norris
Senior Lecture in History
University of Adelaide

Kenneth Pryke
Professor of History
University of Windsor

Donald Swainson
Associate Professor of History
Queen's University

Tom Tanner
Algonquin College of Applied Arts & Technology

Peter Toner
Assistant Professor of History
University of New Brunswick

Brian Young
Associate Professor of History
McGill University

Abbreviations

CAO Commonwealth Archives Office

CHA Canadian Historical Association

CHR *Canadian Historical Review*

CLR *Commonwealth Law Reports*

CO Colonial Office

CPP *Commonwealth Parliamentary Papers*

NLA National Library of Australia

PAC Public Archives of Canada

Proclamations

VICTORIA'S PROCLAMATION

*Copy of historical document of Queen Victoria announcing
Confederation of Canada's Provinces*

A PROCLAMATION

For uniting the Provinces of Canada, Nova Scotia and New Brunswick into One Dominion, under the Name of CANADA.

VICTORIA R.

Whereas, by an Act of Parliament passed on the Twenty-ninth Day
of March, one thousand eight hundred and sixty-seven, in the
Thirtieth Year of our Reign, intituled—An Act for the Union of
Canada, Nova Scotia, and New Brunswick, and the Government
thereof, and for purposes connected therewith after divers Recitals,
it is enacted that it shall be lawful for the Queen, by and with the
Advice of Her Majesty's Most Honourable Privy Council, to declare
by Proclamation that on and after a Day therein appointed, not
being more than six months after the passing of the Act, the Provinces
of Canada, Nova Scotia, and New Brunswick shall form and be One
Dominion under the Name of Canada, and on and after that Day
those Three Provinces shall form and be One Dominion under that
Name accordingly: And it is thereby further enacted, that "such
Persons shall be first summoned to the Senate as the Queen by
Warrant under Her Majesty's Royal Sign Manual thinks fit to approve, and their names shall be inserted in the Queen's Proclamation
of Union." We therefore, by and with the Advice of Our Privy
Council, have thought fit to issue this Our Royal Proclamation and
we do Ordain, Declare, and Command, that on and after the First
Day of July, one thousand eight hundred and sixty-seven, the Provinces of Canada, Nova Scotia, and New Brunswick, shall form and
be One Dominion under the Name of Canada. And we do further
Ordain and Declare, that the Persons whose Names are herein
inserted and set forth are the Persons of whom We have, by Warrant
under our Royal Sign Manual, thought fit to approve as the Persons
who shall be first summoned to the Senate of Canada.

Given at Our Court at Windsor Castle this Twenty-second Day
of May in the Year of Our Lord One thousand eight hundred and
sixty-seven and in the Thirtieth Year of Our Reign.

GOD SAVE THE QUEEN

By the QUEEN.

A PROCLAMATION.

Victoria R.

WHEREAS by an Act of Parliament passed in the Sixty-third and Sixty-fourth Years of Our Reign intituled, "An Act to constitute the Commonwealth of *Australia*," it is enacted that it shall be lawful for the Queen, with the advice of the Privy Council, to declare by Proclamation, that, on and after a day therein appointed, not being later than One Year after the passing of this Act, the people of *New South Wales*, *Victoria*, *South Australia*, *Queensland*, and *Tasmania*, and also, if Her Majesty is satisfied that the people of *Western Australia* have agreed thereto, of *Western Australia*, shall be united in a Federal Commonwealth under the name of the Commonwealth of Australia.

And whereas We are satisfied that the people of *Western Australia* have agreed thereto accordingly.

We therefore, by and with the advice of Our Privy Council, have thought fit to issue this Our Royal Proclamation, and We do hereby declare that on and after the First day of *January* One thousand nine hundred and one, the people of *New South Wales*, *Victoria*, *South Australia*, *Queensland*, *Tasmania*, and *Western Australia* shall be united in a Federal Commonwealth under the name of the Commonwealth of *Australia*.

Given at Our Court at *Balmoral* this Seventeenth day of *September*, in the Year of our Lord One thousand nine hundred, and in the Sixty-fourth Year of Our Reign.

God Save the Queen.

Maps

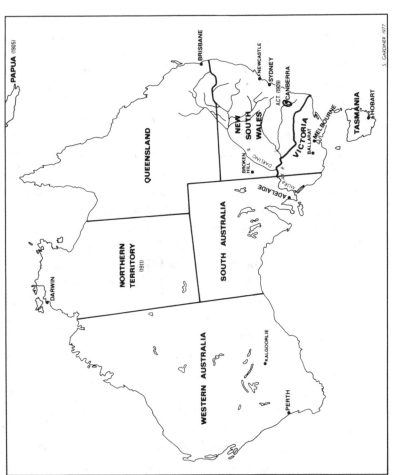

AUSTRALIA ABOUT 1912

S. GARDNER 1977

PAPUA (1905)

BRISBANE

NEWCASTLE

SYDNEY

A.C.T. (1909)
CANBERRA

QUEENSLAND

NEW
SOUTH
WALES

VICTORIA

BALLARAT

MELBOURNE

TASMANIA

HOBART

BROKEN
HILL

DARLING R.

MURRAY R.

ADELAIDE

NORTHERN
TERRITORY
(1911)

SOUTH AUSTRALIA

DARWIN

WESTERN AUSTRALIA

KALGOORLIE

PERTH

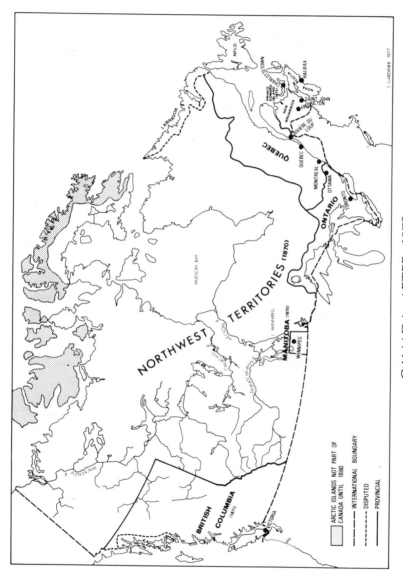

CANADA AFTER 1873

NORTHWEST TERRITORIES (1870)

QUÉBEC

ONTARIO

MANITOBA (1870)

BRITISH COLUMBIA (1871)

LABRADOR

NFLD.

HUDSON BAY

WINNIPEG

VICTORIA

TORONTO

OTTAWA

MONTREAL

QUÉBEC

RIVIÈRE DU LOUP

FREDERICTON

SAINT JOHN

CHARLOTTETOWN

PRINCE EDWARD ISLAND (1873)

NEW BRUNSWICK

N.S.

P.E.I.

HALIFAX

MACKENZIE R.

NELSON

SASKATCHEWAN

S. GARDINER 1977

ARCTIC ISLANDS NOT PART OF CANADA UNTIL 1880

----- INTERNATIONAL BOUNDARY
------ DISPUTED
———— PROVINCIAL

Table of Contents

Introduction

I

The Plans of Mice and Men

BRUCE W. HODGINS

"The primary error at the formation of their constitution," argued John A. Macdonald about the United States, "was that each state reserved to itself all sovereign rights save the small portion delegated." Macdonald, the leader of the Conservatives of Upper Canada, was speaking in 1864 to the Quebec Conference on British North American union. "We must reverse this process," continued the man who would become the first prime minister of Canada after union,

> by strengthening the General Government and conferring on the Provincial bodies only such powers as may be required for local purposes. All sectional prejudices and interests can be legislated for by local legislatures. Thus we shall have a strong and lasting government under which we can work out constitutional liberty as opposed to democracy and be able to protect the minority by having a powerful central government.[1]

"Government at a central and distant point can never be government by the people," declared John A. Cockburn of South Australia. It "may be just as crushing a tyranny under republican or commonwealth forms as under the most absolute monarchy."[2] Cockburn, a leading liberal democrat, was speaking in 1891 to the Sydney Convention on Australian federation. The fathers of Australian federation examined and consciously rejected the centralist sentiments successfully enunciated by Macdonald, sentiments which in 1867 had found expression in the British North America Act. In 1901, J. Quick and R. R. Garran, noted participants in the Australian federal movement and authorities on the resultant Constitution Act, commented critically on the British North America Act. They called it "the semi-federal Constitution of the Dominion of Canada."[3] It was simply too centralist. The provinces

---

1 G. P. Browne, ed., *Documents on the Confederation of British North America* (Toronto, 1969), pp. 94-95.
2 John A. Cockburn, *Australian Federation* (London, 1901), p. 117.
3 *Annotated Constitution of the Australian Commonwealth* (Melbourne, 1901), p. vii.

were under too much supervision. Quick and Garran would not have troubled the Canadian Fathers. Before the Quebec Conference, the *Montreal Gazette* wrote approvingly that the resultant resolutions would achieve "legislative union with a constitutional recognition of a federal principle."[4] A few months later Macdonald secretly reassured one of the very few Upper Canadian Conservatives who opposed the plan that he was certain that within their lifetimes they would "see both Local Parliaments and Governments absorbed in the General Power."[5] In Britain, the Little Englander, Goldwin Smith, seemed to agree: "They intend to create not a federation but a kingdom, and practically to extinguish the independent existence of the several provinces."[6] The Canadian union deliberately emphasized the central supervision of the units and central protection of minorities. The Australian union, in contrast, knowingly emphasized states rights.

In each case, within a short time after union, a pattern would emerge that would tend to reverse the situation. The reasons are complex and elusive but primarily social and cultural. In neither case, in these early years, was the pattern absolutely clear or decisive. Countervailing tendencies certainly existed. Australia was not becoming a unitary state, and Canada was not breaking up; indeed in Canada the electorate seemed to be backing something called a National Policy. Yet by 1880 in Canada and by 1914 in Australia, the trend away from the intentions of the Fathers was significant. It would, with interruptions, complications and contradictions continue. Today, Canada is one of the most decentralized operative federations in the world and Australia one of the more centralized ones. Canada has not disintegrated, though elements of the population and not just in Quebec, talk of separatism or extreme decentralism. In Australia many voices, especially in the Australian Labor Party, see the states as anachronistic and call for the establishment of a unitary system.

The centralist sentiments of Sir John A. Macdonald, the conservative, are echoed in the voices of the Australian social democrats, while the decentralist sentiments of John A. Cockburn, the liberal democrat, find expression in the voices of Canadians from many regions and political persuasions. Australia is a land of diminishing regional cultural differences and an increasingly common political system; Canada remains a land of "limited identities,"[7] with deep-rooted regional diversities and an official commitment to mosaic, not melting pot, a mosaic now based on "a policy of multiculturalism within a bilingual

4 9 September 1864.
5 PAC., Macdonald Papers, Macdonald to M. C. Cameron, 19 December 1864.
6 "The Proposed Constitution for British North America," *MacMillan's Magazine,* March 1865, p. 408.
7 Phrase used by Ramsey Cook and J. M. S. Careless. Note the latter's "'Limited Identities' in Canada," *CHR* 50 (March 1969): 1-10.

framework."[8] In Canada the subordinate federalism of 1867 has been transformed into coordinate federalism and an uneven development of provincial rights. In Australia, the coordinate federation of 1901 has been transformed into state subordination or structural federalism, a system which might be defined as one in which the units survive principally because of habit rather than because of their regional social diversity.[9] Yet in each case the constitutional acts have not been severely altered.

In 1867 the British North Americans were only in part the precarious and divided possessors of half a continent: they were, moreover, living beside an ambitious, mighty, though recently most-troubled nation. The British North Americans were not a single people, though they did all owe allegiance to a common though distant Queen. True, two-thirds of the non-aboriginal people were of Anglo-Celtic stock, but these people were not products of a single temporal migration. The three Maritime provinces were clearly the products of eighteenth-century settlement, more remnants of the first British Empire than creatures of the second. Further east, old and aloof Newfoundland, with its fisheries, had its own unique history which was full of Irish troubles. Upper Canada, like New South Wales, was basically an expanding nineteenth-century creation. Its roots and memory, however, involved (as did those of New Brunswick) a complex eighteenth century counter-revolutionary migration north from the now republican south, by Americans who had often lived there for many generations. Although the Anglo-Celt controlled the commercial life of Lower Canada, the bulk of its people were French-speaking products of the seventeenth century's counter-reformation. They had once been conquered and later felt deserted and alienated. In the late 1830s they had been humiliated again, some would say conquered again.[10] Now individually free and self-governing British subjects, they were at best psychologically fettered, surviving but not maturing as a people. The union of 1867 initially involved only the four principal eastern provinces. (Since 1841, the two Canadas had been forcibly united in a less than happy legislative union.) Beyond the indefinite western border of Upper Canada lay the vast reaches of the North-West, British, but partly and ineffectively ruled by a remote mercantile company; the North-West was a land inhabited by Indian tribes and the increasingly articulate and self-conscious Métis nation, a nation

8 Statement by P. E. Trudeau, Canada, *House of Commons Debates*, 3rd session, 28 parl., vol. 8 (8 October 1971), p. 8545.

9 Michael Stein, "Federal Political Systems and Federal Societies," in *Canadian Federation: Myth or Reality*, ed. J. Peter Meekison, 2nd ed. (Toronto, 1971), pp. 30-42, with acknowledgements to W. S. Livingston and Aaron Wildavsky.

10 Michel Brunet, "The French Canadians' Search for a Fatherland," in *Nationalism in Canada*, ed. Peter Russell (Toronto, 1966), pp. 49-51; Léandre Bergeron, *The History of Quebec: A Patriot's Handbook* (Toronto, 1971), pp. 76-110.

which was the product of the fur trade union of French voyageurs and Indian women. Beyond the distant snow-capped mountains, on the Pacific rim, lay Vancouver Island and the gold fields of British Columbia, in many ways more like Australian colonies than Canadian ones.[11] In 1870 the huge North-West was joined to the new dominion, and within it the tiny Manitoba was created at the Métis centre on the Red River. In 1871 British Columbia joined Canada. After union, a Canada without its central government was unthinkable. Canadians had little in common apart from their external allegiance, their federal government and their rejection—by a majority but not by a consensus—of republican America and its assimilationist democracy. Under the circumstances, the conservative elite of English-speaking Canada constrained themselves to imitate as much as practicable the British constitution and to give as much power as politically possible to the central authorities.

The Australians of 1900, in contrast to the British Americans of 1867, were indeed the possessors of a continent. Nowhere else in the world could there be, as Edmund Barton, who was to become Australia's first prime minister, said, "a nation for a continent and a continent for a nation."[12] Nearly all of its non-aboriginal people were of Anglo-Celtic stock and nearly all of them products of a nineteenth-century (or very late eighteenth-century) migration. The pattern of settlement and development in South Australia, that "paradise of dissent,"[13] was somewhat different, somewhat more North American-like[14] than that of the eastern colonies; Western Australia was somewhat of a latecomer constitutionally and culturally. Sydney was clearly not Melbourne. In Melbourne, Adelaide, Hobart and Perth, people played Australian-rules football; in Sydney and Brisbane it was British rugby. Yet regional diversity was hardly fundamental.[15] Although great rivalries existed, Australians had a common language and a common culture—so much so that many saw no particular need and had no particular emotional desire to establish an Australian government. Already, Australia-wide cricket teams were playing test matches against England.[16] Australians owed allegiance to a common

11 Obvious class divisions and class politics, small agrarian especially yeoman elements, emphasis on exploitive industries, and urban development. Martin Robin, *The Rush for Spoils: The Company Province, 1871-1933* (Toronto, 1972).

12 R. R. Garran claimed that he "jotted down" the famous phrase when Barton "coined" it "impromptu" at a public meeting in Ashfield, called to promote the federation movement. R. R. Garran, *Prosper the Commonwealth* (Sydney, 1958), p. 101.

13 Douglas Pike, *Paradise of Dissent: South Australia 1829-1857* (Melbourne, 1957).

14 Russel Ward, *Australia* (Englewood Cliffs, N.J., 1965), p. 42.

15 Ibid., pp. 78-79 and 92-93. Note also Ronald Norris, "Toward a Federal Union," chapter 10 below and J. J. Eddy, "Politics of New South Wales: The Federation Issue and the Move Away from Faction and Parochialism," chapter 11 below.

16 W. F. Mandle, "Cricket and Australian Nationalism in the Nineteenth Century," *Journal of the Royal Australian Historical Society* 59 (December 1973): 225-46. In 1882 Australia first won a test match in England.

though distant Queen. Isolated in the alien antipodes from their European and northern homeland, "living in a harsh and uncouth land,"[17] they were united by the "tyranny of distance."[18] Most Australians were urban dwellers. Australia had a large urban working class and a democratic elite which emphasized its cultural links with England. The country folk beyond the ranges, the people of the outback, both squatter and shearer, were different from the city folk.[19] But each of the colonies was urban-led. No colony was formed in the outback. The coordinate federalism established in Australia was not based upon an essentially federal society. It had other, more purely political or parochial bases.

Today no Australian state or group of states is a region in the North American sense of the term. Only the original six states exist, although the Northern Territory has potential for a future seventh. The people of the Riverina are ruled from far off Sydney and are separated from their neighbours in the Victorian Mallee, on the other side of the great Murray River, who are ruled from Melbourne. New England remains a part of New South Wales, not a state in its own right nor linked with the neighbouring Darling Downes of Queensland. Australia has no inland states. Broken Hill has little chance of becoming the capital of a mid-western state. Even on the northeast coast, Townsville and Cairns are subservient to distant Brisbane, and in the west, Perth rules an empire about the size of western Europe. The state boundaries do not have important social significance.[20]

In Australia the trend toward increasing initiative at the central level was thus facilitated by the relative lack of regional differences among the Australian people. In Canada the trend toward increasing initiative and power of the unit level was facilitated by the profound vitality of the country's regional diversity.

Not only did the roots of regionalism go deeper in British North America than in Australia, but British North American union was accomplished in the twilight of the pre-democratic era, after the

17 C. M. H. Clark, *History of Australia*, vol. 3: *The Beginning of an Australian Civilization, 1824-1851* (Melbourne, 1973), p. vii.

18 Geoffrey Blainey, *The Tyranny of Distance: How Distance Shaped Australia's History* (Melbourne, 1966).

19 Sean Glynn, *Urbanization in Australian History, 1799-1900* (Melbourne, 1970), especially p. 50.

20 Before becoming Labor Prime Minister of Australia, Gough Whitlam wrote, "We will not return power to the people simply by concentrating assistance for the existing States with their irrelevant State boundaries and malapportioned electoral boundaries." "A New Federalism," *The Australian Quarterly* 43 (September 1971): 17. Note also Don Wright, "The River Murray: Microcosm of Australian Federal History," chapter 15 below, and C. F. J. Whebell, "Non-National Separatism: with Special Reference to Australian Cases Past and Present," *The Politics of Separatism* (University of London, Institute of Commonwealth Studies, collected seminar papers, no. 19, ed. W. H. Morris-Jones, 1976), pp. 19-30.

achievement of responsible government yet before the achievement of political democracy, certainly before democracy became an article of faith.[21] By the time Australian union was accomplished, some thirty-five years later, political democracy in Australia had become a reality. The electorate had to be considered much more directly. In each case union was the achievement of relatively small elites. In each case the populace was involved in the story. In Canada's case the history of the popular side is seen basically in the newspapers and public gatherings, plus two confusing elections in New Brunswick.[22] In Australia's case the populace was involved through the press and political meetings but also and especially in the campaigns and voting for the various referenda; the secret ballot and manhood suffrage existed for the voting in the eastern colonies, and in South Australia women also had the franchise.[23] The Canadian predemocratic political leadership was somewhat more removed from the attitudes of the populace, or more correctly the local, informed elements of the populace, than was its Australian counterpart. The pro-Confederation political leadership agreed upon a union which, while assuring the French Canadians of *la survivance*, would create something as closely akin as possible to the legislative union of the United Kingdom of Great Britain and Ireland. The best phrase to describe this "Macdonaldian constitution"[24] is subordinate federalism. The Macdonaldian constitution, noble in design, was doomed by its elitist origins on the eve of the emergence of political democracy, a democracy which, with strong regionalism and localism, would be anti-centralist. In Canada the progressive, democratic forces were localist and particularist; in the hands of clever, dynamic politicians, especially in wealthy Ontario, these forces could be transformed into pressures for provincial rights.

In Australia these progressive forces were different. By 1890 the great achievements of liberal society lay in the past. Labour groups, led by the Labor Party of New South Wales and its parent the Trades and Labor Council, sought mainly to restrain, reform and "civilize capitalism,"[25] while a few socialist members sought to replace that system. Labour groups had a social programme. If unenthusiastic about federation in 1899, they had a tendency to think of and work for

21 Bruce W. Hodgins, "Democracy and the Ontario Fathers of Confederation," in *Canadian History Since Confederation*, eds. Bruce W. Hodgins and Robert Page (Georgetown, Ontario, 1972), pp. 21-31. Note also Elwood H. Jones, "Localism and Federalism in Upper Canada to 1865," chapter 2 below and the author's, "The Canadian Elite's Attitude Toward the Plan of Union," chapter 3 below.

22 P. B. Waite, *Life and Times of Confederation: Politics, Newspapers, and the Union of British North America* (Toronto, 1962).

23 J. A. La Nauze, *The Making of the Australian Constitution* (Melbourne, 1972).

24 W. L. Morton, "Confederation, 1870-1896: The End of the Macdonaldian Constitution and the Return to Duality," *Journal of Canadian Studies* 1 (May 1966): 11-24.

25 Bede Nairn, *Civilising Capitalism: The Labor Movement in New South Wales, 1870-1900* (Canberra, 1973), p. 6.

the unity of the entire Australian working class, urban and rural. From 1900, Australian Labor had a "federal platform" and together with advanced liberals tended to welcome central initiative, especially in social policy and in matters affecting the racial security of the Australian people.

Ironically, less popular interest seems to have been shown by Australians in their scheme for union than by British North Americans in their scheme, although the latter had no opportunity to choose convention delegates nor to vote on the matter (except peculiarly in New Brunswick). Yet Australian states rights was weakened by the further development toward social democracy, in a society where class division and intrastate divisions were more important than regional, interstate divisions and in which the distance from friends abroad produced a desire for concerted action. The democratic thrust of the Australian union was clear from the beginning. Both the statement by the radical liberal, Charles Kingston, that the union was "the most democratic measure ever framed" and that by his more orthodox fellow South Australian, R. C. Baker, that "never . . . has a more democratic Constitution been submitted for the approval of any people" show the flavour of the times and would have been inconceivable in Canada during the 1860s.[26] Quick and Garran agreed with the Nova Scotian and New Brunswick exponents of a unit-based senate. "The Senate is one of the most conspicuous and unquestionably the most important of all the federal features of the Constitution, using the word federal in the sense of linking together and uniting a number of co-equal political communities under a common system of government." Furthermore, they argued, "the principle of popular election, on which the Senate of the Commonwealth is founded, is more in harmony with the progressive instincts and tendencies of the times than those according to which the Senate of the United States and the Senate of Canada are called into existence."[27]

In Upper Canada, George Brown of the Toronto *Globe* was the leader of the pro-union Reformers or Grits. Like Quick and Garran, this mid-Victorian British-style liberal championed the lower house as the national chamber, with representation based solidly on population. Indeed, for his own Ontario, Brown secured a unicameral legislature which ultimately became the pattern for all of the provinces. Yet Brown denounced "democracy" and feared the "ignorant unreasoning mass."[28] Brown would not have agreed with the following from Quick and Garran:

26 Cited in Ron Norris, "Economic Influences on the 1898 South Australian Federation Referendum," in *Essays in Australian Federation*, ed. A. W. Martin (Melbourne, 1969), p. 138.
27 *Annotated Constitution*, p. 448.
28 *Globe* (Toronto), 23 September 1857. Note also the author's, "The Canadian Elite's Attitude Toward the Plan of Union," chapter 3 below.

The House of Representatives is not only the national chamber; it is the general depository and embodiment of the liberal principles of government which pervade the entire constitutional fabric. It is the chamber in which the progressive interests and popular aspirations of the people will be most likely to make themselves first felt.[29]

The issues which came to the fore in Canada after 1867 generally divided Canadians rather than unified them. After Confederation and especially after the Treaty of Washington in 1871, the threat to Canadian survival from the United States subsided. The recurring depressions of the late century militated against the development of national sentiment. Local issues predominated. Majoritarian ideas grew, but focussed on the local level. At times the distant central authority seemed like an alien marshall to a respectable mob bent on a respectable lynching. Language, cultural and religious[30] issues repeatedly surfaced. In Ontario, people thought that they were Canadians—there was no separatism—but they were Ontarians first.[31] In Quebec, although provincial rights was weak politically until the premiership of Honoré Mercier, 1887 to 1891, concern was almost exclusively for *la survivance* and provincial development.[32] Nova Scotians, as prosperity faded into chronic difficulty, clearly were Nova Scotians first.[33] It was too early at the national level for a social democratic or labour party demanding social welfare and governmental intervention. Only in British Columbia did social democratic parties appear in any serious form before World War One. Furthermore, the late-century blossoming of imperialist sentiment[34] did little to enhance the prestige of a federal government for whom external affairs often produced internal paralysis. While the Montreal "Anglostocracy" obtained the Canadian Pacific Railway, it could not keep its monopoly over the West. Ontarians peopled what became the prairie provinces, and Toronto business secured the ascendancy in the West. But the championing of provincial rights by Ontario did not prevent Toronto and Montreal business from using the federal government to maintain an imperial relationship over the West.[35] These interests endorsed a national or

29 *Annotated Constitution*, p. 448.
30 See Peter Toner, "New Brunswick Schools and the Rise of Provincial Rights," chapter 7 below.
31 See the author's, "Federalism and the Politics of Ontario, 1867-1880," chapter 4 below.
32 See Brian Young, "Federalism in Quebec: The First Years After Confederation," chapter 5 below.
33 G. A. Rawlyk, "Nova Scotia Regional Protest, 1867-1969," in *Canadian History Since Confederation*, pp. 209-24. Note also Kenneth Pryke, "Federation and Nova Scotia Politics," chapter 6 below.
34 Robert Page, "The Canadian Response to the 'Imperial' Idea During the Boer War Years," in *Canadian History Since Confederation*, pp. 291-316, and Carl Berger, *Sense of Power: Studies in the Ideas of Canadian Imperialism, 1867-1914* (Toronto, 1970).
35 See Donald Swainson, "Canada Annexes the West: Colonial Status Confirmed," chapter 8 below.

imperial policy of railway development and high tariffs. They endorsed the withholding of land and other natural resources from the jurisdiction of Manitoba, which was kept inordinately small, and of Saskatchewan and Alberta, whose very creation as provinces was delayed until 1905. Nevertheless, while the Judicial Committee of the Privy Council, with its tendency toward decentralist decisions, undoubtedly misrepresented the aims of the Fathers, it did not misrepresent the sentiments of the people.

Before World War One, despite the resounding defeat of the centralizing amendment concerning industrial powers in 1911, Australia had moved away from the very limited union envisioned by most of the Fathers.[36] Among British North Americans there was no character comparable to Alfred Deakin, no philosopher king who was at the same time a master pragmatic politician.[37] Yet Deakin was hardly displeased at the overall centralizing trend. He had always wanted great national sentiment, and he moved centralist with the times. Between 1901 and 1914, federal politicians, Labor and non-Labor, could capitalize on both the pressure for social legislation[38] and also the growing sense of isolation and insecurity, ironically in a great age of imperial sentiment. This sentiment plus the apparent need for defence and the desire to preserve "white Australia" helped to facilitate the quiet trend toward Australian rather than state solutions.[39] In some areas at least, central action seemed popular, even if there was a contradictory desire on the part of many to confine the sphere of that action. Central politicians could, and did, try to set the pace; though they often met with stiff opposition, it became increasingly clear that the future was theirs. The social dichotomy, which was reflected in the polarization of Australian politics into two competing alliances, made it appear desirable that certain matters should be settled once for the whole nation, and not six times over. The constitution designed for a loose federation by a leadership which, with a few exceptions, wanted only a limited union, a sort of business merger which would establish a common market, incidentally, almost accidentally, gave fiscal superiority to the central authority. This became especially evident after 1910, when the constitutional arrangement for the dispersal to the states of three-quarters of the customs revenue ended, but it was visible even

36 D. I. Wright, *Shadow of Dispute: Aspects of Commonwealth-State Relations, 1901-1910* (Canberra, 1970), and his "An Open Wrestle for Mastery: Commonwealth-State Relations, 1901-1914," chapter 12 below.
37 J. A. LaNauze, *Alfred Deakin: A Biography*, 2 vols. (Melbourne, 1965).
38 See Ronald Norris, "Federal Politics and Social Policies," chapter 15 below.
39 See Tom Tanner, "Race as a Factor in the Strengthening of Central Authority: White Australia and the Establishment of Compulsory Military Training," chapter 13 below and also J. J. Eddy, "Imperial Sentiment as a Factor in Centralizing Australian Federalism," chapter 14 below.

before that date.[40] The central government was able to use its fiscal superiority without a great public uproar. Furthermore, men who had been involved in the creation of the Australian nation were appointed to the High Court. The written constitution, the High Court and the central government all worked, though unevenly, to limit the role of the alien Judicial Committee of the Privy Council.

After union, decentralist politicians did exist in Australia, and their sentiment had considerable popular following. In 1906, Sir Samuel Way, Chief Justice of South Australia, claimed that the authority of the central government was "like a foreign occupation."[41] J. H. Carruthers of New South Wales took a position very similar to that of his counterpart Oliver Mowat of Ontario, but Carruthers was premier for only three years (1904-07), whereas Mowat was premier for twenty-four (1872-96). Even W. A. Holman, Labor Premier of New South Wales (1913-16), had strong tendencies towards states rights. Yet states rights in Australia lacked deep social roots. Large social, ethnic or religious forces identified with such rights were absent. Based on isolation and economic frustration, secessionist sentiment would temporarily develop in Western Australia. But Western Australia was not Ontario nor Quebec. It was more like Nova Scotia. When Nova Scotians voted for secession in 1886, it was because they were frustrated not by lack of provincial power but by depression, by alleged lack of justice for the Maritimes, by lack of concern in Ottawa. By 1910 the turnout for Australian federal elections had surpassed the turnout for state elections. Canadian federal politicians would certainly have envied having the sectionally unifying issues open to their Australian counterparts.

Australia in 1914 and Canada in 1880, indeed Canada in 1914 as both sister societies faced the onslaught of World War One, were still federations. They had significantly modified their practice from the intentions of their respective fathers. They had not, however, moved beyond the spectrum of federalism.

Authorities disagree as to the definition of federalism, but most of those in the western world would agree that federalism must involve a major division in the exercise of sovereignty between a central authority and territorially-based unit authorities. This is true among those who classically emphasize the separation of the two levels, the limitation on power, and the coordinate nature of what they see as genuine federalism. It is equally true among those who behaviourly emphasize the need for cooperation, interaction, and concerted effort. Many countries formally have federal constitutions. Few, however, actually operate federal systems.[42] Today, empirically, probably only seven

40 D. I. Wright, "The Politics of Federal Finance: The First Decade," *Historical Studies* 13 (April 1969): 460-76, and his "An Open Wrestle for Mastery," chapter 12 below.
41 Cited in Wright, *Shadow of Dispute*, p. xiv.
42 Geoffrey F. Sawer, *Modern Federalism* (London, 1969) and the author's review of this work in the *Canadian Forum* 51 (July-August 1971). Note also D. J. Elazar,

operative federations exist in the entire world. Four are predominantly English-speaking, or at least flow from some adaptation of the English tradition—though that tradition itself is quite anti-federal; they are the United States, Canada, Australia, and India. Three are predominantly German-speaking; they are Switzerland, Austria and the Federal Republic of Germany. The former are all extensive in geographical size, the latter rather restricted and contiguous one to another. Some might argue that despite its one-party structure Yugoslavia has entered the spectrum. Others might argue that India's recent past irregularities would place that union beyond the spectrum or that in Austria, power is so centralized that its federalism is purely nominal. On the remaining five there is a clear consensus that they exist under a federal system.

When, however, the monarchical and dependent Canadian union was being formed, only the United States and Switzerland existed as genuine federations. They were both republics. Sovereignty in the United States was said to reside undivided in the people and to find limited expression through the two levels of government. A different concept was necessary for Canada. The Fathers wanted to avoid the dangerous doctrine of popular sovereignty. For this reason, to say nothing of the added insecurity which an independent Canada would face before the American threat, the Fathers were united in their desire to preserve the country "under the Crown of the United Kingdom of Great Britain and Ireland, with a Constitution similar in Principle to that of the United Kingdom."[43] The imperial connection was vital in avoiding the technical issue of divided sovereignty and the ideological issue of popular sovereignty, with all its democratic implications. Besides, much of the British North American leadership believed that the current, close and bloody American Civil War had been caused by arguments over the exercise of sovereignty, inflamed by the faith in democracy. Although Macdonald and his colleagues saw the provinces as subordinate entities under an imperial self-governing dominion in permanent alliance with Great Britain, where resided the Queen, the union of 1867 nevertheless made a major contribution to political theory. It established a monarchical federation under a single, if external, sovereign.[44] Victorian Canadian conservatives held as enobling the

"Federalism," *International Encyclopedia of the Social Sciences* 5 (New York, 1968), p. 364; E. R. Black, *Divided Loyalties: Canadian Concepts of Federalism* (Montreal, 1975); and for the classical view, K. C. Wheare, *Federal Government*, 4th ed. (London, 1946).

43 British North America Act 1867, Preamble.

44 It could be argued that it was New Zealand which first attempted such a system. From 1852 to 1876, that colony had what C. Hartley Grattan calls a "pseudo federal system," although the provincial regimes could be and indeed in 1876 were abolished by the central legislatures. *The Southwest Pacific to 1900: A Modern History* (Ann Arbor, 1963), p. 389. Note also G. Rutherford, *Sir George Grey: A Study in Colonial Government* (London, 1961), pp. 234-51 and 588-99; Grey, who was vainly trying to save the provinces after having been the author (as governor) of the constitution and now a

British concept of "due subordination,"[45] or *parva sub ingenti*, the small under the protection of the great, as the motto of Prince Edward Island aptly described it. It was therefore logical that the representative of the crown in Canada should continue to be styled governor general, that the titular head of a province should be styled lieutenant governor and be appointed by the governor general in council, that provincial bills could be reserved for the governor general's pleasure and provincial acts within a year disallowed by him, that the residual power should rest with the central parliament, and that the senate, though based on regional representation, should essentially be a house of life peers formally appointed by the governor general.

When the Australian colonies came to federate, the Canadian example of a monarchical federation already existed. This the Australians took for granted, hardly aware of the contribution Canadians had made to their nationhood. Australia therefore also united "under the Crown of the United Kingdom of Great Britain and Ireland."[46] The democratic Australian political leadership examined the Canadian subordinate federalism and basically rejected it—rejecting more the form and intent of 1867 than the coordinate federalist reality of 1897.[47] It was appropriate that the representative of the crown at the central level in Australia be styled governor general but that the titular head of a state (not province) be styled governor as himself the representative of the crown and appointed by the Queen, that state bills and acts not be subject to central supervision, that the residual power should rest with the state parliaments, and that the senate should be set up as a genuine states house, with equal representation from each state and senators elected by the people for a set term.

Political leadership is, however, ephemeral. The Christian gentlemen from North America, who in 1867 persuaded the British gov-

local politician, claimed in 1874 that New Zealand had set the federal example for Canada and the whole British Empire (see p. 590).
45 S. F. Wise, "Conservatism and Political Development: The Canadian Case," *South Atlantic Quarterly* 69 (Spring 1970): 232-33.
46 Commonwealth of Australia Constitution Act, 1900, Preamble.
47 The Canadian system did have its Australian defenders, rather more in 1891 than in 1897. One, G. B. Barton, who vehemently opposed the American system, wrote approvingly of Canada that "The Dominion Government in fact is a federal one rather in appearance than in reality. The provincial Governments are so completely overshadowed by it that they are lost to the view of the outside spectator. All he can clearly distinguish is an ambitious structure framed and decorated in close imitation of the Houses at Westminster, but bearing no resemblance to those at Washington." In 1867 Macdonald would have agreed; in 1897 it was not the reality. National Library of Australia, N.S.W. Parl. Papers, LVI, A2, pp. 343ff., G. B. Barton, "Notes on Australian Federation and the Draft Constitution Bills Framed by the Conventions of 1891 and 1897," (Sydney, 1897, reprinted from the *Evening News*), p. 17; other important Canadian references are on pp. 16-20, 30, 51, 58-59. The Barton file also contains the revealing "Comparative Analysis of the Australian Commonwealth Bill 1891 and Four Federal Constitutions" [Canada, United States, German Empire and Switzerland], prepared by E. Carlile, Parliamentary Draftsman, Victoria.

ernment and parliament to establish "One Dominion"[48] called Canada, and the Australian gentlemen, who "humbly relying on the blessing of Almighty God" persuaded the British government and parliament to establish "one indesoluble Federal Commonwealth,"[49] generally wished their union to prosper under the original dispensation. Social and rising intellectual forces in the two countries inclined the new nations otherwise.

Some authorities have argued that "a great democracy must either sacrifice self-government to unity, or preserve it by federalism," that federalism amidst diversity is the greatest achievement of the mind of enlightened man, the epitome of liberalism.[50] Others have seen federalism as a permanent or hopefully temporary concession to parochialism and human frailty or to the problems of communication, at worst a necessary though divisive force, at best a device to lessen the weight of technological and bureaucratic bigness.[51] Some see it as a glorified military or economic alliance. Some see it as the hope of the future, leading through the union of countries toward the brotherhood of men. Others, radical decentralists and peace-loving philosophical anarchists, see federalism, if strictly limited, as an unfortunately necessary concession to the problems and realities of the contemporary world.[52] Others, claiming to be shorn of all liberal illusions and myths, see federalism as an unstable structure, securely based, like other human institutions, upon coercion and institutionalized violence. They see a dominant "federating power" and a largely passive but not powerless "federated power"; through conflict, the relative strength of the two or more powers changes on the basis ultimately of their usable political muscle. Thus the basis of the federation changes, or federalism ceases effectively to exist, either through the absorption of the weaker elements or the effective separation from the whole of one or more of the units.[53]

Many of these views, and not just the last mentioned, emphasize the social dimension or roots of federalism, without denying the role of

48 BNA Act, Preamble.

49 Constitution Act, Preamble.

50 Quotation from Lord Acton, "Nationality" [1862], in his *Essays on Freedom and Power* (New York, 1955), p. 148. Acton and these sentiments were endorsed by P. E. Trudeau, "The Practice and Theory of Federalsim" [1961], in his *Federalism and the French Canadians* (Toronto, 1968), pp. 124-50, and by R. C. Cook, *Canada and the French-Canadian Question* (Toronto, 1966), pp. 1-5, 103 and 141.

51 W. L. Morton, "The Conservative Principle in Confederation," in *Canadian History Since Confederation*, pp. 32-47. Note also J. A. Corry, "Constitutional Trends and Federalism," in A. R. M. Lower *et al.*, *Evolving Canadian Federalism* (Durham, N.C., 1958), pp. 92-125.

52 George Woodcock, "A Plea for the Anti-Nations," in *Nationalism or Local Control: Responses to George Woodcock*, eds. Viv Nelles and Abraham Rotstein (Toronto, 1973), pp. 1-11.

53 [Michel Brunet], *Le federalisme, l'acte de l'amérique du nord britannique et les Canadiens français* (Montréal, 1964) and Jean-Marc Léger, "Ce pays qui s'appellera le Québec," *Le Devoir* (Montréal), 4, 5, 7, 8 février 1977.

economic factors or political history. A federal system is thus ultimately based upon the diverse regional qualities of a society, upon what might be called a federal society.[54] In the eyes of the political leadership of British North America in the mid-1860s and of Australia in the late 1890s, their societies were federal. This leadership recognized, however, that the regional diversity of British North American society was much greater than that of Australian society. In Australia the chief differences lay in the operation of economies and in political administration, and distance seemed to magnify the significance of such social diversity as did exist.

Most of the Australian leadership wanted a limited union and most of the Canadian leadership craved a more centralized union. As the federal aspects of Australian society gradually declined or were seen to decline, Australian federalism, directed by dynamic leadership, gradually centralized. As the regionally diverse and pluralistic aspects of Canadian society remained clearly manifest,[55] as Canadian identity remained decidedly limited, Canadian federalism, guided by dynamic provincial politicians, decentralized. In each case the relative strength of democracy and the social and intellectual style of politics were crucial to the change. In each case, the units operated under the British parliamentary system. In Canada, the Ontario legislature led the way in making good its claim to being a parliament equal in status within its sphere of broadening power to the parliament at Westminster. The parliamentary system, on the other hand, did not save the Australian states from a gradual loss of power.[56] Driven socially by comparable populist or democratic elements and without significantly amending their formal constitutions, the two nations were switching sides within the federal spectrum.

54 W. S. Livingston, "A Note on the Nature of Federalism," in *Canadian Federalism: Myth or Reality*, pp. 19-30; and Michael Stein, "Federal Political Systems and Federal Societies," in ibid., pp. 30-42.
55 See W. H. Heick, "Alexander Mackenzie and Canadian Federalism," chapter 9 below.
56 Given the Canadian experience, one must question the generality of the following: "Responsible government in a two or virtually two party system proved to be the force which pushed classical federalism relentlessly to the wall." L. F. Crisp, *Australian National Government*, new ed. (Croydon, 1970), p. 38. See the author's, "Federalism and the Politics of Ontario, 1867-1880," chapter 4 below; Don Wright, "An Open Wrestle for Mastery," chapter 12 below; and Ronald Norris, "Federal Politics and Social Policies," chapter 15 below.

Canada

II

Localism and Federalism in Upper Canada to 1865

ELWOOD H. JONES

I

The emphasis on localism was constantly a part of British North American political experience. Even when initiative and authority came from the government at the British or colonial level there was a strong current of opinion which believed that power and decision ought to rest at the local level. Only in such circumstances would officials be responsive to local feelings and to local conditions. Moreover, in a land beleaguered by communications problems, the more decisions made locally, the better. This concern for localism, for the recognition of differences as well as similarities, and for the acknowledgement of a role for significant local government at the municipal and provincial levels, was a very important ingredient in the events leading to the union of the British North American provinces by 1867.

This union, known as "Confederation" even though it was not a confederacy, was the result of many concerns and actions. Indeed, the timing and achievement of Confederation rested more upon external pressures than upon localism. Of these external pressures none was more significant than the American Civil War. The evident inadequacies of colonial defence prompted British officials to view favourably a project of colonial union, and to promote it vigorously with suitable political pressure.[1] This was reinforced by a widespread fear that colonial miscues could spark a war between America and Britain, and the events surrounding the St. Albans' raid of 1865 justified this

---

1 The best accounts of the coming of Confederation are W. L. Morton, *The Critical Years. The Union of British North America 1857-1873* (Toronto, 1964); D. G. Creighton, *The Road to Confederation* (Toronto, 1965); and P. B. Waite, *The Life and Times of Confederation* (Toronto, 1962).

fear.[2] Within the colonies there was the reverse fear, readily apparent after the Trent affair of 1861, that British North America, or its several parts, might become involved in a war of Britain's making, particularly if the United States found the colonies convenient and accessible points for retaliation.[3] The withdrawal of British military forces, begun in 1864, heightened the central concern of whether these colonies could be protected from the United States while still preserving British institutions.[4]

It became increasingly evident, as well, that any wider colonial union would have to be tied to British imperial policies of develop-ment, defense and trade. Since 1857 there had been growing pressure for the development of the North-West. Much of it was articulated by Edward Ellice and Sir Edward Watkin, on behalf of the Hudson's Bay Company and railway interests, who argued that colonial union was the necessary prerequisite to British guarantees on investment capital. Others, of which George Brown's *Globe* was most vocal, saw the North-West as the guarantee of a future great nation on the northern half of the continent. The apparently slow growth of British North America after 1857 made colonial leaders more anxious and more receptive to these views.[5] At the same time, and for different reasons, Britain was desirous of a smaller burden in colonial affairs. Conse-quently, the colonies had to be more prepared to accept involvement in achieving reciprocal trade with the United States and in meeting the expenses of defence and development without assurance of British intervention. As the union of British North America suited British policy, it was hastened by British efforts. As George Etienne Cartier reported during the Confederation debates, "Confederation was, as it were, at this moment almost forced upon us."[6]

While the timing of this union was dependent upon external pressures, its shape was affected by well-established localist traditions, a widely held nonrepublican ideology, and beliefs about the implica-tions of federation. Federation had been seen as preparation for nationhood, for assuming duties, responsibilities, and pretensions, which the mother country had previously fulfilled to a considerable extent. George Sheppard, the leading opponent of federalism at the Reform Convention of 1859, stated the point quite succinctly: "Federa-tion implies nationality. For colonial purposes only it would be a costly

2 R. W. Winks, *Canada and the United States. The Civil War Years* (Baltimore, 1960), pp. 298ff.

3 Ibid., pp. 101-04. See also, for example, the speech of Hon. John Rose, in *Parliamentary Debates on the subject of the Confederation of the British North American provinces* (Quebec, 1865), pp. 395-96.

4 C. P. Stacey, *Canada and the British Army, 1846-1871* (London, 1936).

5 J. M. S. Careless, *Brown of the Globe*, 2 vols. (Toronto, 1959 and 1963).

6 *Confederation Debates*, p. 55.

encumbrance." There was no point in a union of colonies that did not lead to nationhood. That Reform Convention rejected a union of British North America as premature largely on the grounds that the colonies were not prepared to accept national responsibilities and expenses. George Brown was attracted to the federal union of the Canadas, as opposed to simple and outright dissolution of the legislative union. He insisted that federal union would be preparatory to the union, Confederation, of all British North America. He challenged the convention in grand oratorical style: "Who does not feel that to us rightfully belongs the right and the duty of carrying the blessings of civilization through those boundless regions, and making our own country the highway of traffic to the Pacific?"[7]

The expression "new nationality," coined by D'Arcy McGee and enshrined in the 1865 speech from the throne, became synonymous with a future federation. Most people were frightened by the implications of full independence, and particularly the prospects of commercial or political annexation to the United States that might follow in its wake. Not envisioning that Canada would ever want to break the imperial bond, John A. Macdonald claimed there was no need for independence with Confederation, for as Canada became more significant, England would be less anxious to be rid of Canada.[8] There was a tradition, though, at least as old as the Durham report, that a British North American nationality could protect against further American influence.[9] Those who welcomed independence as a possible consequence of Confederation stressed that it would be practical, and not republican.[10]

During the debates of the 1850s many expressed the view that any union, when it came, would be the product of popular will. It was never clear what this entailed, but there were various suggestions in parliament and in the press after 1864 that the confederation scheme ought to be submitted to the people. Some supporters of Confederation expressed regret that the government was unwilling to go to the people. In a sense, the government confirmed the validity of this regret when it argued that the people, through their representatives in parliament, were making the decision. Representatives were not tied to platforms, and were free to act as they wished on matters that came before parliament, subject only to subsequent electoral decisions. Furthermore, in this instance, it was argued, the people were kept particularly well informed by the superior press coverage since the late 1850s, when federalism had emerged as a significant public issue.

7 *Globe* (Toronto), 11 November 1859.
8 *Confederation Debates*, p. 43.
9 Ibid., pp. 74-75 (Hon. John Ross), p. 110 (George Brown).
10 E. H. Jones, "Political Aspects of the *London Free Press*, 1858-1867" (master's thesis, University of Western Ontario, London, 1964).

While these rationalizations were true, there had been a widespread feeling that Confederation would reflect the will of the people, and might even be a response to popular pressure.[11] This did not prove to be the case, and the coalition government charged with establishing Confederation never encouraged such notions. To them, Confederation was not to be a product of popular pressure.

Most government leaders expressed a strong preference for legislative union. Such offered the basis for strong, stable, British, monarchical government, and the hope for a united people. Nonetheless, there were pressures which prevented the union from being entirely legislative. Even beyond the obvious limitations of geography, there was strong feeling in the Maritimes and Upper Canada in favour of local control of local affairs; Lower Canada needed guarantees of its language, religious and legal rights.

II

The sources of localism were indigenous as well as imported. The basic proposition of localism was that the interests of the people were best served by government closest to the people. Only there could people begin to guard against power, authority, bureaucracy and expense that were pervasive and beyond their control. Localism reasserted itself whenever the decision-making process seemed closed or remote, whenever there was a concentration of power. Power was especially loathsome when that power seemed directed toward enforcing social and political homogeneity. There was no problem when uniformity arose from localism, as for example when all areas nourished the same values and responded against the same corrupting influences. Localism, in fact, had a tendency toward uniformity whenever people sought to translate the domestic truths of thrift, hard work, honesty and the yeoman virtues to politics.[12] Once local control of local affairs was admitted, the results were certain to be beneficent. Power diffused was power defused.

According to Bernard Bailyn, the origin of American politics lay with the radical whigs of the mid-eighteenth century, and with the localist ideas, beliefs, fears and perceptions that underlay their conception of power in British politics. They echoed the British opposition, and its view of the corruptibility of political leadership in British politics, because such a view corresponded with American understanding. As with the opposition Whigs in Britain, Americans did not believe that men could be trusted with power, particularly if that power was exercised beyond the control of the people, or of the colonists. The tendency for man to seek domination meant, it seemed, that power was

---

11 Waite, *Life and Times of Confederation*, pp. 105-07.
12 R. Wiebe, *The Search for Order* (New York, 1968), p. 136.

aggressive and tended to increase at the expense of liberty. Consequently, "the duty of free men was to protect the latter and constrain the former."[13] The fear of power and authority, and the organization and institutions within which they reposed, was at the heart of the localist tradition in America.[14]

The American reading of history, as well as of contemporary politics, reinforced this localist perspective. Sparta, Athens and Rome, it seemed, had flourished so long as civic humanism, and not individual selfishness, prevailed. In the face of ambition and power these cities disintegrated or became centralized empires. The best government was that closest to the people, that with the least bureaucracy.[15] Localism was the cohesive ingredient in an emerging republican ideology. American ideas of the ancients, of the Magna Carta, of the Glorious Revolution and of the Enlightenment were cemented by the fears and assumptions that power corrupts and advances at the expense of liberty, even in England. England's decline, it seemed, was the more tragic because the government was too distant to be affected by American zephyrs. The Americans became increasingly convinced of the dangers of strong, corrupt government distant from the people.[16]

The distrust of arbitrary power was common to all Americans by the 1770s, and was transported to British North America with the Loyalists. The Loyalists had been distinguished from the Rebels largely by circumstances and by their dependence upon Britain in one way or another.[17] Thomas Hutchinson, the governor of Massachusetts, for example, believed in greater local control for the colonies and had argued privately that it was impolitic for Britain to force the Stamp Act of 1765 upon the colonies. However, Hutchinson held a crown appointment, and in any event was not able to accept the need for independence. There had to be other ways of increasing local autonomy.[18] The Declaration of Independence was a radical step because it converted erstwhile monarchical colonies into *de facto* republics.

There were some, and they eventually became Loyalists, who sought some form of local control within the Empire, who saw no reason for incompatibility between local liberty and a general imperial government.[19] Loyalist leaders, however, sought to impose a new set of

13 B. Bailyn, *The Origin of American Politics* (New York, 1967), p. 56.
14 G. Wood, *The Creation of the American Republic, 1776-1787* (Chapel Hill, 1969), p. 520.
15 Bailyn, *Origin of American Politics*, p. 140.
16 B. Bailyn, *Ideological Origins of the American Revolution* (Cambridge, 1967).
17 W. Nelson, *The American Tory* (New York, 1960).
18 E. S. and H. M. Morgan, *The Stamp Act Crisis, Prologue to Revolution, 1765-1766* (New York, 1963).
19 L. F. S. Upton, "The Idea of Confederation, 1754-1858," in *The Shield of Achilles. Aspects of Canada in the Victorian Age,* ed. W. L. Morton (Toronto, 1968), p. 187; W. L. Morton, "The Conservative Principle in Confederation," *Queen's Quarterly* 71 (Winter

beliefs encompassing deference for king, empire and authority and based upon the deeds and sacrifices, circumstantial and voluntary, made during the Revolutionary War. But as Neil MacKinnon has observed, "The select were usurping the Loyalist image and shaping it to their own ends, whereas the great majority were placing greater emphasis upon the democratic principles and instincts that had been their pre-revolutionary heritage. . . ."[20] Local self-government, with leadership drawn from the respectable elements of society, was widely accepted by Loyalists. They introduced the town meeting in Upper Canada, even though legislative power rested with the several Courts of Quarter Session.[21] As Professor W. L. Morton observed, "The party quarrels that were to arise were always over the conventions or the degree of self-government, never over whether there should be self-government in a community of any size."[22] Furthermore, the popular legislatures in these governments were entrusted with distinctive powers, particularly in relation to money.[23]

This Loyalist legacy of localism was reinforced by immigration from Britain. Naturally, as Professor Craig has observed, these immigrants, and particularly the Orangemen among them, were great supporters of Conservatives when the issue seemed to be for the British connection or against Yankee tendencies.[24] But localism was also crucial. Professor Senior has recently argued, for example, that Orangeism was essentially a fraternal religious organization, and consequently a manifestation of immigrant democracy. In this context, he sees the 1830's as "a collision between an immigrant and a frontier democracy." Orangemen were largely preoccupied with local events, more social than political, although nothing was more exciting than an election riot. They sought patronage for local purposes, and were generally more concerned with the areas in which they lived. Events such as the twelfth of July and election campaigns, in which either the British connection or religious nativism were involved, provided the only exceptions for the rank and file, and even there the fun and excitement were at hand.[25]

1965), reprinted in *Canadian History since Confederation, Essays and Interpretations*, ed. B. Hodgins and R. Page (Georgetown, Ontario, 1972), p. 35. See also L. F. S. Upton, *Loyal Whig, William Smith* (Toronto, 1969).

20 Neil MacKinnon, "Nova Scotia Loyalists, 1783-1785," *Histoire Sociale/Social History* 4 (November 1969): 47-48.

21 F. Landon, *Western Ontario and the American Frontier* (Toronto, 1967), p. 221.

22 Morton, "Conservative Principle," p. 35.

23 S. F. Wise, "Upper Canada and the Conservative Tradition," in *Profiles of a Province* (Toronto, 1967), p. 22.

24 G. M. Craig, *Upper Canada, The Formative Years 1784-1841* (Toronto, 1966), pp. 226-32.

25 H. Senior, *Orangeism: The Canadian Phase* (Toronto, 1972), foreword, pp. 34-39 and 96-97.

The Family Compact successfully harnessed localist feelings in Upper Canada. Regional elites did not feel alienated from the major operations of the government because they were readily recognized, and because they were given an important say in the distribution of government favours.[26] The Upper Canadian government through legislation, grants and the local magistrates controlled the local government, but permitted considerable administrative decentralization.[27] Even at election time, the issues were viewed from a parochial angle, for the provincial electorate was essentially the sum of many local electorates. The Bank of Upper Canada was established in York (later Toronto) because the Family Compact was particularly sensitive to Toronto views. And Christopher Hagerman, though a prominent member of the provincial executive, gave priority to Kingston issues.[28]

Localism was not the exclusive property of Conservatives. Reformers drew upon a "transatlantic persuasion" which opposed monopoly or concentration of power and which favoured wider popular involvement in government. Professor Robert Kelley argues that Reformers were united by their view of the enemy: "superiority and special privilege; prejudice and dominating power; wealth and the habit of authority; economic exploitation and insulting airs; religious arrogance; a calm assumption that the nation was coterminous with themselves and that only they were 'loyal.' "[29] This view was derived from eighteenth-century views on the nature and corruptibility of power. It was supplemented, Kelley argues, by an intellectual legacy of which Adam Smith, Thomas Jefferson and Edmund Burke were key. Adam Smith taught Reformers that governments should not use their powers to grant privileges or to enrich a small part of society. The role of government was to regulate business and to prevent or destroy monopolies. *The Wealth of Nations* was a Reform handbook filled with facts and analysis to assist in the formulation of economic policy.[30] Edmund Burke taught that political compassion was pragmatic, for a tranquil society resulted when governments responded to grievances rather than ignored them.[31] Thomas Jefferson, schooled in Adam Smith, feared monopoly and government tied to business, and so

26 Wise, "Upper Canada and the Conservative Tradition," p. 27.
27 J. H. Aitchison, "The Municipal Corporations Act of 1849," *CHR* 30 (June 1949): 107-22.
28 S. F. Wise, "Tory Factionalism: Kingston Elections and Upper Canadian Politics, 1820-1836," *Ontario History* 57 (December 1965): 205-25. The thesis is confirmed by V. Nelles, "Loyalism and Local Power, the District of Niagara, 1792-1837," *Ontario History* 58 (June 1966): 99-114, and in Elva Richards, "The Joneses of Brockville and the Family Compact," *Ontario History* 60 (December 1968): 169-84.
29 R. G. Kelley, *The Transatlantic Persuasion, The Liberal Democratic Mind in the Age of Gladstone* (New York, 1969), p. 54.
30 Ibid., chapter 2.
31 Ibid., p. 99.

warned against the four evils: "speculation, corruption, strong governments and mass degradation."[32]

This world view was inherited by most Reformers of the 1820s and 1830s. Aileen Dunham commented that they represented for the most part the artisans and the small farmers, and had little knowledge of finance and little initiative for business. They opposed both those enterprising men who enjoyed some political monopoly and the financial policies they represented. According to Dunham, if they were progressive, it was in politics, not economic development.[33] Professor Craig observed that while Upper Canada did not necessarily import ideas from the United States, her people showed similar tendencies in religion, materialism and anti-intellectualism. They distrusted strangers, stressed individual initiative and hard work, and welcomed wider involvement of the people in government.[34] American practices, in which local control of local affairs—with elected officials more responsive to local public opinion—seemed an accomplished fact, were the envy of many Reformers.[35] Few, however, were as envious as William Lyon Mackenzie.

Mackenzie believed that Canada was governed by overpaid foreigners. He contrasted this to the virtuous simplicity of American state government which Canada would share as a state of the union: local self-government, universal suffrage, vote by ballot and other features that existed more in Mackenzie's imagination than in American practice. Mackenzie was, however, representative of basic Reform assumptions of the early nineteenth century. He believed that labour was the source of all wealth. In the ideal society the government "secured for every man the greatest possible quality of the product of his own labour, and denied existence to any privileged political, religious or economic interests who might steal from him."[36] Mackenzie feared that Upper Canada would never be a place for the "simple living, hard working, frugal, independent farmers served by honest merchants, craftsmen, small manufacturers, township schools, an honest legislature, and a free press; in short an educated and largely agrarian democracy."[37] He never doubted that the United States was achieving success in this regard.

32 Ibid., p. 137.
33 A. Dunham, *Political Unrest in Upper Canada 1815-1836* (London, 1927; reprint ed., Toronto, 1963), pp. 136-37.
34 Craig, *Upper Canada*, pp. 198-99.
35 Ibid., p. 207.
36 Ibid., pp. 244-46. In a perverse article, J. E. Rea, "William Lyon Mackenzie—Jacksonian?"*Mid-America* 50 (July 1968): 235, argues that the main influence on Mackenzie "was not borrowed abstract theory, but the realities of Upper Canadian political life."
37 Lillian Gates, "The Decided Policy of William Lyon Mackenzie," *CHR* 40 (September 1959): 186-87.

There were basic tensions in localism that had to be faced during the 1840s. The central tension was the concern for retrenchment. Local control was intended to reduce expenditures because local people understood the real needs. It became clear that local control was linked to local financing, particularly as control seemed to follow the sources of revenue. The other major source of tension related to the power and structure of local elites. Local control would not mean much if it were exercised by a closed clique dispensing the patronage generated by the provincial and imperial governments. The power of the Family Compact rested, in fact, with such local elites. One strategy was to dismantle the power at the center in order to open established elites or to create new ones, but the consequence was a new centralism that failed to satisfy the tenets of localism. Yet the alternate strategy was certain to be frustrated if control of patronage remained at the centre. There was also the need to tie political offices to residence rather than ownership of land if the new elite were to be other than a landed one. The events of the 1840s effectively dismantled the power base of the Family Compact and resolved the tensions between the control of policy and the control of financing.

Many of the issues had already been faced in the development of a roads policy, for roads were necessary, and roads were the basis of the influence of the local elites that sustained the Family Compact. However, during the 1820s the government, largely on grounds of financial stringency, contended that except for commercial highways and district roads, roads were a matter of local concern. The financial difficulties stemmed from the frustrations of the government's commercial development policy. There was difficulty in collecting customs duties from Lower Canada, the canals had proved comparatively expensive, and Britain was experiencing trade difficulties. Reformers fought for roads for agriculture, rather than canals for commerce, and after their success in 1830 centralized road patronage to circumvent the Tory local elites. The reversion to the old theory of local responsibility for roads was made by Francis Hincks in the 1840s, but then largely to prevent embarrassment to a government faced with low revenues and local complaints of neglect. Practical considerations dominated.[38]

The triumphs of localism in the 1840s in municipal government and education likewise rested upon the same practical considerations. As with responsible government, achieved in the same years, there was a notion that government ought to be responsive to the will of the people or their representatives. Both drew upon the precedent of British municipal legislation of 1835, based on the Benthamite view

38 M. S. Cross, "Some Aspects of Road Financing and Administration, 1791-1901" (Toronto, n.d.), pp. 5-7, 20-22.

that local politics was the training ground of statesmen. De Tocqueville had expressed the view succinctly:

> Local institutions are to liberty what primary schools are to science; they put it within the people's reach; they teach people to appreciate its peaceful enjoyment and accustom them to make use of it. With local institutions a nation may give itself a free government, but it has not got the spirit of liberty.[39]

Lord Durham's emphasis on responsible government and municipal institutions reflected his agreement. Local people may not always know what is best, but they will make a greater effort and show greater interest because their welfare is directly involved.[40]

By 1850, Upper Canada had a sound local government system. The units of government were fairly small, and allowed for maximum accessibility. Local government was given extensive power and given increased powers of assessment and financial flexibility. Schools were controlled and financed at the local level, even though there was resentment about the increased taxation that accompanied the change to a more general common education. In both education and local government, appointment from the central level was replaced by election at the local level, and residency displaced land ownership as the criterion for eligibility. The relationship between control, interest and finance was settled with the series of interrelated acts of 1849 and 1850—the Municipal Corporations (Baldwin) Act, the Railway Guarantees Act, the Education Act and the Local Assessment Act. Local governments would determine priorities and accept responsibility for their achievements. The provincial government was freed from the embarrassments of establishing priorities and the expense of pork-barrelling to pursue its interests in railway development. The culmination of many considerations, pragmatic as well as idealistic, had produced a reasonably coherent system of responsible government at the provincial and local levels.[41]

III

In many respects, federalism was an American invention resulting from efforts to build a large nation while recognizing localist sentiments and realities. With the Declaration of Independence, the various legislatures became sovereign bodies. They delegated authority to the

39 Alexis de Tocqueville, *Democracy in America*, ed. J. P. Mayer (Garden City, 1969), volume 1, chapter 5, p. 63.
40 Chester New, *Lord Durham's Mission to Canada* (Toronto, 1963), p. 174; also note Ged Martin, *The Durham Report and British Policy: A Critical Essay* (Cambridge, 1972), pp. 11-29.
41 Susan Houston, "Politics, Schools and Social Change in Upper Canada," *CHR* 53 (September 1972): 249-71, and C. F. J. Whebell, "Robert Baldwin and Decentralization, 1841-9," in *Aspects of Nineteenth Century Ontario Essays Presented to James J. Talman*, eds. F. H. Armstrong, et al. (Toronto, [1974]).

Continental Congress, which coordinated the war effort. This confederacy provided government that was close to the people, and that was consistent with eighteenth-century notions of power and sovereignty. Sovereignty was indivisible, but sovereign bodies could delegate power and authority. In the case of Great Britain, for example, sovereignty rested with the monarchy, which delegated its authority to parliament after the Glorious Revolution of 1688. During the various disputes with the colonies, Britain was unable to blend this view of sovereignty with localist assumptions that sovereignty ought to rest in those governments closest to the people, the several colonial legislatures modelled on parliament.

The prevailing views of democracy stood in the way of a rapprochement. Democracy was a system of government in which each individual who was a citizen participated in the affairs of state. Democracies depended on small size and upon civic humanism: every citizen had unselfishly to place the good and welfare of the state ahead of his own ambition. Since democracies depended on the solid virtues of hard work, honesty, thrift and civic responsibility, they were rare and ephemeral. The lamp of history revealed that democracies invariably disintegrated into factions, anarchy or dictatorships. But Americans increasingly saw democracy and republic (the representative form of government) less as theories of government and politics, and more as descriptions of popular government. The democratic, republican governments were close to the people, and responsive to their will. Armed with this rhetoric, the state governments had all the best arguments, for clearly they were closer to the people than any Continental Congress seeking increased powers.[42]

Those favouring stronger central government and a higher calibre of political leadership had to have the localist arguments in their armoury if they were to expect success. They succeeded with popular sovereignty, the theory that sovereignty rested with the people and not with a legislature. The notion that sovereignty should rest in one place was unchallenged, but as the authority of the people could be transferred to all governments it was possible to have a multitude of legislatures all equal, all drawing from the same source of power, and all supreme in those areas delegated to them. Now it seemed as if the anti-Federalists in fighting the distant central government had been fighting the extension of popular authority, and the supporters of the strong central government argued for government resting upon the people. Distance was to be measured in terms of sovereignty, not

42 Richard Buel, Jr., "Democracy and the American Revolution: A Frame of Reference," *William and Mary Quarterly* 3d. series (21 April, 1964): 165-90 provides excellent insights. See also Staughton Lynd, *Class Conflict, Slavery and the United States Constitution* (Indianapolis, 1967) and Jesse Lemisch, "The American Revolution Seen from the Bottom Up," in *Towards a New Past: Dissenting Essays in American History*, ed. B. J. Bernstein (New York, 1967), pp. 3-45.

geography. As Professor Wood has observed, "The more the Federalists stressed the foundation of the new Constitution in the people, the more excited they became with the spectacular significance of the whole constitution-making process."[43] The Federalists had found the only way to explain their emerging theory of federalism, "by making the people themselves, and not their representatives in any legislature, the final, illimitable, and incessant wielders of all power." With federalism it was possible for state and federal legislatures to be equally representative of the people simultaneously.[44]

The question of democracy was not resolved with the discovery of popular sovereignty. Americans still believed that democracy and republicanism were susceptible to the age-old diseases, of which anarchy and dictatorship were the chief, that contributed to their short life. Federalism promised stability, for the many governments would be supported by one another. A system of balances was considered necessary to prevent the extremes of democracy, to ensure continual reassessment of the balance between liberty and authority, centralism and decentralism, executive and legislative power. By guarding against the historical weaknesses, the stability of the new United States of America seemed assured. As democracy was considered a political theory, and not a political faith as it became by the 1820s in America, it was not necessarily anti-democratic to seek modifications. It was rather seen as a matter of making democracy work most effectively. As long as this was political theory, it was possible to admit the problematics of democracy, of problems that flowed from, were inherent in or generated by the political system of democracy.[45] Faith admits of no problematics, and to oppose greater infusions of democracy under those circumstances would be anti-democratic.

In British North America localism did not lead to federalism of the same type, fundamentally because sovereignty was acknowledged to rest with the imperial government, specifically the monarch, and not with the people. The post-revolutionary colonies increased their powers for pragmatic rather than theoretical reasons.[46] As long as the imperial government would make necessary constitutional adjustments, such as occurred in the granting of responsible government, and in uniting the Canadas in 1840 and British North America in 1867, there was no need, it seemed, for fundamental change along the American model. Nonetheless, some of these pragmatic adjustments reflected the significance of localism and Canadian attitudes toward democracy and federalism.

43 Wood, *Creation of the American Republic*, p. 535.
44 Ibid., p. 545.
45 I. Kristol, "American Historians and the Democratic Idea," *American Scholar* 39 (Winter 1969-70): 91. This article is reprinted with others in I. Kristol, *On the Democratic Idea in America* (New York, 1972).
46 W. L. Morton, *Kingdom of Canada* (Toronto, 1963), p. 241.

It was not easy for leaders in British North America to separate the theory of democracy from its practice in the United States. Indeed, American experience was proof that democracy was susceptible to peculiar diseases when the people lost sight of the need for balance. In Canada, democracy was not accepted by faith; it was seen as susceptible to extremes. As the *Globe* expressed it, "Republican institutions are not favourable to genuine liberty."[47] Democracy could triumph at the expense of liberties, the will of the majority could trample the expectations of minorities, and the rule of the mob could threaten everything. In the United States, "It has become a matter of national faith that there is something contemptible in submitting to rule, and that the true position of mankind is one of entire independence of his neighbor," according to the *Globe*.[48] D'Arcy McGee believed that Americans, cherishing their new-found liberty, forgot the need for authority. "As the scythe to the fabled bundle of sticks, as the hoops to the staves, as the helm to the ship . . . so is authority to liberty, in all well balanced governments."[49] British Americans believed in the superiority of British liberties which they contrasted to the excessive and irrational liberty of Americans.[50]

While Canadian government was not based on popular sovereignty, there was a significant popular base which the British were encouraging. One significant aspect of the achievement of responsible government by 1848 was the extension of the cabinet system to force the executive to be in harmony with the legislature.[51]

A similar conclusion can be drawn from Lord Durham's report. Durham emphasized the relative lack of control over local affairs as a major reason for the rebellions in Upper and Lower Canada in 1837 and 1838. He saw this as a factor in "the failure of representative government and of the bad administration of the country." Consequently, in addition to responsible government, Durham proposed "to grant the provinces self-government in matters of purely internal concern." He also advocated a system of municipal government to promote localism, to provide a training ground for provincial politics and to reduce public works patronage at the provincial level.[52]

The British government favoured Durham's other major recommendation for a simple legislative union of Upper and Lower Canada.

47 *Globe*, 30 October 1849, cited by S. F. Wise in his and R. C. Brown's *Canada Views the United States: Nineteenth Century Political Attitudes* (Seattle, 1967), p. 58.
48 *Globe*, 23 November 1861, cited in ibid., p. 87.
49 B. W. Hodgins, "Attitudes toward Democracy in the Pre-Confederation Decade," (master's thesis, Queen's University, 1955), p. 242.
50 S. F. Wise, "Conservatism and Political Development: The Canadian Case," *South Atlantic Quarterly* 69 (Spring 1970): 232-33.
51 W. Ormsby, *The Emergence of the Federal Concept in Canada 1839-1845* (Toronto, 1969), p. 56.
52 Ibid., p. 34, citing C. P. Lucas, ed., *Lord Durham's Report on the Affairs of British North America* 3 vols. (Oxford, 1912), II: 116.

This augured well for future economic development, as there would be a single government for the entire St. Lawrence and because the anti-development animus of French-Canadian politicians might be countered.[53] Durham's report linked localism and federalism, but the British government resisted for essentially the same reasons that motivated them in the 1770s. It seemed impossible to transfer imperial powers to provincial governments without jeopardizing the imperial connection. The central government in British America would assume imperial responsibilities and encourage the belief that the imperial government was unnecessary. The theory that all sovereignty reposed in one place would be shattered, or else usurped. But for the most part the British stressed the pragmatic considerations against a federal union. It would not forward the assimilation of the French, while it would divide political powers even further, increase the risks of radical influence on fiscal and currency policies, and promote local jealousies on other issues. Furthermore, the expenses of a federal union seemed prohibitive.[54]

Nonetheless the tendency towards federalism was nurtured in the legislative union of the Canadas. The attempted assimilation of French Canadians proved to be a policy based on mistaken assumption. British decisions made the policy logistically impossible. Equal representation in the legislature for Upper and Lower Canada coupled with Lord Russell's edict that even without responsible government the executive ought to reflect the legislature assured French Canadians of the political base from which to defend their language and culture.[55] Quasi-federalism characterized the provincial government. Upper and Lower Canada, though one province, each had their own systems of civil law, education, land tenure and Indian administration. The cabinets were characterized by two attorneys-general, each the acknowledged political leader of his section. After 1849, the seat of government perambulated between Quebec City and Toronto.[56] Under these circumstances the formal achievement of responsible government in 1848 was coincidental with the increasing powers of French Canadians but had no direct impulse on the tendency toward federalism. The British government retained the initiative on the constitution and foreign relations, and to some degree trade, but it was increasingly more practical to allow increased local involvement and control.

During the 1850s Upper Canadian localism was most vocally expressed by Reformers. They sought to extend the principles of munic-

---

53 D. Creighton, *The Empire of the St. Lawrence* (Toronto, 1956) remains the classic interpretation.
54 Ormsby, *Federal Concept*, p. 21.
55 Ibid., p. 5.
56 J. E. Hodgetts, *Pioneer Public Service, An Administrative History of the United Canadas, 1841-1867* (Toronto, 1955), p. 55.

ipal government—administrative uniformity, local control and equal rights for all voters—to the provincial level. They also sought to prevent French Canadians from running Upper Canadian affairs as well as Lower Canadian ones. The union that became increasingly federal for Lower Canadians seemed increasingly legislative for Upper Canadians, as Lower Canada forced separate schools upon Upper Canada, prevented implementation of a sabbath bill, and determined the policy relating to the Municipal Loan Fund. To Reform leaders, Lower Canada's power rested upon its influence in the cabinet, and upon the alleged subversion of responsible government in which the will of the executive rather than that of the legislature seemed to prevail. The defeat of the two-day government formed by George Brown and A. A. Dorion added frustration and despair, but confirmed in their minds that Upper Canada would continue to have all the disadvantages and none of the advantages of legislative union.[57]

Reformers had many means to seek to affirm Upper Canadian localism and resist Lower Canadian dominance. The most traditional remedy was to press for representation by population. This was often seen as a means of giving Upper Canada more seats than Lower Canada, for Upper Canada's population was growing more rapidly and yet her seats were fixed to Lower Canada's level, of forty-two until 1853, and sixty-five after. "Rep. by pop." was not defended, however, on such pragmatic grounds. Reformers emphasized that every voter ought to have equal power, and not be limited by where he lived. If the principle of uniformity were recognized at the voter level, then true union would follow, for all would see that they were equal, and internal distinctions would diminish. But in addition to uniformity, "rep. by pop." promised simple justice and a guarantee of Upper Canadian rights.[58] Opponents were unconvinced, for whatever principle might be involved, "rep. by pop." threatened the influence and position of eastern Upper Canada and Lower Canada. Consequently, "rep. by pop." looked increasingly uncertain of success.

Some Reformers, notably Sandfield Macdonald and his journalist allies with the *London Free Press* and the *Cornwall Freeholder*, advocated double majority. Even more than "rep. by pop.," this solution recognized the federalizing tendencies of the union. Each act of the legislature would require a majority vote from each section, and for purely sectional legislation would require a majority from the section involved. There were many pitfalls, not the least of which was how to decide when an issue was of sectional rather than provincial concern. The touchy question of education, for example, pivoted on this very point. Upper Canadians wanted a uniform educational system across

57 Careless, *Brown of the Globe*, I, discusses these issues thoroughly, while Kelley, *Transatlantic Persuasion* provides thought-provoking insights.
58 E.g., *London Free Press*, 19 July 1859.

the province, provided it was nonsectarian. But they were opposed to uniformity if it involved the retrograde step of accepting separate schools in Upper Canada. Consequently, to Upper Canadians, it was a provincial question to extend nonsectarian education to Lower Canada but an Upper Canadian one to extend separate schools to Upper Canada; but the reverse propositions also seemed tenable, at least to Lower Canadians. Nonetheless, the *London Free Press* saw double majority as an expedient temporary device to ensure the passage of practical reforms of interest to both sections.[59]

Double majority was less likely to be accepted than "rep. by pop." Many Reformers sought to maintain the legislative union, for they saw there the best chance for traditional Reform programmes. But by 1859 there was a growing disillusionment with Canadian politics, and its apparent domination by corrupt ministerialists and Lower Canadians. There was an excited anticipation that if changing the men was not the answer, then changing the system might be. The Reform press and its leaders continually discussed the need for constitutional change and better party organization. The culmination came at the Reform Convention held in Toronto's St. Lawrence Hall that November.

Localist feelings dominated the convention.[60] Delegates were concerned with guaranteeing Upper Canadian rights through the instrument of the Reform party. A confederation of all British North America seemed too distant, too expensive, and too unreliable. Annexation by the United States, though feared as a consequence of dissolution of the union, was unthinkable. This meant that if the union were to be dissolved, the dissolution must be followed either by a separate colony of Upper Canada or by a federal union of the two Canadas. The debate narrowed to one between dissolution pure and simple or federal union, with George Sheppard and George Brown, both of the *Globe*, leading the opposite sides.

The appeal to localism began with the keynote address by Malcolm Cameron, MPP for Lambton. He argued that a dissolution of the union would not increase expenses because "people look more narrowly at expenditures when the area of government is smaller." He pointed to the example of the old Home District which was now divided into sixty municipalities. He also noted that the smaller districts, such as Prince Edward county, found it easiest to stay out of debt. Rowland

---

59 E. H. Jones, "The Great Reform Convention of 1859," (doctoral dissertation, Queen's University at Kingston, 1971), pp. 50-52; B. W. Hodgins, *John Sandfield Macdonald* (Toronto, 1971), p. 38; Careless, *Brown of the Globe*, I: 256.

60 The proceedings were published fairly completely by the *Globe, Leader* and *London Free Press* beginning with the issues of November 10 or 11, 1859. See Jones, "Great Reform Convention of 1859," chapter 9; G. W. Brown, "The Grit Party and the Great Reform Convention of 1859," *CHR* 16 (September 1935): 245-65; and E. H. Jones, "Ephemeral Compromise: The Great Reform Convention Revisited," *Journal of Canadian Studies* 3 (February, 1968): 21-28.

Barr and Moses C. Nickerson thought the municipal corporations of Upper Canada were the strongest arguments in favour of federation. Oliver Mowat argued that government was better before the Union when at least English influence prevailed, and the governors lived in Upper Canada. Dr. Daniel Clark appealed to the convention: "Let us have our affairs in our own hands, and then it will be our own fault if we do not rule the country with economy, develop its resources and make it what it ought to be, the brightest diadem of Victoria." Hope Mackenzie described his notion of a future federation in which local legislatures entirely controlled local affairs. William Johnstone, editor of the Iroquois *Chief*, favoured a federation "of a simple, plain, practical character" which would allow more complete control of local matters than "rep. by pop." James Lesslie argued for dissolution pure and simple, on the grounds that, as before the union, there "would be more patriotism, liberality and economy in Lower Canada," as well as simplification and economy for Upper Canada. Donald A. Macdonald, MPP for Glengarry, noted that Glengarry was "free of debt except the loyalty owed to the queen." This appeal to localism came from all sides of the debate, and was reflected in the speeches of the two main speakers, George Brown and George Sheppard. Sheppard argued that with dissolution,

> we shall have the satisfaction of having Upper Canadian interests legislated for by Upper Canadians only, we shall be free from those alliances which all admit to be a source of ruinous demoralization, and it would be our own fault if we did not take care of our own interests.

He also pointed out the danger in federations for central bodies to acquire increased power, and to seek excuses for adding to their glory and influence. George Brown defended federation as an extension of "rep. by pop.," providing the guarantees for each section to manage its own local institutions without controlling those of the other. In so doing, it also struck to the root of the major Upper Canadian grievance of the Union, "the control exercised by Lower Canada over matters purely pertaining to Upper Canada—the framing of our School laws, the selection of our ministers, the appointment of our local officials."

The debate was resolved with a compromise made possible by the understanding that the options were not different. As long as Upper Canada had the essential local powers she desired, a federal government would only be a coordinating body between provinces. If Upper Canada were a separate colony, a diplomatic coordinating body would be necessary. Consequently reference to a general government was replaced with the expression "some joint authority." The compromise was lost in the aftermath of the convention when George Brown pressed his interpretation that the convention meant to endorse federal union. Brown revealed that he was not open to the same localist sentiment that gave validity to the compromise even though he had been the most vocal advocate of Upper Canadian rights during the 1850s. Brown had caught the vision of a larger Upper Canada that extended to the North-West, and this required a more flexible political system that could be influenced by Upper Canada. The local control of local affairs was not as important as Upper Canadian control of British North American affairs. And yet as George Brown deviated in this way he acknowledged the force of local control. The Reformers had affirmed that, for Upper Canada, it was an essential part of any proposal for union, whether of two provinces, or of all.

IV

Localism thrived in Upper Canada, nourished by geography, tradition and even by immigration, and at critical moments after 1840 this localism was tied to emergent notions of federalism. Despite this connection of localism and federalism, Upper Canadian political leaders professed a strong preference for what they considered to be legislative union. With all power concentrated in one government, Canada could enjoy the advantages of the British constitution and its assurances of permanency and stability. It would tighten the bonds uniting the colonies to Britain, while providing, in the words of one legislator, "stability and a more permanent foothold to the principles that obtain in the British Constitution."[61] D'Arcy McGee added that "the two great things all men aim at in any free government, are liberty and permanency. We have had liberty enough. . . . We need in these provinces, we can bear, a large infusion of authority."[62] John A. Macdonald argued that legislative union "would be the best, the cheapest, the most vigorous, and the strongest system of government we could adopt."[63] He went on to emphasize the flexibility of the system. In Great Britain, Scotland had been granted a local veto on local legislation, while the Province of Canada itself had become increasingly federal and instituted such changes as the elective Legislative Council in 1856. Moreover, the legislative union, unlike federal union, rested on distinctly British and monarchical precedents which augured well for maintaining a strong British connection and superiority.

The permanency of legislative union was tied to its monarchical aspects. Cartier claimed that he and his colleagues tried to achieve a "distinct form of government, the characteristic of which would be to possess the monarchical element."[64] This meant that the government would have a permanent executive, "a respectable executive element,"

---

61 *Confederation Debates*, p. 627. The speaker was Col. F. W. Haultain, MPP for Peterborough.
62 Ibid., p. 146.
63 Ibid., p. 29.
64 Ibid., p. 62.

that extended beyond party supporters to all the people. As one member commented, "As the sovereign is permanent ('the King is dead—God save the King!') we have at all times in him a father, whose interest and whose inclination it is to extend his protection equally over the cottage of the poor and over the palace of the rich, and to dispense equal justice to both."[65]

Even George Brown had strong sympathies for a legislative union, if it were practicable. "Rep. by pop.," merging the Reform principles of local control of local affairs and uniformity, was to be the basis of representation in the lower house of the federal government. But Confederation also promised development of the North-West and so the principle of uniformity for all voters was tied to a prospective new nationality that would eventually stretch to the Pacific. Local control of local affairs could be guaranteed with the superior municipal government system, thus providing all the necessary safeguards for economical government without interfering with an expansive dream. The prospect was the more attractive if it could be assumed that Upper Canada would leave its impress on national government.[66]

This view was an extension of the 1859 position, but it also represented a shift in thinking. In 1859, Reformers had pressed for as much power as possible to rest in the local government. When visions of national grandeur seemed distant, they saw the general government dealing only with problems of trade, defence and diplomacy and other issues that involved coordination with Lower Canada. Economy was achieved by local vigilance and national insignificance. But if the general government acquired new significance, chiefly tied to development, then retrenchment was most readily effected by reducing the concerns of the local government.[67] Neither in 1859 nor in 1864, except with George Sheppard, was local government seen as a source of sovereignty, and there was little understanding of the political theory of federalism, as opposed to its external manifestations. Localism expressed itself in practicable terms.

Despite the strong sympathy for legislative union, with its assurances of government that was British, monarchical, stable, permanent and just, legislative union was not practicable. George Brown summarized the views of the Quebec Conference at a Toronto banquet attended by some delegates, November 2, 1864. "In the first place, we had to consider that this country is of immense extent, presenting a vast variety of interests, great and small, for which it would be exceedingly difficult for any one body of men to legislate."[68] Moreover, Lower

65 Ibid., pp. 833-34 (A. Chartier de Lotbinière Harwood, MPP for Vaudreuil).
66 Careless, *Brown of the Globe*, II: 165-71.
67 *Confederation Debates*, pp. 86ff. (George Brown) and p. 676 (Hope Mackenzie).
68 E. Whelan, *The Union of the British Provinces . . .* (Charlottetown, 1865, reprinted Summerside, 1949), p. 191.

Canada was sensitive about her peculiar position of differing, as John A. Macdonald noted, in "language, nationality and religion from the majority."[69] The Maritimes, as was revealed in the debate over the composition of the senate, wanted to retain their individuality, each as separate political organizations.[70] Nor could Upper Canada forget the lessons learned under the union of the Province of Canada. Brown was "persuaded that, by committing all purely local matters to local control, we will secure the peace and permanence of the new Confederation much more effectually than could possibly have been hoped for from a Legislative Union."[71]

The great problem for the Fathers of Confederation was to retain the advantages of legislative union while recognizing the necessity of federal union. Federalism involved dividing sovereignty between federal and provincial governments, and within the federal government. Confederation was simplified by the fact that all sovereignty rested with the British government, and did not have to be gathered together. As always in the past, at least since the Quebec Act of 1774, imperial legislation created a colonial constitution. The umbrella of imperial sovereignty allowed powers to be divided between and within governments by convenience. But even as imperial sovereignty facilitated Confederation, it prevented the federation from emerging. The imperial government could delegate authority, but it could not transfer sovereignty. As Dorion observed, there was no precedent for a "Federal union between mere colonies."[72] No matter how federal the constitution might appear to be, as long as British North America was not independent all sovereignty remained with the imperial government. As long as the new union remained colonial it remained legislative, at least in theory. Those who wanted legislative union consequently avowed that Confederation was not a prelude to independence.[73] And others, such as Christopher Dunkin, noted the practical flexibility of legislative unions, which allowed special position to such as Ireland and Scotland in the United Kingdom.[74]

Nonetheless the union had, in some respects, the appearance of a federal union, for a division of powers at the centre, and between different governments was necessary. The absence of any difficulties on sovereignty allowed the delegates to the Quebec Conference to take a rather pragmatic approach to both questions. The central government continued on the colonial model, with a governor general appointed in Britain, and with a legislative assembly endowed with re-

69 *Confederation Debates*, p. 29.
70 Ibid.
71 Whelan, *Union of the British Provinces*, p. 192.
72 *Confederation Debates*, p. 689.
73 Ibid., p. 43 (John A. Macdonald) and pp. 394ff. (John Rose).
74 Ibid., pp. 527-28.

sponsible government. The legislative assembly was to have representation by population, in recognition of the long struggle in Upper Canada and of the fact that, as nearly as possible, every voter in the union would be treated equally and uniformly. Such a solution was also consistent with the aims of a legislative union, for it tended to make the electorate one. The legislative council, partly for compromise, was to be consistent with a federal principle, and recognize the differences between the different parts. Each of three sections—Upper Canada, Lower Canada and the Maritimes—was to have equal representation. However, the members of this upper house were to be appointed by the central government, the governor general in council, consistent with usual colonial practice, except in the Province of Canada where the legislative council had been elective since 1856.[75]

The distribution of powers between the governments was also handled pragmatically, in accord with the delegates' reading of the history of British North America. As George Brown explained,

> we have given nothing to the local bodies which did not necessarily belong to the localities, except education and the rights of property, and the civil law, which we were compelled to leave to the local governments, in order to afford that protection which the Lower Canadians claim for their language and their laws, and their peculiar institutions.[76]

Care was taken to avoid the apparent American mistake of acknowledging "an inherent sovereign power in the separate States." This meant strengthening the general government, and seeking to avoid "all conflict of jurisdiction and authority."[77] The general government was given control of all the courts, even to the county level, and the governor general in council was to appoint all lieutenant governors. Brown, at least, thought this would result in a "general government working in harmony with the local Executives and in hearty accord with popular sentiment as expressed through the people's representatives."[78] In short, as Professor Waite has argued, "The Quebec Resolutions remained a working outline; their purpose was practical, their ideas empirical, and their solutions sometimes circumstantial."[79]

Professor Waite's analysis of the federal principle in Confederation reaches too sweeping a conclusion, however. He argues that the division of powers between the local and general governments was taken for granted as a problem presenting little difficulty, even though it "bulks so large in any modern analysis of federation." He suggests the reason for little difficulty lies in the fact that the local governments

75 Whelan, *Union of the British Provinces,* pp. 192-94.
76 Ibid., p. 196.
77 Ibid., p. 197; and *Confederation Debates,* p. 33 (John A. Macdonald).
78 Whelan, *Union of the Provinces,* p. 197.
79 Waite, *Life and Times of Confederation,* p. 112.

would have little substance, that they "were apt to be regarded merely as convenience for dissipating sectional prejudice or absorbing sectional prejudice." Power and significance would rest with the central government. The heart of the federal principle lay not with division of powers, he argued, but with the creation of the central government, and under the circumstances with the composition of the senate.[80]

Certainly the senate was the subject of considerable discussion, and the creation of the central government was important to the federal principle. It was, however, controversial because it was such an obvious compromise between American and British practice, and because it had to be discussed in the legislative councils of the old provinces. Except in its superficial sectional balance it completely violated the federal principle, much to the annoyance of those who knew it.[81]

However, to downplay the division of powers as part of the federal principle seems most strange. That the federal principle was poorly understood by most journalists and politicians may be true. Professor Waite is also correct in noting that few—he cites only the London *Times* and the Montreal *True Witness*—understood the implications of a federal system under imperial sovereignty. There simply was no precedent, and there was certain to be encroachment upon the powers of either the imperial or the former colonial governments.[82] The main point was that although imperial sovereignty facilitated the union of the provinces, it did not readily allow the creation of a federal system. Coordinate federalism was impossible without a transfer of sovereignty to all governments created; subordinate federalism was likewise impossible without a transfer of sovereignty to one or another level of government. One aspect of the struggle, therefore, in 1864 and 1865, was to lay the basis for an interpretation of what the theory of Canadian federalism ought to be if and when independence were achieved.

In this task, the distribution of powers was central, and so understood. In the Confederation debates, many speakers alluded to the distribution of powers to point out that the union tended to be legislative, or that they ought to be changed to make the union more truly federal. John A. Macdonald told the legislature that the United States began at the wrong end by treating each state as a sovereignty. The Quebec Resolutions were intended to strengthen the general government, he said, by giving it all the powers incidental to sovereignty.[83] D'Arcy McGee asserted, "[b]ut indeed, sir, the main question is the due distribution of powers."[84] He went on to explain the principle entirely

80 Ibid., pp. 110-11.
81 Ibid., pp. 115-16.
82 Ibid., pp. 108-09.
83 *Confederation Debates*, p. 33.
84 Ibid., p. 144.

in terms of distribution of power, concluding, "it is a principle eminently favorable to liberty, because local affairs are left to be dealt with by local bodies and cannot be interfered with by those who have no local interest in them, while matters of a general character are left exclusively to a general government."[85] The Honourable L. A. Olivier (MLC, De Landaudière) found the Quebec scheme defective because it "gives to the General Government too much power and to the local governments too little."[86] A number of members commented on the certainty of conflict in areas of apparently concurrent jurisdiction.[87]

Confederation was achieved, and the Fathers of Confederation were pleased with the result. Armed with imperial sovereignty, they had pragmatically blended the monarchical and the democratic, the nationalist and the localist, the legislative and the federal. But they had also left confusion in their train, for they never discussed the implications of sovereignty, or even what would happen to imperial sovereignty if British North America ever became independent. Macdonald and his colleagues acted as if this were a legislative union, and as if imperial sovereignty would be transferred only to the federal government. Cartier, and Brown after 1867, insisted that the union was truly federal and had been from the moment the Charlottetown Conference decided responsible government should be the base of the local governments. Because of this confusion, the localism and federalism that shaped Confederation emerged undiminished by the discussions of 1864 and 1865, and in fact, assumed new vigour in the post-Confederation struggles for provincial rights.

85 Ibid., p. 145.
86 Ibid., p. 173.
87 Ibid., p. 178 (Hon. L.-A. Olivier), p. 404 (Hon. John Rose), and pp. 456-57 (M. C. Cameron).

III

The Canadian Political Elite's Attitudes Toward the Nature of the Plan of Union

BRUCE W. HODGINS

The Canadian political leaders who in 1867 accomplished Confederation in British North America believed that they were creating a nation which would be economically progressive and would soon stretch from Atlantic to Pacific. It would thereby acquire the coveted North-West. It would also avoid dreaded absorption by the expansionist United States. The union would employ the federal principle. The Fathers, however, distrusted pure coordinate or classical federalism. They saw it as too American and too republican; empirically it was too fraught with potential for civil strife. Some of the Fathers were determined that their limited federalism should find more expression in the composition of the central legislature than in the pure division of powers and functions between the two levels of government.[1]

The United Kingdom of Great Britain and Ireland contained three kingdoms and a principality, each with differing institutions and protected social structures but with one government and one parliament. The Canadian union was to approximate that form as much as local conditions permitted, especially as much as George Etienne Cartier, the French-Canadian leader who was not an extreme decentralist, would allow. In this Macdonaldian system, this subordinate federalism, diverse provinces would exist with wide, though circumscribed local responsibilities which were unlikely to expand. These responsibilities, it was thought, would include most of the contentious sectarian and sectional issues, especially education. The provinces would have a status somewhat similar to that of the provinces of the British Empire,

1 P. B. Waite, *Life and Times of Confederation: 1864-67* (Toronto, 1962), pp. 110-16. Small portions of this chapter have already appeared in the author's "Democracy and the Ontario Fathers of Confederation," *Profiles of a Province* (Toronto, 1967), pp. 83-91 and reprinted in *Canadian History Since Confederation*, eds. B. W. Hodgins and Robert Page (Georgetown, 1972), pp. 21-31.

such as old Canada, New South Wales and Nova Scotia, but with one great difference: the electorate in the Canadian provinces would participate in the governance of the whole entity and indeed make up the electorate of the new entity, which itself would remain a self-governing dependency of the British Empire.[2]

The Canadian union was, however, an elitist, essentially nondemocratic or predemocratic achievement—even though the populace was concerned and involved in the debate over its desirability and form. Union was primarily the creation of an English-speaking, urban-led, coalition of Conservative and Liberal (or Grit Reform) leaders from Upper Canada and English-speaking Conservative leaders from Montreal. Together they carried along the ascendant conservative (*Bleu*) elements of French Canada and certain forces from the Maritimes. The dominant commercial interests of Toronto and Montreal promoted union. The French-speaking unionists were ably assisted by the Catholic hierarchy and by widespread fears of American annexation. The extremely insecure Maritime unionists were assisted by the diversions, divisions and inadequacies of their opponents, the Irish-American Fenian scare and the political intrigue and pressure of a frugal and defence-conscious British government now determined to secure British North American consolidation. The achievement of British North American union did not involve elected conventions, referenda or, except in New Brunswick, any general elections. Furthermore, manhood suffrage was not the rule in the elections which immediately followed the achievement of union. In the Province of Canada the pro-union political leaders, all dedicated to freedom, British institutions and self-government, openly criticized democratic ideals and assumptions. They lacked faith in majority rule and in the good sense of the common man.[3]

Confederation had, however, another dimension. The English-speaking leaders had to accept the permanent existence of the French-Canadian culture, at least in Quebec and the North-West, and the existence of a Province of Quebec dominated politically by a French majority. They thereby gave up any wistful hope, which any might still have cherished, in the discredited plan advanced by Lord Durham to assimilate that culture. They had to reject the American concept of majoritarian cultural homogeneity. The French-speaking leaders, relatively passive but nonetheless essential to the movement, abandoned much of the comfortable dualism of the Act of Union of 1840. Under that union, Upper and Lower Canada (Ontario and Quebec) each

2 Canada, *Parliamentary Debates on the Subject of the Confederation of the British North American Provinces* (Quebec, 1865, henceforth *Conf. Deb.*), pp. 29-45 (part of speech by John A. Macdonald).
3 Note the author's "Attitudes Toward Democracy During the Pre-Confederation Decade" (master's thesis, Queen's University, 1955).

permanently had the same number of seats in the lower house of parliament, even though growing Upper Canada had now a much larger population. The French also abandoned many of the dualistic contrivances which had grown up since the achievement in 1848 of responsible government, especially the convention of double-barrelled, jointly-led ministries. Without this great compromise or entente, one which involved the notion of a bilateral union of two cultures or two nationalities, no British North America union seems conceivable. The entente was developed informally, ironically almost subconsciously, thanks to the growing sensitivity of that relatively small body of men who had been presiding over the troubled relations between the two communities. It was worked out during the months of June, July and August of 1864, before the Charlottetown Conference. Confederation was thus meant to solve the old dilemma which had paralyzed the Province of Canada.

The essential nature of the union was subordinate federalism and limited biculturalism. The crucial aim was to escape the shackles of the old Canadian union and to establish politically an anti-continentalist, east-west, northern nation still linked protectively to the British crown. The basic structure of the central parliament was representation by population in the elected house of commons and representation by regions in the appointed senate; if, as most expected, the eastern provinces formed a Maritime union then this senate would be based on representation by province.

To John A. Macdonald, the leading exponent of subordinate federalism who was to become the first prime minister, the system would involve the central supervision of minority rights and indeed the continued central supervision of all policy which might have national significance. Unlike British imperial supervision, this supervision would not decline. As localism diminished, as contacts among the regions increased and as distances effectively shortened, people would become Canadians first and foremost. The best and most ambitious young men would seek central rather than provincial office. Macdonald's conservative commitment to "constitutional liberty as opposed to democracy" was a commitment to ordered freedom, due subordination and minority protection by means of a "powerful central government."[4] One of the devices for this supervision would be the normal operation of authority within the political process. Men, not mere institutions, would make the system work. The written document was merely a skeleton; politicians themselves would add the essential flesh.[5] Within that written document, however, were many formal

4 G. P. Brown, ed., *Documents on the Confederation of British North America* (Carleton Library, Toronto, 1969), pp. 94-95.
5 Ibid., p. 98.

devices for supervision, including the right of the central government
to disallow provincial acts and to appoint provincial lieutenant governors who would remain federal civil servants able to promote federal
objectives and reserve provincial bills. Because British North Americans were forming one union, "with the local governments and legislatures subordinate to the General Government and Legislature," it was,
Macdonald argued, "obvious that the chief executive officer in each of
the provinces must be subordinate as well."

> The General Government assumes towards the local governments pre-
> cisely the same position as the Imperial Government holds with respect to
> each of the colonies now; so that as the Lieutenant Governor of each of the
> different provinces is now appointed directly by the Queen, and is directly
> responsible, and reports directly to Her, so will the executives of the local
> governments hereafter be subordinate to the Representative of the
> Queen, and be responsible and report to him.[6]

In the special field of education, which normally was provincial, the
central parliament was given power to pass remedial legislation if
provinces tampered with legal minority rights.

To Macdonald his concept of subordinate federalism was intimately linked to his attitude toward democracy. Like all conservative
Fathers, he rejected both the word democracy and many of those
attributes now considered essential for it. He rejected political equality,
favoured privilege for the propertied and the well-off, and seemed
more concerned about protecting the rights of the minority than
providing for majority rule. He championed the autonomy of a
monarchical British Canada and the supremacy of parliament, but he
rejected the necessary logic of representation by mere numbers and
the need and wisdom of popular appeals on matters as vital as Confederation. Such an appeal, he argued, would be the device of a tyrant,
would "subvert the principles of the British Constitution" and would be
an "obvious absurdity."[7] The sovereign and her governor general,
advised by a responsible ministry, would represent the whole nation
rather than the mere ephemeral majority as did the American president. Macdonald favoured an appointive upper house. But though
secondary to the lower house and though based on equal representation for each section, it was to play a more significant role than George
Brown envisioned. It was to be an appropriate North American version
of the House of Lords. With restrictive qualification for membership, it
would represent the principle of property. "The rights of the minority
ought to be protected," he argued, "and the rich are always fewer in
number than the poor." Such an upper house would provide "a sober

6 *Conf. Deb.*, p. 42.
7 Ibid., p. 1004; and PAC, Macdonald Papers, Macdonald to S. Amsden, 1 December
   1864.

second thought," even though in North America its members would necessarily be persons "springing from the people."[8]

During the Confederation debates Macdonald argued that no one at the Quebec Conference had favoured universal suffrage, and "that classes and property should be represented as well as numbers."[9] As late as 1889, when alarmed by surging democracy and American ideas, he urged greater influence for the "monarchical idea . . . accompanied by some gradation of classes."[10] During the election campaign of 1861, he wrote that the outcome might decide whether Canada was to be "a limited Constitutional Monarchy or a Yankee Democracy."[11] Confederation for Macdonald and others was certainly not directed against Britain. The Quebec scheme involved a deliberate attempt to establish a union with a constitution similar in principle to that of Great Britain. It involved an attempt by British American leaders to create a viable, legitimate nation apart and different from the revolutionary, republican and aggressively democratic nation to the south. In the United States, democracy had allegedly resulted in a lack of moral force, in a weakening of the sense of authority and responsibility, and in government by faction.[12] Macdonald thus disagreed most emphatically with Goldwin Smith, then of Oxford University, who in 1863 wrote: "It would seem that if Canadian monarchy differs from American democracy as painted by its worst enemies, it is only as the Irishman's ride in a sedan chair with the bottom out differed from common walking."[13] To Macdonald democracy was unconservative, illiberal, republican and dangerous; in a phrase, it was un-British and hence un-Canadian.

Finally, the conferring of the residual power upon the central authority would ensure the advantage of national unity and avoid the conflicts of coordinate federalism:

> We have given the General Legislature all the great subjects of legislation. We have conferred on them, not only specifically and in detail, all the powers which are incident to sovereignty, but we have expressly declared that all subjects of general interest not distinctly and exclusively conferred upon the local governments and local legislatures, shall be conferred upon the General Government and Legislature. . . . We have avoided all conflict of jurisdiction and authority, and if this constitution is carried out, as it will be in full detail in the Imperial Act to be passed if the colonies

---

8 Browne, *Documents*, p. 98; *Conf. Deb.*, pp. 33 and 37.

9 Ibid., p. 39.

10 Sir Joseph Pope, ed., *Correspondence of Sir John A. Macdonald* (Toronto, 1921), p. 450, Macdonald to Baron Knutsford, 18 July 1889.

11 Cited in C. B. Sissons, *Egerton Ryerson: His Life and Letters*, 2 vols. (Toronto, 1947), 2: 426.

12 *Conf. Deb.*, p. 33; Browne, *Documents*, pp. 96-97.

13 Goldwin Smith, *The Empire: A Series of Letters Published in the "Daily News," 1862-1863* (Oxford, 1863), p. 108.

adopt the scheme, we will have in fact, as I said before, all the advantages of a legislative union under one administration, with, at the same time, the guarantees for local institutions and local laws, which are insisted upon by so many in the provinces now, I hope, to be united.[14]

Negotiations toward a federal union had been made possible by the coalition, in June 1864, of the Conservative forces of Macdonald and Cartier with the powerful Grit faction of Upper Canadian Reform led by George Brown, the fiery liberal editor of the province's leading newspaper, the Toronto *Globe*. Brown, as leader of the largest single Upper Canadian political bloc, has often been portrayed as a democrat. Was not this British-inspired liberal the champion of representation by population, the critic of sectarian and sectional privilege, and the opponent of slavery and primogeniture? In 1865 Brown was much more moderate than he had been in the fifties, yet in 1857 he wrote in his *Globe* that "democratic theories" were inadequate "to the wants of a mixed society," and that the broader the suffrage "the more we add to the dangerous element." The extension of the franchise, he argued, had to await the "diffusion of education" and "what a mass of ignorance is still to be encountered in every constituency!"[15]

Long a critic of American republicanism, Brown argued that because of democracy, the American political parties had to eschew before the public all questions of high policy in favour of cant phrases and vituperative attacks. "The balance of power," he argued, "is held by the ignorant unreasoning mass; to swing them is the grand aim of the contest and as truth, character, statesmanship, honest policy, and fair argument would be thrown away upon them, both parties by consent—nay by necessity—resort to other expedients."[16] For Brown, the liberal-monarchist, democracy was too closely identified with American democratic republicanism. To him it involved universal suffrage, the inordinately wide use of the elective principle, a lack of respect for authority, and a tendency for government under popular impulses to go carelessly to extremes. He saw democracy as illiberal, as a threat to individualism and free institutions, as promoting the tyranny of the unreasoning majority. Yet he had seen no illiberalism either in his vehement Free Kirk opposition to separate schools for the Roman Catholic minority of Upper Canada, who regarded the religiously-centred classroom as vital to its view of life, or in his own demand for province-wide representation by population without substantial safeguards for the French Canadians of Lower Canada. His acceptance in 1858 of the idea of some internal federation for the Province of Canada was partial recognition that some such protection

14 *Conf. Deb.*, p. 33.
15 23 September 1857.
16 Ibid.

was necessary to persuade French Canadians that representation by population could be operated with justice to all.[17] By 1865 he was much more sensitive to the fears of French Canadians, yet he remained wary of democracy as an article of faith. He opposed an appeal to the people over Confederation, even by means of an election, as being "an insult" to the Queen.[18]

Throughout his career, Brown was the champion of Upper Canadian rights. As a mid-Victorian British liberal, he had implicit faith in the wisdom of an honest simple majority in the lower house of parliament, if chosen through representation by population, by an intelligent, reasonably well-educated and therefore restricted electorate. He long opposed the principle of the double majority advanced by his fellow but rival Reformer, John Sandfield Macdonald. Between 1858 and 1864 he considered various schemes to solve the disruptive problems of the Province of Canada by redividing it through some form of federation. Sometimes these schemes seemed to imply a centralized federation, other times, a rather decentralized one. He did not, however, articulate any clear doctrine of federalism.

During the summer of 1864, after the coalition had been formed, Brown seemed confident that deliverance from what he had long considered to be French-Canadian dominance was at hand.[19] While recognizing the continued existence of French Canada, he became convinced that Upper Canadian Reformers were about to gain the ascendancy over a united British North America. They would be led by members of the new Toronto business community like himself. He naively thought that he, or probably his colleagues, would emerge victorious rather than John A. Macdonald; Macdonald, the Conservative, had a much smaller Upper Canadian following and had suffered a humiliating Upper Canadian defeat in the last election, that of 1863. Brown, therefore, then saw the existence of provincial governments mainly as a device to guarantee the French in Quebec their cultural survival and remove them from interference in Upper Canadian social institutions, especially education.

During the negotiations leading up to Confederation, Brown advanced extremely centralist arguments. He was, after all, a leading Toronto businessman who had long had his eyes on the North-West, and centralist institutions under the dominance of a Toronto-led Upper Canadian progressive electorate would facilitate business expansion. Back in 1859 it had been his fear for the preservation of the

17 J. M. S. Careless, *Brown of the Globe*, vol. I: *The Voice of Upper Canada, 1858-1859* (Toronto, 1959), p. 280.
18 *Conf. Deb.*, p. 991.
19 This is what Brown meant when on 27 October, after the Quebec Conference, he wrote to Anne Brown, his wife, "Is it not wonderful? French Canadianism entirely extinguished." PAC, Brown Papers.

common market of the non-American part of the St. Lawrence-Great Lakes basin that had helped induce him to oppose radical decentralism within the Province of Canada.[20] Speaking in camera at the Quebec Conference in 1864, Brown argued that Upper Canadians did not want expensive local governments nor ones which would take up "political matters." Fixed legislative terms for a unicameral body and centrally appointed lieutenant governors "would bring these bodies into harmony with the General Government." He proposed the direct election of executive officers with fixed terms, probably subject to removal; they would serve as a council actually presided over by the lieutenant governor, without any premier. Full responsible government was unnecessary, considering "how insignificant are the matters agreed at Charlottetown to be left the local Governments."[21]

During the Canadian debates on the Quebec Resolutions, in February 1865, Brown argued that complete legislative union was not administratively practical nor would it produce justice in taxation; besides, politically it could not have been secured. Yet the proposed scheme had "all the advantages of a Legislative union and a Federal one as well." The major powers, especially in the economic sphere and concerning the appointment of judges, were "retained" at the central level; the divisive issues were "thrown over on the localities." By central supervision of local measures, he asserted, "we have secured that no injustice shall be done without appeal in local legislatures." Important powers were central powers, and in the central legislature representation by population would finally be secured, thereby bringing "complete justice" at last to Upper Canada. The securing of that in the plan "alone, renders all the blemishes averred against it utterly contemptible in the balance."[22]

Then in 1866 he again publicly advanced his arguments. Having recently resigned from the coalition cabinet, he was no longer restrained by any pressures for solidarity. The occasion was the debate in Ottawa, at the final session of the provincial parliament, on the proposed constitution for Ontario. The full responsible cabinet system was unnecessary at the new provincial level, he argued. Department heads needed not to be in the legislature, and the model for provincial regimes ought to be contemporary county councils.[23] All of this was totally unacceptabale to Cartier and French Canada. John A. Macdonald knew this and successfully opposed the proposal, as did John Sandfield Macdonald, the rather centralist leader of the opposition.

20 Note Elwood Jones, "Ephemeral Compromise: The Great Reform Convention Revisited," *Journal of Canadian Studies* 3 (February 1968): 21-28.
21 Browne, *Documents*, pp. 113-14, 142.
22 *Conf. Deb.*, pp. 108 and 92.
23 *Globe*, 3 August 1866; and Canadian Library Association (microfilm), *Parliamentary Debates*, 3 August 1866.

The latter, who had voted against the union because he considered even his namesake's federalism as too divisive and costly, now argued mildly that it would be a serious violation of responsible government to have provincial lieutenant governors appointed by the central government.[24] But the combined wills of John A. Macdonald and Brown prevailed. No signs existed here from Brown, the tribune of Upper Canada who was to become the spiritual father of provincial rights, of that fine balance and noninterference which within two years he would argue as the basis of all true federalism, Canada's included.

Some of Brown's leading disciples, especially Oliver Mowat and Alexander Mackenzie, would not have shared these extremely centralist sentiments, but they did not clearly record their opposition. Basically they were satisfied with their leader and what he was achieving. Mowat and many other Reformers had favoured in 1864 an elective upper house for the new union; Brown effectively argued in favour of an appointed upper house so that, and he was correct, such a chamber might be politically weak.[25] For Ontario, he successfully argued against any upper house at all. In late 1864 Mowat was appointed to the bench and therefore was not involved in the crucial Assembly debates over federalism. Mackenzie, a staunch advocate of union, seems to have been confused as to its federalist details. He claimed both that he would have preferred a legislative union if that could have been "adapted to our circumstances" and also that the new union was essentially the same as that proposed by the Reform Conventions of 1859, but geographically "carried to a greater extent."[26] Certainly he advocated none of the concise coordinate federalism which in 1872 he claimed he had always advocated.[27] The same might be said of William McDougall, still a Reformer but now seriously distrusted by Brown, because in 1862 he had temporarily abandoned representation by population in favour of personal political office. Although McDougall had once, back in 1850, been a political radical, none of the three men in 1865 could have been called or would want to have been called democrats.

In Lower Canada the two leading English-speaking proponents of union were A. T. Galt and T. D. McGee. As Minister of Finance in the coalition, Galt designed the financial clauses of the British North America Act and represented the Protestant forces of Montreal and the Eastern Townships. The great orator and prophet of Confederation, McGee represented the Irish Catholics. Galt was a no-nonsense pragmatic conservative who saw Confederation essentially as a business merger and feared the growth of democratic tendencies; yet he

24 *Leader* (Toronto), 28 July 1866; and *Globe*, 28 July and 3 August 1866.
25 *Conf. Deb.*, pp. 80-90; and Peter Waite, *Life and Times of Confederation*, p. 82, especially note 40.
26 *Conf. Deb.*, pp. 421-34.
27 *Globe*, 8 February 1872.

flirted with republicanism. The English of Lower Canada particularly feared provincial rights because they were about to become an exposed minority in the new Province of Quebec, a tempting economically privileged minority. Galt argued that the provinces would be simply "municipalities of larger ground"; if a local legislature clashed with the central government, the lieutenant governor would report the situation to "superior authority."[28] In these sentiments, Galt was totally backed by the *Montreal Gazette* and the *Quebec Chronicle*.[29]

In many ways, McGee, the former radical liberal who had become a staunch monarchist and philosophical conservative, was really an apologist for the Montreal business community.[30] Yet better than any other he caught the vision of a new nationality, of a future greatness for a transcontinental, monarchical and non-American New Britannia of the North.[31] He used the word federation but virtually explained it away in centralist British terms which saw the units as subordinate municipal entities.[32] Long the champion of state-supported parochial schools, McGee extolled the central supervision of minority rights.

In the Conservative, Christopher Dunkin, the Lower Canadian opponents of the scheme had a brilliant mind. Galt's equal in his analysis of figures, he incisively criticized the financial clauses of the scheme of union; many of his prophecies turned out to be correct. Bitterly anti-democratic, he condemned the union as too liberal, insufficiently centralist and insufficiently British. "I have no fancy for democratic or republican forms or institutions, or indeed for revolutionary or political novelties of any sort," he said. "The phrase 'political creation' is no phrase of mine." Only God could create. Man could only "attend to" and develop His creations, and if growth were to be healthy, it "must be slow."[33]

In the negotiations preceding Confederation it was the French-speaking members of the Canadian cabinet, the *Bleus*, who emphasized provincial autonomy. Thus French-Canadian politicians, the hierarchy, and journalists were the people who most talked the jargon of federalism. The *Rouges*, or French-speaking liberals, who opposed Confederation, claimed it was centralist and assimilationist and would sacrifice the French-Canadian nationality. Even Cartier and Premier E. P. Taché believed that strong French-Canadian ministers in the central government and a strong Lower Canadian voice in the central

28 A. T. Galt, *Speech on the Proposed Union of the British North American Provinces* (Montreal, 1864), pp. 14-15.
29 *Gazette*, 2 and 9 September 1864; *Chronicle*, 10 September and 29 October 1864.
30 Robin B. Burns, "D'Arcy McGee and the Economic Aspects of New Nationality," *CHA Report, 1967*, pp. 95-104.
31 Thomas D'Arcy McGee, *Speeches and Addresses chiefly on the Subject of British-American Union* (London, 1865), pp. 8, 86-90, 110, 129, 131 and 195; *Globe*, 19 June and 6 July 1863; and *Conf. Deb.*, pp. 143-46.
32 Ibid., p. 145.
33 Ibid., p. 483.

parliament would better protect the rights of their nationality than would the provincial legislature. The *Bleu* veteran, Joseph Cauchon, particularly accepted a great deal of centralism. Nevertheless in its attempt to beat down the *Rouge* assault, the *Bleu* press emphasized the high degree of provincial autonomy in the proposed union. *Le Courrier du Canada* (edited by J. C. Taché), a paper close to Premier Taché, emphasized that the central government would not be allowed to interfere in any provincial affairs and that the central parliament would not be able to touch education, administration of justice, and the provincial economy.[34] Thus in Lower Canada, Conservative pro-union newspapers were saying exactly the opposite things. The English press emphasized the centralism of the plan, and the French press claimed that the union would establish in fact several "*Etats souverains*," states completely independent within their spheres, delegating certain rights to the central authority.[35] The latter, at least in 1864, also emphasized that the situation was critical, that the alternative to Confederation was American annexation and assimilation.

This hardly made the French-Canadian political leadership or that majority of French-speaking members of parliament that did indeed vote for union convinced constitutional federalists. They were ambivalent. The jargon and the institutional expressions were frequently federalist, but the preconceptions and primary motivations were based on the concept of *la survivance*. In 1865 Cartier and Premier Taché were not primarily concerned with the rights of provinces but with the rights of the French-Canadian minority in a British North American union. Some of these rights would find expression in the jurisdiction of the Province of Quebec; others would find entrenched expression in central jurisdiction and in French-Canadian politicians at the central level. For them, the arrangement was basically bilateral not multilateral. It was an arrangement between two cultural groups more than a union of three or four provinces. Cartier and Taché were not particularly concerned about the status of Nova Scotia or New Brunswick. Over Brown's initial objections, they were able to limit the power of provincial majorities by establishing a degree of protection for Catholic minorities outside of Quebec, a protection readily accepted for the Protestant minority within Quebec.

Constitutionally, and this was more than mere form, "the Queen's most Excellent Majesty, by and with the advice and consent of the Lords Spiritual and Temporal, and Commons"[36] created the dominion of Canada. The original provinces did not and could not so create. The

34 11 juillet and 26 décembre 1864; note P. B. Waite, "*Le Courrier du Canada* and the Quebec Resolutions, 1864-1865," *CHR* 40 (December 1959): 294-303.
35 *Gazette*, 24 August and 2 and 9 September 1864; *Le Canadien* (Quebec), 24 août 1864; note also *La Minerve* (Montreal), 30 août 1864 and note 34 above.
36 BNA Act, Preamble.

British North America Act created Ontario and Quebec, which immediately beforehand had no separate provincial existence. But
thanks largely to the French Canadians, the provinces obtained considerable if very circumscribed power, including the vital cultural
spheres of education and "property and civil rights."[37] The act contained numerous and complicated guarantees for minorities, but the
guarantees in education were expressed in religious terms, "Protestant" and "Roman Catholic," rather than linguistic terms. Most of the
separate school supporters in Ontario had been of Irish and Scottish
rather than French descent; politically the Franco-Ontarians were
even more insignificant than the Acadians of New Brunswick. The act
said nothing about the Acadians or about any French rights in the
Maritimes. Only Section 133 explicitly concerned language:

> Either the English or the French language may be used in the debates of
> the Houses of the Parliament of Canada and of the Houses of the Legisla-
> ture of Quebec; and both those languages may be used by any person or in
> any pleading or process in or issuing from any Court of Canada estab-
> lished under this Act, and in or from all or any of the Courts of Quebec.

> The Acts of the Parliament of Canada and of the Legislature of Quebec
> shall be printed and published in both those languages.

These were minimum guarantees for French outside of Quebec and,
perhaps more importantly, for English within Quebec. Territorially,
the act guaranteed some bilingualism in Quebec. It did not do so in
Ontario, but neither did it prohibit it; some even considered bilingualism to have been established in Ontario since the beginning.[38] The
act, in fact, protected English in neither New Brunswick nor Ontario; it
was merely silent. Many of the *Bleus* who thought about it believed that
the union guaranteed the educational rights of the Catholics in the
Maritime provinces and that, in the spirit of the age, educational rights
for Catholics covered linguistic and cultural rights.[39] There is little
evidence that the Maritime majority either understood or accepted this
idea.

   More than most English-Canadian Fathers of Confederation, Cartier and the other members of the *Bleu* elite, drawn almost exclusively
from the over-abundant professional middle class, feared the growth
of democracy as a political creed.[40] French Canada was certainly not a

37 BNA Act, Section 92.
38 E.g., Egerton Ryerson. C. B. Sissons, *Bilingual Schools in Canada* (Toronto, 1917), p. 27.
39 Note Ralph Heintzman, "The Spirit of Confederation: Professor Creighton, Bicul-
    turalism and the Use of History," *CHR* 52 (September 1971), especially 249-51; H. B.
    Best, "George Etienne Cartier" (doctoral dissertation, Laval, 1969), p. 391; but also
    note D. J. Hall, "The Spirit of Confederation: Ralph Heintzman, Professor
    Creighton, and the Bicultural Compact Theory," *Journal of Canadian Studies* 9
    (November 1974): 24-43.
40 Joseph Tassé, *Discours de Sir George Cartier accompagnés de notices* (Montréal, 1893), pp.
    269, 347, 376; *Conf. Deb.*, pp. 27, 57-60, and 571; for E. P. Taché note ibid., pp. 6-11,
    240-42, and *Gazette*, 8 July 1861.

democratic society, and it was probably becoming a less open society. Cartier deeply admired mid-century British parliamentary institutions with their alleged order and balance. He was deeply monarchist. A government founded on universal suffrage, he argued, "*ne peut durer longtemps*"; not just numbers but "*la proprieté et des classes*" had to be considered.[41] He defended an appointed upper house dominated by the men of property, and he saw to it that the new Quebec would have one. The defender of *la survivance* yet the solicitor for the Grand Trunk Railway, Cartier extolled the identification of the French-Canadian "*nationalité*" with "*le sol*,"[42] yet looked forward to the expansion of Montreal capitalism, which was clearly in English-Canadian hands. The implications of majority rule, popular sovereignty and American assimilationism naturally troubled him.

Yet Cartier was a moderate, secular Catholic, educated by his friends, the rather Gallican Sulpicians of Notre Dame de Grace in Montreal. Sulpicians were waging a long battle with the growing forces of ultramontanist reaction, represented in Montreal by the exclusivist and vehemently anti-liberal Bishop Bourget. Bourget seemed more ultramontanist than his inspiration, Pope Pius IX. The ultramontanists correctly never really trusted Cartier, who in comparison with them was a liberal radical. The moderate hierarchy, centred in Quebec City, backed Cartier and the federal scheme, first privately and then very officially. Bourget, like his hated enemies, the anti-clerical and agnostic *Rouges*, disliked the centralist aspects of the scheme and feared for the survival of the French-Canadian nation. Only with difficulty was Bourget kept relatively quiet and made ultimately to accept with resignation the new political order.[43] The hierarchy, both moderate and ultramontane, opposed the doctrine of democracy; in 1873, a spokesman for the ultramontanists was to call the idea of popular sovereignty "*un non-sens, une absurdité.*"[44]

At the Charlottetown and Quebec Conferences the main dialogue was between Canadians and Maritimers. In fact, at times, it was amongst the divided Maritimers themselves. The basic Canadian entente had been worked out by members of the Canadian ministry before they left for Charlottetown. Macdonald, Brown, McGee and others talked in 1865 about the Quebec Resolutions being a "treaty" or a "pact," agreed on by the provinces.[45] True enough. This was to prevent the provincial legislatures from altering various clauses. Legis-

41 Tassé, *Discours*, p. 269, also pp. 32, 53, 66, 270-71, 275, 498, 528, 602, 713-14.
42 Ibid., p. 65.
43 Waite, *Life and Times*, pp. 137-38 and 300-01.
44 "Luigi," *Le Don Quickotte Montréalais sur sa Rossinante ou M. Dessaulles et la "Grande Guerre Ecclésiastique"* (Montréal, 1873), p. 70.
45 *Conf. Deb.*, pp. 16 and 31-32 (Macdonald), p. 88 (Brown), p. 28 (McGee), p. 720 (McDougall); note George F. G. Stanley, "Act or Pact: Another Look at Confederation," *CHA Report, 1956*, pp. 1-25.

latures had to accept, they hoped, the whole package. This did not mean, of course, that Confederation was a result of a provincial compact. Furthermore, the Province of Canada and not the Provinces of Ontario and Quebec drew up the so-called "treaty" of the Quebec Resolutions. Besides, only Canada approved of these Resolutions. The London Resolutions were different from the Quebec Resolutions, and the British North America Act was slightly different from both. Ambitious provincial leaders who later advanced the compact theory were clearly historically wrong. The extra-legal cultural entente, which in spirit pervaded the entire provincial Canadian political elite, was quite different and vital. The French-Canadian cultural nationality would be able to prosper within the new political nationality. Although concentrated primarily in Quebec where it was the majority, the French-Canadian nationality could survive and expand in many other parts of the new country.

Clearly, Cartier believed that the French would have rights in the North-West, even though most of his compatriots seemed rather apathetic.[46] The great compromise, the rejection of assimilative majoritarianism, initially held. This was particularly significant because the North-West was the chief interest of Brown and the Grits. For Cartier, the French had historic ties with the huge area, and it might yet become another Lower Canada. The idea of the Pacific railway also captured his adventuresome mind. Others suggested that union would reunite the *Québecois* with the Métis and the Indian tribes of the plains, so that "*nous serons chez eux comme 'chez nous.'* "[47] It was Cartier, aided by Brown's former lieutenant William McDougall, who was chiefly responsible for negotiating the transfer of the Hudson's Bay Company lands to the new dominion. The tiny Manitoba carved out of this, at the junction of the Red and Assiniboine, had a population in 1871 of 14,000, over half of whom were French-speaking. Quebec supplied the model for the Manitoba Act. Section 22 guaranteed the continued existence of denominational schools, and Section 23 maintained official equality of English and French. Over half the members of the first provincial assembly were French-speaking, and the first premier, Marc Girard, was a recent émigré from Quebec. Nothing was said about French rights when British Columbia entered the union in 1871, nor when Prince Edward Island joined in 1873. The North-West Territories Act of 1875 provided that a school system when established

46 A. I. Silver, "French Canada and the Prairie Frontier, 1870-1890," *CHR* 50 (March 1969): 11-36, emphasizes how little interest most *Québécois* had in the North-West in contrast to their focus on their own frontier. Heintzman, in his article (see note 39), discusses in detail the expectations of Cartier and a few others concerning the North-West and Cartier's appreciation of the favourable response accorded these expectations by theEnglish-Canadian political leadership during the Confederation years.

47 *Le Courrier de St. Hyacinthe*, 19 décembre 1867.

would be on the dual model. An amendment in 1877, among other things, extended the guarantee of Section 133 of the British North America Act to the two languages in the territories.

The events of 1870 transpired under the Conservative-dominated regime of Macdonald and Cartier. The acts of 1875 and 1877 were passed under the Liberal regime of Alexander Mackenzie. The dual structure, however, did not last in the North-West, and its destruction is a long story. Yet clearly it was in the generous and elitist Canadian spirit of 1864-67 that it would last. Brown, himself, at the time claimed that it had always appeared to him that "the opening up of the North-west ought to be one of the most cherished prospects of my honourable friends from Lower Canada."[48]

In the legislative assembly of the Province of Canada, in March 1865, the Quebec Resolutions were approved by a vote of ninety-one to thirty-three.[49] The vote fortunately contained a double majority, that is a majority from Upper Canada and a majority from Lower Canada; it also contained a majority of English-Canadian members and, very narrowly, a majority of French-Canadian members. It contained the negative votes of only seven Upper Canadians. The seven were led by John Sandfield Macdonald, ironically the proponent of the double majority, who then believed in union but not federalism; three or more of his coincidental followers were, however, radical Grits who favoured more decentralism. The twenty-six Lower Canadian assemblymen who voted negatively included Dunkin and the unitarian liberal, L. H. Holton. Holton was another brilliant man of figures, most genuine in his breadth of vision and advanced social ideas who believed the plan to be fraught with trouble for the future; it was too centralist, too conservative, and too unsettling for French Canada.[50] Holton was a close friend and associate of A. A. Dorion. the *Rouge* leader.

The largest, most articulate and intelligent group to oppose union in the Canadian provincial parliament was the anti-clerical and rather democratic *Rouges* from the Montreal area. Although decentralist and sometimes narrowly nationalistic, their criticism of Cartier and the scheme of union was often most incisive. The plan was, argued Dorion, "the most illiberal constitution ever heard of in any country where constitutional government prevails." It was too centralist, too assimilationist, too capitalist, too reactionary and undemocratic; the whole scheme was "absurd from beginning to end."[51] On the road to transformation or oblivion, in the face of increasing attacks from an increasingly ultramontane, anti-liberal and powerful Church, the

48 *Conf. Deb.*, pp. 103-04.
49 Ibid., p. 962.
50 Ibid., pp. 147-48, 704-09, 937-41, 996-97 and 1021.
51 Ibid., pp. 245-69 and 694-95; also "Address to the Electors of Hochelaga," as reported in the *Globe*, 9 November 1864.

Rouges were largely dismissed. When decades later they achieved respectability under the Gladstonian Wilfrid Laurier much of their constructive uniqueness, but not their decentralism, would have disappeared. Cleansed of free thought and of social democracy, they would prove fitting allies of Mowat's Grits, and unwitting supporters of Ontario Orangemen in the destruction of the Macdonaldian constitution.[52]

Confederation was basically the achievement of a pre-democratic elite at the very time when ideas of political democracy and concepts of local majoritarianism were growing, especially in Upper Canada. The thrust for union came from Conservative and Reform leadership in Upper Canada and Conservative leadership in Montreal. This leadership was not decentralist. Devoted to parliamentary monarchy, these leaders were convinced that pure federalism was a weak, divisive form of government, one that had helped cause the recent bloodshed in the United States. Worried about American economic, cultural and political expansion, they believed that the imperial relationship was basically good and essential for Canadian survival. The threat to Canadian self-government came not from Britain but from internal dissension and the United States. Self-government combined with the concept of subordination under limited monarchy was uplifting not degrading. While capitalism was the only economic system conceivable, it must operate, they argued, under state direction. The business and political elites were logically connected. It was natural, they thought, that Toronto and Montreal should, with a gesture toward Halifax, dominate the union. No leaders advocated laissez faire, although Conservatives tended to favour more state involvement, preferment and direction than did Reformers. Religion was essential to public morality. Conservatives tended to favour a collective Christian church establishment, while Reformers tended to argue that, although society and politics were Christian, a strict separation of church and state should prevail. Reform leaders tended to be strongly Protestant, both Calvinist and evangelical, and to be critical of the authoritarianism of Catholicism, the unprogressive nature of French Catholics, the propensity to corruption of Irish Catholics and the lingering assumptions of superiority held by some Anglicans. Conservative and Reform leaders tended to believe that the role of government in society would remain in the future roughly what it was in the present; therefore, the financial demands on the central authority would remain much greater than those on the provincial authorities. The provincial units would help satisfy the French and certain particularist forces in the Maritimes. Relatively minor issues, often contentious under cultural pluralism,

52 Lovell C. Clark, "The Conservative Party in the 1890's," *Canadian History Since Confederation*, pp. 261-79.

could be handled by the provinces, thus removing much of the trouble which had brought old Canada to the brink of disaster.

The French Canadians achieved the degree of special status which they did, largely because their conservative political and religious leaders had enough power, albeit mainly negative or passive, to make sure that they were not ignored. They were dealing personally with a relatively small number of English Canadians who had gradually and with difficulty, learned to appreciate their problems and sensitivities. Politically, Cartier had leverage. The French-Canadian people appear not to have been at all enthusiastic about union; most perhaps saw it as better than annexation, if, as their leaders said, the status quo could not long be preserved. To Dorion and the *Rouges*, it was a bad, illiberal deal for French Canada, and quite a large minority seems to have agreed with them.

In English Canada, especially in Ontario and later Manitoba, there were many people who shared neither the centralist views of their political leaders nor, in some cases, their generous spirit toward the French. Often localists, they were not convinced of the virtues of cultural diversity, bilingualism and serious compromise. In the proud Maritimes most people would be unwilling to accept meekly a union so dominated by "Upper Canadians" and so unsympathetic to their problems and unique ways. Furthermore, most Ontarians, including those who settled in the North-West, most Maritimers and British Columbians, most Conservatives as well as Reformers, most Orange Irish, Green Irish and Grits, had never really heard of the great cultural compromise or entente by which the political elite of old Canada had made Confederation possible.

IV

Federalism and the Politics of Ontario, 1867-80

BRUCE W. HODGINS and ROBERT C. EDWARDS

It was probably inevitable that Ontario would be the pivotal province in the Canadian union. It had the largest population and greatest growth potential; as Upper Canada, it had supplied both the intense dissatisfaction with the old constitutional arrangements and also the bulk of the leadership in promoting the new system. Sir John A. Macdonald, the first Conservative Prime Minister, and in 1873 Alexander Mackenzie, the first Liberal Prime Minister, were Ontarians. Yet Ontarians and their provincial government led in the overthrow of the grand national design of that first Prime Minister, the chief architect of the union. "It is a commentary on the vanity of political calculations," wrote Norman McLeod Rogers forty years ago, "that before two years had elapsed Macdonald was compelled to acknowledge the failure of the precautions so carefully taken to avoid an issue on the question of provincial rights."[1] Although it was not obvious until 1896, it is evident to the careful historical observer that by 1880 Ontarians had frustrated Sir John A.'s grand design.

This change took place during the Ontario premierships of three men: John Sandfield Macdonald (1867-71), Edward Blake (1871-72) and Oliver Mowat (1872-96). All, particularly Mowat, played a role in altering the system. But more important than any provincial government was the deep abiding Upper Canadian, now Ontarian, commitment to self-government and local authority and the developing grass roots concept of majoritarian populist democracy. To this commitment was added the fact that Ontarians had never really understood the grand design. Furthermore, the growing young dominion was such a vast land with such great cultural and physical diversity that no success-

---

1 Norman McLeod Rogers, "The Genesis of Provincial Rights," *CHR* 14 (March 1933): 17.

ful central government, however sympathetic, could ever hope to satisfy ethnocentric Ontario, the country's most powerful unit.

Yet for the centre all was not lost. Ontario business interests and others wanted a central government able to give leadership in economic development, especially outside Ontario. Although the imperial role of the central government in restraining Ontario legislation and in protecting provincial minorities, especially in the Maritimes and the West, had a short life, the economic imperial role, with Ottawa as the joint agent of the rival Toronto and Montreal elites, lived on. In 1878 Ontarians, in endorsing the National Policy of protective tariffs, gave Sir John A. Macdonald and his Conservatives, for the first time in their own right, a clear popular majority (52 per cent). The next year, an Ontario plurality (48 per cent) reendorsed the Ontario system by reelecting Oliver Mowat and his provincial Liberals to office in Toronto.

The first premier of Ontario was John Sandfield Macdonald, the leading Ontarian to have opposed the Confederation scheme. Now, ironically, finding himself heading an anti-Grit coalition government, he attempted to operate the Macdonaldian system. In the August-September elections of 1867, which he and Sir John A. had won, he had tried to explain his position. He still believed in the integrity of the St. Lawrence valley. He still had misgivings about the cost and efficacy of federalism, and he still believed that people rather than constitutions had been the source of the old trouble. He would attempt to work the system. He believed that it was necessary to "harmonize" the two levels of government, and to keep from power the "extreme wing of the Reform party," that is, the Grit element led by his old foe, George Brown. But although he would work closely with Sir John A., the Prime Minister, he would remain a Reformer and subservient to no one.[2]

During the four years of his premiership, Sandfield never did become a dupe or flunkey of the central government. In fact he contested with the federal authorities on many matters and actually increased the prestige and the status of Ontario. But this secular, tolerant Scottish Catholic from Cornwall near the border of Quebec, whose commercial ties had been with Montreal, not Toronto, was insufficiently Upper Canadian. He was not a champion of provincial rights, and he under-estimated the capacity of Brown and his *Globe* to tap the wells of localist and particularist sentiment found throughout the province. From the commencement of the Canadian union, the bulk of Ontarians appear not to have endorsed or understood the essence of the new constitutional system and indeed to have dissented from both their premier and their prime minister on this score.

2 *Globe* (Toronto), 25 and 30 July 1867; *Leader* (weekly, Toronto), 2 August 1867.

Sandfield did not take exception to Sir John A.'s careful examination and private comment and criticism of Ontario legislation. Apart from the official exchanges which were published, the two first ministers engaged in a heavy private correspondence. Late in 1868, Sir John A. complimented Sandfield on his "vigor and ability" and on the "management of your comparatively untried Legislature." Although only two Ontario acts were disallowed and no bills were reserved, Sir John A. often urged Sandfield to make changes. Arguing back and forth with civility, they shared the triumphs. On balance, however, the Kingston man in Ottawa found that the Cornwall man in Toronto went "too far"; he was too inclined to paddle "his own canoe," particularly in a reform, even radical direction unchecked by an upper house.[3] Three acts passed during the second session ending in January 1869 caused the most trouble. The first, attached to the supply bill, provided for extra pay, over and above salary paid by the Canadian government which made the appointments, for judges of the superior courts of Ontario. The second provided for possible removal by the lieutenant governor in council of county court judges, though these judges too were centrally appointed and removable by the governor general. The third established for members of the legislative assembly rights and privileges approaching those of members of the British house of commons. The Prime Minister and other Canadian authorities asked the Ontario government to repeal these laws. The Premier replied officially with what even the Prime Minister, who was also Minister of Justice, characterized as "a very able State paper." Sandfield was firm on the first and third items and somewhat conciliatory on the second. On the first matter Ontario would and did pass a substitute act paying judges of the Court of Error and Appeal who were in fact the same persons as the superior court judges in the original bill. Nevertheless, after clearing the matter privately with Sandfield, Sir John A. had the original one disallowed for fear that the Colonial Office might order the new one vetoed after the twelve-month deadline for stopping the original. On the second act Sandfield also had a substitute passed, sticking to principle but making it clear that no usurpation of central authority was intended; this act survived, perhaps because the Prime Minister was ill when it would have been considered. On the matter of privileges and amenities for members of the legislature, Sandfield dug in, logically arguing that if it could grant privileges to a court or municipal council it could grant them to itself, and that if not, it "would

3 Numerous letters in the PAC, John A. Macdonald Papers: e.g., J. A. Macdonald to R. Stephenson, 8 October 1871, refers to the canoe and Macdonald to Macpherson, 7 February 1871, refers to the radicalism; and PAC, John Sandfield Macdonald Papers (J.S.M. Papers); e.g., J. A. Macdonald to J.S.M., 14 December 1868, refers both to J.S.M.'s "management" and his "going too far"; and Canada, Department of Justice, *Correspondence, Reports of the Minister of Justice and Orders-in-Council upon the Subject of Provincial Legislation, 1867-1884*, ed. W. E. Hodgins (Ottawa, 1886).

be unable to maintain its dignity, and would be more feeble than a Justice of the Peace, who has a right to punish for contempt." It was of no avail. Here he was really fighting the privileges of the governor general. The act was disallowed. It was not replaced until 1875, after Quebec had safely secured one similar to the disallowed Ontario act; meanwhile the Ontario legislature continued to behave as if the act had not been vetoed.[4] The claim that the Reformer Macdonald was under the thumb of the Conservative Macdonald was "baseless."[5]

Sandfield's problems with Sir John A., however, revolved around political rather than constitutional questions. With the Grit leadership articulating popular sentiment in favour of Ontario rights, the outcome of these political problems had significance for Canadian federalism. In the spring of 1868 the Prime Minister had William Howland, a Coalition Reform member of the dominion cabinet, appointed as lieutenant governor of Ontario without consultation with the Ontario Premier. This, of course, suited the Prime Minister's civil service view of that office. But for Sandfield, the old Baldwinite, patronage was the crucial device whereby a responsible government shored up its power and prestige. The Prime Minister was well aware of this as far as he himself was concerned, but he failed to comprehend the extreme vulnerability of the Reform Premier in a dominion-provincial Coalition increasingly identified with the Conservative tradition. There were other similar events. Nevertheless, Sandfield with reluctance accompanied Sir John A. that summer on his successful mission to Halifax to win over a much more truculent Reformer, Joseph Howe, to the cause of Confederation and the Coalition. Then the next year, Sir John A., after having the ill-fated McDougall, the Reform leader in the dominion cabinet, appointed to the post of lieutenant governor of the North-West Territory, brought old Sir Francis Hincks, recently returned from the governorship of British Guiana, into the cabinet as Reform leader and Minister of Finance. Now Brown, the Grits and Sandfield all knew that Hincks was no real Reformer; in fact they all thought of him as the reprehensible scoundrel who had disrupted the old Reform party in 1854. The Prime Minister, thinking that it was quite a coup, knew that Hinck's appointment could enrage Brown; he failed to see how it would isolate

4 W. E. Hodgins, *Correspondence*, pp. 37-67, including the Report of Mr. Attorney General [Sandfield] Macdonald, 1 September 1869; J.S.M. Papers, J. A. Macdonald to J.S.M., 14 December 1868, 29 October and 4 November 1869, and 20 January 1870; Macdonald Papers, J.S.M. to J. A. Macdonald, 6 November 1869, J. A. Macdonald to J.S.M., 18 November and 18 December 1869.

5 Adam Shortt and Arthur Doughty, eds., *Canada and its Provinces*, vol. 2: *The Province of Ontario* (Toronto, 1914), p. 108. Despite the wisdom of this source, writers have often accepted Grit propaganda on this matter; e.g., J. C. Morrison, "Oliver Mowat and the Development of Provincial Rights in Ontario: A Study in Dominion-Provincial Relations, 1867-1896," *Three History Theses* (Toronto, 1961), pp. 60-63 and 185-92.

Sandfield.[6] Despite Grit denunciation, the Coalition was still essential in Toronto, but it was wearing pretty thin in Ottawa. Sandfield's only really capable cabinet colleagues, Matthew Cameron and John Carling, were Conservatives. Sandfield's position depended on the credibility of the Coalition, and, as it turned out, the viability of the Macdonaldian system depended to a considerable degree on the political isolation of the Grits for yet a few more years. Sandfield's stand on federalism was further undermined by the unpopularity in Ontario of the "better terms" for Nova Scotia and the federal government's handling of the Red River troubles, including its negotiating with alleged revolutionaries.

Meanwhile, the *Globe* and the Grit opposition, building on genuine feelings for local self-determination and on old Upper Canadian prejudices and frustrations with the direction of the administration in Ottawa, were maturing the alien doctrines of classical or coordinate federalism. But the ingredients of the doctrines were all present by the summer of 1867. Indeed, although Brown did not recognize these ingredients during the Confederation negotiations when he was a dedicated centralist, they were present much earlier among many of the secondary Grit leadership. Between the summer of 1864 and the eve of Confederation, Brown was convinced that, through representation by population and other devices, Upper Canadians would dominate the union; naturally, the liberal and progressive commercial elite of Toronto would lead, in alliance with the prolific yeoman farmers. By detouring east to bring in the Maritimes, the North-West could be secured and made an extension of Upper Canada, not constitutionally but in terms of values and institutions. The superior political skill of Sir John A. and the disunity of Reformers or Liberals throughout the new dominion frustrated all that. Most of the leading Maritime politicians who supported Confederation, even if they had been Liberals, joined with the Coalition. In Ontario, Sir John A. had, through the Lieutenant Governor, engineered the appointment of Sandfield as Premier, and Sandfield had, in Brown's view, treacherously endorsed the Coalition.[7]

For Brown the only answer was classical federalism. Henceforth—without admitting, probably even to himself, that he had changed his mind—all behaviour would have to be judged deductively from the abstract Platonic model of pure federalism. Without in any way abandoning representation by population or the quest for Ontario rights and influence in Ottawa, Ontario would have to be strengthened. To achieve this, Sandfield would have to be denounced

6   Macdonald Papers, Hincks to J. A. Macdonald, 20 September, 7 and 9 October and 8 November 1869; J. A. Macdonald to Hincks, 18 October 1869 and J. A. Macdonald to John Carling, 19 October 1869.
7   Bruce W. Hodgins, *John Sandfield Macdonald: 1812-1872* (Toronto, 1971), pp. 86-88.

and eliminated, and the immoral ruse of Coalition exposed and destroyed.

"Monstrous" was the way the *Globe* on July 30, 1867, described Sandfield's claim that there ought to be an attempt to "harmonize" politically the two levels of government. The "Confederate system" had been established "for the purpose of securing to the separate Provinces the management of their own affairs."[8] "Under a Federal system," the *Globe* lectured its readers, provincial governments "are essentially independent of the general authority. If they were not independent, their existence would be useless." It would be "as improper" for the "Confederate Government" to interfere in provincial affairs as for the imperial government "to dictate to our Confederate Government." Behind the Ontario Premier was John A. Macdonald who, in the first month of its operation, had seriously violated the constitution.[9] The two chief ministers, argued the *Globe*, had brought "our system of government into contempt."[10] "Separation of parties" went along with the division of powers. The source of past conflict lay "in sectional not in political strife." Federalism properly practised could keep sectional issues out of the general legislature. Reformers would "do battle for equal rights to all classes and circles irrespective of locality."[11] Through Coalition and the French vote, Sir John A. hoped to maintain Tory dominance over Canada, the *Globe* believed, but federalism and political cooperation with Maritimers would prevent this once the elections were over.[12] The two Macdonalds had to be defeated. Sandfield's position violated the federal principle which made the government and legislature of Ontario "within its own limit independent of the General Government altogether."[13] Sandfield, the *Globe* argued, wanted a legislative union and that was what the Coalitionists were seeking, but federalism prevented coercion.[14] Sandfield was, the *Globe* concluded on August 14, 1867, a greater threat to the union than Joseph Howe because Sandfield was working from within to destroy the provinces. But the Coalition won the elections, and Brown remained frustrated.

For the next four years Brown's *Globe* attacked Sandfield and the Macdonaldian system of subordinate federalism. Sandfield's behaviour in Ottawa—he was also a federal member—was that of "the veriest dummy and the most slavish ministerialist in the House," it wrote on December 6, 1867. Later, on June 11, 1869, it claimed that Sandfield was actually plotting to undermine the Ontario government

8 18 July 1867. Brown himself had used the word "harmony" in 1864.
9 23 July 1867.
10 20 July 1867.
11 23 July 1867.
12 26 July 1867.
13 31 July 1867.
14 7 August 1867.

and legislature to create a legislative union. He was bringing "them into contempt" to pave the way for the curtailment of their power and the ultimate "dispensing with them altogether." Confederation was designed, the *Globe* claimed on April 4, 1870, "to give us all control over local Provincial matters, insofar as that is compatible with national unity."

In the Ontario legislature, Edward Blake, who soon became the effective leader of the anti-government forces, expressed similar sentiments. As part of the reconciliation of Joseph Howe, Sandfield in 1869 in Ottawa had voted with his namesake in approving "better terms" for Nova Scotia. When the legislature met in Toronto, so vehement and increasingly effective was Edward Blake's denunciation of "better terms" that although Sandfield beat back twelve resolutions against the move, on the thirteenth, calling for a constitutional measure to prevent future bilateral fiscal deals, he had his own forces support it; he thus prevented major desertions.[15] Yet Blake himself was inconsistent in that he had, as a legalist, successfully urged Sir John A. to disallow Sandfield's act extending the British parliamentary privileges and immunities to assemblymen,[16] and in February 1871 he introduced a motion censuring the federal government for its handling of Louis Riel's "execution" of Thomas Scott.[17]

The Premier's opponents also criticized him for the specific manner in which he conducted his administration. Robert Baldwin, his old mentor, had unapologetically but deftly used the legitimate Victorian instrument of patronage to reward the faithful. Sandfield used it similarly but with such blunt frankness that castigation by the opposition was simple if hypocritical. Yet others condemned him for not giving sufficient offices to his fellow Catholics. At one and the same time he was accused of being both prodigal and parsimonious. Allegedly over-emphasizing the role of the executive, he was criticized for obtaining from the legislature an undifferentiated grant of one-and-a-half million dollars from the huge Ontario surplus to aid in the construction of northern development railways. But the very existence of the big surplus and Sandfield's reluctance to spend it turned out to be a political liability. Most significantly, however, the *Globe* led the attack by merging its firm endorsement of classical federalism with its abusive personal attacks on the Premier whom it claimed to be without honour, competence or integrity.[18]

The Grit leader was able to accomplish such a phenomenal transformation in his approach toward federalism without any discernable

15 *Globe* and *Leader*, 24 November 1869.
16 Macdonald Papers, Blake to J. A. Macdonald, 30 November and 28 December 1868.
17 *Leader*, 3 February 1871.
18 21 December 1870.

protest either from those of his lieutenants who remained loyal to him or indeed from his rank and file supporters. To most of the Grit voters, Confederation meant deliverance from French and Montreal dominance, a potential for greater progress, representation by population, cheaper and more honest administration, the restoration of Upper Canadian self-government, a vague national destiny, and, to those land-hungry who were interested, the imminent acquisition of the North-West. Confederation was an elitist achievement. Yet in Upper Canada, concepts and assumptions of political democracy were growing, and they emphasized localism. The bulk of the Grit rank and file or, perhaps more accurately, the local leadership, seems always to have favoured local self-government, both municipal and for Upper Canada. These people seem hardly to have been aware of Brown's extreme centralism of 1864-66. They had been preoccupied with other aspects of his position. A few, like the editor of the Hamilton *Times*, had warily and somewhat imperfectly sensed this difference. Decentralized government, closer to the people and based on popular sovereignty, was always best. The *Times*, in the fall of 1864, had demanded a "direct decision" by the people on the matter of Confederation. If this were not done, then it could imagine no issue in the future important enough "to justify an appeal to them. The polling booths thereafter may as well be turned into pig-pens and the voters' lists cut up into pipe-lighters."[19] In 1867 the *Times* was still consistent. Coalition was totally indefensible, its Reform practitioners betraying the people for office. If Ottawa could dictate to Ontario on the selection of its premier, then "the people have been deceived and cajoled into Confederation by false pretexts and false representations." But now the *Globe* agreed.[20] George Brown had joined his Grit followers.

Although quite nervous about certain allegedly republican and American aspects[21] of the new governmental system, ordinary Orangemen of Ontario had also been attracted to Confederation by the promise that the new system would finally free them from French and Catholic domination of their local affairs. Despite the commitment of the Order's political leadership to the necessity of the alliance of John A. and the Conservative party with the French *Bleus*, this form of localism had long been a strong force among the rank and file Orangemen, especially those in and west of Toronto.[22] While it clearly contradicted his own political and constitutional thinking, John A. had

19 *Times* (Hamilton), quoted by the *Union* (Ottawa), 24 November 1864. See P. B. Waite, *Life and Times of Confederation: 1864-1867* (Toronto, 1962), p. 122.

20 *Times* (Hamilton), quoted and endorsed by the *Globe*, 17 July 1867.

21 Macdonald Papers, M. C. Cameron to J. A. Macdonald, 3 December 1864 and W. F. Powell to J. A. Macdonald, 18 December 1864.

22 Note H. Senior, *Orangeism: The Canadian Phase* (Toronto, 1972) and J. Wearing, "Pressure Group Politics in Canada West Before Confederation," *CHA Report, 1967*.

used this sentiment to rally Orange support behind the Confederation movement. Unlike the localism of the Reformers, Orange localism had few philosophical underpinnings and, unable to outgrow its ethnic and religious roots, was less likely to develop into a clear doctrine of classical federalism and decentralism. More an expression of anti-French and anti-Catholic feeling, Orange localism was to some extent a pragmatic response to the failure of centralism, in the form of the Act of Union, to solve the "French problem" by assimilation. Both unaware and misguided about the real nature of the new system, Orangemen saw Confederation and federalism as new weapons in the struggle against the French and Catholic menace. Thus caught up in their particular brand of localism, Orangemen across the new province had united behind Confederation; during the election campaigns of 1867, the Orange "workhorse" had played a significant role in delivering a victory to each Macdonald.[23]

Eventually, however, Sandfield ran afoul of the Orangemen because of Sir John A's handling of the Red River crisis, especially the killing of the Orangeman, Thomas Scott, in March 1870 by Riel's provisional government. The cries of "Popish plots" and "Rebellion against the Queen" had first aroused the Orangemen, but the "murder" of Scott crystalized their feelings into a howl for revenge against Riel and his Métis followers. In Ottawa, Macdonald found himself trapped between his two main blocs of support, as Quebec Catholics rallied to Riel's support. Although Macdonald dealt with the crisis by means of the controversial Manitoba Act,[24] his efforts to mollify the aroused Orangemen, without offending the Quebec Catholics, met with cries of betrayal from the Orangemen who had supported him so strongly in 1867.[25]

Ontario Reformers, eager to exploit the crisis for political advantage and reflecting their own anti-French bias, had played a leading role in arousing Ontarians, whether Grit or Orange, against Sir John A.'s actions. In the first stages of the crisis the *Globe* had stressed localism; it demanded that "the right of self-government" on the Red River should be conceded "without delay," that the local council should contain more local people and that Riel's early actions were "innocent" if "absurd." The federal government's actions, through McDougall, had shown its "incapacity"; the trouble "lay in ignoring altogether the opinions and feelings of the inhabitants."[26] Early in 1870, it was calling

---

23 Note H. Small, "A Study of the Dominion and Provincial Election of 1867 in Ontario," (master's thesis, Queen's University, 1968).
24 Note W. L. Morton, *Manitoba: A History* (Toronto, 1957) and G. F. G. Stanley, *Louis Riel* (Toronto, 1963).
25 Note G. T. Denison, *The Struggle for Imperial Unity* (Toronto, 1909), pp. 10-48 for an interesting personal account of this period.
26 26 July, 30 August, 17 November, 19 and 31 December 1869.

the insurgents "ignorant," though their demands were "reasonable enough"; the federal authorities and the priests were the real wrong-doers, while again the destiny of Upper Canadians was being frustrated and endangered.[27] Once Riel committed "murder in cold blood" by killing Scott, the *Globe*, still blaming Ottawa and fearing American intervention, demanded Riel's punishment, the sending of troops and the immediate securing of the North-West to the dominion.[28] Thereafter it denounced the Prime Minister for holding discussions with Riel's emissaries who were demanding provincial status.[29] But the Manitoba Act passed, and the military force secured the area.

By 1871, the Reformers under Blake were attempting to focus Ontario's indignation onto Sandfield's government in Toronto. Blake introduced a resolution in the Ontario legislature that was tantamount to censure of the federal government for its handling of the Manitoba affair; it demanded that Scott's "murderers" be brought to justice. M. C. Cameron, Sandfield's Conservative colleague, successfully turned aside the motion by arguing that the entire affair was a matter for the federal government and not for the provincial authorities of Ontario. By persisting with his doomed resolution, despite its quite obvious conflict with Reform advocacy of classical federalism, Blake effectively smeared Sandfield as a mere "puppet" who would "dance to any tune that Macdonald of Kingston likes to start."[30] Playing on the traditional Orange and Grit fears of French domination, the *Globe* charged that Sandfield was subservient to a federal government dominated by French Catholics and that a vote for his government meant a vote for "French domination at Fort Garry."[31] Although the leadership of the Orange Order soon rallied to Sandfield and the Coalition,[32] the rank and file found little satisfaction in the Premier's position or in the complexities of the federal system. Sandfield could no longer count on a solid Orange vote.

Among the Irish Catholics of Ontario, Confederation and federalism had initially aroused deep suspicions. Isolated in an over-whelmingly Protestant population and faced with rising sectarian animosities, the Irish Catholics had committed themselves to the unitary constitutional arrangements of the Act of Union and to the politics of a "siege mentality." Within this context, the Irish Catholics of Upper Canada had succeeded in securing many important benefits, especially in the area of educational and religious rights. The effectiveness of this approach reached its peak with the passage of the Upper Canada

27 1, 4, 12 January 1870.
28 30 and 31 March 1870.
29 22 April and 2 May 1870.
30 *Globe*, 15 February 1871.
31 Ibid., 14 March 1871.
32 Ibid., 24 February 1871.

Separate Schools Act of 1863 which, thanks to the votes of Lower Canadians, further extended the rights of state-supported separate schools despite the bitter opposition of the majority of Upper Canadian assemblymen. Under such beneficial circumstances, the Irish Catholics were naturally very suspicious of Confederation and feared the localist aspects of federalism that were so attractive to both the Reformers and the Orangemen. Without the direct support of their French co-religionists, they feared that their hard-won religious and educational rights might well disappear once a local Upper Canadian or Ontario legislature—probably dominated by Reformers and certainly dominated by Protestants—gained control over local affairs. Eventually, most Irish Catholics were reconciled to Confederation by the insertion into the plan of the educational guarantees to the minorities and by Macdonald's constant assurances that under his guidance it would be a legislative union "in all but name." Thus, despite Brown's efforts for a reconciliation between Irish Catholics and Reformers during the election campaigns of 1867,[33] the Irish Catholics of Ontario, especially the hierarchy, worked hard for both Sir John A. and Sandfield and contributed significantly to their victories.[34]

Sandfield's position among Ontario's Irish Catholics, however, deteriorated considerably during his years as premier. Although a Catholic himself, Sandfield was a liberal and secular Highland Scot whose relations with the Irish Catholics had always been strained. During the 1867 campaign, Brown and the Reformers had attempted to exploit Sandfield's well-known "contempt for the Irish" with little success.[35] This undercurrent of Irish Catholic resentment gradually expanded as a result of Sandfield's alleged "unkept promises of patronage for Catholics."[36] The focus of Irish Catholic dissatisfaction shifted to the limited public and political roles they seemed to play in Ontario. Sandfield did little to calm their unease. By 1869-1870 this unease was sufficient to produce strong initial support from every segment of the Irish Catholic community for the Catholic League, an organization which "aimed at securing more patronage for Catholics and more direct participation by Catholics in politics."[37] Well aware of the situation, Brown once again appealed to them to shift their political loyalty to the Reform party which would guarantee them "a full share of Parliamentary representation according to their numbers and

33 Ibid., 10 July 1867. Note PAC, Alexander Mackenzie Papers, G. Brown to L. Holton, 10 and 19 June, 5 July 1867.
34 Macdonald Papers, J. A. Macdonald to Bishop Lynch of Toronto, 3 July 1867, Note Lynch's open letter of support for the "coalitionists" in the Toronto (weekly) *Leader*, 2 July 1867.
35 *Globe*, 13 August 1867.
36 PAC, J. J. Murphy Papers, "Reminiscences of Mr. Justice MacMahon."
37 Hodgins, *John Sandfield Macdonald*, p. 11.

generous consideration in all public matters."[38] By 1871, such appeals were finding many sympathetic Irish Catholic ears.

Sandfield had also come into conflict with the Irish Catholics in the area of educational rights and privileges. Concerning the question of separate schools, Sandfield had consistently taken a middle course: although personally opposed to separate schools, he supported the right of the Catholic minority to have such schools. In 1863, while Premier of Canada, he had supported the controversial Separate Schools Bill which he clearly intended as the final settlement of Catholic educational demands. Now, the tangled question of state aid to university education challenged again his commitment to the separation of church and state. Sandfield, like Brown, favoured the secular University of Toronto. He was strongly opposed to the current practice of annual grants to the denominational colleges, whether Catholic or Protestant. These colleges were very small, and such grants were costly and inefficient. In February 1868 Sandfield announced that the grants would be ended in eighteen months.[39] This decision immediately aroused the Catholic community against Sandfield and his Chief Superintendent, Egerton Ryerson. The *Canadian Freeman* and other Irish Catholic organs raged against the decision as an example of Catholic helplessness in the face of an overwhelmingly Protestant provincial legislature,[40] while the hierarchy urged Sir John A. to use his power or influence to change Sandfield's decision.[41] In addition, the Catholics were further aroused by the introduction of a second bill aimed at reorganizing the entire primary and secondary school system without providing for the creation of secondary separate schools. Once again the Catholic hierarchy and press expressed its hostility to and alarm at Ontario's educational policies. Thus, by his refusal to provide Irish Catholics with desired patronage and by his unsympathetic attitude toward Catholic educational demands, Sandfield alienated many Ontario Catholics and greatly weakened the bond of mutual self-interest which had united the Coalitionists and the Ontario Catholics in 1867.

Tensions were also growing between the economic interests of the rival urban centres, Toronto and Montreal. In the area of banking legislation, this rivalry had a major impact on the nature of Canadian federalism during the first years of Confederation. For half a century, the Bank of Montreal, while acting as the agent for Montreal-based economic interests and Conservative political interests, had been dominating the Canadian banking system.[42] The Bank of Montreal's

38 *Globe*, 19 June 1871.
39 Hodgins, *John Sandfield Macdonald*, p. 96.
40 *Canadian Freeman* (Toronto), 10 December 1868.
41 Macdonald Papers, J. A. Macdonald to J. Williamson, 13 January 1868.
42 Note R. C. McIvor, *Canadian Monetary Banking and Fiscal Development* (Toronto,

financial hegemony had always been resented by Toronto-based business interests, especially those of a Reform mind, who saw it as a reflection of external control of local affairs and an obstacle to Upper Canadian economic development. In 1866, the "imperial" role of the Bank of Montreal had been demonstrated by its actions leading to the failure of the Bank of Upper Canada.

This event served as the catalyst for the creation, in 1867, of the Bank of Commerce in Toronto. Intended to be the financial agent of the expanding Toronto capitalists, its political leanings were emphasized by the presence of George Brown as a major shareholder and by the selection of William McMaster, the leading Toronto Reform financier, as president. Its first confrontation with the Bank of Montreal came in 1869 when E. H. King, General Manager of the Bank of Montreal, attempted to institutionalize Montreal's financial hegemony in the new nation by means of a federal bank bill. According to the original terms of the bill, the Bank of Montreal would have assumed a role much like Biddle's Bank of the United States; it would have controlled all credit through its exclusive role as issuer of dominion bank notes. Due to the combined efforts of Toronto's financial interests, led by Senator McMaster, and of the other regional financial interests, the bill was eventually withdrawn and revised to allow for the development of a branch system as the basis for the modern Canadian banking structure.[43]

Although the Bank of Commerce could not yet challenge the dominant position of the Bank of Montreal, it had established its independence and was not to be subservient. This defeat of financial centralism by regional interests represented an important setback to Macdonald's original concept of Canadian federalism. Crucial to his political and economic thinking had been the necessity of Central Canadian (read Montreal and Conservative) domination of Confederation, but that domination—or, at least, the Montreal and Conservative aspects of it—had now been successfully challenged by the Toronto-led regional financial interests. In an attempt to counterbalance Montreal's influence with the federal government, Toronto economic interests looked increasingly toward the Ontario provincial government as an alternative political base to advance their interests. Of necessity, the Ontario government should be in Reform hands rather than Coalitionist or Conservative hands. Premier Sandfield Macdonald himself was deeply committed to the St. Lawrence River-Eastern Ontario region and to subordinate federalism and was a close friend to E. H. King and other Montreal financiers.[44]

1958) and M. Denison, *Canada's First Bank: A History of the Bank of Montreal*, 2 vols. (Toronto, 1967).
43 Joseph Schull, *100 Years of Banking in Canada* (Toronto, 1958), pp. 22-27. Note V. Ross, *A History of the Canadian Bank of Commerce*, 2 vols. (Toronto, 1922).
44 *Mail* (Toronto), 3 June 1873; J.S.M. Papers, J.S.M. to E. H. King, 1 June and 4

Unfortunately for the other regional economic interests who had supported the Commerce during the controversy surrounding the banking question, the underlying premise of Central Canadian economic domination of the country had not been the point of the Commerce's attack, but rather how the instruments and spoils of that domination would be shared. When necessary, the rationale of Central Canadian common economic interest still held true for Toronto as well as Montreal. When in 1870 Macdonald settled the Red River crisis with the Manitoba Act, neither Toronto economic interests nor Reform political interests attacked the clearly "imperial" economic relationship established between the new province of Manitoba and the dominion government. Although linguistic and religious concessions were granted the Métis, the dominion government was careful to maintain complete jurisdiction over public lands and natural resources, even though all the original provinces had control in these vital fields. A Manitoba government, especially one dominated in its first years by the Métis, might not grant the generous terms necessary for economic, especially railway, development in the West nor welcome the anticipated flood of Ontarian settlers. Few Central Canadians were prepared to take that chance. Prairie land and resources, even in a Prairie province, would be controlled by Central Canada for "the purposes of the Dominion."[45] Brown and the *Globe* could criticize Macdonald's inept handling of the political arrangements surrounding the creation of Manitoba, but the economic imperialism and the constitutional inequality were not much objected to by the champions of classical federalism in Ontario. On the question of land, both Macdonald and Brown were liberal imperialists like Lord Durham and E. G. Wakefield.

Sir John A. Macdonald had been the architect of subordinate federalism. Preferring British-style legislative union, the great conservative had bowed in 1864 to political realities, especially the feeling of insecurity which Cartier expressed on behalf of French Canada, and also the problems of distance, lack of intercourse, sectional interests and the feebleness of national sentiment. Nevertheless in 1867, he sincerely believed that gradually parochialism would decline; as the country matured and developed materially, practice would approach that in the United Kingdom. Meanwhile, relations between the general and provincial governments would be more imperial than classically federal. The BNA Act was only a skeleton; the political process, dominated by himself and other forward-looking Conservatives, would

November, 1868, King to J.S.M., 5 and 11 June and 5 October 1868, 25 and 27 January and 25 March 1869, 5 August and 18 November 1871, Horace Forbes to J.S.M., 17 June 1870; and Mackenzie Papers, King to Mackenzie, 21 December 1871 and Mackenzie to King, 25 December 1871.

45 Manitoba Act (1870), section 30. Note Chester Martin, *"Dominion Lands" Policy* (Toronto, 1973), pp. 5-13.

supply the flesh of the new system. In October 1868 he wrote privately that, despite his earlier hopes, he was apprehensive that a "States Rights" battle might soon arise. But the powers of the central government "in its relations with the local Governments" were so much greater than those of the American government that "the central power must win." Meanwhile, the continuation of dual representation would help maintain "a certain sympathy." Central authorities should take no more note of the "status or position" of provincial governments, he argued, "than they would to the prospects of the ruling party in the corporations of Quebec or Montreal."[46]

But, above all, Sir John A. was a practical politician. The majority of his own Ontarians did not seem to want centralism, certainly not unless the central government clearly implemented their local priorities and policies, and for many who sincerely believed in government close to the people not even then. Without admitting a change, the Prime Minister adjusted practice toward the reality. This adjustment began even before Sandfield fell from power. Sir John A's failure was in never fully comprehending Sandfield's precarious position and never attempting seriously to try to sell his own constitutional position to the electorate.

On June 8, 1868, he issued his famous paper on disallowance. The relationship between the dominion and the provincial regimes was, on the matter of disallowance, he pointed out, virtually the same as that between the imperial government and the colonies. He noted, however, that disallowance by British authorities of legislation passed by self-governing colonies was naturally in rapid decline. But residents of a province, unlike colonials in the imperial situation, were primarily represented in the dominion parliament. Thus the dominion power of disallowance would not decline, and indeed the dominion would be called upon to disallow provincial acts "much more frequently" than was the case with Whitehall; nevertheless, provincial legislation "should be interfered with as little as possible." Disallowance, not judicial review, would be the chief supervisory device for keeping provincial legislation constitutional and within jurisdictional limits. It would also be a device to prevent action detrimental to the interests of the country generally and stop legislation in concurrent areas that clashed with dominion legislation. If a provincial measure were only partly defective or if it were "prejudicial to the general interests of the Dominion," then the province, time permitting, would be given the opportunity of changing the legislation itself.[47] Earlier he had pointed out that legislative injustice to provincial minorities was detrimental to the national interest and would be counteracted.

46 Macdonald Papers, Macdonald to Brown Chamberlain, 26 October 1868.
47 Hodgins, *Correspondence*, pp. 61-62.

In practice, as already noted, only two Ontario acts were vetoed during his first term of office (to 1873), and one of these had already been replaced. Three acts from other provinces were disallowed. The other method of formal dominion control over provincial legislation was in reservation of bills by the lieutenant governor for consideration by the governor general in council. No Ontario bill was reserved until the Orange Incorporation Bill of 1873. But many bills from other provinces were reserved.[48] Sir John A. insisted throughout that lieutenant governors were subordinate dominion officials, but while Sandfield was Premier he did not push that matter very hard in Ontario.

It was on the political level that Macdonald was endangering his hold over Ontario and promoting the isolation of Sandfield. While the Grits preached classical federalism and Ontario rights, the Macdonaldian system was losing by default. Many Ontarians objected to "better terms" for Nova Scotia; they saw it as a unilateral adjustment of the terms of Confederation. Macdonald allowed Quebec to prevent a settlement concerning the division of the old joint debt of the Province of Canada on which debt allowances were based.[49] Many believed that he withheld self-government on Red River too long and then that he was too pliable and conciliatory with French-speaking Métis rebels. He and Cartier seemed to be too generous in their commitments securing British Columbia's adhesion to the union.

Macdonald was also too unsympathetic to Upper Canadian interests and attitudes, said the Grits, and he allegedly even dominated the Ontario government. The first task was to destroy Sandfield's government and establish Ontario rights. That was the Blake-Grit call during the provincial election in the spring of 1871. For the Macdonaldian system, the campaign was not a propitious one. The Canadian Prime Minister was in the American capital engaging in very trying negotiations which would lead to the Treaty of Washington between Britain and the United States, a treaty which would not be warmly received in Canada. He thought he would be able there to write all the letters and pull all wires necessary to keep at least all the non-Reform factions of the Coalition working for Sandfield who could cope with the Reform elements. The Prime Minister also thought that he would be home before the voting. Although he tried to help from Washington, the diplomatic negotiations left him little time, and they dragged on past the election. Meanwhile, sittings of the Canadian parliament —with the chief away—pinned down other leading federal Conservatives. Furthermore, the frequently infirm Sandfield himself took se-

48 Twenty-one. G. V. LaForest, *Disallowance and Reservation of Provincial Legislation* (Ottawa, 1955), pp. 102-06.
49 J. A. Maxwell, *Federal Subsidies to Provincial Governments in Canada* (Cambridge, 1937), pp. 53-56.

verely ill; he was less than eighteen months from death. The *Globe* almost implied that Sandfield was personally responsible for Riel and the execution of Scott. Blake called for the help of the Almighty in the hour of crisis in "our national existence."[50] Although the results were inconclusive, the astonishing fact was that the Coalition had not fared worse.

The growing articulation of an Ontario version of federalism fundamentally at odds with that of Macdonald and the few other principal architects of the union and the political weakness of the Coalition cost Sandfield several seats. Although John Carling held his urban London seat, the Grit hold on Protestant, rural and small-town southwestern Ontario was not only reestablished but intensified. It would become the anchor of Mowat's Liberal Ontario ship. Although Sir John A. had seemed to be ignoring the sensitivities of the Reform wing of the Coalition, it was his own Conservative wing which seemed to have suffered most. That was not where the irony ended. Sandfield was also convinced that many of the Irish, Green as well as Orange, had defected;[51] many of the Green would never return. One of their leaders, Hugh MacMahon, a criminal lawyer from London who had helped in the formation of the Catholic League, had angrily and bluntly told Sandfield in February that he had repeatedly broken his promises concerning patronage for Irish Catholics. Claiming that he could never be a real Grit, MacMahon nevertheless worked hard to defeat the government.[52] In the hinterland around Cornwall, Sandfield's own brother, Donald Alexander, Liberal MP for Glengarry, kept up his friendship with George Brown and inclined many of his liberal Scottish Catholics to their Grittish Free Kirk kinsfolk.

Sandfield was determined to hold on. It was unclear which way several newly-elected Reformers would vote. He asserted that he meant to meet his accusers though he might be at death's door and have to be carried to the house "in a blanket."[53] When the legislature met in December, eight crucial seats were unoccupied. The Grits, taking political advantage of the stringent new Controverted Elections Act, one of Sandfield's impolitic reforms, had challenged the results in five constituencies. In the Assembly Blake narrowly won several votes. With some justification, Sandfield claimed that with so many vacancies, with several government members excluded on dubious grounds, he had not clearly lost the confidence of the house. But the tide was flowing away. One of his third-rate Reform ministers defected. Several Reform backbenchers followed. On December 19, 1871, Sandfield and

50 Hodgins, *John Sandfield Macdonald*, pp. 112-13. Note the *Globe*, 14 March and 23 April 1871.
51 Macdonald Papers. J. S. M. to J. A. Macdonald, 24 March 1871.
52 Murphy Papers, "Reminiscences of Mr. Justice MacMahon."
53 *Leader*, 24 May 1871.

the Coalition resigned. The next day Edward Blake, with Alexander Mackenzie in the cabinet, initiated over thirty-three years of Liberal rule. The Macdonaldian system of Canada had suffered its most severe blow.

Sandfield's claim that unjust partisanship had inspired the controverted election cases was strengthened early in 1872 when his forces, even though now in disspirited opposition, won four of the five seats challenged by the Grits plus one which they themselves had challenged. The only exception was Stormont, the area next to Cornwall, where brother Donald helped deliver the verdict to the new regime.

Blake's cabinet included the Catholic, R. W. Scott, until then the Conservative member for Ottawa. This was a portent of the future. Scott had been speaker and undoubtedly had been in collusion with Blake on procedures relating to the confidence votes. The author of the Upper Canada Separate School Act of 1863, which Brown had then so vehemently denounced and which became the system guaranteed to the Catholics by the BNA Act, Scott was a hero to many Irish Catholics. He was a lumber baron and railway man of the Ottawa valley, a serious commercial rival of John Sandfield whom he disliked personally.[54] His adhesion, while it afforded the new opposition the chance of deriding the Grits for their previous sanctimonious attacks on the principle of coalition, brought important new regional, commercial and ethnic strength to Blake. It also weakened the commitment of eastern Ontario, old "Central Canada," to a strong federal government focussed commercially on Montreal. It also indicated that, at least for the party leadership, bygones would be bygones; the Catholic minority would be safe now under Grit rule. Dedicated to Ontario rights, a broad, pragmatic Liberal party was forming.

From the beginning, Premier Blake made his position abundantly clear. "With reference to what might be called external relations," he told the house, the new administration totally rejected the concept held by the previous one that the two levels of government "should be allies"; instead, between levels there should be an attitude of "neutrality." "Each Government should be absolutely independent of the other in the management of its own affairs." Ontario would not interfere in the affairs of Canada or another province, and the Ontario administration would accept absolutely no interference in its own affairs. If the central authorities, however, undertook measures which "infringed" on Ontario rights or interests, Ontario would have to act. Attitudes of both "alliance" and "hostility" had to be eschewed.[55] From the editorial desk of the Globe, George Brown went even further. The greatest scandal of the previous regime had been its subservience to Ottawa;

54 Hodgins, John Sandfield Macdonald, pp. 90, 104 and 115-17.
55 Globe, 23 December 1871.

this subservience "crippled and neutralized" its power to assert the rights of Ontario while allowing "intolerable" intervention.

> "Hands off" will be the warning to Sir John A. Macdonald and his colleagues in future, so far as Ontario is concerned. Her ministers will insist first, that she shall be subject to no external interference in her local affairs; and secondly, that her just protests, in all that concerns her interests as a member of the Confederation, shall be respected.[56]

While the first demand was rigid classical federalism, the system that the Fathers had specifically rejected, the second demand, involving as it did a sort of Ontario veto over Canadian policy, had even greater implications for national authority.

Blake was actually premier for just over ten months, and after March 2, the legislature was not in session. During this time, Sir John A. suggested changes in only one Ontario act, and the Premier accepted the suggestion.[57] Meanwhile, Blake carried on a fairly intensive but not then public dispute with federal authorities over the northwestern boundary of the province. Later, under Mowat's regime, the whole controversy was to become public, extremely acrimonious and protracted. Blake, during his short administration, took an uncompromising position which probably produced equal dogmatism on the other side. Macdonald suggested that the two appointed commissioners, one provincial and one federal, should basically engage in marking the border north of Lake Superior on a line due north of the confluence of the Ohio and Mississippi, the alleged western boundary in 1774 of the old British Province of Quebec. Blake insisted that this interpretation was totally wrong, that the western boundary of old Quebec, according to Governor Carleton's instructions, went up the Mississippi to its source and that the western boundary of Ontario would have to be on a line north of that source; otherwise Ontario would make claims for even more of the North-West. The two governments were unable to agree on any procedures to settle the matter.[58]

Sir John A. now seemed to have recognized that his grand design had, with Sandfield's defeat, suffered a setback. Privately, he completely blamed Sandfield for the defeat, claiming that the Premier had thrown the game, which had been "in his own hands," through lack of "pluck" to use the large Ontario surplus and moneys supplied for northern railways in a sufficiently partisan way to have shored up the necessary support.[59] Perhaps. But the big problem was the sentiment of

56 Ibid.
57 Hodgins, *Correspondence*, p. 102.
58 Morrison, "Mowat and the Development of Provincial Rights in Ontario," pp. 101-11.
59 Macdonald Papers, Macdonald to Sir John Rose, 30 November 1871 and Macdonald to Carling, 23 December 1871.

so many Ontarians. In the forthcoming election Macdonald would find this out.

Meanwhile, he chose not to act in order to protect the minority rights of New Brunswick Catholics with regard to their own schools.[60] Probably he did so largely in an attempt to protect himself from severe criticism in Ontario, not only from his Grit foes[61] but more importantly from his uneasy Orange supporters. Obviously disallowance would also have aroused the New Brunswick majority. In 1871 the New Brunswick legislature followed the other provinces in setting up a provincial school system supported by local rates coupled with the continuation of legislative grants. The act prohibited both the granting of local taxes and provincial moneys to denominational schools and also the teaching by persons in religious garb in tax-supported institutions. The Catholics had had their own schools supported in part by the legislature. They had existed "at the time of union," but they had not been guaranteed "by law." Now they could exist only as private parochial schools. As it turned out, the courts were to find the new provisions legal. Clearly Macdonald could in 1872 have disallowed the act. By his own public and private statements in 1864 and 1865 he should have disallowed the act. The act violated the spirit of Confederation. It violated, in spirit, the historic rights of minorities. Whether or not Confederation implied any rights as such to the French-speaking *Acadiens* of New Brunswick, the BNA Act did imply minority rights to the Catholics generally. In New Brunswick there were more Irish than French Catholics. The removal of minority rights, the removal of rights held prescriptively, was surely a matter "affecting the interests of the Dominion generally," that had been, in 1868, one of the stated grounds for disallowance. An argument could even be sustained that the act, while legal, was "unconstitutional" in the nonfederal, British sense. The Fathers did not intend that disallowance should be used exclusively to stop what central authorities considered illegal action. That had not been the British practice. Such a limitation would not have suited subordinate federalism or the convictions of John A. Macdonald, British-American conservative.

In the New Brunswick case, nonaction (except that of supporting in the Commons a mild motion of regret) suited Prime Minister Macdonald, the beleaguered, retreating politician. He was even able to persuade an ailing Cartier to go along with what in effect was abandonment of the Catholics—French and Irish—in New Brunswick. Cartier was persuaded to argue that federal intervention concerning minority education in New Brunswick might be used as an argument

60 Peter M. Toner, "The New Brunswick Separate Schools Issue" (master's thesis, University of New Brunswick, 1967).
61 *Globe*, 30 May 1872.

for future intervention in majority French education in Quebec—a dubious constitutional hypothesis. Certainly the Montreal hierarchy and many others were unconvinced. To a considerable extent because of his negative stand, Cartier was personally defeated in Montreal later that year.[62]

But, during the parliamentary session of 1872, Macdonald was more concerned about other matters. He had been pilloried over the Washington Treaty; he had been unable to obtain sufficient British backing against the Americans so as to secure compensation for Fenian damages and also protection of Canadian fisheries. When instead, the British finally guaranteed a loan of 2.5 million pounds to help finance the Pacific railway, parliament hesitatingly ratified the treaty. The United States was thus reluctantly committed to a recognition of Canadian existence. Macdonald also secured passage, over bitter, "thrifty middle class," Liberal objections, of the Pacific railway bill designed to complete a line across the continent in ten years. Objections were based on the purported haste, on the public cost to benefit a private company and on extreme generosity to remote British Columbia.[63] He also obtained the passage of the Dominion Lands Act, linked in his mind with the railway. Based on the American Homestead Act of 1862, it provided for the granting of lands in the North-West, both territorial and provincial.[64]

Ontarians were demanding and securing more autonomy, and Macdonald was retreating from the protection of minorities not looked upon with sympathy by the majority of Ontarians. Despite these setbacks, Macdonald was still unfolding the outlines of an expansive nation-building policy. First, the North-West and now British Columbia had been brought into Confederation, and a Pacific railroad was promised that would link Canada *a mare usque ad mari*. Yet, for many Ontarians, Macdonald was seen as the despoiler of the Canadian destiny promised by Confederation. The North-West had become part of Canada only by the sacrifice of Ontario blood and honour at the feet of Riel, the Métis halfbreed, and his treacherous rebels. British Columbia had been literally bribed into union by over-generous terms and the promise of an expensive early railway project which alarmed Ontario's notoriously tight-fisted farmers. Furthermore, that railway was to be launched by a British loan "secured" by Macdonald through Canada's acceptance of the degrading and immensely unpopular Treaty of Washington.

62 Brian Young, "The Defeat of George-Etienne Cartier in Montreal-East in 1872," *CHR* 51 (December 1970): 386-406.
63 W. L. Morton, *The Critical Years: The Union of British North America, 1857-1873* (Toronto, 1964), pp. 267-69.
64 Martin, *"Dominion Lands" Policy*, pp. 10-16 and 140-42.

Those Ontarians who thought about a transcontinental country seemed to want a nation ethnocentrically modelled on old Upper Canada and dedicated to unrestricted material progress. "We hope to see," declared the *Globe* on 2 June 1869, "a new Upper Canada in the North-West Territory—a new Upper Canada in its well regulated society and government—in its education, morality and religion." The small but significant Canada First movement[65] also expressed this sentiment. Inspired by the memory of D'Arcy McGee, the "martyred prophet" of the "new nationality,"[66] a group of young, urban, pseudo-intellectuals, nearly all from Ontario, had banded together in 1868 to promote Canadian nationalism and oppose sordid partisanship and compromise. Initially the group expressed a romantic vision of the potential "Men of the North," a fusion of Norman French, Anglo-Saxon English, and Celtic Scots and Irish in "the icy bosom of the frozen north," thereby creating a new "super race."[67] This "pan-Canadian" mythology was quickly corrupted by the group's response to the Red River crisis of 1869-70 and to the Treaty of Washington of 1871. Disillusioned by Macdonald's politics, Canada First became in reality Ontarian, even Torontonian, rather than Canadian in outlook. The aim was now "a great Anglo-Saxon Dominion across the Continent."[68] Concerning Riel, Canada Firsters joined Orangemen and Grits in demanding revenge for Scott's "cold-blooded murder" and denouncing Macdonald for negotiating with "emissaries of murderers."[69] Through public meetings, demonstrations and the press, they provided leadership in rallying Ontario opinion against the handling of the crisis. Equally vehement were their denunciations of the Treaty of Washington. But here they struck a note for the future that Macdonald would later be able to use; they demanded the development of a national economic policy, a policy which evolved into a clear-cut call for protective tariffs.[70] When later endorsed by Macdonald and the Conservatives, the National Policy would be met with favour in Toronto and other urban centres by both the rising manufacturing elite and their labourers.

65 For detailed description and analysis of the Canada First movement see D. R. Farrell, "The Canada First Movement and Canadian Political Thought," *Journal of Canadian Studies* 4 (November 1969): 16-25; D. P. Gagan, "The Relevance of 'Canada First,'" *Journal of Canadian Studies* 5 (November 1970): 36-44; and Carl Berger, *The Sense of Power* (Toronto, 1970), pp. 49-77.
66 University of Western Ontario, James Coyne Papers, H. Morgan to J. Coyne, 10 February 1890. H. Morgan was one of the "old five" who began the Canada First movement.
67 R. G. Haliburton, *The Men of the North and Their Place in History* (Montreal, 1869), pp. 1-10. Haliburton was another of the "old five."
68 *Globe*, 4 August 1870.
69 *Daily Telegraph* (Toronto), 4 April 1870.
70 Note the platform advanced by the Canadian National Association in broadsheet: "Canada First: Address of the Canadian National to the People of Canada" in W. A. *Foster's Canada First Scrapbook* (Canadian Library Association Microfilm).

For the present, Macdonald was in serious trouble. Yet despite severe political warning signs, including Sandfield's defeat, Macdonald headed into the federal election of 1872 with surprisingly high hopes. To an old friend, Macdonald wrote, that he had "a most triumphant session, not having experienced a single check of any kind. The opposition were completely demoralized and I am going to the country with good hopes of success in Ontario."[71] Some fences had been mended over the long winter. The Catholic hierarchy, whose support Sandfield had lost provincially, had been courted by Macdonald with considerable success. By May 1872 Archbishop Lynch of Toronto, the leading Catholic clergyman in Ontario, was assuring Macdonald that there would be "no difficulty in keeping the Catholic vote as of old in your interest."[72] Brown's doctrinaire and bitter anti-labour stance during the Toronto typographical strike and Macdonald's act legalizing trade unions, modeled on that of Gladstone's of the previous year, had strengthened the Conservative hold on the cities generally and on the emerging urban working-classes in particular.[73] Sensing the beginnings of a sentiment in favour of protective tariffs, he encouraged the new Conservative organ in Ontario, the Toronto *Mail*, to cultivate it carefully: "The paper must go in for a National Policy in tariff matters, and while avoiding the word 'protection' must advocate a readjustment of the tariff in such a manner as incidentally to aid our manufacturing and industrial interests."[74] Although the "National Policy" was never articulated and probably not even fully accepted by Macdonald in 1872, its vague outlines were beginning to appear.

In Ontario, it was, however, only in the cities and among the strongly Catholic ridings that Macdonald was able to maintain his support. Across the rest of the province, Ontarians swung strongly Liberal. The farmers and commercial interests reacted overwhelmingly against Macdonald's failure to get reciprocity in the Treaty of Washington. Even Eastern Ontario, that bastion of Conservatism and Orangeism, was split, as some Orangemen "punished" Macdonald for his handling of the Red River and Riel affairs. In the end, Macdonald carried only thirty-eight of Ontario's eighty-eight seats compared with the Coalition's forty-six out of eighty-two in 1867.[75] It had been a severe

71 Macdonald Papers, J. A. Macdonald to J. Rose, 18 June 1872.
72 Ibid., Archbishop Lynch to J. A. Macdonald, 9 May 1872.
73 Note D. G. Creighton, "George Brown, Sir John Macdonald and the 'Workingman,'" *CHR* 24 (December 1943): 362-76; B. Ostry, "Conservatives, Liberals and Labour in the 1870's," *CHR* 41 (June 1960): 93-127.
74 Macdonald Papers, J. A. Macdonald to T. C. Patterson, 24 February 1872.
75 Note H. A. Scarrow, *Canada Votes: A Handbook of Federal and Provincial Election Data* (New Orleans, 1962); Donald Swainson, "The Personnel of Politics: A Study of the Ontario Members of the Second Federal Parliament" (doctoral dissertation, University of Toronto, 1968); Henry J. Morgan, ed., *The Canadian Parliamentary Companion, 1873* (Montreal, 1873); and Canada, *Census of Canada, 1871* (Ottawa, 1873).

defeat for Macdonald, but strong support in Quebec and the West gave him a slim majority in the new House. Ontarians had rejected Macdonald's cultural dualism on one hand and his alleged bungling of economic policy on the other. His policies had failed to be sufficiently Ontarian in nature and intent. A majority of Ontarians seemed prepared to return to their traditional voting habits and looked to the Liberals on the national level as they had to some degree on the provincial level a year earlier.

Meanwhile, during the only legislative session which Blake faced as premier, his administration in 1872 had pushed through an act prohibiting dual representation. By preventing an individual from sitting in both the Ontario and Canadian parliaments at the same time, the act had emphasized and assured the separateness of the two bodies. Duel representation had been an important element in Macdonald's plan of "harmonizing" the two levels of government; its prohibition by the Ontario government was a severe blow to his concept of subordinate federalism. The end of dual representation for Ontarians also had very important implications for the leadership of the Liberal party. Blake and Mackenzie, as members of both houses, were now themselves faced with the choice of remaining at the provincial level or moving to the federal level where, under good leadership, the Liberals might shortly bring down the Macdonald administration. Both clearly preferred the centre, but it was essential that the Ontario Liberal party should be left in hands capable of holding back the opposition which, after all, had only been narrowly overthrown. Within the Assembly, no one with sufficient prestige and leadership ability seemed to exist. Outside the Assembly, Brown no longer wanted his old role as leader. The only remaining Liberal with the necessary qualifications was Oliver Mowat who, since 1864, had been Vice-Chancellor of Ontario. Since the late 1850s Mowat had been a leading Reformer and, before his appointment to the bench, had been part of the Reform wing of the "Great Coalition" which had laid the foundations of Confederation. Throughout October 1872 Brown, Blake and Mackenzie combined to persuade Mowat to leave the bench and return to active politics as premier of Ontario. Although he was initially hesitant, they convinced Mowat that "the future of Ontario was at stake" because the federal government's centralizing tendencies under Macdonald were threatening to turn provincial autonomy into "a delusion and a

Macdonald carried eight out of the eleven ridings where the Catholics represented over 35 per cent of the vote and, in the urban centres of Toronto and Hamilton, he carried four out of five ridings. In the Eastern Ontario ridings (from and including Peterborough to the Quebec border), Macdonald carried only nineteen out of twenty-nine ridings compared to twenty-six out of twenty-nine in 1867. It was the loss of some Irish Catholic support as well as Orange "revenge" that cost Macdonald several ridings.

sham."[76] Blake and Mackenzie would carry on the struggle in Ottawa, but a strong hand was needed at the helm in Toronto itself. A long-time defender of Upper Canadian rights, Mowat soon accepted the challenge. In October 1872 he became Premier and Attorney General of Ontario.

The Ontario opposition naturally made much of Mowat's rejection of "the legal monkhood"[77] in favour of a return to an active political life. The sanctity of the bench, Conservatives argued, was being desecrated by Mowat; his decision would set a precedent which might lead to the growth of the American system of "political" judgeships.[78]

In Ottawa, Macdonald was far from happy to see his old political foe return. The personal-political feud between Macdonald and Mowat had begun in the mid-1850's when Mowat, having articled in Macdonald's law office, rejected Conservatism and entered politics as a Brownite Reformer. In 1861, this animosity produced an incident in the Assembly that saw Macdonald threaten to "slap" Mowat's "chops" and, without Sandfield's physical intervention, might easily have led to a donnybrook.[79] Some suggested that in 1864 Macdonald had deliberately, with malice aforethought, manipulated Mowat's retirement to the bench in order to remove him as a political opponent.[80] Their initial communication now, however, reflected little hostility. Instead, they were the picture of perfect, if hollow, correctness. Macdonald wrote, after accepting Mowat's resignation as Vice-Chancellor, that he hoped that for "the good of the country" Mowat would "try to work the new machine with the construction of which we had so much to do, with as little friction as possible."[81] To this Mowat replied:

> I have ever felt greatly interested in the success of Confederation, and I agree with you that its success will be aided by proper relations being maintained between the Dominion and local Governments as such, even when these are not in the hands of the same political party.[82]

A very considerable gulf, however, existed between what "little friction" meant to Macdonald, the advocate of subordinate federalism, and what "proper relations" meant to Mowat, the staunchest of provincial rightists.

Nevertheless, for the twelve months during which Macdonald remained Prime Minister before his fall in November 1873 both giants

76 G.R.W. Biggar, *Sir Oliver Mowat: A Biographical Study*, 2 vols. (Toronto, 1905), 1: 152.
77 Macdonald Papers, J. A. Macdonald to Mowat, 25 October 1872.
78 Ibid.
79 Note D. G. Creighton's account in *John A. Macdonald: The Young Politician* (Toronto, 1952), pp. 308-14.
80 Biggar, *Mowat*, pp. 133-34.
81 Macdonald Papers, J. A. Macdonald to Mowat, 25 October 1872.
82 Ibid., Mowat to J. A. Macdonald, 29 October 1872.

would continue to avoid the kind of open personal clashes which would become commonplace after Macdonald's return to power in 1878. For Macdonald's part, his heavy losses in the 1872 federal elections made him exceedingly cautious about provoking a new quarrel in Ontario; for Mowat's part, he was still mainly concerned with learning his job and establishing his leadership as premier.

One incident regarding the question of the constitutional power and position of the lieutenant governor effectively illustrates this mood of uneasy peace between Mowat and Macdonald. Assuming that the lieutenant governor had such inherent, prerogative powers, Mowat had him appoint a number of provincial Queen's Counsels. As federal Minister of Justice, Macdonald immediately questioned the legality of such appointments. It was Macdonald's opinion and that of the law officers of the crown that only the governor general, as the Queen's direct representative, had such prerogative powers; the lieutenant governor, as the governor general's representative in the province, had no such powers.[83] The question was clearly one of equality versus subordination. It was of fundamental importance to each man's concept of Canadian federalism. So long as the lieutenant governors were considered merely subordinate officers of the governor general and in no way direct representatives of the crown, so long would the provincial government be distinctly subordinate to the federal government. Despite the issue's importance, however, neither Macdonald nor Mowat were yet prepared to dig in. Thus, when Macdonald suggested that the Ontario legislature could "confer by statute such power on its Lieutenant Governor"[84] Mowat, while refusing to recognize the principle of the lieutenant governor's inferior powers and position,[85] accepted this solution to a rather embarrassing question and passed the necessary acts in the next session.

Perhaps better than Macdonald and his provincial allies, Ontario Liberals had recognized that the success of Macdonald's concept of subordinate federalism depended ultimately on the ability of its supporters to give flesh to what was merely a constitutional skeleton created by the BNA Act. To do so, Macdonald needed to accustom, by careful and sustained use of the central authority's superior powers, both the Ontario government and the majority of Ontarians to its primary position. The provincial government was to become merely a "harmonized" extension of the federal government's dominating presence in the life of Ontarians. Ontarians would come to see the federal government as the paramount agent and defender of their interests, while the provincial government would be no more than a large local council. Hence the importance of isolating the Liberals from political

83 Ibid., J. A. Macdonald to Mowat, 23 December 1872.
84 Ibid.
85 Biggar, *Mowat*, pp. 188-89.

power on the provincial scene for the first decades of Confederation. A Liberal administration in Toronto would hardly be likely to accept with grace such a role and, making full use of its power, would challenge the federal government's dominance in provincial affairs. Thus, the fall of Sandfield's administration in December 1871 had been a severe blow. Yet to be truly successful, the Liberals themselves needed to remain in power and, to do so, first Blake and now Mowat concentrated on increasing the strength of the provincial Liberal party. If the power and prestige of the provincial government in Mowat's hands could be effectively used and expanded, the federal government would be denied its role as the single focus of the loyalty and identification of Ontarians. Without that role and the political and social support it implied, Macdonald's design of subordinate federalism would remain lifeless. Thus, the power and prestige of the provincial government had become interchangeable with the political power of the Mowat administration; to increase one was to reinforce the other. Throughout the 1870s, Mowat was to turn this maxim into a political reality.

On one hand, by the careful use of the province's legislative powers, Mowat broadened the basis of his administration's support across a wide spectrum of social, economic and religious groupings. The most striking of these was his success in continuing the policy of reconciliation with Catholics that had been begun by Brown and carried forward by Blake. One device involved his adept handling of the Orange incorporation question. This issue made its initial appearance during Mowat's first legislative session as Premier, when two private bills to incorporate the "Loyal Orange Associations of Eastern and Western Ontario" were introduced. The Order had built up substantial holdings of both property and money over the years that, without legal incorporation, had to be held in trust by individuals. This procedure was awkward and difficult to administer and, in one case at least, had resulted in a severe financial loss when one such trusted individual embezzled $20,000.[86] Furthermore, Orangemen sought an act of incorporation as a symbol of their organization's status and legitimacy in the life of Ontario. This desire had always been a special concern of the Orange mind;[87] incorporation was seen as final vindication, after decades of frustration and denial. Naturally, Catholic reaction was immediate and intense. In the legislature, it was spearheaded by the leading Catholic Reformer of the day, C. F. Fraser, who attacked the Order as "a standing actual menace against Catholics" and demanded that the legislature not sanction the bills which had for their purpose "the perpetuation of religious strife."[88] Archbishop Lynch warned that

86 Canada, Parliament, *House of Commons Debates*, 19 March 1883, p. 258.
87 Note H. Senior, *Orangeism: The Canadian Phase*.
88 *Globe*, 7 and 20 March 1873.

"dreadful consequences" would result if the Order were given the legal recognition it desired.[89] Neither Mowat nor Brown's *Globe* could understand the intense hostility aroused by what seemed merely a legal convenience.[90] Mowat brushed aside the growing controversy as an over-dramatization of the symbolic importance of an act of incorporation and, despite the opposition of the rest of his cabinet, voted in favour of the bills. However, instead of ending the controversy, the passage of the bills only served to heighten religious tensions in the province; Mowat soon realized that it was becoming a political necessity to avoid responsibility. Consequently, the Lieutenant Governor was advised to reserve the bills for the Governor General's pleasure; this, in effect, was an attempt to shift the responsibility to Macdonald's shoulders. Macdonald, however, had no intention of allowing Mowat to trap him into antagonizing either the Orangemen or the Catholics. After reading Mowat a lesson in constitutional practice, Macdonald returned the bills to Mowat declaring that, since the bills concerned the ownership of property, they were "solely and entirely within the jurisdiction and competence of the legislature of the province."[91]

Meanwhile, Mowat had been able to shape his own solution to the incorporation question. He had the legislature pass a bill which "provided for the incorporation of benevolent, provident and other societies" by means simply of making a declaration before a judge who would then issue certificates of incorporation. In effect, what this bill did was to remove the implications of special sanction in the original incorporation bills but still to provide the means for Orange incorporation.[92] Such a solution had strong precedent in the established legislative practices of both Britain and the United States whereby private or special legislation was not allowed when a general law was applicable. Fraser, who was now a cabinet minister, accepted the general act as a "middle course" which Catholics could live with "in the interest of peace and good feeling."[93] Such a solution was also acceptable to the vast majority of moderate Protestants. Most Orangemen, however, had come to see their special incorporation as something akin to a moral right and were convinced that Catholic influence had robbed them of their desired recognition. Determined to have their special incorporation, Orangemen refused to make use of the general incorporation act and continued to reintroduce their own bills

89 Toronto Archdiocesan Archives, Lynch Papers, Archbishop Lynch to T. B. Pardee, 20 March 1873, as cited in Margaret Evans, "Oliver Mowat and Ontario, 1872-1896: A Study in Political Success" (doctoral dissertation, University of Toronto, 1967), p. 141.
90 *Globe*, 7 March 1873.
91 Hodgins, *Correspondence*, p. 80.
92 Evans, "Oliver Mowat and Ontario," p. 146. Note *Statutes of Ontario*, 1874, c. 34.
93 *Globe*, 10 March 1874.

in almost every session up to 1882 when they shifted their attack to the federal legislature.

Naturally, Mowat's solution to the incorporation issue had gained him new support among Ontario Catholics, particularly among the hierarchy. The Reform policy of reconciliation with Ontario's Irish Catholics had now turned the corner toward success. The gains made in the strong Catholic ridings in 1871 were solidified. In the 1875 provincial election, despite a slight loss in the Liberals' share of the popular vote, they picked up three new predominantly Catholic seats, and Catholic votes turned several marginal seats into victories.[94] More important than the immediate electoral benefits, a "basis of understanding" between the Reform party and the leadership of the Catholic community was taking shape beneath the surface of provincial politics. C. F. Fraser had been accepted by the Catholic hierarchy as Catholic spokesman in the Mowat cabinet to such an extent that, in 1876, Archbishop Lynch publicly broke with the major Catholic newspaper in Ontario, the *Irish Canadian*, because of its violent attacks on Fraser.[95] Mowat fostered the practice of consulting Lynch about legislation of particular importance to Catholics; relations became friendly, almost intimate, in the late 1870's. While Mowat probably did not quite obtain a majority of Catholic votes in either 1875 or 1879, his politically adept handling of Catholic relations, particularly the Orange incorporation issue, produced a steady increase of Catholic support for his provincial administration. At the same time, the loss of this Catholic support pushed the frustrated Conservative opposition into an increasingly greater dependence on Orange support. Over the next two decades, this dependence would lead Conservatives into the political wilderness on the back of the "Protestant horse" and eventually move the bulk of Catholic voters behind the Mowat administration.

Mowat also built up the power and prestige of his administration by adopting a policy of centralizing local powers into the hands of the provincial government. Almost every session after 1872 saw new bills introduced and passed which effectively increased the power, particularly the patronage power, of the provincial government at the expense of the municipalities and county councils. Certainly the most important and controversial of these was the Crooks Act of 1876 dealing with the control of liquor licenses. Previously, the control of liquor licensing had been in the hands of each municipality. Baldwin's Municipal Act of 1849 and the Dunkin Act of 1864 had emphasized this aspect of local autonomy. Neither act, however, had provided sufficient control of the

---

94 In all, they picked up four seats where the Catholic vote was 35 per cent or over, compared to 2 in both 1867 and 1871. Of those seats with 20 per cent or more, they won 11 of 29 compared to 4 of 26 in 1867 and 8 of 26 in 1871.

95 Franklin Walker, *Catholic Education and Politics in Ontario: A Documentary Study* (Don Mills, 1964), p. 41.

liquor traffic in the eyes of the growing temperance lobby which continued to press for more effective legislation. Now, according to the terms of the Crooks Act, this licensing power was removed from municipal hands and placed in the hands of commissioners appointed by the provincial government. The Mowat administration argued that such an act was justified not only as a response to temperance feeling but also as a reflection of the increasing demand for efficiency and reform in the administration of public affairs in Ontario. In the eyes of the Conservative opposition the Crooks Act was not so much a bill to satisfy the demands of temperance advocates as a measure "to vest in the Government, to centralize in the Executive, the powers heretofore vested in the municipalities."[96] The Crooks Act, the Conservative *Mail* argued, was merely another instance in a long list of actions aimed at transferring local powers to the Mowat administration:

> And here it may appropriately be remarked that the reforms for which this administration takes credit, all lean to the side of centralization. The Government centralized the patronage of county printing; it virtually centralized the appointment of issuers of marriage licenses; it centralized the power to sell enormous tracts of the people's land without the people's consent; it centralized, as in the case of the Central Prison, the power to let contracts without regard to the peremptory proviso of the Public Works Act; it centralized as in the case of the Municipal Loan Fund Distribution Act, the power to determine the method in which municipalities should expend their grants; it is striving to centralize in itself the power of expelling members and granting them no appeal to the people and now it proposes to centralize in itself the power of controlling the local liquor traffic.[97]

This policy of centralization on the provincial level was concentrating a very considerable amount of patronage into the hands of the Mowat administration. The Crooks Act had created a small army of commissioners, drawn "from the ranks of local Grit politicians,"[98] the *Mail* charged, who would be needed to maintain and enforce the Act. Furthermore, since these commissioners would have the sole power of granting or withholding liquor licenses, the Mowat administration would have a very effective form of economic blackmail at its disposal. Conservative tavern owners who valued their licenses would certainly think twice before opposing the Mowat administration in the future. By means of centralizing formerly local powers across a wide spectrum of social and economic concerns, Mowat had found a highly effective means of greatly reinforcing the power and prestige of his administration in relation to both its provincial opposition and the federal government. With Mowat the great centralizer, conservatism in Ontario politics often became the champion of local autonomy.

96 *Mail*, 21 January 1876.
97 Ibid.
98 Ibid.

Mowat was, however, not as successful as expected in gaining the support of the federal Mackenzie administration in his campaign to expand Ontario's constitutional powers. Although Mackenzie, Blake and the Ontario wing of the federal Liberal party were sympathetic to many of Mowat's demands, the pressures and responsibilities of the national power introduced unexpected tensions. In Mowat's hands, the theory of coordinate federalism was becoming the vehicle of "Ontario rights," the justification for each new demand designed to increase the power of his administration and of the Ontario legislature. For Mackenzie, leader of the national Liberal party, coordinate federalism could not become such a vehicle if it were to have any real meaning and support outside of Ontario. Nor could the Mackenzie administration allow itself to be seen, in the eyes of the rest of the country, as merely the agent of Ontario interests. Claiming to be strict legalists, Mackenzie and especially Blake emphasized the enumerated division of powers and rejected most of the supervisory aspects and the broad "peace, order, and good government" phrase of the BNA Act. Blake had long advanced the theme of firm "neutrality"[99] in relations, constitutional or otherwise, between the dominion and provincial governments. As Premier of Ontario in 1871, he had demanded "that each Government should be absolutely independent of the other in the management of its affairs."[100] No subordination, harmonious or otherwise, was implied in such a stance. For both Mackenzie and Blake, coordinate federalism was to be based on the independent equality of status, within their respective jurisdictions, of the dominion and provincial governments. To give life to such equality, the Mackenzie administration avoided use of the power of disallowance except in cases where the provincial legislation clearly interfered in the dominion's jurisdiction. Such a stance did not inhibit its use of disallowance; during its five years in office, a surprising total of twenty-one provincial acts were disallowed.[101] Where the formal division of powers offered no clear delineation as to which level held legislative jurisdiction, the Mackenzie administration generally allowed such contentious legislation to operate until a judicial decision could establish responsibility. In dealing with the Crooks Act, Blake found that some of its provisions raised "a question as to Licenses which is *sub judice*"; nevertheless, he recommended that it "should be left to its operation" until a court decision could clarify the full extent of Ontario's licencing power.[102] In 1878, the Mackenzie administration itself passed its own liquor control legislation, the Scott Act, which strengthened and made applicable

99 *Globe*, 23 December 1871.
100 Ibid.
101 Morrison, "Mowat and the Development of Provincial Rights in Ontario," pp. 177-233.
102 Hodgins, *Correspondence*, p. 138.

throughout the dominion the pre-Confederation Dunkin Act. Under the Scott Act, counties and cities could, by local option, vote themselves dry. Mackenzie intended that this act not conflict with the licencing power of the Crooks Act, but Macdonald would later use it to challenge that act. Concerning property reverting to the crown by escheats or forfeiture, the Mackenzie administration even suggested that its own disallowance of an Ontario act claiming control of such property should be reconsidered. Eventually a compromise solution was developed that satisfied both governments without surrendering either's constitutional position.[103] Thus, a spirit of compromise and a willingness to avoid public confrontation dominated the approach to constitutional relations on both sides. Such a spirit undermined subordinate federalism but did little to expand the area of Ontario's jurisdiction.

A similar spirit infused negotiations to resolve the question of Ontario's northwestern boundary.[104] Stalled in 1872, discussions quickly resumed once Mackenzie's federal Liberals took power. By the summer of 1874, Mackenzie and Mowat had agreed to appoint a three-man commission to adjudicate the boundary while a temporary or conventional line was established for administrative purposes. Over the next four years, the Mowat administration, aided by several prominent Ontario federal Liberals, such as David Mills, waged a continuous public and private campaign to assure Ontario of a favourable settlement. Mackenzie was sympathetic to Mowat's arguments, but to Mills' suggestion that Ontario's claims "might extend indefinitely Westward at least as far as the Rocky Mountains,"[105] he warned that such grandiose assertions "would be simply pushing a somewhat strained legal argument beyond what it would bear."[106] Furthermore, "the smaller Provinces regarded this large Province with suspicion," as one concerned Ontarian warned, and such claims only reinforced their desire "to limit the boundaries of Ontario as much as possible."[107] Finally, in August 1878 the commission met and without explanations or reasoning issued its decision which was overwhelmingly favourable to Ontario. The land westward to the Lake of the Woods and northward to the English and Albany Rivers and southern James Bay was awarded to Ontario. Empire Ontario was born. Spanning the entire Great Lakes system and spreading westward to the prairies, Ontario had grasped the means to social, political and especially economic domination of all Canada west of Montreal. For the moment, however, Macdonald on

103 Morrison, "Mowat and the Development of Provincial Rights in Ontario," pp. 195-99.
104 Ibid., pp. 95-176.
105 Provincial Archives of Ontario, Irving Papers, D. Mills to O. Mowat, 7 November 1874.
106 Ibid., A. Mackenzie to O. Mowat, 30 September 1876.
107 Globe, 1 December 1875.

returning to power in September 1878 refused to ratify the award which he saw as an election ploy by the now-defeated Mackenzie administration. Soon dominion and Ontario officials would be openly struggling for control of the disputed area.

In rejecting Mackenzie, Ontarians did not reject coordinate federalism. In fact, although the defeat was severe, it was not overwhelming. His share of the popular vote dropped only from 52.8 per cent to 48.2 per cent. Macdonald won 62 of Ontario's 88 seats, but 34 of those were carried by less than 150 votes. In a province of nearly two million, Conservatives polled perhaps only 8,217 more votes than the Liberals to win their "landslide."[108] Mackenzie, more an administrator than a politician, seemed incapable of responding sufficiently to the challenges of the times. Less adept at the use of patronage, he was unable to attract the Catholic vote the way Mowat could on the provincial level. Most of those Orangemen who had voted for him in 1872 and 1874 soon went back to Macdonald, especially after 1875 when Governor General Dufferin, with Mackenzie's support, granted an amnesty to most of the leaders of the Red River uprising. When, in 1877, the Orangeman Thomas Hackett was shot during an Orange parade in Montreal, enraged Orangemen argued that the "real murderer" was "Alexander Mackenzie because he refused him the protection to which every British subject is entitled."[109] The Green and Orange Irish continued to hate and fear one another, but both disliked Mackenzie.

Mackenzie frequently earned the hostility of both sides of a controversy. When, amid depression in December 1876, railway workers struck the Grand Trunk over lay-offs and wage-cuts, Mackenzie had refused a demand from the Grant Trunk management to use troops to control the strikers. Yet, Mackenzie and Brown's *Globe* made it clear that they were more in sympathy with the hard-pressed railway than the strikers. As doctrinaire liberals, both Mackenzie and Brown opposed trade unionism. The Grand Trunk was ultimately forced to settle with the strikers, but not before Mackenzie had earned the hostility of each group.[110] Similarly, those Ontarians who opposed the Pacific railway demanded that Mackenzie shelve this costly bit of nation-building indefinitely, while those who favoured it resented Mackenzie's decision to follow Macdonald's plan of routing the line

108 J. M. Beck, *Pendulum of Power: Canada's Federal Elections* (Toronto, 1968), pp. 29 and 37; note also Dale Thomson, *Alexander Mackenzie—Clear Grit* (Toronto, 1960), p. 346, and D. Lee, "The Dominion General Election of 1878 in Ontario," *Ontario History* 51 (Summer 1959): 172-90.

109 *London Herald*, quoted in *Sarnia Observer*, 22 July 1877 and Mackenzie Papers, A. Mackenzie to L. Holton, 23 July 1877.

110 Note S. Ayer, "The Locomotive Engineers' Strike on the Grand Trunk Railway in 1876-1877" (master's thesis, McGill University, 1961), and A. W. Currie, *The Grand Trunk Railway of Canada* (Toronto, 1957).

across northern Ontario to Montreal, thus threatening to give that city, not Toronto, economic dominance over the West.

An increasing number of Ontarians, especially the financial and manufacturing interests and thus also their labourers, were dissatisfied with Mackenzie's lacklustre handling of the depression. Concerned about American competition in a tight market, these people saw protective tariffs as a vehicle of market protection, assured growth and prosperity. Such economic self-interest also fitted nicely with the rising tide of economic nationalism which saw protective tariffs as a convenient form of nation-building. A policy of protective tariffs was certainly not in conflict with Mowat's view of Ontario's paramount role in Confederation. Indeed, with Ontario the centre of manufacturing in Canada, such a policy would assure Ontario's economic domination, unchallenged by foreign competition. Led by such organizations as the Manufacturers' Association of Ontario, the demand for protective tariffs had spread rapidly both in Ontario and beyond.[111] Mackenzie and the Liberals rejected such demands and accused the manufacturers of wanting "protection simply for your own interests."[112] Macdonald, who had flirted with protection in 1872, had finally swung fully behind it by 1876. During the budget debate of that year, Macdonald had moved his famous motion for protective tariffs to aid "the struggling manufacturers and industries as well as the agricultural productions of the country."[113] By the time of the 1878 election, protective tariffs had become enshrined as the "National Policy" and, linked with the Pacific Railway and immigration, had given the Conservatives both political élan and the solid support, financial and otherwise, of Ontario's manufacturing interests.

Although a slender majority of Ontarians had rejected Alexander Mackenzie, they did not reject Oliver Mowat and his emerging "Ontario system." In the provincial election of 1879, Mowat carried 58 seats to 29 for his Conservative opponents; an increase of 9 seats from 1875. In terms of popular vote, however, Mowat had merely held his own, capturing as in 1875, 48 per cent of the vote in comparison with 47 per cent for the Conservatives, now led by W. R. Meredith.[114] The solid opposition of Orangemen, still fighting the Orange incorporation battle, seems to have cost him votes but not seats; Catholic and moderate Protestant support more than balanced any losses. Rural and small-town Ontario held for Mowat, but new gains were made in the urban and manufacturing centres where his policies of "development" and "improvement"[115] won votes which nine months earlier had gone

111 Note S. D. Clark, *The Canadian Manufacturers' Association* (Toronto, 1939).
112 Mackenzie Papers, A. Mackenzie to C. Raymond, 8 April 1874.
113 Canada, Parliament, *House of Commons Debates*, 7 March 1876, p. 489.
114 Evans, "Oliver Mowat and Ontario," pp. 499-508. Popular vote percentages from Martin Robin, ed., *Canadian Provincial Politics* (Toronto, 1972), pp. 204-05.
115 Ibid.

to Macdonald and the National Policy. Such a small swing was hardly a paradox. Faced with Mowat's wide-ranging developmental policies, the provincial Conservatives had become the advocators of frugality and retrenchment. In the election campaign, Meredith had sounded surprisingly like Mackenzie as he presented a platform built on "sweeping measures of economy"[116] and vigourously attacked Mowat's so-called extravagance in government expenditures. Such an appeal, however, failed to attract those Ontarians who saw Mowat, as they had seen Macdonald, as the agent of Ontario's expansion and development. In this sense, the election victories of Macdonald and Mowat were consistent; federally and provincially Ontarians had opted for policies and politicians committed to growth, material progress and, above all, Ontario. While Macdonald had found the key in his National Policy to unite Central Canadians behind him politically and economically, Mowat had tapped much the same vein in Ontario to assure the destruction of Macdonald's concept of subordinate federalism. By making himself an equal partner in Ontario's future, Mowat had already won the constitutional battles of the 1880s.

By 1880 federal-provincial politics in Ontario had effectively altered the direction of the Canadian union. The great classic battles between Macdonald and Mowat, with the latter almost consistently the victor, lay ahead. Ontario, territorially, would gain what it wanted in the North-West; Mowat would win the "Rivers and Streams" controversy. Although the federal Scott Act would survive, the more important Ontario Crooks Act and with it basic Ontario control over liquor licenses and regulation would be sustained. But the pattern of development was already clear. Mowat was a great politician. On the other hand, so was Macdonald, and even in provincial elections, Conservatives were securing only one percentage point less than Liberals. This change in the operation of federalism did not originate with politics.

The change originated in Ontario society. Most Ontarians, regardless of how they voted, did not understand, or, understanding, did not accept, the subordinate federalism of the Macdonaldian constitution. They did not want its centralism, its cultural dualism, or its federal protection of minority rights. They wanted internal autonomy. Although many Ontarians, Grit and Tory, were dedicated localists, and some were local democrats, a plurality was prepared to accept or acquiesce in Mowat's centralizing of power in the hands of the provincial administration rather than Macdonald's insufficiently sympathetic

116 Ibid. For the fullest statements of the Conservative platform see the following pamphlets: *The Local Elections* (Toronto, 1879); D. L. Macpherson, *The Ontario Government: A Trenchant Exposure of Extravagance, Incapacity and Corruption; A Series of Deficits* (Toronto, 1878), and D. L. Macpherson, *Letter on the Increasing Expenditure of Ontario* (Toronto, 1879).

supervision of affairs from Ottawa. The economic and political elites had a province to develop, an Ontario system to build; for many, Mowat was their agent.[117] Although the chief architects of union had been Upper Canadians, Confederation had been an elitist achievement. A broader spectrum of Ontarians rejected, consciously or unconsciously, the fundamental nature of that Confederation. As good Anglo-Saxon pragmatists, they set about to change the system. In this task they were aided both by the easily absorbable theories of classical federalism floating about North America and by their optimistic Victorian Protestant conviction of self-righteousness—"sleek, bigoted, and stentorian."[118] After all, Upper Canada, now Ontario, had a great manifest destiny to dominate, one way or another, the "British" half of the continent.

On the other hand, the basic National Policy did not conflict with Ontario interests, especially as interpreted by many of its urban elements. Fully autonomous at home, Ontario could participate through the National Policy in the building of a great east-west transcontinental imperial system. Not devotees of laissez-faire or free trade, they would create a new expansive mercantilism, centred in Toronto, the Queen City of the West, and linked to the old imperial centre across the seas, a newer, freer, more viable empire of the greater St. Lawrence.

Most Ontarians voted the same way, Liberal or Conservative, in federal and provincial elections. Some few made a varied choice each election. A small minority, which included many Irish Catholics and many of the manufacturing elite, voted Macdonald federally and Mowat provincially. This minority produced what was to become the stability of the dialectic. The important point was that in Ontario something approaching a consensus existed among Liberal and Conservative voters that subordinate federalism was inappropriate. Therefore, without making significant changes in the BNA Act, Ontarians decisively altered Confederation.

117 Michael Bliss, "The Protective Impulse: An Approach to the Social History of Oliver Mowat's Ontario," in *Oliver Mowat's Ontario*, ed. Donald Swainson (Toronto, 1972), pp. 174-88; H. V. Nelles, "Empire Ontario: The Problems of Resource Development," in ibid., pp. 189-210; and H. V. Nelles, *The Politics of Development: Forests, Mines and Hydro-Electric Power in Ontario, 1849-1941* (Toronto, 1974).
118 Waite, *Life and Times of Confederation*, p. 328.

V

Federalism in Quebec: The First Years After Confederation

Brian Young

Even without the added strain of Confederation, Quebec in the 1860s was labouring under serious economic and social ills.[1] In addition to traditional ethnic and religious difficulties, there was a growing metropolitan struggle between the province's two major cities, Montreal and Quebec City. Aggressive and expansionist, Montreal's entrepreneurs dominated the province. The concentration of industry in Montreal's harbour and canal area brought an increase of 56.6 per cent in the city's population in the decade 1851-1861 and another 18.7 per cent from 1861-1871. Powerful Montreal families such as the Molsons, Redpaths, Ogilvies and Allans strengthened their hold on the province's brewing, banking, refining, milling and transportation industries. Montreal's stranglehold had been increased by the completion in 1859 of the Victoria Bridge, the only rail link in the province between the north and south shores of the St. Lawrence. In the face of this challenge, other cities in Quebec became what one journalist described as "sloughs of despond." In particular, Quebec City suffered from the growing north-south orientation of trade and the decline in its square timber business. While the ancient capital retained her political and ecclesiastical power, she became a peripheral economic centre.

The province's political parties reflected these tensions. The leader of the Quebec wing of the Conservative Party, or *Bleus*, was George Etienne Cartier. Preoccupied with heavy responsibilities in Ottawa, including a major cabinet portfolio, Cartier became isolated from the provincial reality. In his Montreal base, he found it increasingly difficult to bridge the clashing ambitions of the old Grand Trunk Railway and the aggressive Pacific railway interests. At the same time,

---

1 A general treatment of economic tensions is contained in Jean Hamelin and Yves Roby, *Histoire économique de Québec, 1851-1896* (Montreal, 1971).

his party's long-standing alliance with the Roman Catholic Church was weakening in the face of growing clerical support for aggressive right-wing theology. As early as 1861 a struggle for power in Montreal between the Sulpician and Jesuit orders had implicated the *Bleu* leadership. Cartier backed the Sulpicians while Ignace Bourget, the Bishop of Montreal, supported the stricter Jesuits. The publication of the *programme catholique* in 1871 emphasized the political importance of these religious differences. This ultramontane document called on Catholics to give their political support to uncompromising candidates far to the right of mainline *Bleus*. Although its base of support was much smaller, the province's Liberal party, known as the *Rouges*, experienced the same difficulty in maintaining a united front. While radical *Rouges* like Joseph Doutre insisted on the traditional platform of religious and economic liberalism, more moderate members of the party like A. A. Dorion, Henri Joly and Wilfrid Laurier, moved to encroach on the centrist position of the weakened Conservatives. These moderates called for an end to the perennial bloodletting between the *Rouge*-dominated *Institut Canadien* and the Catholic hierarchy. In 1871 the moderates formed a short-lived but important movement, *le parti national*. To attract nationalist and ultramontanist support they opted for peace with the Church, political liberalism, economic expansion, efficient government and improved communications. Capitalizing on Cartier's weakness and the commercial and religious divisions in his riding of Montreal-East, *le parti national* succeeded in defeating the *Bleu* leader in 1872.

The defeat of Quebec's leading politician emphasized the difficulties of holding responsibilities in Ottawa while trying to maintain control of provincial affairs. Within his own riding of Montreal-East, Cartier was unable to straddle the gap between the national interests of his party and the particular demands of his constituents. Powerful entrepreneurs were able to apply pressure on him within the riding and in Ottawa. His opponent ran as defender of local French-Canadian interests; Cartier had to defend himself against charges that he was a *vendu* to the Grand Trunk Railway. As a federal politician Cartier was also embarrassed by having to explain the reality of the country's religious diversity to his strict ultramontanist Bishop.[2]

Despite the outward signs of stability, Quebec was characterized in the Confederation period by deep political, social and economic divisions. The federal structure grafted onto the province in 1867 had been a conservative and empirical solution to the larger problems facing the politicians of British North America. Given the ethnic rivalry, the regional differences and the *ad hoc* division of administra-

2 Cartier's defeat is examined in detail in the author's article, "The Defeat of George-Etienne Cartier in Montreal-East in 1872," *CHR* 51 (December 1970): 386-406.

tive structures in the union period, it had been impossible to impose a legislative union. By default many Conservative politicians had turned to federalism as the best means of ensuring political stability and economic expansion. After Confederation many of the same politicians worked to ensure the centralization of the new state and the dominance of Ottawa over the provinces.

Unlike its sister province, Quebec made little attempt to emphasize its autonomy in political and economic matters in the early years after Confederation. Some Quebec politicians even regretted that Canada had opted for a federal system. M. W. Baby, a Conservative advocate of legislative union, believed federalism had been a mistake for French Canada because it "is now admitted on all hands that the English members, thirteen in all, control the legislature, and we have a system more expensive than the old one and of no avail to protect the French element."[3] Despite Baby's pessimism, there was always some opposition in the province to federal domination. In the first session of the provincial legislature in 1868, Provincial Treasurer Christopher Dunkin spoke out against efforts to subordinate the province and argued that the provincial and federal legislatures should have "the character of coordination." Narcisse Belleau, the first Lieutenant Governor of the province, protested against the centralizing tendencies of Ottawa and the arrogance of Langevin and other federal officials. He was joined by Cauchon's *Le Journal de Québec*, which attacked Langevin for damaging "the independence of our provincial institutions." There was also resentment against the divided loyalty of politicians who sat in both the provincial and federal legislatures. The dual representation issue allowed Wilfrid Laurier to revive the old *Rouge* legacy of local autonomy; in 1871 he urged that the provincial legislature be independent "from any federal control."[4] Within the province, F. G. Marchand led Liberal opposition to dual representation but he was embarrassed by the fact that both the provincial and federal leaders of the Liberal Party exercised it. Before 1874 bills to abolish dual representation were blocked by the Legislative Council. *Le Journal des Trois-Rivières*, a Conservative and ultramontanist newspaper, was worried about the arbitration of the pre-Confederation debts of Ontario and Quebec; perhaps the silence of Cartier and Langevin on this issue was because "their role as federal ministers entirely absorbed their duties as provincial deputies?"[5]

Bleu leaders in Quebec reflected the conservatism and practicality of their allies in other provinces. They sought stability and a continua-

3 Archives of the University of Montreal, Baby Collection, M. W. Baby to George Baby, 16 December 1869.
4 *Le Journal de Québec*, 4 July 1873; Quebec, *Report of the Royal Commission of Inquiry on Constitutional Problems* (Quebec, 1956), 1: 61, 63.
5 *Le Journal des Trois-Rivières*, 14 November 1870.

tion of the *status quo*, control of patronage, a denial of political power to the *Rouges* and commercial development for their constituencies. The *Bleus* achieved these goals by careful manipulation of the nationalist issue, the implementation of conservative, British institutions, the strict control of the party at both the provincial and federal levels, the subordination of the provincial government to its federal counterpart and by reassuring the province's English minority. In the decade after Confederation, *Bleu* leaders exemplified what Arthur Lower has called "the cunning of experienced hands."[6] While loudly defending French Canada from external threats, they quietly extended their control over the province.

　　Leaders like George Etienne Cartier, Hector Langevin, and Joseph Cauchon had been nurtured on the politics of Lafontaine. A common feature of this experience had been the realization that British institutions—responsible government, the cabinet system and parliamentary committees—along now with a new, formalized federal system could satisfy demands for commercial expansion and cultural autonomy while ensuring their own continued dominance over French Canada. Both before and after Confederation, conservative French Canadian leaders rejected the radical experiments of France and the United States and accepted federalism as a compromise solution. Cartier was typical in applauding the British Conquest which saved French Canada from "the shame" of the French Revolution. Thirteen years after Confederation, Langevin praised life under the British flag as offering "perfect freedom, but no license."[7] Younger Conservatives followed the examples of their mentors. In the first election campaign after Confederation, J. A. Mousseau wrote of "a heart beating with indescribable joy" that only a hundred years after the Conquest, Britain had restored "our complete autonomy." Joseph Chapleau was another who subscribed to the rhetoric of his *Bleu* elders. Although he speculated privately that Quebec's role in Confederation was "to carry water to the mills of others," his public pose was as a defender of the system. He interpreted the federal union as "an idea of conciliation between the different nationalities" and described Confederation and the Conservative party as the defenders of "the autonomy of our Province."[8]

<hr/>

6 A. R. M. Lower, "Theories of Canadian Federalism," in A. R. M. Lower et al., *Evolving Canadian Federalism* (Durham, N.C., 1958), p. 8.

7 J. Boyd, *Sir George Etienne Cartier* (Toronto, 1914), p. 319; Langevin is quoted in *The Pacific Railway Speeches Delivered . . . in the House of Commons, 1880* (Montreal, 1880), p. 49.

8 Mousseau's election pamphlet was quoted by W. Laurier in Canada, House of Commons, *Debates*, 12 March 1879, p. 330; Archives of the Province of Quebec, Labelle Papers, J. Chapleau to Curé Labelle, 27 November 1883; Montreal *Gazette*, 25 September 1878.

Although they often spoke in favour of provincial autonomy, *Bleu* leaders like Cartier and Langevin were centralists in the Macdonald tradition. Most *Bleus* supported double representation whereby politicians could sit simultaneously in the provincial and federal legislatures. Sittings of the Quebec Legislative Assembly were timed to coincide with recesses of the House of Commons. In general, French-speaking Conservatives showed little respect for the provincial, or "local" house as they preferred to call it. "You are at the helm of the ship," P. J. O. Chauveau, the first Premier of Quebec (1867-73), wrote to Macdonald, "well, I have done the best way I can to paddle the smaller skiff."[9] The province's English-speaking Conservatives agreed. The Montreal *Gazette* was probably representative of this feeling when it urged biennial sessions of the provincial house as an economy measure; it also attacked the development of parties at the provincial level since the assembly should deal with "local questions from local stand-points." A year after taking power in the province, Chapleau in 1880 assured the Prime Minister that his government would attempt "to harmonize the action of the Province with the general progress of federal institutions."[10] Minimizing the importance and independence of the provincial government went along with attempts to reassure the province's influential English minority. English-speaking members like Alexander Galt had long had a powerful voice in the Conservative Party; Galt was instrumental in promoting the idea of federation in the late 1850s and in winning over Cartier. The special electoral districts established in the Eastern Townships, the Protestant school system confirmed in the first session of the provincial legislature and the nomination of English judges and cabinet ministers were part of the careful attention paid to the English minority by Cartier, Langevin and other *Bleu* leaders. In 1867 Galt and Christopher Dunkin successfully blocked Joseph Cauchon from forming the province's first ministry. This was by way of retribution for Cauchon's opposition in 1865 to the principle of autonomous Protestant schools. A decade later, federal leaders used their influence with Premier de Boucherville to ensure that six out of the twenty-four seats in the Legislative Council were retained by English appointees even though the percentage of English in the province was declining.[11]

If the *Bleus* were avowed centralists on most economic and political issues, they found it practical to defend provincial autonomy in the New Brunswick school question. The suppression of Catholic schools in 1871 by the New Brunswick government embarrassed French-

9 PAC, John A. Macdonald Papers, P. J. O. Chauveau to J. A. Macdonald, 19 July 1867.
10 Montreal *Gazette*, 25 March 1882; Macdonald Papers, no. 86537, J. Chapleau to J. A. Macdonald, 31 October 1880.
11 Macdonald Papers, H. Langevin to J. A. Macdonald, 18 January 1877.

Canadian Conservatives; important ultramontane leaders like Bishop Bourget called on them to defend the faith by disallowing the provincial act. The *Bleus* skirted the issue and finally diverted it to the courts. In voting against a motion of disallowance Langevin described the British North America Act and its provisions for provincial autonomy as "*le palladium de nos libertés provinciales.*"[12]

Like their *Bleu* counterparts, the *Rouges* were adept politicians who proved quite flexible in adapting to the exigencies of a federal system. By 1874 the major *Rouge* critics of Confederation were out of public life. The *parti national* with its plank of provincial autonomy was dormant, Jean-Baptiste-Eric Dorion was dead, his brother Antoine was on the bench, and radicals like Médéric Lanctot had been destroyed. Most Liberals proved to be able compromisers. While Wilfrid Laurier was an opponent of dual representation, the provincial Liberal leader, H. G. Joly, sat in both the federal and provincial legislatures until 1874. Luther Holton, an outspoken Quebec Liberal, described the provincial legislature as "moribund," and in 1878 refused to join the Joly cabinet. Joly's provincial administration, like its Conservative predecessors, was weak and subservient to Ottawa. "Where none but Provl [*sic*] interests are concerned," he complained to Francis Hincks, "where the autonomy and self Govt of the Province are in Question, is the Province not to be heard?"[13]

Between 1867 and 1873 the fledgling Quebec government was dominated by Sir John A. Macdonald and his French-Canadian lieutenants; Macdonal never permitted Quebec to be an exception to his restricted concept of provincial sovereignty. The Prime Minister rewrote provincial bills that did not suit him or that did not conform to the wishes of prominent Montreal Conservatives like Hugh Allan:

> I have read Chauveau's bill with not a little astonishment. It gives the local legislature infinitely greater power than we have here or the Lords or Commons have in England. The Bill will not do at all but you need not say anything to him about it. I will draft a Bill which I think will hold water and do all that is necessary and will give it to you when you come up.[14]

The provincial Premier was sometimes the last to learn of the Prime Minister's decision. "By the way," Macdonald wrote Premier Chauveau in 1869, "the disallowance of your privileges of Parliament Act will come out in the next Gazette with that of the Province of Ontario. Cartier and Langevin both thought this would be better than your repealing it."[15]

12 H. Langevin to Jean Langevin, 22 June 1873, quoted in A. Déslilets, *Hector-Louis Langevin: Un père de la confédération canadienne* (Quebec, 1969), p. 238.
13 *L'Evènement*, 10 November 1875; Archives of the Province of Quebec, Joly Papers, H. G. Joly to F. Hincks, 12 April 1879.
14 Macdonald Papers, J. A. Macdonald to H. Langevin, 28 December 1869.
15 Ibid., J. A. Macdonald to P. J. O. Chauveau, 30 November 1869.

With Cartier ill and preoccupied with Ottawa affairs, Macdonald's usual emissary to Quebec City was his Minister of Public Works, Hector Langevin. The Conservative party in Quebec functioned as a single unit, and Langevin does not seem to have drawn any particular distinction between provincial and federal matters; he believed that his influence on events in the provincial capital was necessary *"pour mettre la Confédération en mouvement."*[16] One of Langevin's major duties was to reinforce the weak Chauveau administration. Worried that the government of the "trembling and fearful" Premier would collapse, Langevin treated Chauveau as a loyal subordinate.[17] He criticized provincial expenditures and spent long periods in Quebec City to reconcile differences. Langevin also met on occasion with the provincial cabinet to ask for specific provincial measures concerning patronage, railway subsidies, education, or the licensing of inns and grocery stores. Nor was Langevin the only liaison between Quebec City and Ottawa. For important matters the entire provincial cabinet travelled to Ottawa to meet with their federal counterparts.[18]

Langevin's influence in provincial affairs was not restricted to the Chauveau period. When the Premier resigned early in 1873, Langevin went to Montreal for the weekend and helped construct the Ouimet cabinet subject, in the words of a prominent Liberal, "to the approbation of Sir John and the Ottawa Cabinet."[19] Even when the Conservatives were out of power in Ottawa their influence was still felt in Quebec City. In September 1874 the Tanneries scandal forced another restructuring of the Quebec cabinet and again Langevin was involved. The task was difficult, he wrote Macdonald, but he approved the choice of Charles Boucher de Boucherville as premier and the addition to the cabinet of A. R. Angers and J. G. Robertson. The growing provincial debt and Boucherville's inept handling of railway and financial policy brought Conservative leaders back to the province in 1878. The provincial Treasurer had sent Macdonald his tax legislation for approval: "As our House reopens the day after tomorrow, and as I would like to present the financial statement as soon after the opening as may be possible, may I ask if you have had time to look over the draft act that I sent you?"[20] Entangled in a web of railway politics Premier Boucherville had weakened his party by choosing a route for the government railway which favoured the Terrebonne County interests of L. F. R. Masson and Joseph Chapleau. In doing so, Boucherville had alienated

16 Désilets, *Hector-Louis Langevin*, p. 195.
17 Archives of the Province of Quebec, Chapais Collection, H. Langevin to Jean Langevin, 11 February 1868.
18 The whole provincial cabinet went to Ottawa in March 1873 and in February 1884 all but Premier Ross waited upon the federal cabinet. Ibid., H. Langevin to Macdonald, 28 January 1879.
19 PAC, Mackenzie Papers, no. 257, A. A. Dorion to A. Mackenzie, 11 February 1873.
20 Macdonald Papers, L. R. Church to J. A. Macdonald, 15 January 1878.

powerful Conservatives in neighbouring counties and in Montreal. Macdonald was prepared to come to Quebec himself to avoid a "disastrous" breakup, but Langevin was able to assure the Prime Minister that he had "come to an understanding" with Boucherville's leading *Bleu* opponent.[21]

The system of dual representation was a useful tool in enforcing the will of the *Bleu* leadership. Among the Conservatives who sat in both the provincial and federal legislature in 1867 were Langevin, Cartier, Joseph Cauchon, Christopher Dunkin, George Irvine, John Jones Ross, L. A. Sénécal and Premier Chauveau. Committees of the provincial legislature were another source of influence. Of the above members, only Langevin did not sit on the important provincial committee on railways, canals, telegraph lines and mining and manufacturing corporations. The use of federal patronage was a less subtle form of control. A militia post, a judgeship, an appointment to a government commission, a federal contract, a lieutenant governorship, or a senate seat were treasured plums. For the less prominent the federal government had positions in the Post Office, Customs Department or Intercolonial Railway; for errant sons of constituents the North West Mounted Police offered a respectable and yet distant career. Pressures from Ottawa could also be used to encourage entrepreneurs with federal contracts to donate to party coffers at the provincial level. Joseph Chapleau, like Langevin and Cartier, played the patronage game to good effect. Chapleau's brother served as secretary to Langevin and some of his great respect for Macdonald may have been due to handouts he received from the Prime Minister. In 1879 Chapleau, leader of the opposition in Quebec after the formation of the brief Liberal regime of Henri Joly, asked Macdonald for the "paltry sum" of £2000 and reminded the Prime Minister that "times are hard," "elections frequent" and that the government had been "stingy" with him.[22]

The financial terms of Confederation reinforced Quebec's subservience to Ottawa. Over half of the province's income was in the form of a federal subsidy. Despite the warnings and admonitions of federal politicians, the province's financial situation steadily deteriorated. In 1876 the provincial Liberal leader predicted that Quebec would have to accept a legislative union if it did not curtail its spending. Alexander Galt, a leading architect of the financial arrangements of Confederation, wrote to the new Premier in 1878 that "you have a most difficult task before you, if the Province is to be saved from bankruptcy. If you fail, then Confederation must give place to a legislative union."[23] Railway subsidies were the main cause of the province's financial em-

21 Ibid., H. Langevin to Macdonald, 28 January 1879.
22 Ibid., J. A. Chapleau to Macdonald, 13 May 1879.
23 Joly Papers, no. 425A, Alexander Galt to H. G. Joly, 20 April 1878.

barrassment. Government expenditures to aid railway construction jumped from $48,171 in 1871 to $1,013,099 in 1875; by 1882 the province had spent $12,537,980 for a railway joining Quebec City, Montreal and Ottawa. To pay for its railway expenditures, Quebec repeatedly had to make provincial loans and by 1880 debt charges accounted for 23 per cent of the province's total expenditures.[24] Provincial politicians of both parties, while publicly avowing provincial autonomy, directed public revenues to railways that would lock the province into a transcontinental economic grid.

In the years immediately after Confederation, the strong presence in Ottawa of Cartier, Langevin and other prominent *Bleus* had assured the attentiveness of the Macdonald government to the needs of Quebec. However, the provincial administrations of Gédéon Ouimet (1873-74) and Charles Boucher de Boucherville (1874-78) had little leverage with the federal Liberal government of Alexander Mackenzie. After Dorion was named to the bench, the Mackenzie administration had only weak representation from Quebec. Nor was the appointment to the federal Liberal cabinet of the renegade Conservative, Joseph Cauchon, a success. *Persona non grata* with both Liberals and Conservatives, Cauchon was finally put out to pasture as Lieutenant Governor of Manitoba. The outspoken attack by Mackenzie's Postmaster General, Lucius Huntington, on the alliance between the *Bleus* and the Roman Catholic hierarchy damaged efforts by provincial Liberals to moderate the hostility of the Church. Whereas Macdonald, Cartier and Langevin had administered patronage in the province with ease and for useful political goals; Mackenzie's fussing over the temerity of French-Canadian office-seekers led to weak appointments. The Prime Minister was not opposed to railways, but he objected to the constant demands for railway subsidies from the *Bleu* backers of Quebec's north shore railways. The Prime Minister did show concern for the state of Quebec finances, and in 1876 helped the province float a loan on the British market. On the issue of a Canadian supreme court, Mackenzie was bolder than John A. Macdonald. As Prime Minister, Macdonald had backed off from establishing a supreme court in the face of opposition from his Quebec advisers, Cartier, Langevin and Thomas Chapais. Mackenzie went ahead and instituted the court despite the protests of French-Canadian Conservatives who worried about the treatment of Quebec civil law in a federal court. His Minister of Justice, Télésphore Fournier, argued that a supreme court on which two of the six judges would be French Canadian would be an improvement on the Privy Council in England.[25] For a few months in 1878 there were

24 Quebec, *Sessional Papers, 1882-83*, no. 71; *Report of the Railway Commission* (Quebec, 1882-83); S. Bates, *A Financial History of Canadian Governments* (Ottawa, 1939), p. 148.
25 P. B. Waite, *Canada, 1874-1896: Arduous Destiny* (Toronto, 1971), p. 39.

Liberal governments in both Ottawa and Quebec City. Mackenzie and Premier Henri Joly were able to make minor agreements such as the cession of federal property in Quebec City for the construction of a station for the province's railway. However, the period of Liberal dominance was shortlived.

Joly and the Liberals had been brought to power in March 1878 by Lieutenant Governor Letellier's dismissal of the Boucherville government. Late in 1877 relations had deteriorated between Letellier, an outspoken Liberal, and the Conservative cabinet. In addition to growing personal hostility, Letellier contested the cabinet's financial and railway policies and its practice of excluding him from their counsels. After dismissing the Conservatives he invited the Liberals to form a government. The Lieutenant Governor's precipitous action augmented the debate on federalism in Quebec. Provincial and federal elections in 1878 did not ease the situation. In Quebec, Joly's government, with a majority of one, barely maintained its hold on office. The federal election brought John A. Macdonald back to power supported by an overwhelming Conservative vote in Quebec. The resulting months of debate in both Ottawa and Quebec City gave both Liberal and Conservative orators an opportunity to argue their diverse concepts of federalism. The Conservatives, sounding like good Whigs, emphasized the constitutional rights of the people and pressured Macdonald to dismiss the Lieutenant Governor. Israel Tarte, Joseph Chapleau and Conservative newspapers charged that the Liberals had gained power by authoritarian tactics. The Lieutenant Governor, the Montreal *Gazette* charged, had been backed by George Brown and Alexander Mackenzie in "filching power in the Province of Quebec." In a speech to the House of Commons, Langevin concentrated on the unconstitutionality of the Lieutenant Governor's action:

> If the Crown could set aside the laws passed by both Houses of Parliament, then our Responsible Government and constitution would come to nothing, because the Crown alone would rule the country.... The will of the people, as expressed by their representatives, had always been respected. Whenever votes of money had been given by the people through Parliament, the Queen had been most thankful to her faithful Commons, and it was left for Mr. Letellier to do otherwise, and violate the Constitution of the country.[26]

Not surprisingly, the Liberals loudly defended provincial autonomy. "Our federal system is a fraud," an angry Mackenzie exclaimed, "if this Parliament is to constantly exercise surveillance over the actions of the local legislatures and local Governors." To Wilfrid Laurier, the Lieutenant Governor should be left in office as a matter of liberty and self-government:

26 Canada, House of Commons, *Debates*, 12 April 1878, p. 1944.

... what I ask in the name of the Province to which I belong is that we be allowed the privilege of being governed according to our own standard —that we should be allowed the privilege of being badly governed, if being governed by ourselves meant bad government; but, at all events to be governed by ourselves. This I ask in the name of liberty and self-government.[27]

In October 1879 the Joly government fell. Recurring difficulties over its north shore railway policy, the mounting provincial debt, lingering bitterness from the Letellier affair and a hostile Conservative majority in the Legislative Council contributed to the Liberal's collapse. The new Premier, Joseph Chapleau, brought a new strength to provincial leadership. Never a lackey to Macdonald, Chapleau was, however, an experienced professional politician who understood the reality of power in the Canadian federal structure. While solicitous of Macdonald, the Premier was an old hand at hard bargaining with the federal government. Throughout much of his tenure, Chapleau pressed the Prime Minister to resolve Quebec's deepening financial crisis. In October 1880 he warned Macdonald that "the financial existence of the province" depended on the sale of the provincial railway and that a decision could not "be long delayed without exposing our Treasury to a disaster."[28] Chapleau wanted the federal government to increase its subsidy to Quebec, to purchase the government railway or to force the Canadian Pacific Railway to buy it. In March 1882 he settled for half a loaf. The Canadian Pacific bought the line from Montreal to Ottawa; the remaining section from Montreal to Quebec City was sold to Chapleau's friend and crony, Louis Sénécal.

While Chapleau used all the traditional *Bleu* tricks to wangle aid from Ottawa, politicians in other provinces acted as watchdogs against any special concessions to Quebec. In 1884, for example, Edward Blake attacked the flexible system of provincial subsidies as "destructive of the independence and autonomy of the Provinces" and urged that they be placed on a "permanent and lasting basis." He pointed out that the system of subsidies wrecked economical government by the provinces and had an adverse "moral and financial influence" on the Confederation agreement.[29]

The most important theoretical attack on the increasing centralization of the Macdonald system came from Thomas J. J. Loranger. Member of a prominent Conservative family and a judge of the provincial Supreme Court, Loranger was worried by Quebec's loss of corporate identity. Confederation seemed to be working to the detriment of French Canada: "Political Union, which, for other nations

27 Mackenzie is quoted in Dale C. Thomson, *Alexander Mackenzie: Clear Grit* (Toronto, 1960), p. 350; Laurier was speaking in *Debates*, 12 March 1879, p. 329.
28 Macdonald Papers, no. 86519, Chapleau to Macdonald, 15 October 1880.
29 Canada, House of Commons, *Debates*, 12 April 1884, p. 1529.

means increased force, natural development and concentration of authority, means, for us, feebleness, isolation and menace, and Legislative Union, political absorption!" To counteract the increasing focus on Ottawa, he emphasized the autonomy of the provinces, the independence of the lieutenant governors and argued in favour of what became known as the compact theory:

> In constituting themselves into a confederation, the provinces did not intend to renounce, and in fact never did renounce their autonomy. This autonomy with their rights, powers and prerogatives they expressly preserved for all that concerns their internal government; by forming themselves into a federal association, under political and legislative aspects, they formed a central government, only for interprovincial objects, and, far from having created the provincial powers, it is from these provincial powers that has arisen the federal government, to which the provinces have ceded a portion of their rights, property and revenues.[30]

These protests had little effect before 1887. In accepting the subordination of Quebec to Ottawa, the politicians may only have been accepting the reality of the province's situation. Confederation had locked Quebec into a federal state in which, for the moment at least, the great powers lay with the central government. At the same time, expanding railways were tying Quebec into transcontinental systems. The province's major city, Montreal, was making its bid to be the metropolis of the new Canadian state. The city's bankers, shippers and entrepreneurs, caught up in the rush for capital, western trade and new industries, had little time for constitutional niceties or federal-provincial relations. The Liberal party, never a serious threat to the *Bleus* before 1878, was still exorcising itself of the devils of old radical *rougeism*. The *Rouge* leaders—A. A. Dorion, L. A. Jetté, Wilfrid Laurier, and Henri Joly—were moderates for whom provincial autonomy was only one of many planks which had to await the accession to power.

The province torn after Confederation by divisions between Quebec City and Montreal, religious controversies, recurring scandals and a mounting economic crisis, lacked both the strength and the desire to do battle with the centralizers. Only with Honoré Mercier's accession to the premiership in 1887 would Quebec politicians learn to exploit effectively the issue of provincial rights.

30 T. J. J. Loranger, *Letters Upon the Interpretation of the Federal Constitution* (Quebec, 1884), p. 7. For more on the compact theory see R. Arès, *Dossier sur le pacte fédératif de 1867* (Montreal, 1967) and Ramsay Cook, *Provincial Autonomy, Minority Rights and the Company Theory, 1867-1921* (Ottawa, 1969).

VI

Federation and Nova Scotian Politics

KENNETH G. PRYKE

In 1864 Canadian politicians found themselves caught up in a sudden wave of support for the union of British North America. This pressure, which gave an indelible imprint to the whole Confederation movement, sprang from the belief that union provided a solution for Canadian frustrations and drew a blueprint for Canadian ambitions. Quite naturally many Nova Scotians were unwilling to jeopardize their own future because incompetents had driven the Province of Canada into political and economic bankruptcy. Neither were Nova Scotian merchants willing to have their province used as a dumping ground for Canadian manufacturers, nor to help finance the expansion of Canada to the west. Thus, Canadian interest in colonial union was likely to turn Nova Scotians away from the project, particularly as many spokesmen defended the scheme in Canadian terms. Acceptance of the scheme was not made any easier when it was remembered that the Nova Scotian Conservatives had used the idea of union as ammunition against responsible government in the 1850s and that it had been advocated as a want in Nova Scotia's ability to conduct its own affairs.[1]

This Canadian aggressiveness for union tended to obscure the fact that developments outside of the province were gradually making some form of colonial association both desirable and necessary. Of primary importance was the British determination to reduce its obligations to British North America, an intent which was hastened by the American Civil War. Britain's partial withdrawal from North American affairs was particularly significant for the Maritime colonies with their strong dependence on British military power. This arrangement

---

1 A particularly useful account of the Confederation struggle may be found in P. B. Waite, *The Life and Times of Confederation, 1863-1867* (Toronto, 1962). The author of this essay has a monograph, to be published by the University of Toronto Press, which deals with Nova Scotia in the period of 1864 to 1875. This is a revised and extended account of an earlier study "Nova Scotia and Confederation, 1864-1870" (doctoral dissertation, Duke University, 1962).

included the usual forms of military defence, but of even greater importance was Nova Scotian dependence on British naval power to support the province in its long-standing economic struggle with American fishermen over the use of the inshore waters of the Maritimes. Confederation was offered as a substitute for Britain's military might; but the notion that the colonies had to unite in order to resist American military power had a slightly preposterous ring to it.[2] The changes occurring in British colonial policy did necessitate some alterations in colonial relations, but in Nova Scotia Confederation tended to be interpreted as the cause of the change, not an answer to it. By 1867, however, it was apparent to Joseph Howe and other leaders of the struggle against union, that Nova Scotia could no longer rely on direct support from Great Britain, particularly in purely domestic matters.[3]

If Nova Scotia were to be deprived of British power, it would appear to be faced with two alternatives: either join with its neighbouring British colonies, or enter the American union. The choice was hypothetical, as few Nova Scotians really wanted union with the United States, even if it could be found that the United States wanted to accept the province. For many Nova Scotians, however, it was difficult to make a choice as to which was the worse of two evils. In the opinion of Nova Scotians, the Confederation scheme devised by the Canadians merely gave constitutional and political form to the subordination of their province by the Province of Canada. Charles Tupper, Premier of the province,[4] recognized the strength of this argument, but he at-

2 *Morning Chronicle* (Halifax), 18 January 1865; 31 March 1865.
3 Harvard University, Houghton Library, Howe Papers, Stairs to Howe, 28 February 1867. PAC, Howe Papers, J. Howe to W. J. Stairs, 29 March 1867. A perceptive review of Howe's position on Confederation may be found in J. Murray Beck, *Joseph Howe: Anti-Confederate* CHA booklets, No. 17 (Ottawa, 1965).
4 The Conservatives, under the leadership of J. W. Johnston formed the government in 1863 following the defeat of the Liberal party in the general elections of that year. On the appointment of Johnston as Judge-in-equity in 1864, Tupper, the Provincial Secretary, became premier. He continued in that office until Confederation. The controversy over union swept across party lines and a coalition ministry was formed with Hiram Blanchard representing the Liberals and P. C. Hill the Conservatives. In provincial general elections, held in September 1867, this government, which supported Confederation only managed to elect two supporters in an assembly with thirty-eight members. An anti-Confederate ministry was formed in November 1867, with W. Annand, a Liberal, and member of the Legislative Council, as premier. House leader in the assembly was at first M. I. Wilkins, a Conservative but he was gradually supplanted by W. B. Vail, the Provincial Secretary, who was also a Conservative. The Annand-Vail ministry carried the provincial general election of 1871, though with a reduced majority. Vail resigned as provincial secretary in September 1874 and entered the federal cabinet. He was replaced in December by P. C. Hill, who had recently announced his conversion to the Liberal party. The government suffered several losses in the December 1874 provincial general election and the ministry survived in the assembly until 1878 only with the support of several avowed independents. With the retirement of Annand in 1875, P. C. Hill became premier of his province until his defeat in the general election of September 1878 by the Conservatives under Simon Holmes.

tempted to make it palatable by pointing out that the union scheme merely recognized a political situation which had existed for some time.[5] In the midst of the controversy over the merits of Confederation, however, it was all too easy to confuse cause and effect. Tupper's thrust was bold and perceptive, but the Confederation scheme did undoubtedly violate a distinctive sense of "Nova Scotianess," which amounted to a strong, if newborn, form of nationalism. While this feeling could be parochial, it was probably very similar in nature to the drive which led the Canadians to expand their frontiers. It would thus be fruitless to praise the Canadians for their vision of the future and fault the Nova Scotians for their petty chauvinism.

For many Nova Scotians a highly contentious aspect of Canadian domination within Confederation related to the development of the provincial economy. These Nova Scotians wanted the protection of the British government precisely because they wished to develop their economic ties with the United States. British ships riding at anchor in Halifax harbour were visible evidence that Nova Scotians could trade at Boston without fear of unpleasant political repercussions. Confederation, however, raised the possibility that American power might not be checked and that economic continentalism would be followed by political subordination to the United States. As an alternative, or even in addition to this, the Canadians might try to clip Nova Scotia's economic ties with the United States in an attempt to exploit the Nova Scotian market for Canadian advantage.

Tupper tried to avoid the controversy over trade by contending that Confederation would lessen the economic dependence of the province on the United States by fostering manufacturing in Nova Scotia. He tried to represent the Confederation question as a choice between a new industrial society and the old mercantile economy of wood, wind and water.[6] In using this argument Tupper was trying to present Confederation as a product of political nationalism fusing with the doctrine of progress through technology. Basically, however, the link between Confederation and the nature of the economy was not so much a causal argument to be determined by quantitative data as a conceptual point to be determined by perception. Certainly it was not accurate to suggest, as Tupper did, that the industrial interests were in competition with the mercantile economy. Throughout the 1850s and 1860s both the mercantile and industrial economies tended to develop together, sometimes promoted by the same men and, to a large extent, in the same regions of the province. This occurred in part because the

5 Nova Scotia, House of Assembly, 1865, *Debates*, 10 April 1865, p. 211.
6 D. A. Muise, "The Federal Election of 1867 in Nova Scotia: An Economic Interpretation," Nova Scotia Historical Society, *Collections* 36 (1968): 327-51. See also his "Parties and Constituencies: Federal Elections in Nova Scotia, 1867-1896," CHA, *Historical Papers, 1970*, pp. 183-202.

mercantile economy, with its emphasis on ships and shipping, needed a substantial industrial base for its operation. Tupper's dichotomy, therefore, distorted the nature of the economy. There remained substantial concern, however, as to the impact of Confederation on the economic continentalism coupled with political separateness that was favoured by many Nova Scotian merchants. Yet there still existed the dilemma of whether the changes feared by the Nova Scotians would be brought about by Canadian policies or by policies initiated from within the United States.

The fear of falling under the control of the Canadians with its unpleasant consequences was compounded for many Nova Scotians by the necessity for a federal system of government. Critics of the scheme argued that the need for a federal system merely emphasized the lack of that harmony of interests which was essential for the creation of a state. To some extent the rejection by many Liberals of a federal system reflected their notion that a house of assembly expressed the will of the people. Since there was but one people it was axiomatic to some Liberals that there could be but one assembly.[7] In this they were reflecting a strong Nova Scotian concern for a balanced government with the assembly cast as the voice of the people. This eighteenth-century tradition, which was also to be found in the other Maritime provinces, did not appear so prevalent in the upper provinces. The creation of several legislatures also bothered the Conservatives who envisaged an endless state of confusion, which could jeopardize the role of the central government as the creator of order and stability in the proposed state. ⸝

7 The Maritimes were greatly influenced by the political traditions of the pre-revolutionary British colonies in North America. The political traditions of these colonies, in turn, were oriented around such old British constitutional issues as the need for a balanced constitution and the nature of political liberty. This emphasis has been recently analyzed by J. P. Green, "Political Nemesis: A Consideration of the Historical and Cultural Roots of Legislative Behaviour in the British Colonies in the Eighteenth Century," *American Historical Review* 75 (December 1969): 337-60. The Maritimes inherited this tradition, in part, through a direct migration of people and in part because Great Britain imposed a traditional form of colonial administration on the Maritimes. Thus the anomaly developed in the nineteenth century that while Great Britain developed the cabinet system of government, many Nova Scotians continued to adhere to the eighteenth-century belief in the necessity of having a division of power. By the 1840s the Reformers, lacking any feasible alternative decided to press for the adoption of the cabinet government. Control of the government to counteract the economic and political power of the influential. The Reformers (later to evolve into the Liberals) tended to ignore the issues raised by the Conservatives about a balanced cabinet and merely repeated that the assembly, as the people's house, could never be a threat to liberty. Thus it was left to the Conservatives in the 1850s to raise again such eighteenth-century issues as the need for a separation of powers as opposed to the advantages of cooperation. For an examination of some elements of this debate at mid-nineteenth century see K. G. Pryke, "Nova Scotia and Prince Edward Island Consider an Effective Upper House," *Dalhousie Review* 50 (Autumn, 1970): 330-43.

In spite of its many objections to union, Nova Scotia nevertheless found itself in Confederation, mainly because of the role played by Great Britain. Many Nova Scotians refused, however, to accept reality, and under the leadership of the provincial government they demanded that they be released. But slowly they began to recognize that Confederation was part and parcel of England's new colonial policy. Joseph Howe was one of the first of the anticonfederates to acknowledge this and also to realize that continued opposition to union could only harm his province. When he decided to accept union, he also conceded that Macdonald's concept of the role of the federal government was legitimate. Howe's entry into the federal cabinet in 1869 was not intended as a repudiation of the anticonfederate cause. It was meant as an affirmation of the fact that under the new political regime Nova Scotia could best be served in Ottawa. Thus, the acceptance of Confederation did not necessarily imply a complete rejection of previous arguments. Neither was it inevitable that the provincial government would fall heir to the anticonfederate tradition.

Howe firmly believed that the provincial governments had been robbed of any useful role within Confederation, but the manner in which he left the anticonfederate party weakened his position in the province and obscured the validity of his argument. The bitter feud between Howe and the provincial government continued until Howe's death in 1873. It was interpreted by Sir John A. Macdonald as a contest to determine whether the province would be controlled by Ottawa or Halifax.[8] The provincial ministry believed that the outcome of the quarrel with Howe would determine whether they had any political influence whatsoever in the province. Macdonald's version, however, was more likely to appeal to those who feared provincialism and wanted a firm government upon which to establish a stable, social order. At the same time, however, Macdonald's appointment of such regional leaders as Howe to his cabinet, and indeed his entire policy of provincial representation in the cabinet, catered to sectionalism. The sectionalism inherent in Macdonald's cabinet system, however, was reduced by Macdonald's insistence on deciding for himself who were the appropriate representatives of the various provincial and ethnic interests. This was partially shown by the way Macdonald recruited Howe, but it was much more apparent in his earlier selection of Sir Edward Kenny of Halifax as the cabinet representative of the Irish in British North America. Neither Howe nor Kenny were the unqualified nominees of the special interest they were supposed to represent, and both of them remained dependent for power on their position as cabinet ministers. It remained obvious that regional interests, however,

8 PAC, John A. Macdonald Papers, 115, John A. Macdonald to Charles Tupper, 15 February 1869.

were to be expressed in and through the cabinet and Howe could feel with complete sincerity that his province could not be protected unless he entered the federal cabinet. Howe was not the only provincial spokesman to feel this way; Sir George Etienne Cartier was another notably partisan cabinet member. Tupper was another leader who both before and after Confederation had maintained that provincial interests could best be safeguarded in Ottawa. Throughout this period Tupper always balanced his arguments for a national policy with appeals to provincial interests.

In opposition to Macdonald's approach, some Nova Scotians began to adopt the position, which later became identified with the Liberal party, that the provincial governmental structure, both legislative and executive, since it was elected by the people of Nova Scotia, was the most suitable body to speak for and on behalf of the province.[9] This approach had great appeal for the provincial ministry because the Macdonald view gave no significant place to provincial governments. Although Macdonald's system provided for the adjustment and survival of regional and provincial interests, it was not a genuine theory of federal-provincial relations. The Liberal theory had some attraction for those who wanted to establish a role for the provincial governments. Yet the Liberal argument that the constitutional powers of the provinces should be respected was a means of denying the sectional role of the federal cabinet, rather than an appeal to pure provincialism. The Nova Scotian Liberals interpreted Macdonald's theory of federalism as an attempt to exalt the cabinet, which was part of the executive arm of government, to a position superior to the house of commons. If the members of cabinet were to act as agents of special interests, then they would act very much like tribal chieftains, forcing their followers in the commons to accept compromises worked out in cabinet. At the same time many Liberals were reluctant to argue that the commons should become the protector of regional interests, because they believed that the commons, in expressing the will of the people, should become the binding force of national unity. Thus in order to handle the problem of regionalism the only recourse available was to recognize the role of the provincial legislatures and governments. The disagreement between the Liberals and the Conservatives over the position of the provinces within Confederation thus basically involved a dispute about the nature of parliament and the role of the cabinet. The Conservatives preferred to charge the Liberals with attempting to diminish the power of the federal parliament. Yet in principle, the Liberal recommendations could enhance and reinforce the position of the federal parliament because it would be in a better position to ignore sectional or provincial interests. Nor was there any

9 Nova Scotia Assembly, 1869, *Debates*, 18 May 1869, pp. 67-77.

immediate threat that acknowledgement of a role for the provincial legislatures and governments would lead to an instant demand for increased provincial powers. Nova Scotia, for example, was too limited in size to hope to have much influence. Moreover, the powers allotted to the provinces by the BNA Act had been designed with Quebec's particular needs in mind, not Nova Scotia's. The constitutional duties assigned to the province thus had little political appeal and could not be used to support a provincial rights movement.

The contrast between the Liberal and Conservative theories became obvious in Nova Scotia when the Mackenzie government was formed in 1873. The Nova Scotian Liberals, although successful in both the federal and provincial general elections of 1874, had difficulty in replying to the appeal to sectionalism inherent in the Conservatives' attacks on the Mackenzie government.[10] The Liberals' criticism of regional representation in the cabinet and the respect for the constitutional powers of the provinces were, according to the Conservatives, merely a cover for a weak federal government which would accept the parochialism of Ontario.[11] Inherent in this position was the assumption that sectionalism could be mobilized in support of a strong central government and used against the provincial governments.

The criticism levelled against the Nova Scotian members of the federal cabinet was justified because both ministers were utterly incompetent. The problem with the Nova Scotian members in the Mackenzie cabinet was not due to any attempt by the federal Liberals to ignore the quota system for the different provinces that had been initiated by Macdonald. Whatever his personal preferences might have been, Mackenzie accepted the fact that Nova Scotia was entitled to two cabinet ministers. When it came time for Mackenzie to select the two ministers, however, some of the Nova Scotian members insisted that they should select their own representatives. The rebellion of Nova Scotian members of the Commons had actually begun the previous spring. At that time almost all the Nova Scotian members, men who then were identified with Macdonald's ministry, refused to accept the appointment of a Conservative whip. Their demands on first Macdonald and then Mackenzie were an assertion that they, and not the two ministers in the cabinet, represented the province and that they should have major influence in determining government policy. Elected supporters of the government from Nova Scotia ought even to decide who should be their province's federal ministers. They were, also, no doubt, expressing the traditional Nova Scotian emphasis on the role of the assembly as opposed to the power of the executive. Pressed for time, Mackenzie allowed the Nova Scotian caucus to select

10 *Evening Express* (Halifax), 3 January 1874.
11 *Evening Express*, 7 January 1874; *British Colonist* (Halifax), 13 January 1874.

the two cabinet ministers, but unfortunately, as noted, neither of the two nominees were competent. With the support of elements of the party outside of the parliamentary caucus Mackenzie succeeded in replacing one of the two in September 1874 with W. B. Vail.[12] Mackenzie dared make no further attempt to defy the Nova Scotian caucus, and so the second of the two ministers remained in office. Mackenzie was so frustrated by his inability to be rid of his unsatisfactory colleague that he even considered the possibility of abolishing that minister's department.[13] Mackenzie's difficulties with his Nova Scotian colleagues were by no means at an end, because W. B. Vail failed to make a successful transition from provincial to federal politics. A conflict of interest charge eventually led to his resignation, and his defeat in a by-election in January 1878 enabled Mackenzie to bring in the much more able and influential member from Halifax, A. G. Jones.[14] The change, however, came too late to reverse the political decline of the party in the province. Thus the insistence on the power of caucus, which had influenced some members to support Mackenzie in 1873, added considerably to his difficulties in office and contributed to the party's defeat in 1878. Mackenzie's troubles also made clear the point that although Macdonald had been railroaded out of office by the Pacific scandal, this issue was, in several respects, the occasion and not the cause of Macdonald's downfall. Since 1867 a number of problems had been developing which had given Macdonald an increasing amount of trouble. Mackenzie inherited these difficulties, which proved to be a major influence on the fortunes of his own government.

In spite of considerable attention to the political position of the cabinet and to the constitutional rights of the provincial governments, the Liberals passed over the issue of the proper relations between the federal and provincial parties. The federal government, because of its greater political and financial resources, could afford to ignore the wishes of the provincial ministry. Both the federal government and federal members took their supremacy for granted, but sooner or later this was bound to cause friction with the provincial ministry and with the latter's supporters at the local level. Following Confederation, the provincial Premier, William Annand, tried unsuccessfully to utilize his considerable power in the province to force Macdonald to deal with him on politically sensitive appointments in the province. When the governments changed in 1873 Annand immediately renewed his demand, but Mackenzie was no more receptive to Annand's proposals

12 K. G. Pryke, "The Making of a Province: Nova Scotia and Confederation," CHA, Historical Papers, 1968, pp. 41-42.
13 Sister Teresa Avila Burke, "Mackenzie and his Cabinet, 1873-1878," CHR 41 (June 1960): 134.
14 Dale C. Thomson, Alexander Mackenzie: Clear Grit (Toronto 1960), pp. 319-20.

than Macdonald had been.[15] During 1874 some commentators in the province suggested that the only way to avoid a conflict between the two levels of government was to create federal political parties which would have no relation whatsoever with the political parties involved in provincial politics.[16] Most politicians ignored this proposal as well as the less drastic notion of creating federal and provincial factions of the same political party. The Liberals were able to avoid the issue partly because the new Premier, P. C. Hill, was far too weak politically to forego any aid or assistance he could obtain from Ottawa. Thus, during the Mackenzie administration the provincial and federal political parties were closely identified. While this prevented unseemly quarrels, it also meant that some federal members suffered from being identified with unpopular members of the local legislature, to the extent that several federal seats were subsequently lost.[17] The experiences of both Macdonald and Mackenzie left little doubt that the relations between the federal and provincial parties could be as significant as any pronouncement concerning the constitutional position of the provincial government. Indeed, in many respects, the manner in which political relations were conducted provided an accurate picture of Ottawa's real attitude towards federal-provincial relations.

The Liberals' inability to deal with the problems of provincialism was particularly obvious in matters dealing with the economy. Prior to union many Nova Scotians had feared that their provincial economy would be disrupted and exploited by the Upper Canadians.[18] Their suspicions appeared to be confirmed following Confederation when parliament extended the tariff system of the old Province of Canada to the Maritimes. This tariff had obviously been designed by the Upper Canadians to suit their own interest, but Macdonald, displaying a strong sectional bias, rejected all criticisms from Nova Scotia as being completely unjust and unwarranted.[19] Nevertheless, Macdonald was soon forced to withdraw some of the most objectionable duties, and by 1870 the Nova Scotians had even managed to secure marginal protection for their coal mining industry. This achievement represented, for the time being, at least, the limits of Maritime influence on Canadian economic policies. In 1871 the members from the upper provinces forced the withdrawal of the duties on imported coal, even though at the same time they had to forego protection for Ontario grain. Central

15 *Report of the Board of Trustees of the Public Archives of Nova Scotia* (Halifax, 1952), Mackenzie to Jones, 24 December 1873, pp. 36-38.
16 *Halifax Evening Reporter*, 2 December 1874; 4 December 1874.
17 PAC, Alexander Mackenzie Papers (microfilm), E. C. Church to Mackenzie, 27 September 1878.
18 Nova Scotians, prior to Confederation, used the term "Canadians" to refer to residents of the Province of Canada. They continued to use this term following union, but for the sake of clarity I have adopted the term "Upper Canadian."
19 Macdonald Papers, 111, Macdonald to McCully, 2 January 1869.

Canadians were obviously not prepared to suffer much inconvenience for the sake of Maritime interests.

This attitude was even more clearly revealed the same year during the course of negotiations in Washington over American access to the inshore waters of the Maritimes. Although this dispute was widely known as the fisheries issue, it really involved a struggle between Nova Scotian and American merchants for control of the fisheries trade. The American negotiators offered economic concessions of particular significance to the New England-Maritime region.[20] Macdonald, who wanted to use the Maritime fisheries to obtain benefits for the upper provinces, successfully thwarted the American offer,[21] but he was finally forced to accept American entry into the inshore waters in return for the duty free export of fish to the United States and an unspecified sum of money. Details of these negotiations became public during the provincial general elections, and the provincial ministry, supported by a lobby of coal mine operators, immediately raised a cry against this blatant display of Upper Canadian parochialism.[22] Such a charge made it difficult to develop a bond with the Ontario Liberals, and after the provincial election, the Nova Scotian Liberals decided that criticism of the treaty should be directed at Macdonald and the British government, not at Ontario.[23] Thus the Treaty of Washington indirectly served to strengthen Confederation, because if the colonies could not depend on Great Britain, then they had to work together for mutual protection. Furthermore, the treaty provided public justification for the Nova Scotian anticonfederates in abandoning their isolation and seeking an alliance with the Liberal party in Ontario.

The general acceptance of the fishing terms of the Treaty of Washington, which satisfied many of the merchants in the province,[24] was undoubtedly helped by the revival of the economy in 1871.[25] Nova Scotians began to note, with a sigh of contentment, that Confederation had not been accompanied by a sudden destruction of the economy. Shipbuilding continued to expand, enthusiastic speculators drew up plans for railways, and capitalists developed the extensive coal deposits of the province. Unlike the earlier developments in mining areas, which prior to union had been financed principally from American sources, the new expansion was undertaken by such prominent Montreal capitalists as Sir Hugh Allan, J. J. C. Abbott and George Drummond. It was also noteworthy that these men were also associated

20 Allan Nevins, *Hamilton Fish: The Inner History of the Grant Administration* 2 vols. (New York [ca. 1936], 1957), II: 475-76.
21 Goldwin Smith, *The Treaty of Washington* (Ithaca, 1938), p. 63.
22 *Morning Chronicle* (Halifax), 1 May 1871.
23 Ibid., 17 February 1872.
24 *Tribune* (Yarmouth), 21 June 1871.
25 Howe Papers, 9, Howe to Archibald (private), 4 November 1871.

with the Conservative party. The changes in Nova Scotia thus were leading to fuller economic and political integration of the province with the other regions of the country. In future the province would be subject, in particular, to the metropolitan influence of Montreal. Montreal's position as a seaport and its interest in Nova Scotia's coal mining and iron smelting indicated that it would have a more beneficial and positive impact on Nova Scotia than would Toronto.

The mood of euphoria in Nova Scotia was somewhat exaggerated, for a sharp depression began to make itself felt in 1874. Several of the mines had to curtail production drastically, because Nova Scotian coal could neither penetrate the Canadian market above Cornwall, nor breach the tariff walls surrounding the American market. Ship-building also came to a sudden halt as trade generally declined. Bankruptcies increased rapidly, reaching a peak in 1877, and a number of Halifax commission merchants went out of business the following year.[26] The cause of this business recession in Halifax was partly due to a change in transportation routes. Products, in a steadily increasing volume, were being shipped from the West Indies to American ports[27] where they were processed and then sent to the upper provinces by rail. Thus the shipowners and merchants had cause to fear a permanent decline in their trade through Halifax, as well as to Montreal. After 1876, when the government-owned Intercolonial Railway link to Quebec was completed, they also had to contend with a marked increase in the amount of goods sent to Nova Scotia from the upper provinces.

Although several of the problems facing Nova Scotia had been developing for some time, it was the Liberals who were forced to develop suitable solutions to them. Many proposals were made, and they varied from subsidies to enable coal operators to break into the Ontario market to demands that the government-owned Intercolonial Railway reduce its rates to remain competitive with the American railways.[28] Whatever the merit of these proposals, they tended to be ignored in favour of an argument over the merit of free trade as opposed to a protective tariff. The Nova Scotian Liberals, under the banner of free trade, marched to the defense of the true principles of political economy and maintenance of low taxation. Yet their commitment to the principles of free trade were undoubtedly hazy, as some were quite prepared to accept the benefits of incidental tariff protec-

26 Statistics on insolvency are to be found in Canada, Parliament, House of Commons, *Sessional Papers 1879*, 9, Annex to the Report of the Minister of Agriculture. See also the *Monetary Times*, 17 May 1878; 9 August 1878; 4 October 1878.
27 Mackenzie Papers, Jones to Mackenzie, 27 April 1875.
28 Canada, Parliament, House of Commons, *Journals*, 1876, Appendix 3, Report of the Select Committee on the Causes of the Present Depression of the Manufacturing, Mining, Commercial, Shipping, Lumber and Fishing Interests.

tion and had no strong objection to government intervention in the economy. Indeed, one of the professed champions of free trade was A. G. Jones who, as early as 1872, had tried to convince the Conservative finance minister to impose a tariff of 55 per cent on refined sugar in order to justify the construction of a sugar refinery in Halifax.[29] Jones apparently believed that without some assistance from the government, the mercantile economy of the province would collapse, leading to an immediate demand for a full-scale protective system. Even if the other provinces should agree, Central Canadians would exact such heavy concessions that the cost to the province of a protective system would far outweigh any benefits.[30] Thus, Jones's objection to protection was not directed against the use of tariff for protection of selected industries but against the belief that such a policy required a uniformity in political and economic interests, which was not present in Canada. In this he differed from those who wanted to use an economic policy as a means of developing a national political consciousness.[31]

Jones's scepticism concerning the feasibility of adjusting the various economic and political interests of the country was probably deepened by his experiences with the Liberal government. In 1874 the first Liberal budget included an increase in the duty on refined sugar, which would benefit both Montreal and Halifax. Due to the pressure of members from both Ontario and Quebec this had to be withdrawn. The following year the government, by an order-in-council, again tried to change the duties on sugar but these plans also had to be withdrawn. Jones thought that the opponents of the duties on sugar, who were led by Luther Holton of Montreal, were "*selfish* and *unreasonable*."[32] Jones was in no mood to be sympathetic in 1876 when Luther Holton attempted to obtain increased tariffs on manufactured goods, and the Nova Scotian members successfully opposed any increase in tariffs.[33] Jones's inability to obtain protection for Nova Scotian interests confirmed his opposition to expenditures on any major project, such as the railway to the west, which would prevent the government from undertaking various smaller projects in the different regions of the country.[34] For Jones no policy could be termed national which excluded the interests of any region. In line with this approach, Jones tried to persuade the government to adopt lower freight rates on the Intercolonial Railway so that Halifax could compete with Portland during the winter season,

29 *Morning Chronicle*, 11 January 1878, Jones to Sir F. Hincks, 28 January 1873.
30 Ibid., 28 May 1878; 9 August 1878.
31 PAC, Charles Tupper Papers, Rev. Hugh McLeod to Senator J. Bourinot, 17 July 1878.
32 Mackenzie Papers, Jones to Mackenzie, 7 May 1875.
33 Sir Richard Cartwright, *Reminiscences* (Toronto, 1912), pp. 157-58. In his account Cartwright traces the opposition of the Maritimes to a dislike of high tariffs without making any allusions to Jones's attempts to obtain a higher tariff on sugar.
34 Mackenzie Papers, Jones to Mackenzie, 10 October 1876.

for freight carried by the Grand Trunk Railway from the west.[35] Jones gained a small point when the government declared Halifax to be a winter mail port. He almost gained his chief objective in 1877 when the manager of the government railway agreed to reduce the freight rates on grain shipped from the west. However, Mackenzie saw no reason why the Ontario taxpayer should subsidize Halifax, and he cancelled the agreement and relieved the manager of any power to make further policy decisions.[36]

Jones's inability to gain government recognition of the economic aspirations of Nova Scotia provided Charles Tupper and the Conservative party with an opportunity to appeal to those in the province who felt that some action, any action, was preferable to inaction. Without offering any specific details as to how they would implement it,[37] the Conservatives suggested that their self-avowed National Policy would, like a patent medicine, be a universal cure for the ills of the farmer, merchant, banker and manufacturer. Behind their programme lay the premise that all the regions of the country, and all the interests of the different economic and social classes were basically compatible. The emphasis on a protective tariff system on manufactured goods, however, as well as on the need to establish Halifax as a winter port really was aimed at reinforcing the economic and political position of the well-to-do. This was made explicit in the contention that the state had a duty to provide employment for workers in order to prevent any threat to the social order from restless, unemployed men who might be tempted to engage in anarchy, or even communism.[38] Furthermore, the more able and deserving workingmen might be able to develop their own businesses and move out of their class.[39] It was, therefore, obvious that the Conservatives had an ambiguous attitude towards the prospect of a growing, propertyless, urban, working class. In a more open appeal to working men, the Conservatives returned to their theme of social justice by promising that they would equalize the taxation burden on all classes.[40] Workers would no longer have to pay (as they did at present) a higher rate of taxation on their tobacco than did the wealthy. In this way false distinctions between the rich and the poor would be abolished. Thus the Conservatives made no claim that all classes would benefit equally from their National Policy, but in appealing to a levelling instinct, present in the province, they managed

35 Ibid., 28 April 1876.
36 Ibid., Mackenzie to C. J. Brydges, 21 December 1877. For correspondence concerning attempts to develop Halifax as a winter port in 1878 and 1879 see Canada, Parliament, House of Commons, *Sessional Papers*, 1879, p. 113.
37 *Morning Chronicle*, 27 May 1878.
38 Evening Reporter, 8 June 1878; 19 June 1878.
39 Ibid., 28 August 1878.
40 Ibid., 18 May 1878; 20 May 1878; 29 July 1878.

to present their programme as a means of balancing social order with social justice.

The stress on the role of the state as the creator of peace and order obviously linked the platform of 1878 to the entire policy followed by the Conservatives in Nova Scotia since Confederation. In some respects the stress on a protective tariff was new, but traces of this programme had been present for some time. Indeed much of the opposition in Nova Scotia to developing interprovincial trade came from the belief that the Central Canadians were hostile to developing trade patterns which were equitable to all sections of the country. Certainly since Confederation it was the Central Canadians, and not the Nova Scotians, who had been particularly active in blocking government measures designed to promote interprovincial trade. Thus the question in the federal general election of 1878 was not so much whether the Nova Scotians would now forget their hostility towards Upper Canadians and continue their support for the principles of free trade, but whether they had any confidence in the good faith of the Upper Canadians. Jones, for one, had little doubt as to the outcome of the elections, and he helped persuade Mackenzie to postpone the election until the fall, but the delay merely enabled the Conservatives to develop more arguments to use against the Liberals. Throughout the campaign Jones continued to support a free trade policy, but he privately believed that his campaign had been harmed by the refusal of the Minister of Finance, Richard Cartwright, to make any concession to the Halifax sugar interests.[41] However just the complaint, Jones undoubtedly lost the support of many merchants who had played a prominent role in his previous campaign.[42] Not only Jones but his entire party was badly defeated. The Conservatives won a large majority of the federal seats and also swept the provincial election which took place the same day.

A conspicuous feature of the 1878 election campaign in Nova Scotia was that the debate accepted the framework of Confederation. The contest was fought over policies which revolved around the political union established in 1867. This was in marked contrast with the election campaign of 1867 and illustrated how, in a short space of time, the province had accepted its new position. This acquiescence might be regarded as having been temporary and half-hearted, particularly in view of the "repeal" campaign waged in 1885 and the Maritime rights movement of the twentieth century. Yet the later agitation, particularly that of the twentieth century, had its own origins, and it represented a departure from, and not a continuation of, the political attitudes present in the province around 1867.

41 Mackenzie Papers, Jones to Mackenzie, 18 September 1878.
42 Ibid., James B. Duffus to Mackenzie (private), 11 July 1878.

Certainly, in the 1870s, the Liberals had little interest in increasing the powers of the provincial government and curtailing those of the federal authority. While bearing in mind the economic concerns of their region, they wanted rather to advance political unity in Canada. They were in agreement with the Conservatives as to the necessity of preserving the supremacy of the federal government, but they differed about the way in which sectional interests and national unity could be made to coincide. The Liberals' scepticism towards the adoption of a national economic policy may have reflected a deep-seated provincialism, but this was undoubtedly due to their awareness of the political and economic realities of Canada. Liberal doubts, however, were no match for Conservative promises to safeguard provincial interest, to preserve social order, to revive prosperity and to introduce social reform. The Conservatives' paternalistic theory of the state appealed to law and order; by catering to a levelling instinct, this theory syphoned off discontent which might have supported a more fundamental movement for political reform. Thus the election of 1878 affirmed that Nova Scotia accepted union. It was particularly significant that the arguments being used and the policies being adopted in Nova Scotia were similar to those being debated or implemented in the other provinces.

VII

New Brunswick Schools and the Rise of Provincial Rights

PETER M. TONER

Because it was one of the first constitutional crises after Confederation, the New Brunswick Schools Question provides an unusual opportunity to observe the way in which the Fathers of Confederation applied the provisions of the BNA Act to the conduct of dominion-provincial relations. This dispute clearly indicates a political reluctance on the part of Macdonald and Cartier to interfere in contentious provincial matters; they placed a higher value on political survival than on the principle of duality. It is surprising that such a significant dispute remained neglected by historians for many years, and unfortunate that when it was given its proper recognition, the New Brunswick Schools Question should have been so poorly understood and so badly used by historians. The tendency has been for historians to view the dispute as merely the opening salvo in the struggle over the true test of Canadian duality, French-language education outside the province of Quebec.[1]

In the light of later educational disputes, all directly concerned with language of instruction, this is understandable but hardly excusa-

1 As eminent an historian as W. L. Morton is a case in point. In an otherwise commend-able article, "Confederation, 1870-1896," *Journal of Canadian Studies* 1 (May 1966: 11-24) he implied that the real basis for the dispute in New Brunswick was linguistic. Although he disagreed with Morton on other points, L. C. Clark also accepted the linguistic nature of the New Brunswick Schools Question in his reply, "David Mills and the Remedial Bill of 1896" (ibid., 1 [November 1966]: 50-52). More recently and more seriously, Ralph Heintzman weighed in with his misinterpretation of the New Brunswick Schools Question ("The Spirit of Confederation: Professor Creighton, Biculturalism, and the Use of History," *CHR* 52 [September 1971]: 245-74). While attempting to prove that the BNA Act was a bicultural compact, Heintzman argued that the refusal of the Macdonald government to protect the Acadians of New Brunswick constituted the first blow to the principle of duality. Again the assumption that denominational schools meant French-language education was repeated in defiance of the facts. His further assumption that Cartier and Langevin cherished the dual nature of Confederation may also be questioned. Their actions speak louder than their words.

ble. The New Brunswick Schools Question was one of religion, not language, and cannot be employed as a precedent in later disputes. The majority of New Brunswick's Catholics, both Catholic bishops, most Catholic priests, and a disproportionate majority of the Catholic schools were Irish. More significant is the fact that throughout the debate on the New Brunswick Schools Question, language of instruction was never an issue. Despite the fact that many New Brunswick Catholics were French-speaking, the Common Schools Act was never challenged on the grounds that it prohibited instruction through the medium of French.

The absence of the language issue did not make the dispute less bitter—quite the contrary. In New Brunswick the Irish loomed far larger in the hatreds and fears of the majority than did the French. Although it was not the only factor,[2] the Irish threat, real and imagined, contributed decisively to New Brunswick's tardy acceptance of Confederation. In 1865, the Irish in New Brunswick, led by T. W. Anglin of Saint John, opposed and helped defeat the prospect of union with Canada. But if there was nothing unusual in such opposition in 1865, the rise of Fenianism changed matters considerably. In April 1866 New Brunswick was threatened with a Fenian invasion, which was met by mobilizing military force and the patriotic fervor of the loyal people of New Brunswick. In the eyes of the majority the threat was obvious, and not merely external. The Fenians were Irish Catholics, therefore Irish Catholics were Fenians. The Fenians condemned Confederation, which the Irish of New Brunswick also opposed, therefore loyalty demanded support for Confederation.[3]

At the height of the crisis, the Lieutenant Governor of New Brunswick, Arthur Hamilton Gordon, forced the resignation of the anti-confederate government, formed a new ministry committed to Confederation, and called elections on the issue.[4] The equation in the public mind of Catholicism with treason forced the hand of the Catholic hierarchy of the Maritimes. Up to this point, only Archbishop T. L. Connolly of Halifax had supported Confederation;[5] now the others began to change sides. On 10 April 1866, C. F. MacKinnon, Bishop of Arichat, Nova Scotia, issued a circular which endorsed Confederation as the best means of nullifying the Fenian threat.[6] Closer to home, James Rogers, Bishop of Chatham, New Brunswick,

2 See W. S. MacNutt, *New Brunswick, A History: 1784-1867* (Toronto, 1963); W. L. Morton, *The Critical Years* (Toronto, 1964); and D. G. Creighton, *The Road to Confederation* (Toronto, 1964), for the background to Confederation in New Brunswick.

3 H. A. Davis, "The Fenian Raid on New Brunswick," *CHR* 31 (December 1955): 316-34; P. M. Toner, "The New Brunswick Separate Schools Issue, 1864-1876" (master's thesis, University of New Brunswick, 1967), pp. 16-21.

4 MacNutt, *New Brunswick*, pp. 446-50.

5 David Flemming, "Archbishop Thomas L. Connolly, Godfather of Confederation," Canadian Catholic Historical Association *Report*, 1970, pp. 67-84.

6 *Morning Freeman* (Saint John), 10 April 1866.

addressed a series of public letters to confederate politicians, which urged Catholics to prove their loyalty by supporting Confederation.[7] When the election returns were complete, Archbishop Connolly and his suffragan bishops believed that the resounding success of the Confederation party was in great part the result of their timely intervention, and that the Catholic Church and its people should be rewarded for their efforts.

The reward which Connolly sought was in the field of education. In 1864, the government of Nova Scotia had adopted a school system which standardized education throughout the province. Henceforth, instruction would be nondenominational and only through the medium of English. The Catholics of Nova Scotia had objected to the new system, which ended public support for their schools, and Connolly felt that the new federal government should guarantee denominational education by extending the Lower Canadian school system to all provinces. When the Archbishop lobbied the Fathers of Confederation at the London Conference for such a concession, he was opposed by the French-Canadian delegates, George Cartier and Hector Langevin, who refused to allow the federal government the necessary legislative powers to alter the system of education in any province. If the federal government gained this power, then presumably the French Catholics of Lower Canada would be at the mercy of an English Protestant majority in the House of Commons. Connolly's only reward was the vague and dubious wording of Section 93 of the BNA Act. Although education was to be a matter of provincial concern, this section provided federal protection for denominational privileges established by law at the time of union.[8] The separate and dissentient schools of the Province of Canada were clearly protected by Section 93, and equally clear was that Catholic schools in Nova Scotia could only be established on provincial initiation. The position of Catholic schools in New Brunswick was not specified and rather vague. If the existing confessional schools of New Brunswick had been established "by law," they were protected by Section 93. A brief examination of contemporary New Brunswick school legislation is necessary to determine the legal status of confessional schools in that province.

The "Act Relating to Parish Schools" of 1858 was the law in 1867.[9] It had been passed to rationalize and partially control the hodge-podge of schools which had grown up to answer local needs. The parish schools were partly financed by local means and partly by direct government grants. Teachers were licensed by the government. For present purposes, the critical passage in the act is Section 8, which dealt

7 Archives of the Diocese of Chatham (New Brunswick), Papers of Bishop James Rogers, Pastoral Letter, 6 January 1874.
8 Canada, Parliament, *Sessional Papers*, VI, 1873, No. 44.
9 Ibid.

with the duties of teachers, who were enjoined to instill and inculcate the principles of Christianity, providing no pupil was forced to read from religious books or join in acts of devotion to which his parents or guardians objected. Scriptures were to be read in parish schools, and the Douay Version was prescribed for Catholic pupils. Thus, according to the law in effect at the time of Confederation, teachers were obliged to teach religion, religious books and acts of devotion were expected, and Scriptures were to be read by all consenting pupils. Teachers of Catholic pupils were specifically ordered to use the Douay Bible. These were matters specified by law, and most schools which operated within the bounds of the Parish Schools Act were "denominational" to a certain degree. In towns and cities, almost all schools were sponsored by religious denominations. There were Catholic schools, Anglican "Madras" schools, Baptist schools, and Presbyterian schools, all operating within the bounds of the law of the province. Only in the thinly-settled, religiously mixed areas did common, or nondenominational, schools exist.

But the 1858 Act was truly unsatisfactory. It did not provide for a standard system of teacher training, nor did it provide for suitable financial backing. By the late 1860's, many demanded a complete reform of the school system, and the provincial government was receptive to the idea. Essentially, this government was a pro-Confederation coalition, some would say it was in the vest pocket of Leonard Tilley, federal Minister of Finance and strong supporter of Sir John A. Macdonald. It was also an anti-Catholic government, elected during the 1866 backlash against Fenianism. And it was a progressive government, heir to the reform traditions of the 1850s. A nonsectarian, free and compulsory school system, supported by universal taxation, was well in line with that tradition.

In 1870, the provincial elections were based mainly on the issue of reform of the school system. Support for reform came from both sides of the legislature, and opposition came from many assorted quarters. Some objected to the proposed taxation of property to support schools, but most of the criticism was directed at the nonsectarian principle. Many Protestants initially objected to the loss of their schools, and others felt that religion could not be separated from the general process of education. But the centre of resistance came from the Catholics, who saw the proposed reforms as hostile to their interests. The government was returned and it soon formed a new coalition based on the need for reforming the school law. The new legislation appeared in 1871, was debated in and out of the legislature and was passed by a small majority. Entitled "An Act Relating to Common Schools,"[10] it was the focal point of crisis for the next five years.

10 Ibid.

The Common Schools Act did everything its creators had promised and threatened. Schools would be free, compulsory, nonsectarian,
supported by direct taxation, with standard curriculum and textbooks.
The new legislation was to become effective on 1 January 1872 and all
schools seeking public funds were to conform to the provisions of the
act by that date. Since direct legislative grants were suspended any
school operating outside the act would be deprived of all forms of
public financial support. The Board of Education, which was responsible for implementation of the new law, issued regulations which went
beyond the wording of the act. All religious symbols, images, devotions
and garb peculiar to any denomination were banned from schools.
Orange sashes were thus proscribed, but for Catholic schools which
depended upon the use of teaching nuns and brothers, this was adding
unnecessary insult to injury.

Catholics, both lay and clerical, protested to the board, the provincial government, to their MLAs, all to no avail. They also petitioned the
dominion government, claiming protection under Section 93 of the
BNA Act. When school district meetings were held in January 1872
Catholic-dominated districts refused to assess for school purposes,
passed resolutions condemning the nonsectarian principle and waited
for assistance from Ottawa.

Macdonald, in his capacity as Minister of Justice, was forced to
consider the merits of the Catholic position. He was also a politician
facing an election. There were three "Catholic" seats in the Commons
from New Brunswick and two were filled by members of the opposition. Tilley controlled most of the remaining dozen New Brunswick
seats, and had a strong influence over the New Brunswick government.
The members of the New Brunswick government were Macdonald
supporters, but they already had reason to be wary of him. When the
Treaty of Washington was signed, they objected to many of its provisions, especially American use of the Saint John River. In vain they
attempted to persuade Nova Scotia and Prince Edward Island to help
them block the treaty.[11] New Brunswick had been beaten on the Treaty
of Washington; if beaten again on the Schools Question, the New
Brunswick government might become very hostile during the federal
elections.

On the other hand, Macdonald had little to gain from disallowance
of the act. Even if he gained the three Catholic seats in New Brunswick,
he stood to lose many of the other seats, thus neutralizing his gain. In
addition, he also stood to lose the critical Orange vote in Ontario if he
leaned too far in support of the Catholics, and that meant a long stretch
on the wrong side of the House of Commons. Macdonald examined

11 J. P. Mansfield, "New Brunswick and the Treaty of Washington" (master's thesis,
University of New Brunswick, 1958), pp. 51-82.

the Common Schools Act and the Parish Schools Act, and found a way out: the former repealed the latter, and did not relate to separate, dissentient, or denominational schools. Nor, in his opinion, did the Parish Schools Act establish such confessional schools. Section 93 protected confessional schools established by law, and since the statutes of New Brunswick established parish schools rather than separate, dissentient or denominational schools, Macdonald argued that the Governor General had no right to intervene.[12] Political reasoning, aided by an extremely narrow reading of the Parish Schools Act, allowed Macdonald temporarily to dodge a volatile issue.

Naturally, the matter did not rest there. Two New Brunswick MPs, T. W. Anglin and John Costigan, carried the Catholic cause to the House of Commons. On 29 April 1872, the New Brunswick Schools Question was debated for the first time.[13] Anglin told the House that New Brunswick Catholics had been deprived of their rights by the new school law, and that it was the duty of the dominion government to restore those rights. It was also the duty of all Catholic MPs to support him in this matter. Macdonald replied that education was a provincial matter, and therefore, the system of schools in New Brunswick was not the concern of the House of Commons. If the Common Schools Act operated against the interests of the Catholics, they should apply to the provincial authorities for redress. If Macdonald ever believed in federal supremacy or in the force of Section 93, he dismissed both in that short and very blun;t speech. Sir George Cartier echoed the Prime Minister by insisting that the dominion government had no right to intervene in provincial matters. He dismissed pleas for justice to minorities, noting that at the time of Confederation, only in Ontario and Quebec had special provision been made for minorities.

Towards the end of May, Costigan rose in the House to move that the Governor General be advised to disallow the Common Schools Act as contravening Section 93 of the BNA Act.[14] He said that the act interfered with educational rights held by Catholics at the time of Confederation and was unconstitutional. Cartier warned his supporters that if the House were to intervene in New Brunswick, then the Catholic schools of Quebec might also be subject to such intervention. At least Cartier was consistent. In 1866, he had opposed a constitutional extension of separate schools to preserve Quebec supremacy in its education system; six years later he opposed federal intervention in education for exactly the same reason. If Cartier had ever believed in the principle of duality, it did not apply to Irishmen in New Brunswick.

Cartier could not carry all his supporters with him. Some of his *Bleu* backbenchers, especially those of an Ultramontane persuasion,

---

12 Rogers Papers, "Extract of the Report of the Minister of Justice," 6 January 1872.
13 Canada, Parliament, *House of Commons Debates*, 1871, III, cols. 197-206.
14 Ibid., cols. 705-11.

were wavering, and one, Roderick Masson, openly argued against
Cartier's position. Masson said the Common Schools Act violated the
letter and spirit of Section 93, and justice demanded that the House aid
the minority in New Brunswick. The act could be disallowed without
endangering Catholic education in Quebec. The *Rouge* leader, A. A.
Dorion, agreed with Masson. Catholic rights in Quebec were well
protected, and the House would never tamper with them. The New
Brunswick government had exceeded its jurisdiction, and the House
should disallow the act. This was one of the very few times Dorion
urged federal intervention in provincial affairs. One may only assume
that he detected political advantage in such a position; he could make
an election issue out of Cartier's stand on the New Brunswick Schools
Question.

Debate on Costigan's motion resumed on 22 May.[15] J. H. Gray of
Saint John moved that the motion be amended to indicate the jurisdiction of the New Brunswick government. Gray was a Father of Confederation, yet his view favoured provincial rights, an odd position for a
Macdonald supporter. The *Bleu* Premier of Quebec, P. J. O.
Chauveau, still allowed to sit in the Commons, moved yet another
amendment calling for an amendment to the BNA Act to extend
separate schools throughout the dominion. This had been Connolly's
position in 1866. Cartier had opposed it then, he would oppose it now.
Most of New Brunswick's MPs demanded a recess to consider this
important proposal. During the interval, Macdonald sent a whip to
offer Costigan a compromise.[16] If Costigan would accept Chauveau's
amendment, Macdonald would try to have it passed. At first Costigan
and Anglin were inclined to accept, but to do so would have been an
admission that Section 93 had offered no protection for denominational schools in New Brunswick. Up to that point, the entire position
of the Catholics had rested upon that protection. Macdonald also had
problems. Tilley offered his resignation if the government decided to
support Costigan's motion or Chauveau's amendment.[17] Such a resignation would have invited disaster for the Macdonald party, especially
in New Brunswick.

On 29 May, when debate resumed, a Conservative, Charles Colby,
moved an amendment expressing regret that the Common Schools Act
was not satisfactory to Catholics. Costigan demanded that Macdonald
indicate which amendment he preferred, Chauveau's or Colby's. Macdonald chose Colby's. Costigan demanded to know why the government had changed its mind. But Chauveau rose to withdraw his
amendment, without reason or apology. Macdonald and Cartier had
restored order to the Conservative ranks. Colby's amendment was

15 Ibid., cols. 758-66.
16 Rogers Papers, Anglin to Rogers, 22 May 1872.
17 PAC, John A. Macdonald Papers, Tilley to Macdonald, 25 May 1872.

approved by a majority of seventy-five. Alexander Mackenzie, leader of the opposition, moved that the House obtain the opinion of the law officers of the Crown. Having accepted this action, the first parliament of Canada washed its hands of the New Brunswick Schools Question.[18]

The federal elections of 1872 returned Macdonald and the Conservatives with a reduced majority. Cartier lost his Montreal seat, and was forced to seek another in the new province of Manitoba. The Schools Question played a large part in Cartier's defeat and in the elections all over Quebec.[19] During January 1873, Catholic school districts in New Brunswick continued to resist school assessments and maintained Catholic schools by private donations. Catholics in Protestant districts had been prosecuted for nonpayment of taxes, and in February the New Brunswick Supreme Court handed down decisions on most of the appeals. In appeals based on the constitutionality of the Common Schools Act, the court ruled for the Crown. But the court found that the assessment provisions supporting the act were imperfect and dismissed cases based on the mechanics of taxation. The New Brunswick government immediately passed a series of assessment acts designed to close these loopholes, and these were submitted to Ottawa for routine approval. This action provided an opportunity to bring the Schools Question back to the House of Commons and obtain a decision from what was potentially a more receptive group of MPs. One of the cases relating to the Common School Act was being appealed to the Judicial Committee of the Privy Council. If Ottawa approved the assessment acts, the basic position of one of the parties in that action would be altered. Anglin also noted that disallowance of these acts would ruin the new school system.[20]

While the parliamentary friends of the New Brunswick Catholics were preparing to do battle, Bishop Sweeny of Saint John went to Quebec, Montreal and Ottawa to rally support. Through the services of Anglin, he received assurances from the *Rouges* and the Grits. This was soured when on 5 May Macdonald tabled the decision of the law officers of the Crown. Their opinion was unfavourable to the Catholic position and upheld Macdonald's policy of nonintervention.[21] On 10 May Sweeny met with the *Bleu* caucus with no satisfactory result and came to the conclusion that only a statement of support from the Quebec hierarchy would rally that caucus. He immediately left for Quebec City, where the Quebec bishops were scheduled to meet. There then appeared in Ottawa a delegation from the New Brunswick

18 *Debates*, cols. 898-909.
19 Brian Young, "The Defeat of George-Etienne Cartier in Montreal-East in 1872," *CHR* 51 (December 1970): 386-406; Rogers Papers, Anglin to Rogers, 13 September 1872.
20 Rogers Papers, Anglin to Rogers, 13 March 1873.
21 PAC, Governor General's Numbered Files, Kimberly to Dufferin, 7 April 1873.

government, which attempted to counteract Sweeny's influence. These men were in the Commons gallery on 14 May when Costigan moved in favour of disallowance of the assessment acts.[22] Macdonald again took the position that education was a provincial matter, and that the House had no right to interfere. He argued that the BNA Act would be worthless if the House passed this motion and, more to the point, warned that the rights of Quebec would be tossed out the window if the House could overturn valid provincial legislation. It was obvious that the *Bleus* held the balance of power on this issue.

Sir Hector Langevin, upon whose shoulders the mantle of Cartier had fallen, attempted to hold his followers in line. Speaking only in French, he said there was nothing the House could do except to ensure that Ottawa would be unable to interfere with education in Quebec. He pleaded with his followers to defeat the motion. Alexander Mackenzie stated that although he was normally opposed to separate schools, he favoured the Costigan motion because the matter was before the Privy Council, which might settle the issue once and for all. He might also have added that passage of the motion would embarrass the government and weaken Macdonald's tenacious grip on the seals of office. The motion was declared an open question, and when the House divided, Macdonald suffered a great personal defeat. The entire opposition supported the motion, supported by over half of the *Bleus*.[23]

Although Costigan's motion did not involve confidence, it was a blow to the Macdonald government, which was labouring to conceal its financial connections with the Pacific Railway Company. The Prime Minister had been instructed by the House to advise the Governor General "to do that which he says will tear our constitution to tatters."[24] On 19 May Anglin rose in the House to ask what action had been taken on the Costigan motion. Macdonald replied that in view of the decision of the law officers, he could not advise the Governor General to act upon the motion without the advice of the imperial authorities. The same day, the Quebec bishops drafted a letter of support to Sweeny and Rogers which said:

> Si donc, pour acquitter d'un devoir sacré, Vos Grandeurs jugent convenable, dans leurs sagèsse et leurs prudence, de réclamer aupres du Parliament Impérial où du Gouvernement Fédéral pour la défense et le respect plus éfficaces de leur droits, Elles nous trouveront tout disposés à les appuyer dans cette demand si légitimé, et avec nous, nos ministres et nos législateurs Catholiques, nous osons nous en porter garants.[25]

All the elements necessary for a decisive confrontation were now present. The government refused to be bound by a motion of the

22 *Morning Freeman*, 15 May 1873.
23 Canadian Library Association, *Debates of the House of Commons, 1873*, pp. 181-83.
24 *Morning Freeman*, 17 May 1873.
25 Rogers Papers, The Hierarchy of the Province of Quebec to Bishops Rogers and Sweeny, 19 May 1873.

House of Commons, and the Governor General chose to ignore the advice of his elected parliament in favour of the advice of the imperial government, and all this on an issue which was dividing the governing party. Furthermore, the Catholic hierarchy of Quebec had pledged the support of their parliamentary supporters. Anglin and Costigan decided to topple the government with a pointed motion of nonconfidence based on the failure of the government to act upon the advice of the House of Commons. It seemed probable that the government would fall.

That was as close as the New Brunswick Catholics ever came to victory in their struggle. That night, at the insistance of Langevin, the Quebec hierarchy reversed its position. Telegrams were sent to *Bleu* dissidents and to Anglin and Costigan advising against further action.[26]

Bishop Rogers later insisted that the Quebec bishops, while quite sympathetic, had been unwilling to allow the defeat of the Macdonald government on the New Brunswick Schools Question. He believed that this stand was merely an extension of Cartier's position during the London Conference.[27] The role of the bishops is difficult to defend. A Catholic minority lost longstanding educational rights; Quebec, the principal bastion of Catholicism in Canada, failed to rise to the challenge. Rather than become the champion of minority rights, Quebec retreated to provincial isolation and a policy of federal nonintervention. Quebec's reward? A few extra weeks in office for a corrupt government. In the long term, Quebec's failure to protect Catholic rights in New Brunswick backfired in Manitoba and Ontario. If Quebec had adopted a position of minority rights in 1866 and 1873, indeed, a position of true duality, the effects of the Manitoba School Bill and Ontario's Regulation 17 would probably have been drastically reduced if not prevented.

The battle in New Brunswick really ended with the failure to unseat the Macdonald government. Further incidents were merely anti-climatic. The Conservatives were soon defeated over the "Pacific Scandal," and the new Liberal government did not owe its elevation to power to the New Brunswick Schools Question. Had this been the case, they might well have been forced to take action but as it was, they were able to adopt a position of provincial rights and reconfirm the basic Macdonald stance. In 1874 the New Brunswick government went to the polls shouting "The Ticket, the Whole Ticket, and Nothing but the Ticket!" and whispering "No Popery." The opposition, almost completely identified with the Catholic cause, was virtually annihilated. The Judicial Committee of the Privy Council ruled the Common Schools Act "intra vires" of the BNA Act, confirming all previous

26 Ibid., Anglin to Rogers, 20 May 1873.
27 Ibid., Rogers, Pastoral Letter, 19 March 1891.

political and legal decisions. A final desperate attempt to settle the issue in the House of Commons degenerated into a vicious squabble amongst the Catholic MPs, each blaming the other for the 1873 failure.

Superficially, the issue was minority rights, but implicitly the issue was the relative powers of the federal and provincial authorities, and indeed, the basic nature of Confederation. Macdonald, the prophet of the strong central authority, the man who insisted that the federal government was the defender of minorities, could have found in Section 93 of the BNA Act and Section 8 of the Parish Schools Act sufficient grounds for disallowance of the Common Schools Act. Contrary to what he and Cartier said in and out of the House, this would not have allowed federal intervention in Quebec's school system, because sectarian schools were specifically protected in that province, and also because it would have been politically impossible. Rather than invoke the principle of strong central government in the New Brunswick Schools issue, Macdonald found it politically expedient to withdraw behind a barrage of voiced good intentions and expressions of sympathy. The province of New Brunswick, on behalf of the advocates of provincial rights, stole a march on Ottawa while Macdonald and Cartier counted votes.

The New Brunswick Schools Question was one of the first constitutional crises faced by the dominion of Canada. For the first time, the division of powers contained in the BNA Act was called into question. If Macdonald had stood firm on the federal responsibility to maintain minority rights and reaffirmed the federal responsibility to maintain "good government" throughout the dominion, and had used his power of disallowance, the power and prestige of Ottawa would have been enhanced. Instead, he capitulated without a struggle, and federal power and prestige suffered a tragic defeat.

VIII

Canada Annexes the West: Colonial Status Confirmed

Donald Swainson

The early history of the Canadian West[1] is characterized by dependence and exploitation. The area and its resources were controlled from outside, for the benefit of several distant centres, whose relative importance changed from time to time. London, Montreal and Toronto, the major and competing metropolises, were flanked by such lesser competitors as Minneapolis-St. Paul, Benton and Vancouver. A prime result of this pattern of development has been a continuing resistance to outside controls. At the same time, the character of western people and institutions has been heavily influenced by forces outside western control. Even indigenous peoples were largely defined by the forces that controlled the region. The interplay of these factors has played a large part in moulding the character of the West and in determining fundamentally its role in Canadian federalism.

I

The pattern of dependence preceded federal union and for the West is the context within which federalism must be viewed. It began in the seventeenth century when English traders established themselves in posts around Hudson Bay. Chartered in 1670 as the Hudson's Bay Company, this "Company of Adventurers of England tradeing [*sic*] into Hudson's Bay"[2] tapped an enormously profitable trade in furs. To this prestigious and powerful firm the Crown delegated vast responsibilities and valuable privileges:

1 In this essay the "West" refers to the territories that became the provinces of Manitoba, Saskatchewan and Alberta. Rupert's Land consisted of the Hudson's Bay Company territories. The North-West Territory included the other British lands in the northwest. British Columbia was separate and is not considered in this essay.

2 E. E. Rich, *Hudson's Bay Company, 1670-1870*, 3 vols. (Toronto, 1960): 1: 53.

[T]he Company was granted the "sole Trade and Commerce of all those Seas Streightes Bayes Rivers Lakes Creekes and Soundes in whatsoever Latitude they shall bee that lye within the entrance of the Streightes commonly called Hudsons Streightes together with all the Landes and Territoryes upon the Countryes Coastes and confynes of the Seas Bayes Lakes Rivers Creekes and Soundes aforesaid that are not actually possessed by or granted to any of our Subjects or possessed by the Subjects of any other Christian Prince or State". They were to be the "true and absolute Lordes and Proprietors" of this vast territory, and they were to hold it, as had been envisaged in the grant of October 1669, in free and common socage. . . . These lands were to be reckoned as a plantation or colony, and were to be known as Rupert's Land; and the Company was to own the mineral and fishing rights there as well as the exclusive trade and the land itself.[3]

For two hundred years, the Hudson's Bay Company was the (more or less) effective government of Rupert's Land, an enormous territory stretching from Labrador through the shield and the prairies and into the Arctic tundra in the West. It included most of what are now the provinces of Manitoba, Saskatchewan and Alberta. Control over the West was thus vested in a firm centred in London and exercised in the interests of commerce.

Montreal businessmen (whether French before the Conquest, or British after) refused to recognize the HBC's trade monopoly, and wanted to share in the profits. In spite of enormous overhead costs French traders penetrated the West in the middle of the eighteenth century, and entered into competition for the favour of the Indian fur gatherers. After the Conquest Montreal's challenge to the Hudson's Bay Company's monopoly was even more serious. Numerous Montreal-based traders entered the field, but the most famous and effective were organized late in the eighteenth century as the North-West Company. This marvel of capitalist organization exploited the wealth of the shield and the prairies. It opened the rich Athabasca country and its agents penetrated north to the Arctic and west to the Pacific. The Nor'Westers introduced the influence of Montreal into the mainstream of western life. The vicious competition between Montreal and London for the control of the western trade, however, proved too costly; in 1821 the Hudson's Bay Company and the North-West Company amalgamated. But both Montreal and London continued to exercise great influence in the West. And, of course, the officers and men of the reorganized Hudson's Bay Company remained a powerful force in the West until Canada annexed the area in 1870.

Children of mixed white and Indian blood were an inevitable result of the presence of fur traders in the West. By the late eighteenth century these people were a numerous group on the prairies. They can

3 Cited in ibid., 1: 53-54.

be very roughly divided into two sub-groups: English-speaking half-breeds and French-speaking Métis. The former tended to be relatively settled and to have close ties with the white communities in the Red River Valley. The Métis were more autonomous and distinctive. During this period, they developed into a powerful force.

As a people, the Métis were very much a product of the fur trade. Like many other unsophisticated and indigenous peoples, they were manipulated by the great business firms that exploited the natural resources of their area. The North-West Company employed them first as labourers and hunters. The trade war between the fur tradeing giants increased their utility, especially after Lord Selkirk established his famous settlement in the Red River Valley in 1811-12. Selkirk's colony and the HBC functioned as interdependent units, and challenged the viability of the NWC operations west of the Red River. The NWC could not declare war on one without fighting the other. Consequently it declared war on both, and the Métis became its prime weapon. The leaders of the NWC encouraged the growth of a primitive nationalism; the Métis were encouraged to believe that the Red River settlers threatened their claim to western lands, a claim inherited from their Cree and Saulteaux mothers. Cuthbert Grant, a Scottish-educated half-breed, was appointed Captain of the Métis by the North-West Company, and his followers became a small private army. They harassed the Selkirk settlers, a process that culminated in 1816 in the battle of Seven Oaks where Grant's men massacred Governor Robert Semple and twenty of his settlers. But in spite of its superior military strength, the NWC, primarily for geographical reasons, could not sustain a protracted campaign against the Red River colonists and the HBC. Consequently, the firms united in 1821; the West was pacified.

The four-year struggle (1812-1816) against the Selkirk settlers was a decisive event in western history. It marked the beginning of the Métis as an organized and self-conscious group. After 1821, they continued to accept Grant's leadership. They founded Grantown on the Assiniboine River west of the restored Selkirk settlement and made that village their capital; for the next seventy years they were at the centre of prairie history.

After the union of the firms, Cuthbert Grant and his people were coopted by the controlling interests. The Metis defended the growing and prosperous community of Selkirk settlers, their former enemies, from the Sioux. In 1828, Grant was made Warden of the Plains of Red River, with responsibility for enforcing the Hudson's Bay Company trade monopoly. During these quiet years of the 1820s and 1830s the Métis of Grantown organized and refined their most important institution, the famous buffalo hunt, which provided important food reserves for settlers and traders alike, and an economic base for the Métis.[4] The implications of the hunt were endless. It was organized along military lines and was easily adaptable to military and political purposes. The Métis, self-confident about their identity and proud of their place in western society, referred to themselves as the "New Nation" but nonetheless they remained dependent on buffalo and fur traders.

The Métis were created as a people only after the arrival of white traders in the West; the Indians had peopled the prairies for several millennia. It might be argued, however, that European influences recreated Indian society; these forces certainly revolutionized Indian history. When white men first came to North America the Indians who inhabited the western plains lacked horses and guns. The acquisition of these items, combined with trade, radically altered Indian society. In some instances, and for a brief period, the result was startling. A recent historian of Alberta illustrates:

> For a few vivid decades Blackfoot culture, based upon horses, guns and unlimited buffalo, rose rapidly into the zenith of the rich, colourful and glamorous life which many regard as the apogee of plains culture. Prior to 1730, during the long era which the Blackfoot called the dog-days they travelled on foot and used dogs for transport. About that year, the acquisition of horses and guns swept them rapidly onward and upward until slightly over a century later they were at the peak of their spectacular horse-based culture. . . . Though horses and guns had made the Blackfoot aggressive, they also provided the leisure which led to the flowering of their social life.[5]

Revolutionized Indian societies were highly vulnerable to external forces. They could not manufacture either guns or ammunition; traders could (and did) cause social calamities through the introduction of liquor and a variety of diseases; trading patterns could not be controlled by Indians. More important, the buffalo could be liquidated and settlement could destroy the basis of Indian independence. In the mid-nineteenth century these successful western Indian societies were in a delicately balanced position. European contacts had changed the very character of their society; at the same time they were dependent upon and vulnerable to white society. Further white encroachment in

---

4 For a superb account of the buffalo hunt, see Alexander Ross, *The Red River Settlement* (London, 1856), Chap. XVIII.

5 James G. MacGregor, *A History of Alberta* (Edmonton, 1972), pp. 17, 24. For further illustrations see Stanley Norman Murray, *The Valley Comes of Age: A History of Agriculture in the Valley of the Red River of the North, 1812-1920* (Fargo, 1967), p. 13: "By 1800 the Sioux and Chippewa tribes also had acquired horses. Because these animals made it possible for the Indians to hunt the buffalo over great distances, these people soon spent most of the summer and fall roaming the vast prairie west of the Red River. As they became more nomadic, the Indians placed less emphasis upon agriculture, pottery making, weaving, and the idea of a fixed dwelling place. In years when the buffalo were numerous, they could live from the hunt alone. Such was the case between 1800 and 1840 when the Sioux and Chippewa experienced degrees of luxury and leisure they had never known."

the West could destroy them. That encroachment of course quickly occurred, and in the 1870s the western Indians were swamped. A recent student of Canadian Indians comments: "For the sake of convenience, and recognizing the arbitrariness of the choice, we may use the date 1876, that of the first Indian Act, as the beginning of what we call the "colonial" period. From the point of view of the European, the Indian had become irrelevant."[6]

The full complexity of mid-nineteenth-century prairie society cannot be revealed in a few paragraphs. The main characteristics, however, can be delineated. The West was inhabited by French-speaking Métis, English-speaking half-breeds, officers and men of the Hudson's Bay Company, Selkirk settlers and a handful of missionaries, retired soldiers and free-traders. Except for the Indians, these groups were all centred around the forks of the Red and Assiniboine Rivers, where a pluralistic society emerged. Reasonable amity usually prevailed, although the Métis could not be controlled against their will by the aging and increasingly ineffective HBC regime. This was a civilized society, with its own churches, schools and law courts. Its various components produced their own indigenous middle-classes, leaders, institutions and traditions. Several religions were sustained within the settlement and promoted amongst the Indians.

At the same time these diverse western societies were fragile and derivative. W. L. Morton describes the Selkirk settlers as "Scottish crofters on the banks of the Red."[7] Indian society had been recreated through European contact and persons of mixed blood were a product of liaisons between fur traders and Saulteaux and Cree women. Employees of the HBC were often of British birth. None of these groups had sufficient cultural integrity or autonomy to retain their distinctiveness and independence without a considerable degree of isolation from the larger North American society. As Bishop Taché observed about immigration into the West: "[T]he movement [of immigration] is an actual fact, and we must cease to be what we have hitherto been, an exceptional people."[8]

They were dependent on more than isolation. Economically they needed the fur trade and the buffalo hunt. Buffalo products were sold to traders, settlers and Americans at Minneapolis-St. Paul. The fur trade supplied cash, employment and markets. Agriculture, "subsis-

---

6 E. Palmer Patterson, *The Canadian Indian: A History Since 1500* (Don Mills, 1972), pp. 39-40. Different dates apply in different areas: "Thus, by 1865 the plight of the Indians in the Red River Valley was a pathetic one, and for the most part their culture no longer had any effect upon this area" (Murray, *Valley Comes of Age*, p. 15).

7 W. L. Morton, "Introduction to the New Edition" of Alexander Ross, *The Red River Settlement* (Edmonton, 1972), p. xx.

8 Cited in A. I. Silver, "French Canada and the Prairie Frontier, 1870-1890," *CHR* 50 (March 1969): 13.

tent, riparian, and restricted,"[9] was nonetheless an important enterprise. Markets were obviously extremely limited. The large-scale export of commodities was hardly reasonable and, even within the West, Red River Valley farmers had no monopoly on food production as long as the buffalo survived. The agricultural sector of the western economy thus remained modest.[10]

Within the West some of these groups, particularly HBC officials, Indians and Métis, could exert tremendous authority; their futures, however, were in the hands of forces that could not be contained. They had sufficient group-consciousness to defend collective interests, and to varying degrees they were all willing to resist encroachments from the outside. The Métis revolted against the locally enforced trade monopoly; HBC officials became dissatisfied with the treatment meted out to them by their London superiors. The Scots settlers resented the suggestion that the area could be disposed of without prior consultation. A willingness to resist in spite of dependence and relative weakness was a striking western characteristic long before the West was annexed by Canada. It is an important component of the western context of federalism.[11]

II

The Central Canadian context is equally important. French-Canadian explorers penetrated the West in the eighteenth century, and thereafter the West was always a concern of at least some Central Canadians. The connection became somewhat tenuous after the union of the fur

9 W. L. Morton, "Agriculture in the Red River Colony," *CHR* 30 (December 1949): 321.

10 Murray, *Valley Comes of Age*, pp. 44 and 48: "[T]here can be little question that the economy of the Selkirk colonies stagnated soon after they were able to produce a surplus. The major reason for stagnation in Red River agriculture was the limited market for farm produce, and this situation developed primarily out of the economic prerogatives of the Hudson's Bay Company. . . . [I]t continued to rely upon supplies brought from England and pemmican furnished by the metis hunters." In short, "agriculture did not become really commercial under the fur company regime. . . ." Morton points out that Red River agriculture lacked both "an export staple and transportation" ("Agriculture in the Red River Colony," p. 316).

11 There has recently been considerable discussion of western "identity." Debate on this question will doubtless continue. It can be argued that this persistent willingness to resist is one of the most distinctive western characteristics and is certainly a part of any western "identity," and that it long antedates Confederation. P. F. W. Rutherford, however, dismisses Métis influence: "Unlike other regions in the dominion, the western community was essentially a product of events set in motion by Confederation" ("The Western Press and Regionalism, 1870-96," *CHR* 52 [September 1971]: 287). Morton, however, comments: "Louis Riel was a more conventional politician than William Aberhart . . ." and "[t]his was the beginning of the bias of prairie politics. The fears of the Metis had led them to demand equality for the people of the Northwest in Confederation" ("The Bias of Prairie Politics" in *Historical Essays on the Prairie Provinces*, ed., Donald Swainson [Toronto, 1970], pp. 289 and 293). What is more "western" than this recurring "demand" for "equality"?

companies in 1821, but it was never lost; there was always full cognizance of the fact that Rupert's Land was British territory.

A more pointed interest became evident in the late 1840s, and the nature of that interest illuminates Central Canadian attitudes about what the West was, what it should become and how it should relate to what was then the Province of Canada. This interest, while by no means partisan in nature, centred in the Upper Canadian Reformers. It can be illustrated by an examination of two of its representative manifestations: the campaign of the Toronto *Globe* to annex the West and the organization of the North-West Transportation Company.[12]

The *Globe* was the organ of George Brown, who emerged in the 1850s as the Upper Canadian Reform leader. It was a Toronto newspaper that spoke to the farmers of what became western Ontario, but at the same time represented many of the metropolitan interests of Toronto's business elite. Its interest in the North-West tended to be economic and exploitative. Underlying this early tentative interest in the West was the assumption that the West would become an economic and social adjunct of Upper Canada. On 24 March 1847, for example, Brown reprinted Robert Baldwin Sullivan's lecture, "Emigration and Cololization." While primarily concerned with Upper Canada, Sullivan also discussed settlement possibilities in the North-West. He viewed the West as a potential settlement area for Upper Canadians. In 1848 the *Globe* claimed the West for Canada, and dismissed the rights of the Hudson's Bay Company. The West, it argued, was "capable of supporting a numerous population. This wide region nominally belongs to the Hudson's Bay Company, but in point of fact it does not seem to be theirs."[13] The *Globe*'s interest petered out in 1850, but revived after a few years. In 1856 it published a series of revealing articles by an anonymous correspondent, "Huron": "I desire to see Canada for the Canadians and not exclusively for a selfish community of traders, utter strangers to our country; whose only anxiety is to draw all the wealth they can from it, without contributing to its advantages even one farthing."[14] He pronounced the charter of the Hudson's Bay Company "null and void" and declared that "[t]he interest of Canada require that this giant monopoly be swept out of existence. . . ." "Huron" was emphatic on this point:

> The formation of a Company in opposition to the Hudson's Bay Company would advance the interests of Canada; it would consolidate and strengthen the British power on the continent. . . . In the organization of

12 For a more detailed discussion by the present author see *Ontario and Confederation*, Centennial Historical Booklet No. 5 (Ottawa, 1967) and "The North-West Transportation Company: Personnel and Attitudes," Historical and Scientific Society of Manitoba *Transactions*, Series III, No. 26, 1969-70.
13 *Globe* (Toronto), 14 June 1848.
14 Quotations from articles by "Huron" are from *Globe*, 18 and 31 October 1856.

[opposition to the HBC], every patriot, every true Canadian, beholds results the most important to his country.

According to the *Globe*, westward expansion was an urgent need because of a shortage of settlement land "south of Lake Huron." "[Canada] is fully entitled to possess whatever parts of the Great British American territory she can safely occupy...."[15]

Interest in westward expansion was by no means confined to the *Globe*. In 1856 the Toronto Board of Trade indicated interest in western trade.[16] Various politicians took up the cause and the matter was aired in both houses of parliament.[17]

In 1858 a Toronto-based group made a "quixotic" and "abortive"[18] attempt to penetrate the West through the incorporation of the North-West Transportation, Navigation and Railway Company (known as the North-West Transit Co.).[19] The project, designed to link Central Canada and the Red River Valley by a combination of rail and water transport, was premature and unsuccessful, but its promoters' attitudes towards the West were both representative and persistent.[20] The objects were the exploitation of such likely and unlikely western possibilities as buffalo hides, furs, tallow, fish, salt, sarsaparilla and cranberries, "the opening [of] a direct communication between Lake Superior and the Pacific..." and the opening of trade with the Orient. "[W]e place before us a mart of 600,000,000 of people [in China] and [our project will] enable us geographically to command them; opening the route, and leaving it to the guidance of commercial interests, Canada will, sooner or later, become the great tollgate for the commerce of the world." By "Canada," of course, was meant Toronto, and these promoters dreamed of controlling a great empire: "Like the Genii in the fable [the East Indian trade] still offers the sceptre to those who, unintimidated by the terms that surround it, are bold enough to adventure to its embrace. In turn Phoenicia, Carthage, Greece, Rome, Venice, Pisa, Genoa, Portugal, Holland and lastly England, has won and worn this ocean diadem; Destiny now offers [the East Indian trade] to us."

15 Ibid., 10 December 1856.
16 Ibid., 4 December 1856.
17 Province of Canada, *Journals of the Legislative Council of the Province of Canada*. Being the Third Session of the 5th Provincial Parliament, 1857, vol. XV, pp. 60, 80, 184, 195; Province of Canada, *Appendix to the Fifteenth Volume of the Journals of the Legislative Assembly of the Province of Canada*. Being the 3rd Session of the 5th Provincial Parliament, 1857, vol. XV, Appendix 17.
18 Joseph James Hargrave, *Red River* (Montreal, 1871), p. 143.
19 Province of Canada, *Statutes*, 1858, pp. 635ff.
20 Material that follows is from *Memoranda and Prospectus of the North-West Transportation and Land Company* (Toronto, 1858); Allan Macdonnell, *The North-West Transportation, Navigation and Railway Company: Its Objectives* (Toronto, 1858) and *Prospectus of the North-West Transportation, Navigation and Railway Company* (Toronto, 1858).

During the 1850s a dynamic and expansive Upper Canada saw the North-West as its proper hinterland. It was regarded as a huge extractive resource, designed to provide profit for the businessman, land for the farmer and power for Toronto.

While cultural attitudes are sometimes difficult to identify, it was probably assumed that the North-West would be culturally as well as economically dependent on the St. Lawrence Valley. J. M. S. Careless, for example, suggests that "Brown used the North-West agitation to complete the reunification of Upper Canada's liberal party, merging Toronto urban and business leadership with Clear Grit agrarian strength in a dynamic party front."[21] Brown's "party front," which wanted "French Canadianism entirely extinguished,"[22] was dedicated to majoritarianism and the sectional interests of Upper Canada. While the nature of Reform attitudes towards French Canada is debatable, it is hardly likely that the same men who strove to terminate duality in Central Canada sought to extend it to the North-West. Some Lower Canadian leaders (both French- and English-speaking), especially those identified with Montreal business, were interested in westward expansion for economic reasons. There was, however, little French-Canadian enthusiasm for expansion westward.[23] French-Canadian attitudes emanated from the nature of Lower Canadian society, which was profoundly conservative and lacked the buoyant and dynamic qualities of Upper Canada: "Not movement but stasis, enforced by the very nature of the task of 'survival', was the keynote of French-Canadian society."[24] French Canadians lacked confidence in the economic viability of the North-West, in major part because of pre-Confederation missionary propaganda that emphasized difficulties relating to the West. It was generally assumed that "western settlement was the sole concern of Ontario"[25] and that large-scale French-Canadian emigration would threaten French Canada's ability to survive. Thus there existed no Lower Canadian force to counter-balance Upper Canada's drive westward or Upper Canadian assumptions about how the West should be used. The only additional British North American region that could have possessed western ambitions consisted of the Atlantic colonies: New Brunswick, Nova Scotia, Prince Edward Island and Newfoundland. Their traditional orientation was towards the Atlantic, not the interior. The Atlantic colonies were not about to launch an imperialistic venture in the 1860s.

21 J. M. S. Careless, *The Union of the Canadas: The Growth of Canadian Institutions, 1841-57* (Toronto, 1967), p. 206.
22 PAC, George Brown Papers, George Brown to Anne Brown, 27 October 1864, cited in Donald Creighton, *The Road to Confederation* (Toronto, 1964), p. 182.
23 For an analysis of French-Canadian attitudes see Silver, "French Canada and the Prairie Frontier."
24 Ibid., p. 29.
25 Ibid., p. 15.

Apart from Montreal business ambitions the field was clear for Upper Canada, but little could be done until a new political order was established in Central Canada. The constitutional settlement embodied in the Act of Union of 1840 broke down during the 1850s. The complexities of Central Canadian politics during the 1850s are not germane to this discussion, although it should be noted that a prime reason for the breakdown of Canadian government was the incompatability between the uncontrollable dynamism and expansionism of Upper Canadian society on the one hand, and the conservative and inward-looking society of Lower Canada on the other.

The new order was worked out by the Great Coalition of 1864 that was committed to the introduction of "the federal principle into Canada, coupled with such provision as will permit the Maritime Provinces and the North-West Territory to be incorporated into the same system of government."[26] The solution was Confederation, which was established by the British North America Act of 1867. It created a highly centralized federation that included the Province of Canada (divided into Ontario and Quebec), Nova Scotia and New Brunswick, and that made explicit provision for the inclusion of the remaining British North American territories:

> It should be lawful for the Queen, by and with the Advice of Her Majesty's Most Honourable Privy Council, on Addresses from the Houses of the Parliament of Canada, and from the Houses of the respective Legislatures of the Colonies or Provinces of Newfoundland, Prince Edward Island, and British Columbia, to admit those Colonies or Provinces, or any of them, into the Union, and on Address from the Houses of the Parliament of Canada to admit Rupert's Land and the North-western Territory, or either of them, into the Union. . . .[27]

Confederation was thus the constitutional framework within which the West was destined to relate to Central Canada.

The nature of the new confederation had profound implications for the West. The system was highly centralized, so much so that in conception it hardly qualified as a federation in the classic sense. The Fathers of Confederation wanted a strong state that could withstand American pressure. Heavily influenced by trade considerations, they saw federation in mercantilistic terms. As children of the empire as it existed prior to the repeal of the corn laws, it is not surprising that their federal model was the old colonial system, modified to involve "the citizens of the provinces . . . in the government of the whole entity":[28]

> The purpose of the Fathers of Confederation—to found a united and integrated transcontinental Dominion—was comparable with that of the

26 Cited in Chester Martin, *Foundations of Canadian Nationhood* (Toronto, 1955), p. 314.
27 British North America Act, Section 146.
28 Bruce W. Hodgins, "Disagreement at the Commencement: Divergent Ontarian Views of Federalism, 1867-1871," in *Oliver Mowat's Ontario,* ed., Donald Swainson (Toronto, 1972), p. 55.

mercantilists: and in both designs there was the same need that the interests of the parts should be made subordinate to the interest of the whole. The Dominion was the heir in direct succession of the old colonial system. It was put in possession of both the economic and political controls of the old regime. On the one hand, it was given the power to regulate trade and commerce, which had been the chief economic prerogative of Great Britain; on the other hand, it was granted the right to nominate provincial governors, to review provincial legislation and to disallow provincial acts, the three powers which had been the chief attributes of Great Britain's political supremacy.[29]

In his more optimistic moments, John A. Macdonald went so far as to predict the demise of the provinces: "If the Confederation goes on, you, if spared the ordinary age of man, will see both local parliaments and governments absorbed in the general power. This is as plain to me as if I saw it accomplished."[30]

It is true that Lower Canada and the Atlantic colonies were part of the new dominion, but the effective pressure for the new settlement came from Upper Canada. French Canada realized the inevitability of change, but generated little enthusiasm for Confederation. She could offer no better alternative and hence acquiesced (not without considerable protest) in the new arrangement.[31] The creative role was played by Upper Canada, and for that section Confederation was a great triumph. The new system was posited on the abandonment of dualism and, through representation by population in the House of Commons, the acceptance of majoritarianism, albeit with limited guarantees for French Canadian culture within the Province of Quebec. Majoritarianism was very much to the advantage of Ontario, which, according to the 1871 census, had 1,600,000 persons—or 46 per cent of Canada's 3,500,000 people. This translated into 82 of 181 seats in the House of Commons. The first prime minister was an Ontarian, as were the leading lights of the opposition—George Brown, Edward Blake and Alexander Mackenzie. In the first cabinet Ontario, the wealthiest province, had 5 of 13 places. Even the capital was an Ontario city.

The Ontario Liberals became the leaders of the nineteenth-century provincial rights agitation and Ontario emerged as the bastion of provincial rights sentiment, but while the federal scheme was being defined most of Ontario's leaders, regardless of party, concurred on the utility of this "quasi federal" scheme.[32] This is hardly surprising. The Reformers or Liberals were the larger of the two Ontario parties, and doubtless looked forward to a great future as the rulers of *both*

29 Donald Creighton, *British North America at Confederation* (Ottawa, 1939), Appendix II, *The Royal Commission on Dominion-Provincial Relations* (Ottawa, 1940), p. 83.
30 PAC, John A. Macdonald Papers, 510, Macdonald to M. C. Cameron, 19 December 1864, cited in Creighton, *The Road to Confederation*, p. 165.
31 See Jean Charles Bonenfant, *The French Canadians and the Birth of Confederation*, Canadian Historical Association booklet No. 10 (Ottawa, 1967).
32 See Hodgins, "Disagreement at the Commencement."

Ontario and the dominion. Although they realized this aim by 1873 and ruled simultaneously in Toronto and Ottawa for five years, they suffered humiliating defeats in 1867 at both levels. The deep autonomist drives within Ontario society quickly reasserted themselves and Ontario's Liberals began their protracted assault on Macdonald's constitutional edifice. This should not obscure the fact that quasi-federalism met with little Ontario opposition during the mid-1860s.

The acquisition of the North-West would take place within the context of Canadian federalism. The Fathers of Confederation tended to assume that the " 'colonial' relationship with the provinces was a natural one. . . . It therefore seems more appropriate to think of the dominion-provincial relationship at that time as similar to the relationship of the imperial government with a colony enjoying limited self-government."[33] Ontario Liberals quickly adopted a different approach to federalism; federal Conservatives did not. The West was to be "annexed as a subordinate territory."[34] Ontario's leaders were anxious that expansion take place quickly, and assumed that Ontarians would benefit through the creation of a miniature Ontario in the West. At the same time the settled portion of the West, shaken by the breakdown of its isolation and possessing a tradition of resistance to outside control, was accustomed to colonial status, exploitation and dependency.

III

Canada's first Confederation government was anxious to honour its commitment to annex the West. William McDougall and George Cartier went to London in 1868 to negotiate the transfer to Canada of Rupert's Land and the North-West Territory. Their mission was successful. The Hudson's Bay Company agreed to transfer its territory to Canada; the dominion agreed to compensate the company with one-twentieth of the fertile area in the West, land surrounding HBC posts and a cash payment of £300,000. The initial transfer was to be to the Crown, which would immediately retransfer the area to Canada.

In preparation for the reception of this great domain, Canada passed "An Act for the temporary Government of Rupert's Land and the North-Western Territory when united with Canada."[35] This short act provided that the West, styled "The North-West Territories," would be governed by federal appointees—a lieutenant governor assisted by a

33 J. R. Mallory, "The Five Faces of Federalism," in *The Future of Canadian Federalism*, eds., P.-A. Crepeau and C. B. Macpherson (Toronto, 1965), p. 4.
34 W. L. Morton, "Clio in Canada: The Interpretation of Canadian History," in *Approaches to Canadian History*, ed. Carl Berger, Canadian Historical Readings I (Toronto, 1967), p. 44.
35 This act is reprinted in W. L. Morton, ed., *Manitoba: The Birth of a Province* (Altona, 1965), pp. 1-3.

council. It also continued existing laws in force and public servants in office until changes were made by either the federal government or the lieutenant governor. The act was to "continue in force until the end of the next Session of Parliament."

It has been suggested that this statute does not reveal much about the intent of the federal authorities because it was preceded by such phrases as: "to make some temporary provision" and "until more permanent arrangements can be made."[36] At the same time P. B. Waite notes that it was not a temporary provision at all. After the creation of Manitoba, "the rest of the vast Northwest Territories remained under the Act of 1869, that 'temporary' arrangement. It was re-enacted in 1871 as permanent without any alteration whatever."[37] There is no reason to assume that in 1869 Macdonald and his colleagues intended any very radical future alteration in the statute, which, with the appointments made thereunder, revealed much about Ottawa's attitude toward the West. The area, not a crown colony in 1869, was to join Confederation as a federally controlled territory—not as a province. It was not assumed that the West was joining a federation; rather, Canada was acquiring a subservient territory. Local leaders were neither consulted nor considered. These assumptions emerge even more clearly when the initial appointments under the act are studied. Ontario's ambitions to control the West were symbolized by the appointment of William McDougall as Lieutenant Governor. He was a former Clear Grit who represented Ontario Reformers in the first Confederation government. An imperious and sanctimonious expansionist, he had neither the ability nor the desire to take local leaders, especially those

36 See Ralph Heintzman, "The Spirit of Confederation: Professor Creighton, Bicul-turalism, and the Use of History," *CHR* 52 (September 1971): 256-58. Heintzman comments: "Now even a cursory examination of the text of this Act of 1869 would cast serious doubt upon the worth of this argument" (p. 256)—i.e., that the act revealed the "real intentions of the federal government" (p. 247). "The purely temporary character of the Act is made clear in the preamble.... But all of this informed specualation is quite unnecessary. We have an explicit statement of the intentions of the government from the mouth of John A. Macdonald himself. Macdonald told the House of Commons flatly that the 1869 Act was 'provisional' and 'intended to last only a few months' ..." (p. 257). Heintzman's chief concerns are educational and linguistic rights.
37 P. B. Waite, *Canada 1874-1896: Arduous Destiny* (Toronto, 1971), p. 65. See also Lewis Herbert Thomas, *The Struggle for Responsible Government in the North-West Territories 1870-97* (Toronto, 1956), p. 48. It is clearly possible to debate the implica-tions of the act, but a document that Macdonald's government made the permanent constitution for the North-West Territories cannot simply be dismissed as meaning-less. It is interesting to note that when the statute was made permanent in 1871, with only insignificant modifications, and, of course, the exclusion from its provisions of the new Province of Manitoba, it was justified in its preamble as follows: "whereas, it is expedient to make provision for the government, after the expiration of the Act first above mentioned [i.e., An Act for the temporary government of Rupert's Land], of the North-West Territories, that being the name given ... to such portion of Rupert's Land the North Western Territory as is not included in ... Manitoba ..." (*An Act to make further provision for the government of the North-West Territories*, 34 Vict. Cap. XVI).

who were not white, into his confidence. Certainly the federal government's request that he search out westerners for his council[38] would hardly inspire local confidence. McDougall was regarded as anything but impartial.[39] Initial executive appointments were not likely, with the possible exception of J. A. N. Provencher,[40] to inspire local confidence in a regime that was organized in Central Canada. Two appointments were flagrantly political. A. N. Richards was the brother of a minister in Sandfield Macdonald's Ontario government and Captain D. R. Cameron was Charles Tupper's son-in-law. Even if one accepts the argument that the "temporary" act was indeed temporary, it is difficult to argue that Lieutenant Governor McDougall, Attorney General Richards or Chief of Police Cameron were temporary.

These various decisions made in distant capitals caused an upheaval in the Red River settlement, the only really settled part of Rupert's Land. Red River was, in fact, on the verge of explosion—a point forcibly made to federal and imperial authorities by Anglican Bishop Machray, HBC Governor of Assiniboia Mactavish, and Roman Catholic Bishop Taché.[41] The unsettled state of Red River was a product of many factors. By the end of the 1840s the commercial authority of the HBC had been irretrievably eroded. During the 1850s the isolation of the area was just as irretrievably lost. American traders pushed up from St. Paul and by the late 1850s a Canadian party, allied

38 "Instructions issued to Hon. Wm. McDougall as Lieutenant Governor of the North West Territories, Sept. 28, 1869," in *The Canadian North-West: Its Early Development and Legislative Records*, ed., E. H. Oliver (Ottawa, 1914-15), II: 878-79.
39 For his earlier hopeless insensitivity concerning Red River see W. L. Morton, "Introduction" to *Alexander Begg's Red River Journal* (Toronto, 1956), p. 23.
40 Provencher, a nephew of Bishop J. N. Provencher of St. Boniface (1847-53), was a Central Canadian newspaperman. He had only a minimal contact with the West and was described by Alexander Begg, an intelligent and representative citizen of Red River, as "a pleasant sort of a man who had come up altogether wrongly informed regarding this country . . ." (*Alexander Begg's Red River Journal*, p. 176). Provencher's relationship with the Bishop was his only tie with the West, unless it is assumed that the Métis were French Canadians and therefore identified closely with other French Canadians. The Métis, of course, assumed no such thing, regarding themselves as a New Nation. To assume that the Métis were French Canadian is to commit a sort of historiographical genocide. Heintzman, "Spirit of Confederation," p. 253, for example, comments: "This awareness of the 'canadien' community at Red River was one reason to rejoice in the annexation of the North-West: it meant that the French of the west would be welcomed back into the fold and raised the possibility that colonists from Lower Canada would find themselves 'at home' on the prairies." Presumably, for Heintzman, these 'canadiens' included the Métis. Alexander Begg held the members of McDougall's party in very low esteem. McDougall was characterized as "overbearing," "distant," "unpleasant" and "vindictive." Richards "does not appear to be extraordinarily [sic] clever on Law Subjects although appointed Attorney General." Cameron was "a natural ass" and Dr. Jacques "an unmannerly young fellow" (W. L. Morton, "Introduction," *Alexander Begg's Red River Journal*, p. 176). Is it any wonder that Canada's initial attitude toward the North-West was looked at through a jaundiced eye?
41 George F. G. Stanley, *The Birth of Western Canada: A History of the Riel Rebellions* (Toronto, 1936), pp. 63-64.

with the anti-HBC agitation in Canada, had emerged in the settlement. These Canadians, whose attitudes had been previewed in the 1840s by Recorder Adam Thom and were later to merge with those of Canada First, were arrogant, threatening and racist. They led a concerted assault on the authority of the company, and were instrumental in producing political chaos at Red River during the 1850s. To the Métis especially they represented a threat to their rights and way of life. These justified fears[42] were confirmed by Canadian government officials who entered the area prior to the transfer and offended local sensibilities. Instability was abetted by a "breakdown of the traditional economy of the Settlement" during the late 1860s. In 1868 Red River "was threatened by famine."[43]

The people of Red River could assess Canadian intentions only on the basis of Canadian activities, appointments and laws. The response was resistance, spearheaded by the Métis but reluctantly supported to varying degrees (or at least tolerated) by most people at Red River, except the members of the Canadian party: "Riel's authority, although it originated in armed force, came within a few months to be based on the majority will of the community."[44]

The details of the resistance of 1869-1870 are well known and are not germane to this paper. What is important is that Louis Riel's provisional government was in such a strong strategic position that it was able to force the federal authorities to negotiate on terms of entry. The results were embodied in the Manitoba Act that created the Province of Manitoba.

Provincehood was a victory (more, it might be noted, for the Métis than for the other sections of the Red River community), but Manitoba nonetheless entered Confederation as a dependency, not as a full partner with a federal system. Two broad circumstances explain the continuation of "subordinate"[45] status. First, Manitoba was not constitutionally equal to the other provinces. The Métis leaders and their clerical advisors placed great emphasis on cultural problems. Anticipating an influx of Ontarians, they demanded and obtained educational and linguistic guarantees. The federal authorities were concerned primarily with such larger issues as the settlement of the West and the construction of a transcontinental railroad. To facilitate these policies, in the formulation of which Manitoba had no say, Ottawa retained control of Manitoba's public lands and natural resources "for the purposes of the Dominion."[46] Professor Eric Kierans comments:

42 Morton, "Introduction," *Alexander Begg's Red River Journal*, pp. 29, 40-42, 45.
43 Ibid., p. 17.
44 M. S. Donnelly, *The Government of Manitoba* (Toronto, 1963), p. 10.
45 Morton, "Clio in Canada," p. 44.
46 Manitoba Act, Section 30.

The ownership of the land and resources belong [sic] to the people collectively as the sign of their independence and the guarantee of their responsibility. By British law and tradition, the ownership and control of the public domain was always handed over to the political authority designated by a community when the citizens assumed responsibility for the government of their own affairs.... During the ... hearings [related to the *Report of the Royal Commission on the Transfer of the Natural Resources of Manitoba* (Ottawa, 1929)] Professor Chester Martin ... testified: "The truth is that for 35 years, (i.e., until the creation of the Provinces of Saskatchewan and Alberta), I believe that it will be correct to say, Manitoba was the solitary exception within the British Empire to accepted British practice with regard to control of the crown lands and it still remains, in respect of public lands, literally not a province but a colony of the Dominion." ... In substance, any attempt to grant responsible government to a province or state, while retaining for the Imperial or Federal authority the control of crown lands and revenues, was held to be a "contradiction in terms and impossible."[47]

Just as serious as Manitoba's inferior constitutional position, was her effective status. She was in no way equipped to function as a province with the full paraphernalia of responsible government. She was ridiculously small, limited in 1870 to some 12,000 persons and 13,500 square miles. The province had an extremely limited tradition of representative government and, to complicate matters further, several of her key leaders were fugitives from justice because of their roles in the resistance. As Lieutenant Governor A. G. Archibald explained in 1872: "You can hardly hope to carry on responsible Government by inflicting death penalties on the leaders of a majority of the electors."[48] Perhaps even more important, provincial finances were hopelessly inadequate; the federal government granted "provincial status to an area which was essentially primitive; and it gave financial terms modelled improperly upon those given to the older provinces."[49] Under the Manitoba Act the province received $67,104 per annum in grants. Her own revenue came to only about $10,000. Even by 1875, 88 per cent of provincial revenues were federal subsidies. "During the whole period from 1870 to 1885 Manitoba was little more than a financial ward of the federal government...."[50] The province could not even afford public buildings to house the lieutenant governor and assembly until Ottawa advanced the necessary funds. In 1871 about one-third of provincial expenditures were used to cover legislative expenses.

Thus provincehood was granted prematurely to a jurisdiction that could sustain neither its responsibilities nor the kind of status it ought

47 Eric Kierans, *Report on Natural Resources Policy in Manitoba* (Winnipeg, 1973), p. 1. The severity of this kind of analysis has been questioned. See, for example, J. A. Maxwell, *Federal Subsidies to the Provincial Governments in Canada* (Cambridge, Mass., 1937).
48 Cited in Donnelly, *Government of Manitoba*, p. 16.
49 Maxwell, *Federal Subsidies to the Provincial Governments*, p. 37.
50 Donnelly, *Government of Manitoba*, p. 161.

to have occupied with a federal state. The primary fault lay with the federal leaders: "[T]he Manitoba Act bears on its face evidence both of the inexperience of the delegates from the Red River settlement and of the lack of mature consideration given to the measure by the federal government. The former circumstance was unavoidable; the latter can hardly be condoned."[51] During the early years of Manitoba's history even the outward trappings of real provincehood were absent. For several years the province's immaturity prevented the development of responsible government and the first two lieutenant governors, A. G. Archibald and Alexander Morris, functioned as effective governors rather than as constitutional monarchs. Until 1876 the lieutenant governors even attended cabinet meetings.

Early Manitoba was a colony of Central Canada because of constitutional discrimination and because she had neither the maturity nor resources to support provincehood. But that was not all. With the advent of formal provincial status came an influx of settlers from Ontario, a process that started with the arrival of the Anglo-Saxon Ontarian hordes that dominated Colonel Garnett Wolseley's expeditionary force of 1870. That small army had no real military function. It was sent west in 1870 to appease Ontario—to serve as symbolic compensation for the inclusion in the Manitoba Act of cultural guarantees for the Métis. In extreme form, the expeditionary force was a model of what the later Central Canadian influx was to mean. Local traditions were shunted aside as agriculture was commercialized and society revolutionized. The Indians were unable to assimilate themselves; many Métis sold the land they had been granted to unscrupulous speculators and moved into the North-West Territories. In a symbolic action a group of Ontarians who arrived in 1871 seized some Métis land on the Riviere aux Ilets de Bois. In spite of Métis protests they kept the land and sharpened the insult by renaming the river "the Boyne"! Some Scots settlers sympathized with the Canadians, but like the HBC traders they had to watch the old society die. Within a few years Manitoba was a colony of Ontario demographically as well as constitutionally, politically and economically.

The Province of Manitoba was only a miniscule portion of the territory annexed by Canada. The remaining enormous area was organized as the North-West Territories. With virtually no permanent white settlement, it received even shorter shrift than Manitoba. Its initial government was provided under the "temporary Government" act. That statute was "re-enacted, extended and continued in force until . . . 1871" by the Manitoba Act.[52] Prior to its second automatic expiry in 1871 it was again reenacted without major change, this time with no expiry date. Until 1875, therefore, government for the

51 Maxwell, *Federal Subsidies to the Provincial Governments*, pp. 37-38.
52 Section 36.

North-West Territories was provided under the initial legislation of 1869. During these six years the administration of the territories was somewhat casual. There was no resident governor—that responsibility was simply added to the duties of the Lieutenant Governor of Manitoba. Most of the members of the council were Manitobans who did not live in the territories. The Indians, the largest group of inhabitants, were managed not consulted.

The Mackenzie government overhauled the administration of the North-West in 1875 by securing the passage of "The North-West Territories Act." Although not "fully thought out"[53] it did provide a fairly simple system of government consisting of a separate governor and a council that was initially appointed but that would become elective as the non-Indian population grew. The capital was established at Battleford until 1882 when it was moved to Regina. Mackenzie appointed David Laird, a federal cabinet minister from Prince Edward Island, as the first full-time Lieutenant Governor of the North-West Territories. His first council included neither an Indian nor a Métis who resided in the NWT. There was no elected councillor until 1881.

Prior to 1869 the West was a dependent area, ruled (if at all) in a casual, chaotic but paternalistic manner for the benefit of a huge commercial firm centred in London. Westerners feared that the transfer involved simply a change of masters, not a change of status. The Métis feared that in the process they would lose their life style and culture through an inundation of Ontario settlers. The result was a movement of resistance led by the Métis, but with broad support within the Red River settlement. For the bulk of the West the resistance resulted in no change whatsoever. For a small district on the Red River the result was a tiny, anemic province incapable of functioning as a viable partner within a federal system.

IV

After 1867 Macdonald and his colleagues were not able to maintain "quasi-federalism" over the original components of Confederation, but for the West annexation to Canada involved the confirmation of colonial status. The fifteen years after the transfer was the launching period for the West in Confederation. During those years federal sway on the prairies was virtually unchallengeable.

Ottawa's most powerful instrument was federal possession of the West's public lands "for the purposes of the Dominion." This enabled Ottawa to implement two policies that were crucial to the Canadianization of the West: rapid settlement and the construction of a transcontinental railroad. Extreme difficulties did not prevent the execution of

53 R. G. Robertson, "The Evolution of Territorial Government in Canada," in *The Political Process in Canada* (Toronto, 1963), p. 139 note.

these policies. Public lands were made available to settlers in a variety of ways. Although settlement did not proceed as quickly as the federal authorities desired, Manitoba experienced rapid growth during the 1870s and 1880s. Within a generation of the transfer the territories west of Manitoba had been populated by Ontarians, Americans and Europeans. Consequently the provinces of Saskatchewan and Alberta were established in 1905. The federal authorities had recognized from the outset that a transcontinental railroad was required if the West was to be properly Canadianized. After several false starts, the Canadian Pacific Railway was chartered in 1880. The CPR was heavily subsidized, receiving from the federal government some $38,000,000 worth of track constructed at public expense, $25,000,000 in cash, a railroad monopoly in western Canada for twenty years and 25,000,000 acres of prairie land. The land grant was considered indispensible to the line's success and the success of the railroad was one of the fundamental "purposes of the Dominion." The federal government designed its transportation policies to suit the needs of Central Canadian business, and was not particularly tender towards western interests. As Charles Tupper, Minister of Railroads, put it in 1883: "The interests of this country demand that the Canadian Pacific Railway should be made a success. . . . Are the interests of Manitoba and the North-West to be sacrificed to the interests of Canada? I say, if it is necessary, yes."[54]

Federal Conservative strategists, who were in power during 1867-73 and 1878-96, tied tariff policy to settlement and transportation. They saw the West as Central Canada's economic hinterland. The area was to be settled quickly and become an exporter of agricultural products and an importer of manufactured goods. Central Canada was to be the manufacturing centre. The CPR was to haul eastern manufactured goods into the West and western agricultural produce to market. High tariffs were designed to protect the manufacturing industries from foreign competition and at the same time guarantee freight traffic to the CPR by forcing trade patterns to flow along east-west, not north-south, lines. These basic decisions determined the nature of post-1870 western development. They were made by federal leaders to serve Central Canadian interests and they perpetuated the status of the West as a colonial region.

Federal management of the West during these years should be looked at in micro as well as macro terms, although it is clear that federal authorities had little interest in day-to-day western conditions. If settlement was to proceed in orderly and rapid fashion the Indian "problem" had to be solved. That task involved extinguishing Indian rights to the land and rendering the tribes harmless by herding them onto reserves. The instrument used for these purposes was the Indian

54 Cited in Chester Martin, *"Dominion Lands" Policy* (Toronto, 1938), p. 470.

"treaty." During the 1870s a series of agreements was negotiated between the crown and the prairie tribes. Through these treaties the Indians gave up their rights to their traditional lands in return for reserves and nominal concessions, payments and guarantees. However, they tended to resist being forced onto reserves as long as the buffalo, their traditional source of food, remained plentiful. By 1885 the buffalo were on the verge of extermination and most Indians had been coerced to settle on reservations.

In 1873 Canada founded the North-West Mounted Police, another instrument of federal control.[55] The mounties constituted an effective federal presence on the prairies, chased American traders out of southern Alberta, policed the Indians and Métis, and symbolized the stability and order desired by white settlers. In bringing effective federal rule to southern Alberta they abetted the termination of the international aspect of Blackfoot life. This breakdown of regional international societies was part of the process of Canadianization.

The federal political structure also functioned as a control instrument. Until 1887 Manitoba's handfull of MPs constituted the West's entire representation in the House of Commons. These members tended to support the government of the day because of its immense patronage and fiscal authority.

> Dependent upon federal largesse yet suspicious of eastern dictation, the western attitude towards national politics was often a curious mixture of ministerialism and defiance. Some papers seemed to believe that the electorate should always give a general support to the government, for such support would ensure a continuous supply of federal monies for western projects. At the same time these papers admitted the need to champion regional interests.[56]

During the 1870s and 1880s the West was Canadianized. By the end of the century massive immigration (which incidentally produced a distinctive population mix that helped differentiate the region from Central Canada) combined with basic federal policies had produced a new West, but its status had changed little. The process generated resistance. The government of Manitoba challenged the CPR's monopoly and sought to obtain better financial terms. Farmers in Manitoba and along the Saskatchewan River organized unions and began their long struggle for a host of reforms including lower tariffs and a transportation system sensitive to their needs. Under Louis Riel's leadership a minority of Indians and Métis rose in 1885 in a pathetic and ill-led rebellion. Territorial politicians crusaded for representa-

---

55 See S. W. Horrall, "Sir John A. Macdonald and the Mounted Police Force for the Northwest Territories," *CHR* 53 (June 1972). Horrall notes, pp. 182-83: "To Macdonald the problem of policing the Northwest resembled that faced by the British in India."

56 Rutherford, "Western Press and Regionalism," p. 301.

tion in parliament and responsible government for the North-West Territories.

By the end of the century western resistance to federal control and leadership was a well-established tradition. The West, however, was not strong enough to challenge Canada's great national policies successfully. Consequently the West has remained a subordinate region; the Canadian federation retains its imperialistic characteristics. As W. L. Morton suggested: "For Confederation was brought about to increase the wealth of Central Canada, and until that original purpose is altered, and the concentration of wealth and population by national policy in Central Canada ceases, Confederation must remain an instrument of injustice."[57]

57 Morton, "Clio in Canada," p. 47.

IX

Alexander Mackenzie and Canadian Federalism

W. H. HEICK

He was bound to say that he [had] advocated Confederation not merely as a great political measure essential to the continuation and perpetuation of British political power on this continent, which was his principal object, but as the system of government most suitable to our condition, and under which we would be able to obtain certain great advantages in the administration of our own affairs. It was the constant complaint prior to 1867 that we were subjected as a people to unfair influences. We were placed in the position of contributing from two-thirds to three-fourths of the revenue of the country, while [we] were always unable to obtain for local purposes, such as we tax ourselves for under the present system, one-half of the actual revenue of the united provinces. In this respect he believed the change effected by the Confederation of the provinces was extremely beneficial to us as a province; and he hoped to the Province of Quebec also, by stimulating its people to greater exertions in regard to local affairs, instead of depending upon the general resources.[1]

When he spoke these words in the late winter of 1872, Alexander Mackenzie was already the recognized leader of the parliamentary opposition in Ottawa, although it would be a year before he would assume the mantle, as well as the burdens of that office. It would be a year-and-a-half before he would be able to marshall the parliamentary troops to defeat Sir John A. Macdonald on the issue of the Pacific railway scandal, and thus become Prime Minister of Canada. In that office for five years, 1873 to 1878, Mackenzie was in a position to influence the evolution of the Canadian federal system.

It is the argument of this chapter that the second prime minister of Canada was basically an old line Upper Canadian Grit or Reformer who accepted Confederation in 1867 as a means whereby his part of British North America could achieve "home rule" and extend its

1 Alexander Mackenzie in the House of Commons, quoted in the *Globe*, 8 February 1872.

strength. This dominance would have been best achieved, in theory, through a legislative union. However, the situation required a form of federal union, and Mackenzie supported the Quebec resolutions as the only viable alternative. He fully expected that within this framework ". . . before many years elapse the centre of population and power will tend westward much farther than most people now think. The increase in the representation is, therefore, almost certainly to be chiefly in the west, and every year will add to the influence and power of Western Canada, as well as her trade and commerce."[2] Once in office as leader of the central side of the federal dichotomy, Mackenzie had no national policy to follow. Nor was Mackenzie a first-rate national politician: first, although he had great patriotism, it was primarily oriented towards Ontario and the Empire, not the new Canada; second, he lacked the requisite thirst for power. Therefore, he approached his work of governing the nation on a piece-meal basis, more often than not in response to events rather than as initiator. Mackenzie was quite ready to let power be shifted from London to Ottawa, but not to take power from Toronto (or the other provincial capitals) to Ottawa; in fact he was not always opposed to the opposite, from Ottawa to the provincial capitals, when the occasion arose. However, while Mackenzie was one of the old-time Reformers like George Brown, who were basically satisfied with the situation federally after 1867, there were new liberal elements within the party that pressured for more changes. Federally Edward Blake and David Mills were the most powerful of these new Liberals, while on the provincial level Oliver Mowat gave the leadership.[3]

It is difficult to sort out an answer to the question of Mackenzie's motives and actions as prime minister. His proclivity for the provincial rights argument and the home rule efforts of his home province was in juxtaposition with his response to the pressures generated by the depressed economic conditions to curtail government costs to the greatest degree. Mackenzie's liberal and far-sighted moves as Ontario provincial treasurer in the prosperous early years of the decade do admit of the generous nature of the man. However, the main point in determining Mackenzie's activities as treasurer was the fact that he was working for his native province. In the middle of that decade Mackenzie was in Ottawa, not Toronto, and without the same perspective of the national scene as he had of the provincial.

The most important problem for the Mackenzie government was the construction of the transcontinental railway to British Columbia. To the British Columbians all relationships with Canada, which they

2 *Parliamentary Debates on the Subject of the Confederation of the British North American Provinces, 3rd Session, 8th Provincial Parliament of Canada, 1865* (Ottawa, 1951), p. 425.
3 For the purposes of this chapter the term Reformer will be used to label the Brown-Mackenzie wing of the party and Liberal for the Blake wing.

had just joined in 1871, revolved around the railway. Mackenzie had then opposed, as impossible of fulfillment, the commitment in the terms of union to commence construction within two years of the entry of British Columbia into Confederation and to complete that line within ten years of union. That opposition placed him, as Prime Minister, in a poor position with the people of the western province. After he came to office he should have made the best of the situation by emphasizing the positive side of his government's actions: the hyperactivity regarding surveys (by the end of his term of office in 1878 he was prepared, as Minister of Public Works as well as Prime Minister, to decide upon the location of the whole route); the erection of the telegraph line to the Pacific coast; and the construction of over seven hundred miles of track, albeit all of it far to the east of the province most concerned. Supervision of this activity was the main part of his customary fourteen- to sixteen-hour day. Instead, while this work was proceeding, he attempted, as in all other situations, to be scrupulously honest and above-board. He interpreted the two-and-ten clause as literally as the province did, but this commitment he considered, after he assumed office, even more impossible than he had in 1871 because of the economic stringencies. On the basis of this position he attempted to renegotiate the agreement, an effort which caused him more political discomfort than any other. The whole affair became embroiled in intraprovincial, dominion-provincial, and Canadian-Imperial relations.

Mackenzie's first attempt to revise the 1871 agreement grounded upon the shoals of British Columbian politics. The Prime Minister's envoy, James D. Edgar, found it impossible, on his trip to the west coast, to do anything but intensify the competition between those who lived in the Fraser Valley of the lower mainland and those residing on Vancouver Island and in the Upper mainland region. Neither side being assured of Ottawa's acceptance of their choice of location of the western terminus, both turned upon Edgar and Mackenzie's proposal to extend the time limit.

Reacting in fear of losing their fondest dream, the British Columbians moved to appeal over Ottawa's head to London. Mackenzie became caught from four sides: first, the province; second, the Imperial authorities, primarily the Governor General, Lord Dufferin, who was eager to participate more actively in the governing of his domain; third, the Macdonald Conservatives, in spite of their announced understanding that two and ten had not been meant to be interpreted literally but rather "as soon as possible"; and last, the liberal wing of Mackenzie's own party. Blake and Mills led the party opposition to what they considered an impossibly extravagant project. This internal division approximated in personality and was simultaneous to that connected with constitutional reform as related to the imperial tie to be discussed below. The scenario was played out in the context of a general reluctance by Central and Maritime Canadians, fed by the effects of the depression, to spend any money in a manner from which their parts of the country would gain little immediate benefit.

The efforts of the British Columbia government to invoke the Imperial authority to have the original railway terms met were initially opposed by the Prime Minister. His position was that the situation was an internal Canadian dispute in which the Imperial authorities had no jurisdiction. However, the evolving conditions soon required of Mackenzie that he accept the good offices of the Governor General and the Secretary of State for the Colonies, Lord Carnarvon, to suggest a basis for compromise. The success of these efforts, as well as the continuing work of Mackenzie, caused the province to become amenable to letting the issue lie dormant while the federal government exerted itself concerning the construction of the railway. Thus lay the issue until Mackenzie resigned from office in 1878.

The Pacific railway had been handled in a very pragmatic fashion by Mackenzie. Despite a traditional Reform opposition to Imperial involvement in domestic affairs, he did accept it when the situation permitted no obvious alternative. While the whole episode may have had little fundamental impact upon the evolution of Canadian federalism, it does illustrate the pragmatic approach of the Reform Prime Minister to the questions facing him in office and his willingness to bend constitutional principles in his government's relations with both the province and the Imperial authorities.

The Métis uprising in 1869-1870 left a residual situation in which Mackenzie once again showed his pragmatism. The problem was whether or not his Conservative predecessor had in fact offered an amnesty to Louis Riel and his followers through Archbishop Taché. So long as no Métis were in custody, the question was essentially inoperative. The capture and conviction of Ambroise Lepine, Riel's lieutenant, brought the matter to a point of urgent dispatch. Any action regarding Lepine was important, for what was done with him would give notice as to how Riel might be dealt with, should he be arrested.

Caught, as Macdonald had been, on the twin hooks of Orange Lodge displeasure at any leniency shown to the Métis and French-Canadian anger at any punishment of their fellow citizens, Mackenzie squirmed as hard as his predecessor. This consternation, despite the fact that, as Ontario provincial treasurer, he had been a party to the offer of a $5,000 reward for aiding in apprehending Riel.

Mackenzie's hesitancy to act fit neatly with the Governor General's anxiousness to be as involved as possible in the governing of his realm. Dufferin's power, in his instructions, to grant mercy on his own authority was brought into play. He received concurrence from Lord Carnarvon to invoke this power so long as commutation of the death sentence, and not full amnesty or pardon was involved. For Mackenzie, such a manoeuvre provided the politically least objectionable way out of the matter. Nor did its encroachment on the Reform tradition of stressing responsible government seem to have any bearing upon Mackenzie's activity.

The commutation to two year's imprisonment and permanent forfeiture of political rights was delayed until after the Ontario elections in January 1875 so as to avoid having the expected wrath of the Ontario voter vented upon the Mowat administration. Three weeks later, Mackenzie moved in the Commons an address calling for the granting of general amnesty for events in the Red River uprising; Riel would gain such amnesty after five years banishment.

Such action resolved for most persons the amnesty question. But constitutionally the method of resolving the issue had further repercussions. As the Conservative Ottawa *Citizen* commented in one of its arguments against the government's action: "O Reform! O Responsible Government! Where are thy glories now?"[4] Edward Blake also became concerned with the constitutional ramifications of the Governor General acting without the advice of his Canadian ministers. This action, added to that of Lord Kimberley, the Colonial Secretary who had advised Dufferin in 1873 that he could act on his own discretion in the question of the New Brunswick School Act, caused Blake to instigate efforts to have the Imperial authorities rewrite the letters patent and instructions of the governor general. Once he had begun, Blake was supported in this constitutional crusade by most of his fellow ministers. Mackenzie, although not ready to take the initiative, also agreed.[5] Blake's point was achieved with the appointment of the Marquis of Lorne in 1878; his letters were rewritten to delete any subject upon which the governor general could act without the advice of his Canadian ministers.

Mackenzie's *ad hoc* approach to governing also arose with regard to Senate reform, a problem with clear federal implications. In April 1874 David Mills moved in the House of Commons a motion to have the Senate made more responsive to the people and the provinces. He proposed this be done by conferring upon the provinces the right to appoint their own senators and to define that method of appointment. The motion was talked out by the House but raised again by Mills a year later, again seconded by Blake. It passed first reading but went no further. Mackenzie voted affirmatively after having spoken in its support. He believed it desirable to change the method of senatorial

4 27 January 1875.
5 Ontario Archives, Edward Blake Papers, Mackenzie to Blake, 4 July 1876.

selection, but his administration would move on this subject only when public opinion called for it.[6]

Yet forty-six days after taking the oath as the Queen's first minister, Mackenzie had acted to request the Crown to invoke the powers under Section 26 of the BNA Act and appoint six additional senators. His argument was extreme expediency. The previous government had appointed only its supporters to the Senate, upsetting the political balance established in 1867. The additional senatorial positions were required to offset anticipated hostile opposition in the Senate.[7] The Colonial Secretary, Lord Kimberley, declined to permit such action. His argument was that Section 26 had been intended to deal with an extraordinary situation which had already built to a crisis, not to provide a means to avoid an anticipated problem. Having failed to achieve his immediate ends, Mackenzie declined to press the point. He ignored an embarrassment in 1877 when Macdonald's supporters in the Senate got that body to express great appreciation of Lord Kimberley's action in rejecting Mackenzie's request for the additional senators.

Provincial rights was, since Confederation, a Reform principle. For Mackenzie, as with Mowat, the philosophical undergirdings of this point strengthened his Ontario-oriented political perspective. This fact became obvious in his handling of the New Brunswick schools question. The Roman Catholics of New Brunswick had been trying to have the School Act of 1871, ending public support for denominational schools, removed from the statute books. Efforts to use the courts failed because denominational schools did not have their rights specifically guaranteed by law before 1867. The request to have the Macdonald government disallow the act had failed. Only pressure exerted in the federal parliament remained as a hope to redress these grievances.

The French-Canadian wing of the Conservative party, minus strong leadership after Cartier's death, took up the cause of their coreligionists in the neighbouring province. The fight in parliament was led by a New Brunswick member, John Costigan. In May 1874 he had begun his latest series of manoeuvres by submitting a resolution requesting parliament to seek the amendment of the BNA Act to give denominational schools in New Brunswick the same rights as those schools in Quebec and Ontario. The resolution was withdrawn after extended debate because the Privy Council's decision had not yet been handed down. When Costigan submitted the resolution in the session of 1875 Mackenzie became involved by moving an amendment claiming that it was dangerous to amend the BNA Act in a way which encroached upon the rights of the provinces. This position was con-

6 Canada, House of Commons, *Official Reports of the Debates, 1875*, p. 42.
7 PAC, Privy Council, Orders in Council, 1873, #1711.

tradictory to that which the Reformers had taken in 1872 when Costigan had made his first move in parliament. This flip-flop was doubly enigmatic to Costigan, because the Reformers had just a week before supported the senate reform resolution of David Mills, which would have meant a similar changing of the BNA Act. Mackenzie's argument followed a tight provincial rights position. His language here[8] and three years later in the Letellier case involving the dismissal of the Quebec lieutenant governor,[9] stressing terms such as "compact" and "our written constitution," suggested a rigidity and fundamentalism. To say that he had in this debate demonstrated the acquisition of a national perspective is carrying matters too far. Principle and expediency did not clash in this instance. New Brunswick Roman Catholics had a strong moral right to their separate schools, but a legal right they did not have. The parliamentary resolution to have the Queen use her influence to gain redress from the legislature went for naught. There the matter remained, unresolved until after Mackenzie left office.

Concerning Mackenzie's position with regard to the Letellier matter a few more words are in order. The dismissal of the Conservative de Boucherville ministry by the Liberal Lieutenant Governor, Luc Letellier de St. Just, a former member of Mackenzie's administration, generated an awkward political situation for the Prime Minister. Macdonald, to make the most of the situation to embarrass his opponent, moved a motion of censure against Letellier. In the long-winded fatuous debate that took the better part of four days, Mackenzie used the terms noted above but in a general sense. His specific approach to the Letellier case was simply to duck the principles and call for the Commons to permit the people of Quebec to determine the issues at the imminent provincial election.[10]

The legislation regarding the establishment of the North-West Territories also illustrates Mackenzie's position concerning the federal structure of the country. As his statement at the beginning of this chapter notes, he understood the Confederation experiment to be one in which his home province could develop in its own unique manner. Such freedom, if granted to Ontario, must also be recognized as the privilege of all the other provinces and of any new areas entering into the partnership. Thus the Prime Minister was quite prepared to insert in the 1875 Territories Act a guarantee of separate school rights as was enjoyed by the minority in Ontario[11] and to put his government's support behind the linguistic amendment introduced in the Senate two years later.[12]

8 Commons, *Debates, 1875*, pp. 610-11.
9 Ibid., *1878*, p. 1902.
10 Ibid., p. 1909.
11 Ibid., *1875*, pp. 610-11.
12 Canada, Senate, *Official Reports of the Debates, 1890*, p. 672.

The efforts to establish a supreme court provided a major opportunity for Mackenzie to set forth his position on the federal structure of Canada. A federal state requires a supreme court for judicial review. A body of men trained in the Canadian federal experience was needed so that this important task would not be left to British jurists unacquainted with the peculiar Canadian circumstances.

Macdonald's efforts to pass such legislation had run up against French-Canadian distrust of the concept and Macdonald's own lack of a sense of urgency. The question remained for the Reformers to deal with when they came to office. The introduction of the legislation in February 1875 by Telesphore Fournier, the Minister of Justice, seemed to allay some of the fears of the other French-Canadian members concerning Quebec rights.

Most of the concern over the bill centred on the question of the status of appeals from Canada to Britain after the court was established. David Mills debated the question most thoroughly. He took the traditional position concerning provincial rights to its logical conclusion, that is, the doctrines of strict construction and of separation of dominion and provincial powers. He favoured a supreme court as long as it confined itself to cases arising from federal law. In this position Mills was far beyond even the other Liberals in the House of Commons. His mentor in most political matters, Blake, did not participate in this aspect of the debate. Mackenzie also did not comment upon the question raised by Mills. He knew that neither he nor his government would be a threat to the provinces. With Macdonald out of power, the real threat to the provinces—an over-zealous, meddling, federal executive—was gone, as far as Mackenzie was concerned. The subtleties of Mills' arguments made no impact upon Mackenzie's practical mind. To him the urgent element in the situation was to get the court established.

The most controversial question related to the supremacy of the court centred around clause 47—the Irving amendment. That amendment attempted to restrict the rights of Canadians to appeal beyond the supreme court to the Imperial courts. The argument with the British law officers was carried for the Canadian side by Edward Blake, Fournier's successor in the justice portfolio. Blake's entry into the cabinet in the late spring of 1875 marked his momentary victory over Mackenzie within party councils. It left Mackenzie, although still Prime Minister, not in full control. Blake, with his zealous concern for Canadian autonomy that showed itself also in his efforts to have the letters patent and instructions of the governor general altered, really kept the pressure on London to win his point. "I have no sympathy with a so-called Reform Party," he had recently declared, "which says there is nothing to reform, with a so-called Liberal Party which says there is nothing to liberalize, with a so-called Party of Progress which is determined to stand absolutely still."[13]

Mackenzie permitted Blake to have his head on the matter. In the judgment of Lord Dufferin, his first minister was interested in the issue only from the standpoint of party tactics; without that clause he could not have gotten the bill through parliament. On the other hand, this same astute observer of Canadian affairs believed Blake to be working on the basis of a "morbid hatred of the legal authority of England."[14] The act was proclaimed on 18 September 1875 and efforts began immediately to nominate the justices and establish the court. The Colonial Office had agreed to permit these steps on the condition that any objections by the law officers would be met through parliamentary amendment of the act. During the following winter Blake corresponded with officials in London and followed this action with personal interviews in the summer of 1876. Lord Cairns, the Lord Chancellor, insisted on an amendment permitting special cases to be appealed. The final compromise permitted the clause to stand but with the understanding that it was quite inoperative.

The problem of the court demonstrated again the pragmatic approach of Mackenzie. The work of Blake left Canada with a supreme court, but one emasculated of its most important function in a federal state—the power of final melding of the various interpretations of law within Canada into one Canadian legal code. This power was to remain with the Judicial Committee of the Imperial Privy Council until appeals in criminal cases were abolished in 1939 and in the matter of civil cases in 1949.

Mackenzie's government was plagued by serious financial stringencies during most of its five years in office. These troubles were generated for the most part by the depressed economic conditions which caused a serious decline in federal government revenues. Mackenzie and his Minister of Finance, Richard Cartwright, followed a hard, narrow, orthodox approach to public finance. A balanced budget was a Reform article of faith. Mackenzie's natural proclivities towards parsimonious government at all levels supported his attitude on dominion-provincial relations.

> It is much better in every way, better in the general interest, that each level of government should pursue its own particular line and attend to its own affairs.... It is one of those things upon which we may be allowed to congratulate ourselves ..., that our present system of government, from our school sections upward to the Federal Government, is one of the most artistically correct in the world.[15]

13 *The Nation*, 11 June 1875.
14 Dufferin to Carnarvon, 11 November 1875 in *Dufferin-Carnarvon Correspondence*, eds. C. W. de Kiewiet and Frank H. Underhill (Toronto, 1955), p. 162.
15 Mackenzie in a speech at Unionville, Ontario in the summer of 1877, in Reform Association of the Province of Ontario, *Reform Government in the Dominion, The Pic-nic*

Artistic correctness included financial self-sufficiency. Each level of government should have clearly outlined responsibilities. One of these was to raise, on its own, the monies required to pay for its own activities.

Required by law to continue the constitutional subsidies to the provinces, Mackenzie and Cartwright showed no mercy when it came to the special grants, whose renewals were requested by the provinces concerned. In 1877 the special ten-year grant of $63,000 annually to New Brunswick was ended. The judgment in Ottawa was that the province was spending too much on roads and education and should come to grips with its fiscal situation. The same answer was given to Nova Scotia concerning its special grant of $82,700; over half of the provinces' total expenditures were for roads and education. Local direct taxation, Mackenzie argued, should be imposed to the extent required rather than lean on external resources.

Manitoba's peculiar circumstances created greater problems. Its creation as a province left a political unit with too few people and resources to function properly. In 1874 it requested additional funds from the federal government in order to avoid bankruptcy. Yet federal expenditures in the province were almost one million dollars annually while federal revenues from Manitoba were only $40,000. Such an imbalance could not be permitted to continue, Mackenzie argued, let alone increase. He suggested that Manitoba cease to be a province until such time as it had the human resources to support such an elevated political status. Territorial status, with a governor and small council, should suffice. Were Manitobans to accede to such a proposal, he would be prepared to give sympathetic attention to Manitoba's request for more money.[16] Mackenzie's medicine was too strong for the province, but he remained adamant that in return for more money the province had to take some strong steps to curtail expenditures. In the end the abolition of the Legislative Council was agreed upon in return for a temporary annual subsidy of $28,700 until 1881 when the decennial census would establish a new population base for the province's regular subsidies.

This subsidy was the only such increase granted by the Mackenzie government. The total of the provincial subsidies in fact fell to $300,000 below the 1873 level. Half of this decrease was represented by the termination of various special grants and the other half was due to the effect of withdrawals by the provinces of capital sums credited to the debt allowance account. To Mackenzie, provincial rights meant provincial responsibilities. In the desperate straits of budget time in 1876 he went so far as to suggest to Oliver Mowat a scheme whereby

Speeches Delivered in the Province of Ontario During the Summer of 1877 (Toronto, 1878), p. 56.

16 PAC, Mackenzie Papers, Letterbooks, Mackenzie to Alexander Morris, 16 April 1874.

federal works on interior rivers would be handed over to the province in which these works occurred, thus relieving the national government of the charges for their upkeep. The chief difficulty would be the works on rivers such as the Ottawa where no single provincial jurisdiction existed.[17] The scheme came to naught, but it is worthy of note as a sign of the degree to which the Prime Minister was willing to decrease federal responsibility in a moment of financial embarrassment, whatever the consequences for the federal system over the long run.

The relationship of the federal government with that of Ontario under Oliver Mowat was of a special nature. Ontario was Mackenzie's home province; Mowat's government was of the same political persuasion as was Mackenzie's; the men were friends and had been colleagues politically in earlier days; on their basic approach to federalism the two men were disciples of George Brown. The five years of Reform rule in Ottawa were not the occasion for any serious confrontation between the two governments. The Ontario-Manitoba boundary question illustrates the close and informal relations between Ottawa and Toronto during these years. Most of the negotiations between the two levels of government from 1873 to 1878 on this delicate issue were carried on by private correspondence and personal interviews. As a result of the informal negotiations Mackenzie, much more in sympathy with the case he supported, while he was provincial treasurer, than the federal case he was supposed to support now, agreed to a temporary accommodation. A compromise line was accepted by both sides which would enable the two governments to provide necessary law and order to the territory in dispute until a three-man commission could adjudicate a final boundary line. That commission finally met in 1878 and handed down a report extremely favourable to Ontario. Mackenzie and Mowat were each prepared to accept this decision. It came down too late, however, for action prior to the federal election which altered the whole situation. It could be argued that Ontario had much the better case and that Mackenzie practised wise statesmanship in his attempts to come to a resolution with Mowat. It is much more plausible, however, to judge his actions regarding the boundary as governed more strongly by his feelings for Ontario. A provincialist in a national post, he was unable to fight the national side of this issue as hard as he might. Much later, in 1884, he declared at a mammoth Liberal rally:

> Determined, systematic efforts have been put forth by the federal government, practically to abrogate the Constitution of this country, and we owe it to Mr. Mowat and his Cabinet that those efforts have been successfully resisted.... Long may he live, and may provincial rights always be defended with equal ability.[18]

17 Ibid., Mackenzie to Mowat, 16 February 1876.
18 Charles R. W. Biggar, *Sir Oliver Mowat, A Biographical Sketch*, 2 vols. (Toronto, 1905), I: 425-26.

The Reform interregnum, as Conservatives called the five years from 1873 to 1878, provided an opportunity for the Reformers to guide the new nation's affairs according to their precepts. The leader of the party, Alexander Mackenzie, represented a Reformer whose reforms had been achieved; in this sense at least he was a conservative. A few months before the election which led to Mackenzie's defeat, the *Globe* expressed a judgment, intended to be supportive of the Prime Minister. Rather, in perspective, the statement reveals much of the Reform conservatism of both this newspaper and Mackenzie: "The best proof of the success of Mr. Mackenzie's administration is to be found in the fact that no troublesome or difficult question now presses upon him for solution."[19]

For Mackenzie Confederation provided an opportunity to further his own province's fortune. Therefore, striding the national political stage did not truly become him. Lord Dufferin had quite soon come to see his first minister as one who needed a "little more talent to give him 'initiative' and 'ascendancy' " in order to be a "capital Minister."[20] He never became a "capital Minister." He was prevented from doing so partly by the restrictive effects of the economic depression, but primarily by his Ontario-tinted glasses and his lack of a "little more talent." Because of these deficiencies the Canadian electors rejected him.

In rejecting Mackenzie in 1878 the electorate really did not reject or approve any form of federalism. His basically pragmatic approach to national politics, modifying his initial Ontario-orientated position, had caused Mackenzie to fail to follow any constitutionally consistent pattern based upon well-thought-out philosophical principles.

19 *Globe*, 8 July 1878.
20 PAC, Dufferin Papers, Film #1152, Dufferin to Edward Thornton, 14 April 1874.

Australia

X

Towards a Federal Union

RONALD NORRIS

On 1 January 1901 the six Australian colonies federated under the Commonwealth of Australia Constitution Act. The event was the culmination of decades of spasmodic effort which began with the abortive proposals of Lord Grey in the late 1840s. The constitution was the outcome of heated controversy, exhaustive debate and careful compromise in Australia and Britain in the twilight years of the nineteenth century.

To the student of history, with the wisdom of hindsight, union seems inevitable. In the long run it probably was. But to dedicated federationists such as Alfred Deakin—though we should allow for pride of achievement—to say it was fated was to say "nothing to the purpose." Federation frequently "trembled in the balance," its ultimate accomplishment being secured by a "series of miracles."[1] And for contemporaries, as Harrison Moore observed in 1902, the wonder was less that federation had been so long delayed and more that it had occurred in their time.[2] Moreover, as it happened, the colonies federated at a particular point in time. Had they done so at some other, then union would have been achieved by different means for other ends, and the constitution would have been the creation of other men with different concepts of federalism and democracy. Paradoxically, perhaps, the colonies had first to drift apart before they could see the need to come together. Common interests had to manifest themselves and outweigh differences. Centripetal forces had to overpower centrifugal. The federation movement had to generate energy, overcome inertia and friction, and gain momentum.

The early history of Australia was marked by isolation. The southern continent was isolated from Britain, the Empire, and the civilized

---

1 Alfred Deakin, *The Federal Story*, ed. J. A. La Nauze (Melbourne, 1963), p. 173.
2 W. Harrison Moore, *The Constitution of the Commonwealth of Australia* (London, 1902), p. 55.

world at large. The coastal settlements within Australia, and the six colonies which came to occupy the whole continent during the nineteenth century, were isolated one from the other. These separate colonies gradually secured representative, and then responsible, systems of administration. Distinct and independent political factions and parties evolved to control and manipulate governmental machinery. The political establishments, and the politicians who comprised them, had vested interests in preserving their individual status and identity.

The separate colonies also developed independent economies and economic systems. Producers, and men of trade, commerce and industry had, like their political counterparts, interests to preserve. At first their competitors were mainly fellow colonists from within their own colony, or overseas British. Later, as colonial economies expanded their rivals came to include men in like pursuits in adjacent colonies. Primary producers, manufacturers and businessmen competed for internal and external markets. Wheat from the Wimmera in Victoria and the Riverina in New South Wales threatened, and by the 1880s ended, the dominance of South Australian wheat in intercolonial markets. South Australian wines competed with Victorian and New South Welsh at home and abroad. Exports of Tasmanian apples and potatoes disturbed orchardists and market gardeners on the mainland. Tropical fruits went south from Queensland and reduced the demand for locally-grown temperate produce. The products of Victoria's factories limited opportunities for the growth of manufacturing in other colonies. Sydney fought to retain her position as premier port; Melbourne struggled to remain the financial capital of the continent.

In this way political and economic rivalry and jealousy developed. Colonial politicians paid regard to their own colonies in the interests of themselves and their electors, to whom they were required to make periodic appeals for support. They therefore enacted legislation to foster their primary and secondary industries. These measures, which directly or indirectly hit at neighbouring colonies, increased suspicion and hostility. The colonies fought and feuded over such things as the awarding of the P. and O. mail contract, and the capture of British capital and honours. Rivalry exceeded the bounds of healthy competition.

Probably nothing contributed more to ill-feeling and conflict than divergent fiscal policies, because in this area political and economic factors converged. All the colonies imposed import charges for revenue purposes. Tariff duties and land sales (especially in New South Wales) were the largest sources of colonial revenue in an era before direct taxation. But as trade expanded, customs duties gradually began to assume a protective character, though originally protection against other Australian colonies had not been envisaged or deemed desirable.

Attempts to secure common tariff policies proved abortive because of mutual mistrust, conflicting interests and failure to agree on distribution of revenue. The "free border" agreement between New South Wales and Victoria lasted from 1867 to 1873, when Graham Berry, Premier of Victoria, introduced the first truly protective tariff.

Before Berry's outright protectionist policy, as Geoffrey Serle has argued,[3] there was possibly some hope of reconciliation between the two largest colonies. After its implementation the resulting tariff warfare embroiled all colonies as others retaliated against Victoria and one another. New South Welsh free traders believed that Victorian protectionists had made their common boundary of the River Murray a "barrier as effective as the great wall of China to the elevating influences of civilising commerce."[4] John Robertson held that federation meant "marrying [their] living free trade to the dead carcase of the protection of Victoria."[5] The fiscal issue became, in the famous phrase of Victoria's James Service, "the lion in the path of federation."

Railway battles became one of the more spectacular aspects of tariff warfare and colonial hostility. Initially investment in colonial railways had been cautious, being based upon the criterion of profitability.[6] Ultimately, under the impetus of intercolonial competition, economic considerations gave way to political. Large-scale railway construction and investment, which incurred heavy debts and interest commitments overseas, proceeded with disregard for declining yields on cumulating capital liabilities. In the early 1860s Victoria began to extend trunk lines from Melbourne in attempts to divert the flow of trade away from Sydney. The Riverina was the chief target. New South Wales, in order to retain its trade, responded in kind in the 1870s and 1880s by constructing main lines out from Sydney to defend threatened regions. Brisbane and Sydney disputed the Darling Downs area of southern Queensland. South Australia built rail heads on the Murray to tap intercolonial trade. Rail spurs to the New South Welsh border ensured the supply of Broken Hill ores for smelting in South Australia. Preferential and differential freight rates complemented tariff policies and rail construction. Victorian railways, for instance, charged less than half the normal freight rates for goods transported to and from Melbourne and the Riverina. Ironically, the financial repercussions of this wasteful duplication and competition contributed greatly to the depression of the 1890s, which in turn contributed greatly to the eventual success of the federation movement.

3 Geoffrey Serle, "The Victorian Government's Campaign for Federation, 1883-1889," in *Essays in Australian Federation*, ed. A W. Martin (Melbourne, 1969), p. 14.
4 Ibid.
5 Ibid.
6 N. G. Butlin, *Investment in Australian Economic Development 1861-1900* (Cambridge, 1964), pp. 358-69.

These, therefore, were some of the factors which divided the colonies and kept them apart: isolation and parochialism, the evolution of separate politico-economic vested interests, competition locally and overseas, bitterness engendered by conflicting tariff policies. These were also some of the factors which determined that if the colonies were to come together one day, then union would have to take the federal form. Unification was out of the question. The occasional politician (such as George Dibbs of New South Wales) who proposed a unitary system was usually not only an opponent of federation but an opponent of *any* form of union. Similarly, these factors determined that neither Sydney nor Melbourne nor any other colonial city could become the capital of a federated Australia. Canberra became, as W. K. Hancock remarked, "less a national capital than the monument of a compromise between jealous provincialism."[7]

At the same time as divisive issues fostered separatism, so countervailing forces operated to draw the colonies closer together.

The colonies were the sole occupants of an island continent. Edmund Barton's appeal "a nation for a continent and a continent for a nation" could conceivably have been made nowhere else. Colonists were of the same blood, and they shared the same language and culture. The white settlers and their descendants who peopled the antipodes sprang from a common Anglo-Celtic stock. At times during the second half of the nineteenth century the Chinese had appeared menacing—especially on the goldfields of Victoria and New South Wales—but a variety of restrictive measures had stemmed their influx. By 1901 nearly 96 per cent of the nonaboriginal population had been born in the United Kingdom or Australasia. The "crimson thread of kinship," as Sir Henry Parkes aptly put it, linked the colonies.

In this context colonials, oblivious of ethnic subtleties, generally described themselves as "Anglo-Saxons" or "Britons." Like true Britons, federationists sometimes argued, they should attain nationhood and create a new Britannia in the southern seas. Canada was one such Anglo-Saxon nation (this disregarded the Gauls) which had recently shown the way. The United States was another (they disregarded all but the chosen few) and while the American colonies had unfortunately left the Empire they might one day return. Australian federation might be a step towards imperial federation, or even, in wilder flights of fancy, to one great combination of all English-speaking peoples. Alfred Deakin, the young Victorian liberal, informed a public meeting of the Australian Natives' Association that federation would establish "another stronghold of Anglo-Saxon stock."[8] Henry Dobson, an old Tasmanian tory, told fellow delegates to the federal convention

7 W. K. Hancock, *Australia* (Brisbane, 1961), p. 58.
8 *Age* (Melbourne), 31 May 1898.

of 1897-98 that by federating they would "assist the great movement in the old country for Imperial Federation; . . . and having welded the mother-country and her colonies into one mighty nation under the Union Jack of Old England, [they] shall make manifest to the other nations of the world the power and civilization of the Anglo-Saxon race."[9] J. H. Symon, a conservative South Australian, hinted at a possible "Empire of the English speaking race—a vast and glorious confederation."[10]

The colonies shared the Christian faith. Some sectarian differences existed between Protestants and Catholics, but the Irish-Catholic minorities were widely dispersed throughout the several colonies. The acute regional, ethnic and religious antagonisms, which had divided the two Canadas, were therefore absent. Cardinal Moran, an unsuccessful candidate in 1897 for the second federal convention, urged Catholics to go "hand-in-hand with [their] Protestant fellow-citizens"[11] to vote in favour of federation at the referendum of 1898. The Reverend Dr. Paton, a prominent Presbyterian, claimed it would be a standing disgrace "if people such as they were—of one blood, with a heritage of glorious traditions and privileges, owning allegiance to the same monarch, reading the same English Bible, worshipping the same divine man, Christ—should continue to be separated from each other, to the material and moral injury of all by barriers purely artificial."[12] The Reverend Dr. Jeffries, Congregationalist and pioneer of federation, believed that it had been clear for years that "the great Master of Life was summoning this Australian people to achieve its destiny."[13] The Anglican *Church News* disliked the Puritan overtones of "Commonwealth," declined to "enthuse or blaspheme" over the Bill, but nevertheless counselled faith in chosen leaders as they had secured "such financial terms as will be hard to beat."[14]

The colonies possessed a common political tradition. They adopted, and gradually adapted, British parliamentary institutions with bicameral legislatures and responsible systems of cabinet government. By 1889, when Parkes took up the federal cause in earnest, all colonies except Western Australia had experienced some thirty years of self-government under relatively democratic institutions. Manhood suffrage and the secret ballot—often termed the "Australian" or "Victorian" ballot in Britain and America—had been introduced in several colonies as early as the 1850s. Triennial parliaments—regarded as

9 *Official Record of the National Australasian Convention Debates* (Adelaide, 1897), p. 202.
10 Symon's draft of an article "United Australia" published in the *Yale Review*, August 1900 in Symon Papers, National Library of Australia, Canberra, MS 1736.
11 *Register* (Adelaide), 3 June 1898.
12 Ibid., 30 May 1898.
13 Ibid., 3 June 1898.
14 *Church News* (Adelaide), 3 June 1898.

more democratic than quinquennial—had been established in South Australia and Victoria in the same decade. By 1890 they had become the general rule. Payment of members was the practice in most colonies, and no property qualifications existed for candidates and electors to popular houses. With many of the Chartist points already achieved, progressives turned their attention to refining and extending the democratic process. Abolition of the remnants of plural voting, reduction of residential qualifications, introduction of the initiative and referendum, votes for women and, above all, reform of upper houses were familiar issues. Though differences existed in political styles and stances, the similarity of political institutions, processes and policies emphasized common heritage.

On occasions the colonies shared interests vis-à-vis the imperial government. Britain, with its empire and world wide concerns was, many believed, inclined to neglect the views and interests of her colonies in the antipodes. To British governments these interests were peripheral: to the Australian colonies they were central. During the early and mid-nineteenth century the Colonial Office had seemed insensitive to colonial opinion on questions such as transportation of convicts, local control of land and revenue and self-government. Later, secretaries of state for the colonies appeared to pay insufficient heed to protests concerning French aspirations and actions in the south Pacific. The prospect of the New Hebrides becoming another cesspool for French criminals provoked a degree of colonial unity. But lukewarm interest in the issue in New South Wales and disagreement as to the proper response, effectively undermined the Victorian campaign in 1883 for annexation. The attempted annexation of New Guinea by Queensland in 1883 to forestall rumoured German ambition, though apparently a unilateral action, received widespread colonial approval. The fact that colonial forebodings proved well founded, together with Lord Derby's belated declaration of a protectorate over south-eastern New Guinea, did little to persuade the colonies that they had been well served by the Colonial Office. But disunity had again limited the effectiveness of representations to Britain. If they were to speak with one united voice (though the point was seldom made explicit), perhaps they would be heard more clearly in London. If as separate colonies they had become strong, "how much stronger would they be in dealing with the affairs of the world as a united Australia."[15]

Advances in technology drew the distant colonies closer. Until intercolonial communications and transport developed, the practicality of a national parliament to which all colonies could send members remained dubious. But as the century progressed technical innovations made Australian federation, perhaps even imperial federation,

15 Henry Parkes, *The Federal Government of Australia* (Sydney, 1890), p. 67.

less impractical. The electric telegraph linked the remote Western Australia with the east in 1877. Steamships and iron-clad clippers plied coastal waters and high seas, and the opening of the Suez Canal promised reduced sailing times with Britain. Steam trains connected Sydney and Melbourne in 1883 (calls for federal union were made at the celebration banquet). Travel by rail between all eastern mainland capitals became possible with the Melbourne-Adelaide line in 1887, and the Sydney-Brisbane in 1889. The promise of a federally-financed transcontinental railway was a major inducement for reluctant Perth interests to federate.

Many of these factors combined to foster the growth of a national sentiment. Shared grievances and aspirations emphasized "Australian" concerns. Closer contact, while generating friction and heat, led to an awareness of a similarity of life styles and mores. By about the 1870s native-born outnumbered immigrant (though the *adult* proportion remained a minority until the turn of the century) and increasingly the population appeared to identify with locality of birth and association. The Australian Natives' Association, formed in Melbourne in 1871, had over 7,000 native-born members by 1890. The stridently nationalistic and republican *Bulletin* began publication in Sydney in 1880. The latter part of the nineteenth century saw the beginning of a period of "self-conscious nationalism" in literature.[16] Between 1885 and 1890 a "distinctive Australian school of painting" emerged as members of the Heidelberg group came to terms with the peculiarities of Australian light, colour and landscape.[17]

But the political content of these signs of national consciousness was small and political nationalism, in the sense of a desire for a national government and Australian nationhood, weak. The Australian Natives' Association had as one objective, the encouragement of Australian nationalism and unity, but its strength and influence was unimpressive outside Victoria. Indeed, elsewhere in the nineties, when union came to fruition, it seemed moribund. If anything, the federation movement revived the organization rather than the reverse.[18] The influence of the *Bulletin* has been greatly exaggerated, and its attitude to imperial relations was consistently unrepresentative of colonial opinion. It disavowed Queensland's attempted annexation of New Guinea in 1883, the dispatch of a New South Welsh contingent to the Sudan in 1885, and participation in the second Boer War—in their time, all popular causes. The "Bushman's Bible" predicted that Australians, especially bushmen, would refuse to fight the Boers, and it deplored

16 H. M. Green, *A History of Australian Literature 1789-1923* (Sydney, 1961), I: 345.
17 Bernard Smith, *Australian Painting 1788-1960* (Melbourne, 1962), pp. 71-124 (specific reference to p. 71).
18 See, for instance, Janet Pettman, "The Australian Natives' Association and Federation in South Australia," in *Essays in Australian Federation.*

the imperial connection because it involved the colonies in Britain's foreign wars. Volunteers for South Africa were obliged to compete in skills with horse and rifle to win coveted selection in the 16,000 strong contingents. Symon, a major figure in federation, believed that the spontaneous support had "beyond all controversy made the Empire one. Such a result was worth a war."[19] Republicanism, never strong, was a spent force by the mid-nineties.

The traditional view of nationalism as a radical working-class phenomenon—whether nurtured in bush or city—is singularly inapplicable to federation. The labour movement was normally indifferent or hostile to federal union, which seemed remote from its immediate concerns. Federation diverted attention away from colonial politics, where labour was becoming increasingly active and influential. Trade unions, devastated by strike defeats and depression, and fledgling labour parties, were preoccupied with problems of survival, organization and social reform. The exclusion of working-class representatives from official events in the federation movement did nothing to stimulate support or sympathy. The federation conference of 1890, and the federal convention of 1891 were attended solely by established politicians. They took place before the first labour candidates were elected to parliament. Only one labour delegate gained entry to the federal convention of 1897-98, which drafted the Commonwealth Bill. Labour in New South Wales, Victoria and South Australia campaigned against federation under the bill in the referenda of 1898-99. In Queensland labour was divided. There appears little to support Russel Ward's contention that whereas labour's leaders were not ardent federationists working-class citizens somehow were.[20]

Middle-class nationalism has more relevance because federation was promoted by middle-class career politicians (free trade and protectionist, conservative and liberal), producers, businessmen and professional people.[21] No doubt some prominent federationists were inspired by political idealism as well as baser motives. But nationalists such as Deakin were in a minority in the movement. The majority expressed more mundane notions. Most seemed to look upon a future federal government as a sort of agency dispensing with legal, administrative and commercial problems of an intercolonial nature in the interests of the states. For example, in 1889 Inglis Clark, an architect of federation

19 Symon, "United Australia."
20 Russel Ward, *Australia* (Sydney, 1969), p. 114.
21 See L. F. Crisp, *Australian National Government* (Melbourne, 1965), p. 11 for an occupational analysis of delegates to the federal conventions, and R. Norris, *The Emergent Commonwealth, 1901-10* (Melbourne, 1975), Appendices I and II, for biographical notes on same. See A. W. Martin, "Economic Influences in the 'New Federation Movement,' " in *Historical Studies, Selected Articles,* compiled by J. J. Eastwood and F. B. Smith (Melbourne, 1964), p. 218 for an occupational analysis of members of Federation Leagues.

and the constitution, sought to enlist Barton's support for the good cause on the grounds that only a federal "authority" could remove problems involving joint stock companies, recognition of orders in lunacy, wills and patent laws.[22]

Moreover, federation was initiated by middle-class anglophyles, who, while not necessarily liking all individual Englishmen, prided themselves on their British character, manner and monarchy. Parkes, "Father of Federation," disclosed an intimate regard for Queen Victoria when he contended that

> the woman who sits on the English throne, stripped of all her royal robes and all her royal pendants, is no common woman in the administration of affairs, that she has disclosed a genius for government, a close attention to business, and a keen foresight which has never been equalled by any monarch known to history.[23]

Deakin delighted in his cultured English accent, which was of "exactly the same quality" as that of cultured English gentlemen.[24] But the familiar notion of "dual nationalism" (Deakin was a member of both the Australian Natives' Association and the Imperial Federation League) is deficient. A more appropriate term would be "triple nationalism" as the dual concept lacks the third dimension of identification with, and loyalty for, the particular colony of birth or residence. The words "nation" and "country" were frequently applied to the individual colonies which, for instance, possessed (and indeed still possess) "National Galleries." Such was the strength of state rights sentiments in the late nineteenth century that colonists possibly regarded themselves first as Tasmanians, Victorians, Queenslanders and so on, second as Britishers and third as Australians. Certainly federationists made use of, and evoked, patriotic demonstrations in their campaigns. Enthusiastic audiences cheered, waved flags and sang patriotic songs (*Rule Britannia* seems to have been the favourite). But anti-federationists did similar things with similar results. Their patriotic efforts were directed towards the preservation of the rights, privileges, powers and sovereignty of their existing nation.

The fact that federation eventuated does not necessarily mean that "Australianism" triumphed over "Victorianism" and the like. Nor can Australian nationalism account for the wide variations in support for, and opposition to, federation between and within colonies in the referenda of 1898-1900. The idea that a rising tide of nationalist

22 A. Inglis Clark to Edmund Barton, 19 June 1889, item 62(a), Barton Papers, National Library of Australia, MS 51.
23 *Official Record of the Proceedings and Debates of the National Australasian Convention 1891* (Sydney, 1891), p. 323. Parkes, born in England in 1815, arrived Australia 1839. At the first convention seventeen out of forty-six delegates were born in Australia, at the second twenty-nine out of fifty-four.
24 Deakin, *Federal Story*, p. 70.

sentiment swamped provincialism and carried federation is inconsistent with the public's lukewarm interest in the affair. In 1897 a large number of candidates sought election to the second federal convention, yet polling ranged from a mere 25 per cent of qualified voters in Tasmania to a grand 51 per cent in New South Wales. (Tasmania, incidentally, had the highest proportion of native-born population.) At the first federation referenda in 1898, on which the fate of federation hinged, less than half the qualified electors troubled to poll. In the total of ten referenda, in only one—Victoria in 1899—did a majority of electors support the bill. A presumption also exists that nonvoters tended not to approve federation because the affirmative vote in most colonies had to reach a statutory minimum (80,000 in New South Wales) for the bill to succeed. Whereas citizens might have been confused by conflicting economic appeals to federate—and therefore abstained—according to the Australian nationalism thesis they had the clear opportunity to establish a nation. Public response in these federation events was considerably less than in colonial elections of the period.

The major obstacle to overcoming colonial separatism was the general indifference of parliaments and public to notions of union. Behind this widespread apathy existed a fundamental problem—the lack, up to the 1890s, of a compelling need to federate. The colonies, in the best traditions of whig history, had progressed rapidly from penal settlements to free, self-governing communities within the empire. They were prosperous. Their economies had developed and diversified, especially in the decades following the gold rushes of the 1850s. During the period 1860-90 the gross domestic product increased at an average rate of between 4-1/2 and 5 per cent a year, an economic growth rate probably second only to that of the United States. British investors, with declining opportunities for home investment after 1873, increasingly turned their attention to the antipodes. From 1874 to 1890, British capital "flowed in a rising tide into the Australian colonies."[25] Population increased rapidly. Sixty years after the arrival of the first fleet in 1788, the population, largely as a result of massive immigration, reached 400,000. It nearly trebled during the gold rush decade of the 1850s. By 1890, by which time natural increase exceeded net immigration, it approached 3-1/4 million.

These remarkable advances took place in the security provided by two factors: remoteness of the antipodes from potential predators and membership in the Empire. Australia was insulated by isolation from the dangers and conflicts of the old worlds of Europe and America. On occasions foreign warships—Russian, French, German—appeared on the distant horizon, and in the latter part of the nineteenth century

25 Butlin, *Investment in Australian Economic Development*, p. 335.

European powers began to take more interest in the south Pacific region. Sporadic scares arose. But in fact no aggressor ever attempted, or indeed plausibly could attempt, armed invasion. British garrisons were withdrawn in the 1870s but the "mighty moat"[26] still surrounded the island continent. The Royal Navy patrolled the oceans. Britannia ruled the waves.

Historians have traditionally nominated three basic reasons which supplied the immediate need to federate; the desire for national defence, immigration control and intercolonial free trade.

The belief that the question of defence prompted federation is founded primarily on events surrounding the inspection of colonial military forces by Major General J. Bevan Edwards in 1889. Edwards, a British officer stationed in Hong Kong, recommended a "common system of defence" and "federation of the forces. . . ." These recommendations came in a memorandum attached to his separate reports to the colonial premiers. Parkes, spurred by this advice, immediately took the initiative. In his calls for federation to Duncan Gillies of Victoria, and other premiers, and in his Tenterfield address, he referred to the Edwards memorandum. Thus began, in October 1889, what Parkes himself termed "the first movement worthy of the noble object of bringing all Australia under one National Government. . . ."[27]

The importance accorded this motive for federating seems difficult to maintain. Parkes, in fact, first proposed the immediate consideration of a scheme for federation in a private letter to Gillies on 15 June 1889. The existence of an earlier approach to Gillies than the October one was noted by commentators such as Quick and Garran and Bernhard Wise.[28] Its significance generally appears to have been missed. That is, Parkes opened negotiations with the Victorian Premier in 1889 before Edwards had presented his famous memorandum, indeed before the general had left Hong Kong. The letter, and a second later in June, made no mention of defence or Edwards' memorandum.[29] Parkes gave no reasons for his initiative, except to warn that difficulties in the way of federation would be increased in New South Wales by further delay. Contemporaries suggested a variety of reasons: The lull in colonial politics which induced him to

26 J. A. Cockburn, *National Australasian Convention 1891* (London, 1901), p. 204.
27 Henry Parkes, *Fifty Years in the Making of Australian History* (London, 1892), p. 585. Copies of memorandum and reports in *British Parliamentary Papers*, 1890, 49, C. 6188, *Correspondence Relating to the Inspection of the Military Forces. . . .* See Norris, *Emergent Commonwealth*, for fuller consideration of this and related topics.
28 John Quick and Robert Randolph Garran, *The Annotated Constitution of the Australian Commonwealth* (Sydney, 1901), p. 117. Bernhard Ringrose Wise, *The Making of the Australian Commonwealth* (London, 1913), p. 2.
29 Text first quoted in Serle, "The Victorian Government's Campaign for Federation," p. 50; copy in South Australian Archives, Chief Secretary, 1889/1462. Edwards left Hong Kong 16 June, arrived Darwin 28 June, Sydney 19 July. Dated memorandum 9 October.

consider constitutional problems; his precarious political position (the 1889 election reduced his majority to two); envy of a revitalized Federal Council (South Australia had joined earlier in 1889 and larger delegations seemed likely); personal ambition.

Moreover, the defence issue bears the marks of a manufactured cause. It seems probable that the opportune memorandum, with its opportune "federal" recommendations, was inspired by Parkes and furnished by a compliant Edwards so as to assist the noble aim of federation and the ambitions of both. The General later recounted that after meeting the Premier (but before composing his memorandum), he had become aware that a "consensus of opinion" favourable to federation existed.[30] The "realisation of some common need was required to bring it about." Later Sir Henry saw at once that the memorandum's recommendations of combined action for defence purposes could not be implemented without a federal government. He therefore championed federation. Edwards hoped to become "Inspecting General" of colonial forces to take them into federation. Parkes suggested such a post to Gillies. Edwards, after Gillies rejected the proposal as "premature," aspired to fill the rumoured vacancy in the governorship of Tasmania and thereby to perform the dual roles of inspector general and governor. Parkes telegraphed Edwards, "All going well,"[31] as the General was about to leave Port Darwin on route to Hong Kong. Edwards, in order to advance federation, tried on his return to persuade Admiral Ting, an "old comrade" who commanded the Chinese imperial squadron, to sail his fleet and show his flag in Australian waters.

Whatever the motives of Parkes, it is apparent that neither he nor his contemporaries were especially concerned about questions of defence or security in the late eighties and during the nineties when federation became a reality. Rather, there appears to have been widespread indifference, even complacency, on this score. Australian delegates at the Colonial Conference of 1887 cavilled at the cost of contributing to an auxiliary naval squadron for exclusive use in Australian waters.[32] Colonial premiers begrudged paying for the proposed inspection of military forces. In 1888 Parkes declined to join Gillies in a formal request for the inspection. The tour of Edwards took place only because the War Office persisted with the idea and the Colonial Office accepted the charge. The resultant reports and memorandum aroused

---

30 *Proceedings of the Royal Colonial Institute, 1890-91*, 22, pp. 196-97. Edwards' letters to Parkes January-May 1890 in Parkes Correspondence A68 and A921, Mitchell Library. See Norris, *Emergent Commonwealth*, pp. 109-12.

31 Parkes to Edwards, 30 November 1889, copy, Colonial Secretary 4/902.1, New South Wales Government Archives, Mitchell Library.

32 Great Britain, *British Parliamentary Papers*, 1887, 56, C5091, *Proceedings of the Colonial Conference 1887* (London), pp. 29, 33, 37, 40.

no great alarm or interest. The eighties were prosperous years. During the depression of the nineties the colonies drastically cut defence expenditure. Delegates to the official conventions of the 1890s readily agreed that a federal government should assume responsibility for security. The subject of defence formed one of the principal resolutions for federation enunciated by Parkes at the convention of 1891, and Barton at the convention of 1897-98. The commonwealth government, like central governments elsewhere, should have exclusive control of defence as a matter of course. But they displayed little sense of federating for this purpose. Central control would be more efficient and more economical. Armed conflict was theoretically possible but they were "undertaking federation deliberately without external pressure, without even its being forced on us in any way by the consideration of events, except that we acknowledge that, in the pure evolution of events, if [they did] not come together [they] must gradually fall asunder."[33] Unlike the United States and Canada, which federated under the threat of foreign aggression, the Australian colonies had "no enemy" likely to burn their cities, levy contributions upon them or kill their people.[34]

The topic of defence was given no special place in the "popular" phases of the new federation movement. Only one speaker referred to the subject at the Corowa Conference of 1893. The president of the Bathurst Convention of 1896 observed that the assembly could be "calm and collected" in their deliberations because there was "no present fear of the warlike intention of any great Power . . .":[35] two members alluded to the advantages of federal defence. Campaigners in the federation referenda gave no priority to defence. "Billites" occasionally touched upon the question in their appeals for a vote of "yes." Their stirring speeches, the manifestoes of federation leagues and newspaper editorials sometimes mentioned the issue in passing. More commonly they ignored it altogether. "Anti-Billites" occasionally attacked the Commonwealth Bill because of its defence provisions in their calls for a vote of "no." They feared future federal extravagance in this field (and hence higher taxes) and the possibility of an oppressive standing army. Apparently advocates of federation, astute men experienced in gauging and gaining public support, did not consider that appeals to federate for purposes of defence would influence many people. Apparently opponents, again shrewd campaigners, believed that opposition on the reverse grounds would. Neither lends credence to the traditional view of the vital relationship between federation and defence. In essence it was a nonissue. Perhaps both federationists and

33 P. A. Jennings, *National Australasian Convention 1891*, p. 126.
34 T. Playford, *Official Record of the Proceedings and Debates of the Australasian Federation Conference 1890* (Melbourne, 1890), p. 15.
35 *Bathurst Convention: Proceedings of the People's Federal Convention* (Sydney, 1897), p. 79.

anti-federationists realized that Australian people were not particularly interested in, or unduly concerned about, questions of defence and security at the time federation was put to the popular test. Perhaps they recognized that the period 1889-1899, when the federation battle was fought and won, was free of external threat. In any event the old federation movement sired by Parkes expired when the draft bill of 1891 died of neglect in colonial parliaments. Enthusiasm for federation and the Bill, according to G. B. Barton (Edmund's brother), "was mostly confined to the delegates and their friends."[36] Anti-federationists rejoiced, echoing Sir John Robertson's boast: "Federation is as dead as Julius Caesar." Few mourned its passing.

The legend that Australians were spurred by the urgent need for federation in order to secure a White Australia also dies hard. According to Deakin in his second reading speech on the Immigration Restriction Bill in 1901

> no motive power operated more universally on this continent or in the beautiful island of Tasmania, and certainly no motive operated more powerfully in dissolving the technical and arbitrary political divisions which previously separated us than the desire that we should be one people and remain one people without the admixture of other races.[37]

Historians have taken Deakin's statement as meaning that the demand for uniform, central control of immigration was a compelling motive for federation. But the validity of Deakin's assertion—or the interpretation given it—has been accepted without being tested. The passing in 1901 of the Immigration Restriction Act and the Pacific Island Labourers Act was sufficient proof. Deakin's claim in federal parliament in 1901 contrasts sharply with his utter silence on the issue in his own "inner history of the federal cause," *The Federal Story*, written between 1898 and 1900. An examination of the relationship between immigration and federation suggests that Deakin was speaking less as a founding father recounting history, than as a party politician supporting a bill for which, as Attorney General, he was partly responsible.

The topic of immigration control was neither dominant nor prominent at important stages of the federation movement. Parkes did not mention it in his initiatives of 1889 or at Tenterfield. At the federation conference of 1890, when he canvassed the reasons for federating and the advantages to be derived therefrom in his opening address, he somehow overlooked the question.[38] On the final day he declared the subject important. The remarks of the few other delegates who alluded to it betrayed no sense of urgency. Sir Samuel Griffith tentatively suggested immigration as a federal power. Thomas Playford im-

36 G. B. Barton, *The Referendum in Australia* (reprinted from the *Asiatic Quarterly Review* [July 1900]), *Federation Pamphlets*, South Australian State Library, 2: 3.
37 *Commonwealth Parliamentary Debates*, 4: 4804.
38 *Australasian Federation Conference 1890* (Melbourne), p. 5.

mediately claimed that a national parliament would never need to deal with the question.[39]

Again, the subject was given no special priority at the official conventions of the 1890s. It was not included in the principal resolutions announced by Parkes in 1891 and Barton in 1897. Very few members mentioned the issue at either convention. Some viewed immigration control as a state right. Others argued that Queensland, which employed indentured Pacific islanders in its great sugar industry, would require special consideration. Henry Bournes Higgins, a radical liberal, believed Kanaka labour was "a question which effects that colony alone."[40] Immigration became a concurrent power in the Australian constitution rather than an exclusive federal one which delegates agreed was the stronger form. It appeared twenty-seventh in the list of thirty-nine legislative powers.

The unofficial conferences of the nineties were even less interested in the issue. The Intercolonial ANA Federation Conference failed to include immigration in its list of sixteen "national matters" for federal action.[41] None of the nearly three-hundred delegates to the Corowa and Bathurst gatherings saw fit to mention the pressing problem.

The final opportunity for a public display concerning White Australia came with the federation referenda. Occasional appeals to federate for this purpose can be found in the campaigns in the four south-eastern colonies. But appeals of this nature were the rare exceptions rather than the common rule. Federationists generally ignored the issue. Shortly before the first referendum, for example, the Sydney *Bulletin*, renowned for its rabid racist nationalism, overlooked immigration control in its twenty-three reasons to vote for federation.[42] On polling day it failed to include the subject in its twenty-seven point "Case for the Bill."[43] The White Australia question was more evident and lively in 1899 in Queensland, where Kanakas were in extensive use in the canefields. Several prominent Billites—including Labor's Thomas Glassey and Anderson Dawson—stressed the issue. But Labor parliamentarians were almost evenly split on federation—reportedly eleven to ten in favour. And Labor organs and bodies such as the Brisbane *Worker*, the Bundaberg *Patriot* and the Workers' Political Organisation opposed federation and disowned the views of Glassey. The *Worker* believed that black labour and immigration were "really matters of domestic concern."[44] The *Patriot* charged that federation

39 Ibid.; Griffith, pp. 11-12; Playford, *Official Record of the Proceedings and Debates of the Australasian Federation Conference 1890*, p. 13.
40 *National Australasian Convention Debates* (Adelaide, 1897), p. 17.
41 Quick and Garran, *Annotated Constitution*, p. 151.
42 *Bulletin* (Sydney), 30 April 1898.
43 Ibid., 4 June 1898.
44 *Worker* (Brisbane), 26 August 1899.

was intended to benefit sugar interests and perpetuate "black slavery."[45] Sugar producers, who looked to the continuing use of a cheap, black work force, were not alarmed at the prospect of federation. The *Sugar Journal and Tropical Cultivator*, of Mackay, reported in its pre-referendum edition that growers and manufacturers believed that a federal parliament would be less likely to disturb the *status quo* than a Queensland legislature controlled by, or under the influence of, an emerging Labor Party.[46]

White Australia was thus no more than a peripheral issue in the referenda of the 1890s and the federation movement as a whole. The problem of Asian immigration, which first disturbed the colonies in the 1850s, was commonly regarded as solved. Restrictive measures from the fifties onwards had effectively stemmed the influx of Chinese: at an intercolonial conference in Sydney in 1888 delegates proposed making their legislation uniform. In 1885 the Queensland parliament legislated to end the Kanaka traffic in 1890. Parkes therefore took his initiative when these matters seemed least pressing. The question of other Asian immigration did not arise until the mid and late 1890s, when it was provoked by the Anglo-Japanese Commercial Treaty of 1894. The colonies, led by George Reid, Premier of New South Wales, determined at an intercolonial conference in 1896 to extend their legislation to all coloured races. But this new aspect of an old question produced no public concern such as to stir widespread interest in, or demand for, federation. There were no demonstrations, riots, or strikes, in the nineties against Asian immigration as there had been in earlier decades against the Chinese. The labour movement, which had led the move to restrict Chinese, did not adopt a plank in its party platform calling for the exclusion of all coloured races, alien and British alike, until 1900.[47] Reid's own brief "yes-no" campaign in 1898 seriously jeopardized the federal cause in New South Wales. Queensland's Kanaka traffic was resumed in 1892 when the Griffith government repealed earlier prohibitive legislation. But federationists in other colonies did not, and could not, give prominence to this problem in their campaigns or promise its resolution through union. First, Queensland might not federate. The offending colony boycotted the convention of 1897-98 and conducted its referendum after the south-eastern colonies had voted to federate. Second, many advocates of federation in Queensland approved of, or saw the necessity for, black labour. Griffith was a champion of federation and chief draftsman of the bill of 1891. The *Brisbane Courier*, a resolute defender of the Kanaka traffic, campaigned as enthusiastically for federation as any

45 *Patriot* (Bundaberg), 8 July 1899.
46 *Sugar Journal and Tropical Cultivator*, 15 August 1899, p. 27.
47 *Worker* (Brisbane), 2 February 1900. The word "alien," used hitherto, did not cover Indians, who were British.

major paper in Australia. In the event Queensland's tropical northern and central sugar regions carried the colony into federation against the opposition of the south.

In brief, the idea that the desire for uniform immigration control to secure a White Australia was the compelling motive for federation is a gross exaggeration. The notion is riddled with inconsistencies. The issue was dormant in the 1890s. Deakin was indeed more the politician in parliament in 1901 than the historian.

The influence of intercolonial free trade on federation was more apparent than either defence or immigration, and the belief in its vital importance to the movement rests on firmer foundations. The issue was greatly in evidence in both the old and new phases. No motive was advanced more often or more forcefully than that of federating to achieve internal free trade. As the movement reached its climax in the referenda, so the theme of the benefits to be derived from abolishing customs houses and border duties was trumpeted in all its variations. Paradoxically, the very issue which most divided the colonies came to provide, under different circumstances in the 1890s, the compelling need to unite.

Parkes stressed the appeal of intercolonial free trade early in his campaign, though he did not mention it in his Tenterfield address. "With federation," he told a cheering audience at Albury, "all trace of Customs officers along our borders would be swept away."[48] His original draft of resolutions for the federal conference of 1890 in Melbourne began with the principle of intercolonial free trade.[49] Subsequently, the opening resolutions of the conventions of 1891 and 1897-98 called for "absolutely free" trade and intercourse between the federated colonies.[50] Intercolonial free trade became embedded in the draft bills which resulted from the conventions. Ultimately, Sections 88 and 92 of the constitution embraced the principle and provided that it be implemented within two years of the establishment of the commonwealth. Thus internal free trade became the one policy which the future commonwealth parliament had to put into effect within a prescribed period of time. Whereas colonial citizens necessarily were ignorant of what policies federal ministries might pursue in defence and immigration—if, and when, governments chose to act in these areas—they could be absolutely sure that internal trade would be absolutely free following federation. Billites ensured that they remained in no doubt on this score. The opening up of an unrestricted market within the federated colonies, with trade flowing into its "natural" outlets, became the dominant appeal for federation. In a celebrated academic exchange between R. S. Parker and Geoffrey

48 Parkes, *Federal Government of Australasia*, p. 46.
49 Parkes, *Fifty Years in the Making of Australian History*, p. 604.
50 *National Australasian Convention Debates* (Adelaide, 1897), p. 17.

Blainey concerning the influence of regional economic factors on federation, Parker emphasized the preponderance of economic appeals in the referenda campaigns. Arguments against union consisted "almost entirely of hard-headed economic special pleading . . . ," those in favour were "partly of the same character . . . though naturally of reverse import."[51] In response to Blainey's criticism, Parker withdrew slightly: "economic motives were present, were influential, and in some places at least constituted a crucial element in the campaign."[52] He need not have done so. While his statement about the nature of Anti-Billite appeals was an exaggeration, his view on the Billite ones greatly understated the case.

Even so, none of the reasons advanced for union proved able to overcome disunion until events of the nineties intervened. The Federal Council, the creation of the eighties, lacked adequate executive powers and full membership, with South Australia rarely present and New South Wales always absent. It failed because colonial politicians saw no sufficient cause to remedy these faults. Similarly Parkes's effort of 1889 came to grief. The old federation movement foundered in the depths of more pressing parochial politics. Awareness of the unacceptable nature of existing intercolonial relations and realization of the need to change them, came with financial and economic crisis.

The great depression of the 1890s was a traumatic experience for the colonies. Excessive speculation and over investment in increasingly unprofitable sections of the economy, and declining overseas prices and returns resulted in financial chaos. Victoria's land boom collapsed. Banks closed. Trade stagnated. Revenue declined. Pastoral investment peaked in 1891, and plunged until 1897.[53] The tide of British investment ebbed. Loan raising overseas by colonial governments virtually ceased in 1894, and Victoria was forced out of the London market for most of the decade.[54] Immigration almost stopped, and emigration took place from the eastern colonies to the West Australian goldfields and New Zealand. The rate of population increase during the nineties, as people also delayed marriage or practised restraint, was nearly half that of the eighties and the lowest by far since the settlement of Australia. Unemployment possibly reached 30 per cent of the workforce. Economic progress, which, despite periodic droughts and occasional recessions, generations of Australians had come to regard as the natural order, came to a halt.

51 R. S. Parker, "Australian Federation: The Influence of Economic Interests and Political Pressures," in *Historical Studies: Selected Articles*, eds. J. J. Eastwood and F. B. Smith (Melbourne, 1964), pp. 158-59.

52 R. S. Parker, "Some Comments on the Role of Economic Interests in Australian Federation," in ibid., p. 196. Geoffrey Blainey, "The Role of Economic Interests in Australian Federation," in ibid.

53 Butlin, *Investment in Australian Economic Development*, p. 61.

54 Ibid., pp. 338, 449.

The new federation movement, therefore, had an essential rationale for union and a plausible cause. The campaigns of Barton and the Australian Natives' Association at the depth of the depression in 1893 met with immediate response. Federation leagues, and the conferences at Corowa and Bathurst were preoccupied with financial and economic issues. Federation would remove the vexatious stock taxes. Federation would restore the confidence of British investors in Australia. Federation would facilitate cheaper borrowing overseas. The speech in Sydney in 1893 of Sir Mackenzie Bowell, Prime Minister of Canada, was given wide publicity: dominion loans were oversubscribed at about half the interest rates London once charged the provinces.[55] Above all, federation and its corollary intercolonial free trade would end the internecine tariff warfare, revitalize trade and commerce, and permit unfettered development of natural resources.

In this way the depression lifted the federal cause out of the rut of colonial politics and above the traditional division of party politics. While politically the colonies were independent, economically they appeared less so. The depression devastated colonies regardless of their particular fiscal policies, which assumed less importance. Given the depression, the old attitude that what was good for Victoria was by definition bad for New South Wales—and vice versa—began to soften. Free traders and protectionists could tacitly compromise without compromising their principles. On the one hand for free traders, internal free trade could be supported as a step towards the fading dream of absolute free trade. On the other hand for protectionists, federation promised a common external tariff, which, given the preponderance of protectionist colonies and the Braddon clause,[56] might reasonably be expected to lean to protection. Besides, protectionist Victoria, which the depression struck hardest, required free Australian markets and New South Wales showed increasing tendencies to protectionism. Discredited and ambitious politicians, who led their colonies from boom to doom, could champion federation in the hope that one day they could redeem themselves in a new political arena.

In a sense, therefore, the federation movement became apolitical. Ironically, it has been depicted both as politically progressive —designed to spread enlightened measures—and as politically regressive—calculated to isolate "socialistic" tendencies. Certainly some radicals suspected a conspiracy of conservatives and capitalists. Likewise some reactionaries damned federation as a radical scheme.

55 *Bathurst Convention*, p. 80; *The New Federation Movement* (Bendigo, 1894), p. 9; *Sydney Morning Herald*, 20 November 1893.
56 Later section 87. This provided the federal government with one-quarter of net customs and excise duties as revenue. Often called the "Braddon blot" in N.S.W., which it was supposed to tax hardest. Sometimes called the "Braddon blessing" in small colonies. In 1899, at the insistence of Reid, the clause was limited to ten years and "thereafter until the Parliament otherwise provides."

Basically it was neither, except in the sense that federalism tends to frustrate rapid change. Support for federation, and opposition to it, cut across normal political allegiances. Deadly political foes found themselves allied on the issue. Billite ranks numbered prominent progressive liberals such as Alfred Deakin and Charles Kingston, and staunch conservatives such as Richard Chaffey Baker and William McMillan. At the time of the referenda, Kingston, Premier of South Australia, was attempting to storm the bastion of conservatism, the Legislative Council, of which Baker was president. (In 1892 Kingston paraded the street with a loaded pistol in an attempted duel with Baker—Baker called the police.) Similarly radicals such as Henry Bournes Higgins and conservative diehards such as Sir Normand MacLaurin campaigned against the Bill.

By and large, attitudes to federation owed less to political persuasion than to expectation of economic gain or loss. In this way both sides campaigned on essentially state rights platforms. The main thread of Billite arguments was that federation would benefit significant areas of their colony's primary production, trade, industry and the economy and finance of the colony as a whole: at the same time their colony's rights and privileges would not be materially infringed. Their adversaries argued largely with reverse thrust. In broad terms, colonial electors apparently responded in kind and were seen to have done so by contemporary observers such as Quick and Garran.[57] No colony was as aggressively confident of profit from intercolonial free trade as Victoria (Anti-Billites there dwelt upon constitutional defects of the Bill) and none as depressed. As it happened Victoria proved the most pro-federal in the referenda of 1898 and 1899. None was as wary of trade and financial prospects as New South Wales, where some interests feared for the "free" port of Sydney and many citizens feared the consequences of the "Braddon blot." As it happened New South Wales proved the least pro-federal. Northern and central Queensland hoped for free access to New South Wales for the marketing and refining of sugar; Brisbane and the south feared the unequal free competition of Sydney under federation. The smallest south-eastern colonies, given that the largest were about to unite, could ill afford to stand out. If they did, South Australia and Tasmania, as foreign countries confronted by the external tariff and wealth of the federated states, would meet the same "bankrupt fate" as Newfoundland, that "foggy and foolish island."[58] Western Australia, relatively unscarred by old tariff wounds and buoyant because of its gold rush, hesitated until the eleventh hour. To the extent that fear wrought federation, the fear

57 *Annotated Constitution*. See pp. 209-11, 244 for an interpretation of the campaigns and their results.
58 Symon, *Register* (Adelaide), 2 June 1898.

was less of yellow hordes—warlike or peaceful—and more of the economic consequences of separation or isolation.

When Kingston, Barton, and Deakin reached agreement on the Commonwealth Bill with the British government in London in 1900, the trio, left alone, "seized each other's hands and danced hand in hand in a ring around the centre of the room to express their jubilation."[59] And well might the comrades-in-arms. Past battles had been crowned with success. To the victors the spoils. The future looked full of promise.

59 Deakin, *Federal Story*, p. 162.

XI

Politics in New South Wales: The Federation Issue and the Move Away from Faction and Parochialism

J. J. EDDY

The political preparation of the Austalian colonies for federation proved to be long, practical and apt. Federation did not merely come about. To be achieved, it had to emerge in the late 1880s as a hard new issue against a lively background of deep local loyalties and considerable, if very parochial, political experience. A wide variety of arguments could be, and were, marshalled to support and to oppose the federal idea, but whatever the precise course of events which went to make up the "inner history" of the cause,[1] eventually the hopes, fears, aspirations and intentions of the founding fathers would have to take political form.

The progress to federation required the movement to be accepted successfully into the political framework of each constituent element of the future commonwealth, and obstacles could arise at many points. Clearly the first real *élan* must come from the large and powerful colonies of New South Wales and Victoria. The Victoria of James Service and Alfred Deakin had always seemed enthusiastic for the cause, even before the grave economic depression of the 1890s and its aftermath had underlined the need for national unity and highlighted the weaknesses of provincial separation.[2] But the vital cooperation of New South Wales, the senior colony, was by no means as readily predictable. In all the Australian colonies a shift was taking place in the nature of politics, a shift towards a broadly principled and more disciplined party system and away from the old, more personal arrange-

---

1 Alfred Deakin's phrase from *The Federal Story: The Inner History of the Federal Cause 1880-1900*, ed. J. A. LaNauze (Melbourne, 1963), p. xi.
2 G. Serle, "The Victorian Government's Campaign for Federation 1883-1889," in *Essays in Australian Federation*, ed. A W. Martin (Melbourne, 1969).

ments in which individuals and groups formed and re-formed according to a complex geometry not yet fully understood.[3] Ironically, part of this process was the adoption of free trade and protection as organizing concepts in both Victorian and New South Wales politics, concepts which proved such a daunting hurdle to ardent federalists.

Sir Henry Parkes, Premier of New South Wales, had proposed the establishment of a Federal Council "to pave the way to a complete federal organization hereafter," but the time was not yet ripe, and union remained, in the words of Sir John O'Shanassy, once Premier of Victoria, "a beautiful conception."[4] The 1880s did see spasmodic and discontinuous progress as conferences and conventions were held. A stunted Federal Council, whose existence Deakin considered was the most significant thing about it, did come about in 1886, largely in response to Victorian and Queensland involvement in the affairs of the New Hebrides and New Guinea. But the idea had to have the support of a movement, and the movement had to have momentum, organization and embodiment in a constitution before federation could be examined, analyzed and implemented as a practical, political scheme.

In New South Wales, political attitudes and groupings polarized more fully during the 1890s, and indeed evidence suggests that the effects of this polarization were as permanent, *pari passu*, as the federal constitution slowly being hammered out at the same time. When Henry Parkes made his first and crucial intervention in June 1889 to launch federation as a permanent and negotiable political issue, the process was incomplete. Yet it is in this confused and rather inauspicious context that the new federal thrust had its humble but effective birth: for Parkes's move led directly to the federal constitution of 1891. Parkes, whom Deakin described as a "massive, durable . . . imposing . . . full blooded, large-brained, self-educated . . . Titan,"[5] appears always to have had subtly mixed motives for his activities. His career illustrates the interplay of grand design and petty politics which would continue to be the fate of the federation issue.[6]

The centrifugal tendency of the earlier years succeeding self-government, characterized by a natural parochialism and concentration on the solution of local problems and the realization of local ambitions, was now to be replaced by a convergence which seemed to offer a greater scope and opportunity. Local issues, divisions and

---

3 P. Loveday and A. W. Martin, *Parliament, Factions and Parties: The First Thirty Years of Responsible Government in New South Wales, 1856-1889* (Melbourne, 1966).
4 J. A. LaNauze, *Alfred Deakin* (Melbourne, 1965), p. 108.
5 Deakin, *The Federal Story*, p. 28.
6 G. C. Morey, "From Factions to Parties in New South Wales: The Transition Begins, 1885-1892" (doctoral dissertation, Australian National University, 1974). I am grateful to G. C. Morey for permission to use in the succeeding section his unpublished research on New South Wales faction politics.

peculiarities were and remained paramount, but they proved to contain within themselves the seeds of a national political growth without which pressing social, economic and political problems would have lacked effective solution. There were and would remain outlets other than political by which national enterprise and public idealism could be expressed, but parliamentary government was the ultimate arena in which the polity would be discussed and ways and means devised for carrying out the popular will in legislative and administrative terms. The drive towards federation was seen in hindsight to be part of the progressive advancement of the Australian colonies, but "the impulse towards reform and the impulse towards national union were often rather uneasy bedfellows, and amidst the other excitement of the nineties, the federal movement seemed at times to be losing rather than gaining ground."[7] Its rather halting progress arose in part from the fact that it was a political matter requiring political action, and even among its supporters it cut across the political alignments of the day. Colonial politics had succeeded in channelling the sectional fights of interest groups into the parliamentary arena, and the years of middle-class politics had witnessed the substantial victory—to a larger or lesser degree in each colony—of a recognizable Australian democracy which therefore became a powerful and necessary component of any proposed alteration of the colonial constitutions in a federal direction.

Liberal, democratic and even radical changes were not always brought about from motives of high principle. Victorian liberalism in the colonies, even if it agreed that privilege was to be destroyed and social equality encouraged, had eliminated neither selfishness nor venality. Land taxation, electoral reform, votes for women, factory acts, payment of members, the advocacy of protection or free trade, all could be used as vehicles for politicians to consolidate or increase their own power. Considerations of practical policy had probably always been a more essential and central part of colonial politics than a grasp of principle or adherence to an ideal. Yet most reforms, once accepted, had proved politically irreversible. Federation turned out to be no exception, but many interests had to be satisfied before it could come to political fruition. Federation's cause was ideally sound, but its fortunes fluctuated in the 1890s as it took its place as an everyday issue in the world of colonial politics as they changed to cope more adequately with new social and economic demands. In the clash and clamour of parochial dispute the federal idea could be brought forward as a distraction, or to create a diversion, or to hold out hopes for better and more far-ranging solutions to urgent political and social problems. In turn, local politics, partisan tactics, and lack of vision could hinder or help the furtherance of the federal cause.

7 B. de Garis, in *A New History of Australia*, ed. F. K. Crowley (Sydney, 1974), p. 245.

From the 1870s the issues of free trade and protection had seemed to offer New South Wales, along with the other colonies, a useful and relevant political divide. These were not unreal issues in themselves, and they came to represent ideological orthodoxies held with almost religious fervour. The detailed advantages or disadvantages of this or that application of tariff policy could be written about, spoken about, supported or attacked almost as if they were central political doctrines. "Between free trade [and] protectionist . . . rings we are being rapidly provided with political conscience keepers, self-elected and auto-cratic."[8] Men formed a habit of holding or rejecting these tenets, yet the real pragmatic political issues which had to be debated and which called for practical legislation rather than panaceas could scarcely be con-fined long within the stifling bounds of fiscal policy. Such issues had earlier concerned convictism, the opening of the land, and constitu-tional questions relating to parliamentary franchise and democracy —to say nothing of that politics of personal and clan loyalties which maintained in New South Wales as elsewhere. Not surprisingly, the very nature of parliamentary government—with its necessity of getting out the vote and passing legislation—had brought about quite sophisti-cated traditions of leaders and led, government and opposition, and of embryonic party. These inchoate groups may not have been linked by any comprehensive philosophy or maintained by any great ideal or movement, but they could be coherent, tough and knowledgeable.

During the 1880s there were in New South Wales and other eastern Australian colonies slow changes away from an outmoded politics based on faction or rigid fiscal orthodoxy towards wider and more dynamic parties incorporating a world view which strove to deal realistically with the newer social and political realities of the day —among them the issue of federalism. Certainly a man's belief about free trade or protection could strongly influence his approach to a wide variety of important questions such as land-tax, revenue raising, in-come tax and intercolonial trade. But the groupings formed on fiscal lines had little direct relevance to such pressing Australian issues as the confrontation of labour and capital, demands for better working con-ditions and increased social services—or with the federation of the colonies. Lines tended to become blurred in the emergence of "pro-trade" and "free-tection."

The need to rearrange and remobilize political resources, how-ever, strengthened the already accepted case for party discipline and extra-parliamentary organization at a time when social anarchy was a possibility and political stalemate seemed to block necessary legislation. Besides, it was essential for the forces of the middle classes to regroup tightly to counteract organized minorities which seemed to stand in the

8 *Sydney Morning Herald*, 26 January 1889.

way of desired reform, or exercise too considerable an influence, or represent—as did the nascent Labor party—an entirely new political force. Australians expected their governments to play a forward role in economic and social legislation, but the question of how much interference was the subject of a grand debate. Free-trader Henry Parkes, long an admirer of Gladstone, was by the late 1880s conservative compared with Bernhard Wise, who saw the state's role in more active terms. Protectionists for their part could be old agricultural conservatives, the rural interests, or new democratic radicals seeking increased state intervention. In short, the old bottles could not long hold the new wine satisfactorily. It was against this complex parish-pump background that Parkes raised the federal issue.

Apart from the "vanity, opportunism and an admirable ambition to perform a last service for the country which had brought him fame if not fortune,"[9] and other well-known general motives, Parkes certainly had his own local reasons for acting when he did. He was now leading his fifth ministry. It has been suspected that he saw an opportunity to stave off a threatened defeat of his free trade regime at the hands of the advancing forces of protection by confusing his opponents with a new issue. Perhaps, on the other hand, he felt left out in the cold, lost among new men and new methods in his own free trade camp when the formation of the conservative-dominated Liberal and Political Association of New South Wales (LPA) and the more radically-oriented Free Trade and Liberal Association (FTLA) signalized the reorganization of the party.[10] Yet he was active in both the LPA and FTLA and retained his party headship. The federal issue was not necessary to divide his party; it was already divided.

More probably, Parkes used the new cry to resist the widespread demand for immediate social reform.[11] The radical free traders certainly thought that Parkes's "pother" of 1889-91, his thrust for federation, was a conservative conspiracy to provide an excuse for his failure to implement the party's policy of direct land taxation. Radical pressure within the parliamentary party for a pure free trade tariff and the imposition of direct taxation had forced Parkes in 1888 to introduce sham proposals, but the radicals were not satisfied. Hitherto, radical free trade pressure from outside parliament had scarcely existed. The Free Trade Association was made up, like its protectionist opposite number, of largely wealthy merchants, and did not seek changes in the traditional policy of revenue tariffism, so that the founding of the

9 See chapter 10 by R. Norris above; LaNauze, *Alfred Deakin*, pp. 115-17; and J. A. LaNauze, *The Making of the Australian Constitution* (Melbourne, 1972), pp. 6-9.
10 Morey, "Factions to Parties," pp. 252ff.; A. W. Martin, "William McMillan—A Merchant in Politics," *JRAHS* (1954), p. 209.
11 H. V. Evatt, *Australian Labour Leader: The Story of W. A. Holman and the Labour Movement*, 3rd ed. (Sydney, 1945), p. 17.

conservative-dominated LPA did not create any real pressure. But from April 1889, at least, radical pressure to substitute direct taxation for indirect taxation gradually mounted. For the old political compact, the writing was on the wall.

In April 1889 the New South Wales treasurer, William McMillan, was forced by the protectionists to pledge the removal of the anomalies in the tariff, but it was the increasing clamourings of the FTLA radicals on the issue of the land tax which posed the greatest threat to conservative inaction. In July, the radicals of the FTLA urged that the ministry act, and this was reiterated in August at the FTLA conference. Land tax was declared party policy, and this surely put the conservative-dominated ministry in a very awkward position. Sham tax proposals were out of the question, but a plausible excuse to postpone the unpalatable prospect of direct taxation was needed. Federation provided that excuse.

Parkes, shrewd and perceptive, needed a "delaying issue" as early as June (he was a member of the FTLA conference), but he made his concerted move in October to initiate a federal conference. In November he told Edmund Barton that "the fiscal contention must be left for settlement on a federal basis hereafter," and from that time on always expressed publicly the same opinion. In fact, Parkes became thenceforward a federalist first, and only then a free trader. He was able to shelve the fiscal issue and avoid any necessity of interfering with existing fiscal arrangements. William McMillan, Parkes's treasurer, was not ready to oppose outright this convenient escape route from the obligation to implement "pure free trade." He declared his support for such a delay or "breathing time," so that the people might be afforded an opportunity of reviewing the whole matter from a national instead of a local standpoint, and he said he "would go with Sir Henry Parkes . . . they must trust the federal dominion parliament with the adjustment of this matter of tariffs."[12]

Federation with its fiscal implications brought into the open the fundamental and destructive conflict that split the FTLA in two. The Association's consideration of free trade in its relation to Australian federation extended over four nights in February 1890. The debate clearly revealed a definite cleavage between the pro-federation conservatives, anxious to forestall fiscal change, and the anti-federation or "free trade first" radicals. The traditional conservative-liberal president of the FTLA, Andrew Garran, opened the debate by exposing at length the conservative support for federation as an escape route from free trade obligations. He based his argument on the philosophical contention that free traders as liberals must agree that federation was "of more importance to the general interests of Australia" than free

12 *Daily Telegraph*, 23 November 1889, quoted in Morey, "Factions to Parties," p. 254.

trade; as such, immediate free trade must be sacrificed to the cause of national unity. He then went on to assert that "we can be no parties to foreclosing any question of taxation, on which it would be the duty of the Dominion Parliament to pronounce." For his part he thought a "moderate free trade" tariff would provide the federal government with "all, and more than all" the revenue it required, i.e., he preferred "revenue tariffism."[13] To Garran at least it seems that federation was a means of preserving his preferred system of taxation in New South Wales.

The same probably can be said of Parkes, as the FTLA radicals inferred. The single-taxer, J. A. Dobbie, said: "Sir Henry Parkes' scheme had all the appearance of a dazzling political job."[14] By now, however, the radicals would not be fobbed off, and J. C. Neild's motion that the FTLA Council "deprecates any form of Australian federation calculated to imperil the free trade policy of New South Wales" was carried twenty to ten.[15] All taxation, the radicals thought, was unacceptable except land tax. This was to implement "true free trade."

The minority conservatives in the FTLA fought a rearguard action. They could not bring themselves to support simple single tax. Federation was certainly a movement worthy of encouragement, but the party must stay united. The radicals were in control, however, and conflict erupted again towards the end of 1890. By this time federation was a current topic of party politics. In October the Single Tax League intervened, stating that they had allied their forces with the Free Trade and Liberal Association, in the expectation that the declared policy of the FTLA would be carried out, and they demanded the necessary readjustment of the tariff. At a meeting of the FTLA council some weeks later, the fiery and outspoken single taxer, Alexander Riddell, moved against the postponement of the free trade policy. This was evidence of the strength and pressure of the single tax party in the council. But opinion was not unanimous, and in 1891 there were disputes about the relative merits of revenue tariff and single tax, with Riddell pointing out that the secretary of the protectionists' old extra-parliamentary organization, H. T. Donaldson, was "in favor of inter-colonial free trade and protection against the world" by the imposition of a high revenue tariff, and therefore, that the FTLA were traitors to the cause.[16] The FTLA remained obviously divided about property tax proposals. The phrase "free trade" could mean almost anything—as could the word "protection"—in the new context of the 1890s. In fact the FTLA collapsed. The consistent refusal of the conservatives within the free trade party, both in and out of parliament, ever to specify or

13 *Sydney Morning Herald*, 1 February 1890.
14 Ibid., 22 February 1890.
15 Ibid., 1 February 1890.
16 Ibid., 28 January, 6 February 1891.

implement a policy of real free trade caused party tension. Even on the one issue on which the party was based, there was no agreement. It was this internal party conflict which undermined every other development towards a permanent integrated and disciplined free trade party. The newly-organized Labor party, being more realistic in its programme and more powerful in its simpler organization and discipline, would prove the sort of party able to survive. For Parkes and his like the politics which they had known were passing, and it is perhaps no surprise that they took up the federal cause with increased motivation.

In New South Wales, therefore, the federal issue was injected by Parkes into a factional debate at a time when the political system was gradually changing to accommodate new realities. It was the sort of issue which had the potential of becoming a new cause or movement, to be handled very carefully and judged eventually on its own merits. It called for a balanced and not merely partisan response from radicals, liberals and conservatives—whether they adhered to free trade or protectionist principles, or whether or not they supported the new Labor party.[17] It could open new avenues for development and reform, be seen as a threat to established or entrenched interests, or used as a device for maintaining the status quo. Indeed, the politics of the federal movement could never be entirely divorced from existing and continuing political traditions. Any new issue such as federation had to be integrated into the transitional world where the old factions were trying somewhat desperately to reshape their policies and groupings according to a new pattern—with programmes, party pledges, extraparliamentary organizations, local branches and travelling agents, all aimed at transforming ineffective or unstable group and coalition politics into effective machine politics. Federation had to come down from its lofty pedestal into the market place and make itself heard at a time when various attempts to mobilize political support for apparently cohesive and disciplined parties on fiscal lines were proving inadequate to the task.

The polarization of conservatives and progressives which had begun in the 1880s cut across the divisions formed by free trade and protection. To be successful, federalism had to establish and broaden its appeal just at the moment when most colonial politicians were facing new tactical challenges. The need for recognizable and reliable groupings according to comprehensive policy programmes drove men such as George Reid (soon to be Parkes's successor) and Bernhard Wise —both to play crucial roles in the federal story—to attempt a capture of the wider public for their reconstructed free trade party, in order to assure its indissoluble connection with a democratic principle. The

17 G. N. Hawker, "Factions, Labor and Federation," chapter 10 of *Parliament of New South Wales* (Sydney, 1971).

necessity of combining almost incompatible elements within outdated or unsuitable boundaries placed an extraordinary emphasis on tactics. Even where personal careerism could be discounted, tactical disagreements could and did arise to shatter painstakingly constructed political arrangements. Parkes tried restlessly to shape a new alliance around such issues as federation, free trade, local government reforms and new electoral boundaries: and he was not as ready as men such as William McMillan to bring in the troops during the time of industrial unrest in 1890. Wise, in his turn, failed in 1891 to commit the party to an active policy of reform in order to ameliorate the condition of the masses. Parkes fell from power in October 1891. Conservatism and the promotion of self-interest was a dominating feature of free traders and protectionists alike, and it was not until 1895 that George Reid (Premier, 1894-99) managed to put together a coherent, principled non-Labor party. The advent of the Labor party, which occurred at about the same time in each colony, but whose success in New South Wales was momentous, gave witness to a crisis of confidence in the heart of colonial liberalism and to the failure of capitalist politics to come up with satisfying answers to the needs of the day. The Labor party was firmly based for its support on the trades and labour councils, the unions, and local branches. Its example consolidated the lessons which had been learnt all around and would prove relevant in the later organization of federal politics.

Reid succeeded well for a time in constructing an informal alliance, as he followed Parkes's own example in convincing Labor to award him. "support in return for concessions." This in turn loosened the conservative domination within his free trade party, and enabled him so to transform colonial New South Wales society that the "mounting demands for federation seemed like cries for financial help from the protectionist Southern colonies."[18] Between them, Reid and Labor dealt with many reforms which were in one way or another relevant to federation, e.g., payment of members, elective ministries, referenda, state banking, and many items concerning social welfare.

The protectionists for their part (many of them lapsed free traders) divided into those ready for legislation to meet the challenges of social change, such as E. W. O'Sullivan and W. H. Traill, and the more conservative "revenue" elements such as George Dibbs (Premier, 1891-94) and W. Lyne. There were important differences between urban and rural interests, and further essential divisions and subdivisions separating the approaches of business and finance, industry and agriculture, labour and capital. Urban labourers, for example, in New South Wales at least seem to have felt that whatever duties were

18 N. B. Nairn, *Civilizing Capitalism: The Labor Movement in New South Wales 1870-1920* (Canberra, 1973).

imposed they would pay higher prices and, despite O'Sullivan's efforts to attract the trades and labour councils to protection, they continued to support free trade until the Labor party offered them a clear alternative. When it came to a consideration of federalism, the debate gradually changed from whether federation was a good thing or not to what kind of a federation would prove most acceptable to what group.

Reid had replaced Parkes as free trade leader in 1891 and had astutely moved to the left, moulding a party that was united in principle and policy, prepared to come to grips with the problems of the day. Federalism, which had seen definitive progress in 1891 with the drafting of the constitution, needed new leaders less bound by the puzzling and kaleidoscopic parochial politics of the day to lift the cause out of the cross-currents and swamps of colonial parliamentary politics and practice. By 1893 the Corowa conference had linked the cause to a classically democratic future by calling for the next delegates to be popularly elected rather than appointed, and for the constitution to be voted on through referendum rather than debated desultorily in colonial legislatures. Conservative-dominated until 1895 under Dibbs, who was anti-federalist in tone the protectionists also were divided and suffering from radical attacks. Before he died in 1896, Parkes drifted over to the protectionists with a number of his old free trade conservative followers, and entered into a coalition with Dibbs. This disappointed the radical protectionists and helped consolidate the political divisions in New South Wales into those more keen on democratic reform and others. Divided Labor at the end of the decade would once more blur this emerging scene.

Back in 1891 Parkes had become clearly and genuinely interested in strengthening the free trade electoral organization with the help of J. H. Carruthers, who was actively engaged in organizing, inspecting and rallying the local branches. An efficient network had to be built up, candidates chosen and endorsed, rolls "cleansed" and scrutinized, and problems connected with finance and electoral management solved. Parkes had not been able to maintain the old links based on the decaying personalized factions of the past, and in the late 1880s he had seen the fiscal issue as a means of rallying support. He had almost unintentionally initiated the move away from a politics of pure personality towards a politics of disciplined organization, yet he and Dibbs had really led two rival "syndicates." Alignment according to fiscal doctrine was really inappropriate and out-dated, but it suited Parkes because it possessed the potential for precipitating a two-sided conflict and polarization out of which he had hoped of emerging victor. Before 1892 the conflict *between* the two parties scarcely transcended the unprincipled confines of power pragmatism; it was *within* both parties that the transition to more principled politics took place. Parkes had manipulated an issue of principle for a distinctly unprincipled purpose. Yet the climate was ripe for the emergence of a "politics of principle." There were clearly sufficient diverse approaches, from defensive conservatism at the one extreme to aggressive radicalism on the other. Many intermediate positions were held, but no existing or likely party seemed capable of embodying fully either side of a basic divide. Classical liberals might be attracted by independence and individualism, but most colonial politicians knew the need for pragmatic discipline and party unity, even if that unity could only be obtained through the use of platforms which were in many ways vague and unreal.

In 1892 Parkes, looking to make a return, formed his own party, the chief plank of which would be federalism. Federation could be a unifying cause, but it was in a different category from those which were gradually coming to characterize the colonial parties. It was incapable of becoming in itself alone a fully-fledged political platform: it could, of course, be supported or attacked from either left or right. The Federal League of Australasia was perhaps an attempt to create a new parliamentary political entity, to supersede the fiscal parties and seek Australia-wide support. It was impossible to transmute and organize the provincialism of New South Wales into national patriotism, however, when the field was really colonial party politics. Yet its creation was part of the process by which the federal issue was brought into the public eye. Parkes was himself trying to recover the political initiative from his rivals and successors.

The creation of the Australian Federation League of 1893 by Edmund Barton, a man with a protectionist background, meant that there were two competing organizations. George Reid tried by preference to keep federation out of party politics, yet once it had been introduced it had to be taken into account. Parkes needed the "old system" to maintain his personal dominance, and judged that the federal issue could help him disrupt Reid's course. Reid concentrated more successfully on organization according to the new ideological principles and aimed at party unity based on a belief in social progress. He gave priority to federation as a political goal, but was always vulnerable to the attack that his priority was not high enough. Edmund Barton, a consistent believer in the federal idea, probably would have preferred federation to be accepted as a bipartisan compact. Certainly federalism was clearly in danger of becoming a political football, for it now entered into the calculations of all the competing political groups, and could be seen as either a liberal notion or a conservative plot.

But though the politics and parochialism of New South Wales would continue to influence deeply the course of federal success, there were other, clearer, and apparently more hopeful factors to be taken into account. For though federalism would sooner or later have to be accepted into the internal political structure and adopted by the political community of each colony, there had been created in the intercolonial arena a sphere of inchoate federal politics where the deepest colonial jealousies did not seem capable of presenting a hopeless barrier to the triumph of the cause.

Parkes's initiative had led to the 1891 convention, which not only drafted the eventual federal constitution, but also set a high standard for the rest of the formal meetings leading to the ultimate creation of the commonwealth: a story that is well known.[19] The 1890s would see many disappointments, particularly the years of stagnation which followed the first enthusiasm. Once discussions about the elements of a federal constitution had begun in earnest there could be no real turning back. To the constitution-makers, inheritors of the vast political experience as well as of the pettiness of parochial colonial tactics, fell the task of balancing out their responsibilities towards the parent colonies, the traditions out of which they had themselves come, and the duty they owed to the emerging nation. As J. W. Hackett, of Western Australia, put it, " . . . the problem of making a divided Australia into a single nation was complex: that the wishes of the populace must in the last resort prevail, but that they must be consistent also with the federal will." Talking, thinking, enquiring and arguing about federal powers, the real economic effects of tariffs, the role of a states house, and the creation of a new legal and administrative system with which to face the twentieth century, undoubtedly lifted the nature of political debate within Australia.

Political changes in the other Australian colonies also affected the situation in New South Wales. By the end of the 1890s, Alfred Deakin somewhat optimistically thought that in all colonies "party differences were at once sunk upon any provincial issue or upon any truly national question." The rivalry of New South Wales and Victoria was still tangible, symbolized rather thinly now by the protection versus free trade debate. Victorian politics were dominated in the 1890s by a coalition of liberals and constitutionalists who strove to deal with the effects of the depression. Labor, not able to assert itself as strongly as in New South Wales because of the disadvantages it suffered through the unbalanced distribution of parliamentary seats and because of the different colonial traditions, linked with the Liberals. Deakin thought the patient and tolerant Victorians were "transparently" sincere federalists, not driven by the "necessities of their colony"—unlike South Australia, which "had its eye upon the river waters and traffic of New South Wales," or the parent state, which desired a financial settlement to suit itself and George Reid "though it must be disastrous to less prosperous

---

19 LaNauze, *Australian Constitution* and *Alfred Deakin*, where the story is told brilliantly with dramatic human detail.

colonies."[20] Western Australia had seen its population grow from 53,000 in 1891 to 160,000 in 1897, and there had been dramatic political as well as economic consequences of the discovery of gold. The "ancient colonists" had been supreme 1890-97, but John Forrest's party had declined so that the "challenge of liberalism" and the advent of Labor familiar to the eastern colonies came in the years 1897-1900. Naturally, the attitudes of the "recent arrivals" in the western gold-fields and Perth gave a boost to the federal cause.[21]

Local pressures would remain important right to the finish. Deakin noted that Reid, Turner, Kingston, Braddon and Dickson were all ejected from colonial office at the end, through it was perhaps more relevant for the success of the federal cause that they and Forrest had held such continuous office in their respective colonies during the years 1895-99. By this time the federal momentum was great, so that the colonial delegates were able to claim in their negotiations with Chamberlain that "the Bill was Australian and that they spoke for Australia when asking that it should be passed unaltered." The movement had trembled in the balance, Deakin thought, twenty times in ten years. In an article in the *Morning Post* he wrote that parties in the federal parliament would not break completely with their past, but that "their horizons will be wider . . . and party lines will be drawn not as at present largely by geographical considerations, but by principles of national import."[22]

At the end of the 1890s political groupings were certainly fewer in number, more cohesive and better organized than ever before, with independents a fast vanishing breed. Although the process had started before the emergence of the Labor parties, it certainly did not lose any of its urgency because of that event. Taken at its highest aspiration the Labor party of New South Wales was perhaps the paradigm case of the new party principle, for it was organized as a political party to "civilize capitalism." It claimed to represent a movement wide enough to include all aspects of social life as expressed in the work of democratic parliamentary institutions and all progressive philosophies from cantankerous socialism to social Catholicism.[23] In the political arena Labor aimed to represent the whole people rather than political groupings or the sectional interests of one economic class. It was to have its failures—lack of unity, embarrassing inexperience—and many short-

20 Deakin, *Federal Story*, p. 79; de Garis, in *New History of Australia*, pp. 238f.; S. M. Ingham, "Political Parties in the Victorian Legislative Assembly 1880-1900," *Historical Studies* (November 1950).

21 C. T. Stannage, "The Composition of the Western Australian Parliament 1890-1911," *University Studies in History*, 1966.

22 Deakin, *Federal Story, pp. 147 and 173; Morning Post* (London), 8 January 1901.

23 Nairn, *Civilizing Capitalism*, esp. chapter 13, "Labor, Socialism and Federation"; J. J. Eddy, "Labour and the Civilizing of Capitalism," in *Twentieth Century* (December 1973), pp. 149-63.

comings, but from the beginning the Labor member was meant to represent not only his local and wider community but also was expected to stand firm to the progressive principles of the party.

The Australian Labor parties regarded federation in 1891 with suspicion. There seemed to be more pressing objectives for them in the various parliaments in which they had gained representation, and they could be excused for suspecting federalism as a plot of some kind, for they had no representative in its councils. Not all Labor branches were anti-federation, and the course of the 1890s saw the possible advantages of federalism canvassed in its effects towards the forwarding of democracy. By 1897 the issue was about to be put to the acid test of a popular referendum and could hardly any longer be considered or dismissed as a middle class preserve. There would remain unresolved problems which meant that neither movement could anticipate the smoothness with which the Labor view of egalitarian democracy would blend into the federal commonwealth scene. The men whose energies went into creating the two contemporary movements were different, but the constitutional and political arrangements elucidated by the federal fathers proved perhaps even more receptive to the future Australian Federal Labor Party than the particular colonial political traditions which had seen the advent of political Labor in the 1890s.

The Labor parties were a landmark in Australian politics—and were rapidly and notably successful. "By 1915 Labor governments had been in office in the Commonwealth parliament and in all States, and in every State except Victoria they had gained a majority of seats in the lower house."[24] Labor's rapid rise and national character during the time of federal nation-making and after indicates that, even if federation was in some senses a conservative plot, it could unite Labor too, giving it fresh impetus in the new arena and strengthening its separate parts. If, on the other hand, it was meant as a way to contain the new political forces of organized industrial democracy and enable them to have their practical outcome and expression, federation was again more of a success than bargained for. The Labor parties seem to have had little to lose and everything to gain.

By the time of the 1897 federal convention in Adelaide, many of the outlines of future federal politics could be discerned by perceptive bystanders. The conventions themselves gave a preview of the style and tone; many of the delegates went on into the national parliament. Local patriotism remained, as was natural in federal discourse. Deakin predicted that the parties would be divided chiefly by the line of "more progress and faster" and "less progress and slower." The division of liberal and conservative became obvious early in the preparatory de-

24 D. W. Rawson, review of *Labor in Politics: The State Labor Parties in Australia 1880-1920*, ed. D. J. Murphy (Brisbane, 1975), in *Labor History* (November 1974), pp.61ff.

bates about specific constitutional points concerning the conscious decision to promote or oppose the extension of democratic participation in federal politics, "if we allow that voting for its extension could sometimes reflect a resigned acceptance of the inevitable."[25] Nobody could recognize the ultimate impact of real working federalism on the financial independence of the new states, though Deakin and others doubtless made some shrewd guesses. Everybody knew from experience, however, the difference between conservative and liberal approaches to social, economic and political issues. Constitution-making had its own rhythms, false starts and sudden bursts of progress; minor tragedies could occur at any stage. "The convention having been parliamentary in its origins required to submit its work to its parents," wrote Deakin.[26] The results of deliberations had to be reported back to the separate colonial legislatures. Each clause would need to be examined patiently and carefully, for it was recognized by all that real issues, some of them new and unfathomed, lay behind each dry legal formulation. Finally, public opinion having been roused by a great number of contributory factors, the constitution came to be presented to the colonial parliaments for debate and decision. Yet it seemed that ultimately the movement was capable of creating a new dimension of politics in which the various state or colonial issues would have their echo.

The last struggle for the acceptance of the Constitution Bill by New South Wales saw Reid in his famous yes-no position, with Labor divided and unsure. Yet Higgins in Victoria could oppose the Bill because it was not democratic enough. Various devices were called upon to unlock the treasure chest, and at the end no less than at the very start was there urgent need for clever and hard-headed political manoeuvring to free the national spirits imprisoned within.

Australian federation, as a middle class achievement, faithfully mirrored the aspirations and intentions of its founders, whose political experience led them away from distinct and deliberate efforts to set up a federal union merely as a bulwark against the forces of progress. Federation was not a conservative device, even if it had for some the advantage of restraining and defending society against anarchy or extreme socialism. Federal union left large powers to the states in industrial and social matters, which powers could be expected to check and balance "unwise" or imprudent federal initiatives. Indeed, the aim was to capitalize on the homogeneity of the states without sacrificing too much local independence. The Labor party may well have preferred a unitary system, but that preference, too, was not doctrinaire. Rather, Labor was a pragmatic party and, as it did not expect to be

25 LaNauze, *Australian Constitution*, pp. 119 and 124ff.
26 Deakin, *The Federal Story*, p. 53.

XII

An Open Wrestle for Mastery: Commonwealth-State Relations, 1901-14

DON WRIGHT

The Australian Commonwealth came into being on 1 January 1901. At last, the constitution which had been debated for a decade[1] began to function. But this constitution, the only legitimate basis for the government of the new nation, was no perfect and complete gift from the gods. On that hot summer Tuesday, it was no more than a formal, legal contract—a skeleton of dry bones without sinew, flesh or the breath of life. It would be the work of time, the Australian people and, perhaps especially, their politicians to provide it with that which it lacked.

Writing in the London *Morning Post* on 8 January 1901, Alfred Deakin, Attorney-General and later three times Prime Minister of the commonwealth, pointed clearly to the likelihood that bitter controversy would arise in Australia because "a considerable proportion of the electors of the Federal Parliament are not yet really allied in sentiment nor ripe for concerted action."[2]

There was ample justification for this expectation in the nearly fifty years of independent history which all colonies but Western Australia had enjoyed. During the time, each had been free to develop along its own lines. Ties with the mother country were often more important than those with other Australian colonies. There had been many attempts (some of them successful) at cooperation, but intercolonial relationships had exhibited a high degree of rivalry. Tariff policy had varied from the free trade of New South Wales to the high protection of Victoria, and these differences had led to a long dispute between those two states and South Australia over border duties along

---

1 See chapter 10 by Ron Norris and also J. A. LaNauze, *The Making of the Australian Constitution* (Melbourne, 1972).
2 A. Deakin, *Federated Australia*, ed. J. A. LaNauze (Melbourne, 1968), pp. 7-8.

the River Murray. The same states had been arguing for fifteen years over the use of the Murray waters, while four separate "wars" over railway rates had been going on for years as the four eastern mainland colonies sought to attract trade from neighbouring territories to their own ports.[3]

The mere addition of a new government with jurisdiction over the whole territory of the continent would not solve all this. Federation did not and could not involve a complete break with the past. As Deakin told his English readers, the prejudices of years could not be dissipated by an act of parliament.[4] Some of this rivalry, amounting at times to antagonism, was bound to be transferred to the new relationship with the commonwealth government, especially since the constitution necessarily transferred areas of jurisdiction from states to commonwealth, thus reducing the effective scope of their quasi-sovereignty.

Where the meaning of the constitution was clear, there was little trouble. But since the constitution was only a general statement of principle, it was necessarily vague on many points and room was left for confrontation over a variety of issues, some fundamental and others of the most trivial and ephemeral character. Life was breathed into the new body politic in an atmosphere charged with parochialism, misunderstanding and the inevitable desire of politicians to protect or extend their spheres of influence and their own *amour propre*. The early years of Australia's federal history were a period of tension, but the union survived the strain, though the intentions of the founders were modified in the process.

The seven Australian governments were forced into administrative contact over a wide range of matters. The constitution, as accepted, imposed only an interim financial settlement; the postal, defense and customs departments were immediately transferred to the new government, but others like quarantine, census and statistics and meteorology would be transferred later under separate agreements. The property belonging to these departments had to be transferred with them and compensation paid to the states. A site had to be found for the federal capital. Unless the new system was to be impossibly expensive, and it had been promoted on the ground that it would cost no more per head than a dog license, the federal government would have to rely on the states to perform many services for it until the creation of a full federal establishment was warranted.[5]

3 The view of S. R. Davis that "by the time federation was consumated in 1901, the practice of inter-colonial consultation had become an integral feature of intergovernmental relations in Australia" (S. R. Davis, "Co-operative Federalism in Retrospect," *Historical Studies* 5 [November 1952]: 216), is not in dispute. Unfortunately, consultation all too frequently led not to cooperation but to recrimination.
4 Deakin, *Federated Australia*, p. 10.
5 Many of these matters are referred to in D. I. Wright, *Shadow of Dispute* (Canberra, 1928). See especially chapters 2 and 3.

Fundamentally, three areas of dispute were of vital importance, affecting, as they did, the legal and political status and the power of the seven governments. Two of these had not (and could not have) been anticipated by the founders: the right of the states to continue to communicate directly with the Imperial government through the state governor, as in the past, and not to send all communications through the governor general; and the right of the various governments to tax each other's officers and goods. The third, already referred to, was the financial link. Some discussion, however brief, of these three issues is essential before it is possible to outline the general trend of commonwealth-state relations in the pre-World War I period.

Before federation, the correct channel of communication between a colonial government and the Imperial government was through the governor of the colony to the Colonial Office. At the first federal convention (1891) the question of the continued appropriateness of this was raised. As a result, a clause was inserted in the draft constitution making the governor general the sole channel of communication.[6] An attempt by Deakin and Edmund Barton, later first Prime Minister of the commonwealth, to insert a similar clause at the Adelaide session of the 1897-98 convention found little support.[7]

In this regard the prefederal rights of the states were left completely unimpaired. This was in tune with the desire for a coordinate system of federation with each government exercising quasi-sovereignty within its own sphere. To make the head of the federal government the sole channel of communication would have been to suggest subordinate status for the states, and few were prepared to do that. Nor was it realized by many, as yet, just how greatly one sphere of government would impinge on the other.

In the light of this, it is surprising that Joseph Chamberlain, Secretary of State for Colonies, should, as part of his preparations for inaugurating the new form of government, instruct the states to send copies of their correspondence with the Imperial authorities to the governor general.[8] Probably because his own experience of federal government was limited to Canada, where such a proposal would certainly not have been untoward, Chamberlain failed to realize the political and constitutional implications of his instruction.

The South Australian authorities, always sensitive about matters of status, saw these implications at once and regarded them as vitally important. They protested forthwith to Chamberlain through their

6 For a detailed discussion of the whole complex channel of communications questions see ibid., chapter 1.
7 *National Australian Convention Debates* 1891, pp. 850-64; *Convention Debates* (Adelaide, 1897), pp. 1177-81.
8 Secretary of State for Colonies to Governor N.S.W., 2 November 1900, Commonwealth Archives Office (CAO), CRS A8, 02/403/1.

Governor, Lord Tennyson, while the Premier, F. W. Holder, set about organizing support from the other states. After a dispute lasting seven months (with the commonwealth joining in against the states), a compromise was reached which modified the pre-federal position only slightly. The states were to send copies of communications to the governor general only when they touched on federal or interstate interests. They were to be the judges of this, though the Colonial Office might overrule them if necessary.[9]

This was a sensible solution to the federation's first "diplomatic" dispute. It preserved the real interests of all parties, as well as being true to the general tone of the constitution. The compromise remained undisturbed while Lord Hopetoun and his successor, Lord Tennyson, both of whom had been involved in working it out, held office as governor general.

Lord Northcote assumed office early in 1904 and, from the outset, showed himself an ardent advocate of extension of the commonwealth sphere. On this question he acted with such precipitancy, and on the basis of so little local knowledge, that it must be assumed either that he worked from concepts developed elsewhere (perhaps during his governorship of Bombay), or that someone in the Colonial Office had been urging centralist notions on him. The nature of the response he drew from the Office suggests that the former view is correct.

A series of despatches during 1904-06 failed to persuade the Colonial Office to alter a compromise which it believed was working satisfactorily.[10] In any case, by this time, such an atmosphere of suspicion and mistrust had grown up between states and commonwealth that a new solution could only have been imposed by fiat from Downing Street, if at all. A Chamberlain might have attempted it; but he was long since gone. His successors were not prepared to fight a needless battle with six state governments at the same time and for minimal gains.

The states fared less well on a related but different issue—the channel of communication to be used in matters involving external affairs. Several such questions arose in the period under consideration, some involving complaints by foreign authorities against an Australian state, others involving complaints by Australian citizens against foreign governments.[11] One must suffice as an example here.

9 This correspondence is in the National Library of Australia (NLA), Australian Joint Copying Project (AJCP), reel no. 2138, Colonial Office (CO), 418/9 Nos. 54, 12336 and 16705; AJCP 2142; CO 418/13, No. 7849. See also South Australian Archives (SAA), GRG 24/6, 01/327.
10 NLA, AJCP 2164, CO 418/31, No. 9044, ibid., 2169, CO 418/36 No. 28154; ibid., 2170, CO 418/37, No. 42154; ibid., 2176, CO 418/44, No. 12371; ibid., 2177 CO 418/45, No. 43464.
11 For a detailed treatment of several of these incidents see Wright, Shadow of Dispute, chapter 1.

The *Vondel* case arose in 1901-02 from a Dutch complaint against the alleged refusal of the South Australian authorities to fulfil certain obligations under the Anglo-Netherlands convention of 1856. When Chamberlain asked the commonwealth government to investigate the allegations, the South Australians refused to reply to inquiries, asserting that they would only do so when approached through the constitutional channel, the state governor. For the commonwealth, Deakin, acting as Prime Minister at the time, asserted only that the commonwealth was *A*, not *The*, constitutional channel.

After a full exchange of views, Chamberlain, advised by Sir John Anderson, his most senior official, decreed that, so far as other communities were concerned, federation had created in Australia a single political community for which the commonwealth alone could speak. That government was responsible for everything occurring within Australia and affecting any external community, and communications concerning such matters must pass through its hands.[12]

This was a curious view for the time—for the commonwealth government was certainly not an independent government with international status. Any foreign government seeking redress for an incident occurring in Australia was bound to look for satisfaction, as the Dutch had on this occasion, to the Imperial authorities. That granted, there was much to be said for direct communication with the state concerned, which alone could provide information or punish an offending official. Chamberlain's view certainly went further towards a unitary system of government than did the constitution or most contemporary Australian opinion, including that of Deakin. Again, he (or Anderson) may have been misled by his experience with Canada.

Ultimately, a decade of debate on the various aspects of the channels of communication question led to the conclusion that the states were not subordinate to the commonwealth in matters within their competence, but the area of that competence had been reduced in a way which many believed had not been intended. The states were surprised by this unexpected reduction. They seemed to detect some loss of status and they resented it. They felt that they had, to an extent, been subordinated to their own creation. On the other hand, it had been established that the commonwealth was not merely the agent of the states for the more efficient management of the customs, postal and defense departments. It had an independent authority, and in all matters of external affairs and foreign trade its supremacy was assured. The commonwealth had made good use of an opportunity created by the Colonial Office to improve its position vis-à-vis the states.

12 The most important document is Secretary of State for Colonies to Lieutenant Governor S.A., *Commonwealth Parliamentary Papers* (*CPP*), 2 (15 April 1903): 1165-67.

The role of the Colonial Office, and its emissaries in Australia, the governor general and state governors, is of interest. It is clear that Downing Street desired as much centralization as possible in its communications with the various Australian governments. It would be naive to suggest that this was a mere matter of administrative convenience. Far more likely, Chamberlain and his senior adviser, Sir John Anderson, had their own conception of what the new political order in Australia should mean. This they had no doubt developed from their own participation in a unitary system of government, and from their experience with the Canadian system which, on matters like this, was hardly comparable with the Australian. Working from this foundation, they tended to read into the constitution things which were not there. The men on the staff of the Colonial Office with the best appreciation of the true situation were A. B. Keith and H. E. Dale, but in the early years their advice was not often accepted.

In spite of this centralizing tendency, the Colonial Office did back down over the question of general communications (and, indeed, supported the states when Northcote tried to reopen the question), probably because the true constitutional position could hardly be denied once the states had made their concurrent and vociferous protests. In the matter of communications dealing with external affairs, the position was more obscure. Since its own interests were involved, the sovereign imperial government was in a position to lay down a procedure to be followed. That is exactly what it did. If the reasoning in Chamberlain's despatch of 15 April 1903 was not beyond question, his authority was. He could not prevent the states from continuing to raise and argue about the question. Nor could he prevent his successors from making some small tactical withdrawals in actual practice. But his theory, clearly and forcefully laid down, did continue to govern the discussions. The part played by Northcote in the years 1904-06 has already been discussed. Almost equally prominent at the outset was the South Australian governor, Lord Tennyson, who was concerned to preserve the rights of the state governments and governors. It appears, from his correspondence, that he did not merely follow the wishes of his constitutional advisers, but that his actions were also motivated by personal conviction.[13] No doubt the fear of loss of status was not more pleasing to a governor than to a politician. Quite different was the attitude of his successor, Sir George Le Hunte, who tried to persuade the South Australians that they could adopt Northcote's later proposals without loss.[14] But he had never experienced the pre-federal situation as Tennyson had.

13 See especially Tennyson to Sir Samuel Griffith, 12 August, 1901, Griffith Papers, Dixson Library, Add 453.
14 Sir George Le Hunte to Premier S.A., 12 October 1905, NLA, AJCP 2172, CO 418/39, No. 42156.

However the decisions were reached, and for whatever motives, it seems likely that the solution in each case was a reasonable one and that it met the needs of the developing situation. While the link of empire and commonwealth remained, and while state governors continued to be appointed directly as the monarch's special representatives, it was clearly appropriate for the states to retain the right of direct communication in all purely local matters. If there was only doubtful constitutional justification for making the commonwealth the sole channel of communication in external matters in 1902-03, then the passage of time and the achievement by Australia of an independent international status, rendered such a solution necessary in the long run. But this does not mean that Chamberlain, Anderson and Northcote must be credited with unusual political prescience.

The legal relationship of states and commonwealth was provided for in chapter V of the constitution. Section 109 (commonwealth laws to prevail over those of the states in any case of inconsistency) and section 114 (both states and commonwealth forbidden to tax each other's property) provide the key. Yet there was still need to define the position more closely. This was done in a number of cases settled in the courts during the first decade.[15]

A series of cases in the early years determined that commonwealth officers were liable neither for state stamp duty on receipts given for their official salaries, nor for state income tax on those salaries.[16] Curiously, although these might all have been settled on the basis of the two constitutional provisions mentioned above (sections 109 and 114), the High Court chose to rely on the famous American precedent, *McCullogh v. Maryland*, and to adopt its doctrine of "immunity of instrumentalities." This doctrine held that with a federal constitution it was necessary to read individual clauses in the wider light of the whole document. Thus the legislative and executive powers of the states must be considered in a way which did not fetter the free exercise by the commonwealth of its powers, and the taxes referred to, which might be used in this way were, by necessary implication, invalid.

This rule, almost necessarily, proved to be a two-edged sword. In the *Railway Servants' Case* (1906),[17] the Court decided that it was reciprocal and that it protected state instrumentalities and servants from federal interference. Furthermore, the rule was not limited to taxation

15 The main cases are discussed in D. I. Wright, "The Political Significance of 'Implied Immunities' 1901-1910," *Journal of the Royal Australian Historical Society* 55 (December 1969): 380-99.

16 See especially *D'Emden v. Pedder* (1903-04 *Commonwealth Law Reports* (*CLR*), p. 91; *Deakin v. Webb* and *Lyne v. Webb*, ibid., p. 585. See also *Wollaston's Case* (1902-03), 28 *Victorial Law Reports*, p. 357; *Webb v. Outrim* [*sic*] (1907); *Appeal Cases*, p. 81; *Baxter v. The Commissioners of Taxation N.S.W.* (1907), 4 *CLR*, p. 1087.

17 *Federated Amalgamated Government Railway and Tramway Service Association v. N.S.W. Railway Traffic Employees Association* (1906), 4 *CLR* (Pt. 1), p. 488.

but might extend, as in this case, to the exercise of the commonwealth's arbitration power.

A similar protection was given to the states by the rule known as "implied prohibitions," first enunciated in *Peterswald v. Bartley* (1904) and established in *Barger's Case* (1908).[18] This doctrine sprang from the view that a general consideration of the constitution led to the conclusion that the founders intended a wide area of "reserved authority" to be left to the states. Thus, the specific grants of power to the commonwealth should be so construed as to minimize their interference with the reserved powers of the states.[19] In the cases cited, this was used to give state jurisdiction full ambit in questions relating to intrastate trade, industry and employment.

As a result of the adoption of these principles of interpretation, developed from the general nature of federalism, the states were given far greater protection then would have been the case had the Court relied solely on the specific provisions of the constitution, and this protection continued to be enjoyed until the doctrines were finally rejected in the *Engineer's Case* (1920).[20] This situation may fairly be attributed to the personal, political and juridical philosophy of the three original justices of the High Court, Sir Samuel Griffith, Sir Edmund Barton and R. E. O'Connor. All three had been heavily involved in the creation of the constitution and each came to his new position holding firmly to the concept of federal balance, of the free and unfettered exercise by all governments of their constitutional powers within the limits of their jurisdiction.

But there was one area of constitutional decision in which the states fared less well even though the same principles were apparently involved. Before federation, the states had, of course, not levied duties on their own imports. This was not merely a question of expediency in financial administration, but the consequence of the accepted view that the crown was exempt from such imposts. They assumed that this immunity would continue when the control of customs passed to the commonwealth. This expectation was immeasurably strengthened by section 114 of the constitution which specifically forbad the taxing of state property by the commonwealth.

The first commonwealth government decided to take a hard line on the question and, as a deliberate act of policy, failed to include an

18 *Peterswald v. Bartley* (1904), , *CLR*, p. 497; *The King v. Barger* (1908), 6 *CLR*, p. 41. See also *Attorney-General for N.S.W. v. The Brewery Employees Union of N.S.W.*, ibid., p. 469; *Huddart Parker and Co. Pty. Ltd. v. Moorehead* (1908-09), 8 *CLR*., p. 330; *Federated Sawmill, Timber Yard and General Woodworkers Employees Association of Australia v. James Moore and Sons Pty. Ltd. and Others* (1909), 8 *CLR*, p. 465.

19 See also G. Sawer, *Australian Federalism in the Courts* (Melbourne, 1967), pp. 127-28.

20 *Amalgamated Society of Engineers v. Adelaide Steamship Co. Limited* (1920), 28 *CLR*, p. 129.

exception for the states in its tariff bill, thus leaving the whole matter to be settled on the actual wording of the constitution.

The states were bound to react strongly to this action. The question involved far more than the obvious issue of privilege, though that alone would have been enough to bring on a challenge. Once the guaranteed return of customs duty under section 87 of the constitution came to an end (after 1910) the matter would have grave financial implications. The cost of the states' large public works programmes would be increased substantially.

In April 1903, in the state Supreme Court, New South Wales challenged the commonwealth's right to levy such duties and won. The Court held to the established doctrine that goods the property of the crown were not liable to duty.[21] The commonwealth, which wished to have the matter settled by the yet to be established High Court, did not appeal to the Privy Council, but continued to collect duties on state imports. A long wrangle, mainly with New South Wales, but involving all states by implication, followed, but no positive action was taken for several years.

In the early afternoon of 21 August 1907, J. H. Carruthers, Premier of New South Wales, anxious to cut the Gordian knot, sent a team of carters to Darling Island wharf to collect a shipment of wire netting imported by his government and on which no duty had been paid. The Collector of Customs protested, but no notice was taken until he gathered a group of clerks from his office and they sat or stood on what remained of the netting so that it could not be moved. In his desperate attempt to capitalize on the strong antifederal feeling which he knew had arisen in New South Wales as a result of a recent upward revision of the tariff (New South Wales was traditionally a free trade state) and the commonwealth's failure to select a site satisfactory to the state for the federal capital, Carruthers had committed an act which had to be illegal whatever the situation with regard to the payment of customs duties.

The High Court eventually settled the question by deciding that its rule of "implied immunities" had no application to powers which had been conferred on the commonwealth in express terms and which, by their nature involved control of some operation of the state governments. The regulation of trade and commerce with other countries was such a power.[22]

21 *Attorney-General of N.S.W. v. Collector of Customs for the State of N.S.W.* (1903), 3 Supreme Court (N.S.W.), p. 115.
22 *Attorney-General of N.S.W. v. Collector of Customs for N.S.W.* (1908), 5 *CLR*, p. 818. See also minute, 7 November 1904, by Secretary of Attorney-General's Department (Commonwealth), with Prime Minister to Premier N.S.W., 18 November 1904, CAO, CRS A33, Vol. 8, pp. 108-20; *Sydney Morning Herald and Daily Telegraph*, 22 August 1907; Wright, "The Political Significance of Implied Immunities 1901-1910," note 15

This decision must have been a serious shock to the states, though there was no logical reason why the Court should not impose limitations on a doctrine which was judge made. More difficult to understand was the reasoning that section 114 of the constitution did not give the states a specific guarantee in this instance since the tax involved was paid on the act of importation and not on the goods themselves, an argument which would appear to be invalidated by the simple fact that the tax varied in proportion to the quantity of goods imported.

There can be no doubt at all that the result of the decision was to weaken the legal position of the states vis-à-vis the commonwealth, and to increase their fears about their financial future when section 87 should terminate on 31 December 1910. Yet, politically, the Court's decision was essential. In Australia, state governments have traditionally undertaken a wide range of activities which may involve the importation of goods or equipment. Not all of these were (or are) strictly governmental in character. To leave such large importers free from the restraints of the customs power would have been to wreck the commonwealth's policy of tariff protection and would have involved an even more serious interference with its legitimate functions than the states actually suffered as a result of the decision.

No part of the debate between states and commonwealth in the prewar years was more significant (either immediately or in the long term) than that concerned with financial relations.[23]

Inevitably, the establishment of a federal system of government involves a division of both resources and responsibilities between the centre and the regions. Rarely, if ever, is it possible to match these divisions perfectly. It is never possible to allow for future shifts in the balance of responsibilities or changes in the relative importance of sources of income.

In the Australia of 1901, the major responsibilities shifted to the commonwealth involved little expense. The Customs Department and the Post Office paid their own way, while defense expenditure was of little significance. The states retained the major expenses —development, education, public health and the like.

With regard to resources, the division was quite different. Unless federation was to be rendered nugatory, and the much desired common market lost, the collection of customs revenue had to be given to the central government. This was the major source of revenue for every colony except New South Wales. Direct taxation was generally

above. It was not necessary for Carruthers to commit this illegal act to test the matter. He could have begun action in the High Court at any time during the preceding three years.

23 A detailed account of the major aspects of this question may be found in D. I. Wright, "The Politics of Federal Finance: The First Decade," *Historical Studies* 13 (April 1969): 460-76.

very light, and a sudden shift to it from indirect was certainly politically inexpedient and probably impracticable, in some parts of the country at least.

For five of the colonies, then, it was essential that they should have some guarantee that the commonwealth would return to them a revenue sufficient to meet their continuing obligations (many of which were fixed obligations for interest on money raised on the London market over the years for developmental purposes). The sixth colony, New South Wales, dreaded such a guarantee, since it seemed to imply the early demise of its treasured free trade policy—and New South Wales wanted at least the opportunity to try to persuade its new partners to implement that policy on the national level.

To compound the problems of the founders, the decade before 1900 was one of drought and depression over much of the continent, but, because of important gold discoveries, one of unprecedented prosperity in Western Australia. Nowhere was the period "normal," and this abnormality meant a dearth of reliable information on the basis of which the future might be forecast. Nor could anyone anticipate at that state the probable effects of interstate free trade and the new and as yet unknown uniform tariff.

The constitution as implemented provided that until 31 December 1910 the states collectively were entitled to have returned to them not less than three-quarters of the net customs and excise duty raised by the commonwealth (section 87). This clause provided the guarantee sought by the five states, while the limitation with respect to time was imposed at the wish of New South Wales (at a special conference of premiers in 1899 after that colony had failed to accept the proposed constitution at the first federal referendum in 1898). The limitation was one which all states would quickly learn to regret. Revenue was to be distributed to the states, for a period of at least five years after the imposition of uniform duties, on the basis of a "bookkeeping system" (sections 89 and 93), whereby the expenditure in each state by the commonwealth was deducted from the revenue collected therein and the balance returned to the state each month. After the expiry of the five-year term, the commonwealth could return the money on any basis which it deemed fair (section 94), and after the termination of section 87 it could determine, on its sole responsibility, what moneys were to be returned to the states. There was a further provision (section 96) for special grants to be made to any state which found itself in temporary financial difficulties.[24]

Some of these provisions were hardly federal in nature, involving as they did a rigid keeping of accounts between the states for several years. But they did face up to political reality, for it is improbable that

---

24 For an extended and able account of the actual operation of this clause see R. J. May, *Financing the Small States in Australian Federalism* (Melbourne, 1971).

federation could have been achieved at that time without some such complicated procedure. At least there was nothing "theoretical" or "imported" about them; they were specifically designed to meet existing Australian conditions and prejudices. And if the solution was only interim, that was hardly the fault of the founders, but was rather the necessary consequence of the circumstances outlined above.

From 1903 to 1909, the question of future financial relations was constantly before the politicians and was the major subject of discussion at the annual premiers' conferences. Deakin, in a well-known passage in one of his *Morning Post* articles, recognized that while the states had been left legally free they were "financially bound to the chariot wheels of the central Government." This, he believed, would eventually allow the commonwealth to gain a supremacy over the states which the constitution had not intended.[25]

The state premiers also recognized the importance of the question. Their need to achieve some final settlement before section 87 terminated, and the commonwealth could deal with the matter unilaterally, weighed heavily on them. Unfortunately, some of them seemed to think that while section 87 remained operative they retained some kind of right to force their own solution on the commonwealth. There was no constitutional justification whatsoever for this.

A variety of solutions was suggested to the financial puzzle, including again making section 87 permanent in its operation, and the payment of an adequate annual fixed sum to the states by the commonwealth.[26] But the first positive action was taken towards the middle of 1908 when the Deakin-Lyne government passed the important *Surplus Revenue Act 1908* to enable it to keep its full quarter of the customs and excise revenue instead of returning to the states at the end of each month any unspent portion of this money. The purpose of the act was to allow the commonwealth to accumulate money (by the simple expedient of transferring unspent revenue to trust accounts) for coastal defense and for the federal old age pension scheme, due to begin in July 1909.

The significance of the move was not lost on the states which opposed the act strongly and contested its validity in the High Court where it was declared *intra vires* of the constitution. This hostility was not due primarily to the amount of revenue they expected to lose immediately. The sum was small and could have been covered by other means.[27] In any case, they could only rely on receiving it until the end of

25 Deakin, *Federated Australia* 12 May 1902, p. 97.
26 Reports of annual premiers' conferences appear in parliamentary papers. The best source is *South Australian Parliamentary Papers*, but many also appear in *CPP*. See also the correspondence in SAA, GRG 24/6, 05/682.
27 The total sum in excess of their three-quarters returned to all states together to 30 June 1908 was EA6-7 millions ($A 12-14m). For the challenge to the act see *The State of N.S.W. v. The Commonwealth*, 7 *CLR*, p. 179.

1910. Partly they resented the high handed way in which the commonwealth passed the act in June 1908 and, by making it immediately effective, unexpectedly reduced the expected returns to the states for 1907-08, returns which had long since been committed. More, the move was indicative of a change in commonwealth thinking. It suggested a new determination to find the means to carry out national policies thought to be desirable regardless of the feelings of the states. This high-handedness convinced the states that they were likely to receive short shrift when section 87 terminated.

In August 1909, a premiers' conference agreed that after the termination of section 87 the states should receive a payment of twenty-five shillings ($2.50) a year per head of population. This agreement was to be submitted to a referendum for inclusion in the constitution as a permanent arrangement.[28]

Many, including the Labor Party, opposed the scheme, not because of the very limited growth factor, which strikes the modern mind as a crucial disadvantage, but because its permanent nature tied the hands of the commonwealth and might become an embarrassment should customs revenue decline.

The people did not approve of the constitutional amendment, and the Labor government of Andrew Fisher, swept to power in the election of 13 April 1910, passed an act granting the same amount for ten years and until parliament otherwise provided.

This change allowed the commonwealth to retain greater freedom of action than would otherwise have been the case as it now required only another ordinary act of parliament to vary the arrangement. For their part, the states lost little of real value, since they were given reasonably security and, in any case, by 1920 inflation had halved the value of the grant and a constitutional provision would have been an embarrassment to them. But they could not know this in 1910, and they resented the alteration vigorously.

What the change did assert strongly, and this can hardly be overemphasized, was commonwealth dominance in the field of federal financial relations. This was no more than the constitution as finally accepted allowed, though it was out of step with the real intention of the conventions of 1891 and 1897-98. It was also a portent for the future and to this writing there has been no sign of real willingness to recede from the position of dominance thus assumed. Deakin's prophecy, referred to above, was now well on the way to fulfilment.

Another, different, matter must be touched on: the commonwealth industrial powers referendum of 1911.[29] From 1908, the fight-

28 The 1909 conference was held in secret and no official report was ever issued. However, a substantial reconstruction from a variety of sources, may be found in Wright, "The Politics of Federal Finance," pp. 469-74.
29 For a more detailed account of this (and the related referenda of 1913 and 1919) see

ing platform of the Labor party had indicated its desire to alter the division of power established by the constitution in relation to monopolies, arbitration and industrial regulation generally. This desire was largely the consequence of the failure of Deakin's "new protection" legislation. The "lib-lab" alliance of the early years had sought to pass on the benefits of "old," or tariff, protection to the workers by various legislative devices, but in a series of cases the High Court had declared all these attempts to be beyond the commonwealth's constitutional competence, which was limited to trade and commerce between the states and with other countries. The power of the commonwealth parliament to deal with monopolies and of the Commonwealth Arbitration Court to settle industrial disputes was similarly limited.[30]

Few denied the need for some amendment of the constitution in this respect. P. Mc.M. Glynn, Attorney-General in Deakin's "Fusion" government, produced a lengthy memorandum on the subject in August 1909,[31] and advocated some changes. But such men were not prepared to go as far as the Labor party and, in particular, as M. W. Hughes, Attorney-General in the Fisher government and the man responsible for the new proposals.

Fundamentally, Hughes sought to wipe out the constitutional restriction on the commonwealth's trade and commerce power, to gain power to nationalize or regulate any industry, business or service, to make laws concerning corporations and to create, regulate or control any corporation (including those formed under state law, and also foreign corporations), and, finally, a virtually unlimited extension of the commonwealth arbitration power.[32]

Hughes saw no antagonism between his measures and the maintenance of true state rights. The essential feature of the federal system was that each of the regional and central governments should be free to exercise its quasi-sovereignty in its own sphere. The actual division of powers was irrelevant provided that this condition was not infringed. The existing constitution violated true federal principles with regard to the trade and commerce clauses since there was no clear line of demarcation between state and commonwealth spheres and neither government could act effectively. There was no real danger of unification in the proposals to rectify this situation.[33]

Others saw the matter differently. For Deakin the proposals were a savage violation of the constitution he had helped to build, and a long step towards unification. The success of a federation depended not

C. Joyner, *The Commonwealth and Monopolies* (Melbourne, 1963). See also L. F. Fitzhardinge, *William Morris Hughes*, 1 (Sydney, 1964).
30 See the cases referred to in notes 17 and 18 above. The *King v. Barger* was especially significant.
31 Memorandum by P. McM. Glynn, CPO, 1910, Vol. 3.
32 Joyner, *The Commonwealth and Monopolies*, appendix, pp. 96-97.
33 *CPP*, 63 (11 December 1911): 4697ff.

only on the separation of the spheres in which the various governments exercised their quasi-sovereignties, but "upon the nice relation and co-ordination of the parts; on the preservation or development of local, as well as national, centres of interest, discussion, and opinion." Every federal government had to tread "a narrow path with an abyss on either side"—undue decentralization of government leading to weakness in the national spirit, and over-centralization leading to "democratic despotism." Rob the state parliaments of the powers proposed, which made up four-fifths of their work, and the whole nature of the Australian constitution would be changed.[34]

Deakin was right. Had these changes been affected, which they were not, they would have caused a dramatic shift of power to the centre. Labor men in the states were as aware of this as he. W. A. Holman, Attorney-General of New South Wales, was the most able and forthright of these, and he did his best to defeat the amendments.

The issue here was not merely one of state rights versus centralism. The polarization of Australian politics into a two-party system reflected a social dichotomy which was important in this issue. Deakin might be concerned with constitutional balance, and Holman might argue that the states were the proper governments to introduce social experiments, but others were anxious to further the vested interests of either capital or labour. Such men knew little about the finer points of constitution making and would not have been impressed had they known. Hughes, who had taken no part in the constitutional conventions and had fought against the adoption of many of the provisions of the constitution, was the leading representative of a new generation of politicians who were unwilling to let constitutional forms stand in the way of the achievement of their social ends. That is why this particular issue had to be fought out in the party room, in the parliament, and, above all, on the hustings, rather than in conference or in correspondence between premiers, as with the other issues discussed above. Nevertheless, the whole campaign for change was symptomatic of an increasing trend towards centralism and the incident showed the states again under considerable pressure to maintain their constitutional position.

The Australian constitution clearly intended to establish a system of coordinate federalism, with the various governments equal in status and independent within their own spheres. Some men at the time lamented this, preferring either greater decentralization or greater centralization, but none denied that this was the kind of federalism actually created.

Geoffrey Sawer has pointed out that this coordinate federalism, with its special characteristic of no formal subordination is much easier

34 Ibid., pp. 4802ff.

to apply among the regions or units themselves than it is between the units and the centre. The national government usually controls the main sources of wealth, the military power, the international stage; its laws prevail if there is a clash. More important, "there is a qualitative difference between the position of the Centre and that of a Region, because the Centre represents within its area of competence both the people of the particular Region and those of all the other Regions."[35]

Perhaps, then, there was never any real probability that the intended position could be maintained in its integrity. Among contemporary observers, Deakin, at least, held this view. He argued that in the Australian circumstances either commonwealth or states would be master, in spite of the interdiction of the constitution. From the beginning, he noticed a trial of strength proceeding quietly, with the states challenging the commonwealth individually and each being defeated in its turn. They were unable to combine against the commonwealth because of their own divergent interests. There was no doubt in his mind that the commonwealth would eventually dominate—its financial superiority would be the true source of this dominance. Without any formal change in the constitution, a "vital change" would come about in the relations between commonwealth and states. The commonwealth would acquire "a general control over the States" and every extension of political power would be made by its means and would go to increase its relative superiority.[36]

It is the argument of this chapter that Deakin's prophecy, one which he made with great equanimity, was fulfilled, and for the theoretical and practical reasons given by Sawer. By World War I (or even by 1910), the broad outlines of the future development of relations were becoming clear.

As a result of the solution forced on them in the seemingly endless debate about channels of communication (external affairs), the states had been made to accept a measure of subordination in political status. Yet, clearly, they were not as completely subordinated as they would have been if the commonwealth government and the Colonial Office had had their way entirely and had been able to compel all communications to be sent in copy to the governor general regardless of their subject matter. The Melbourne *Argus* had said early that there was a real sense in which "[t]he independent Governor . . . [is] the sign and symbol of the sovereign state."[37] That is why the states fought this issue so bitterly, and at such great length, and why they were bound to resent such inroads as were made into the governor's power to communicate directly and without supervision with the imperial authorities.

35 G. Sawer, *Modern Federalism* (London, 1969), pp. 117-18.
36 *Morning Post*, 12 May 1902; Deakin, *Federated Australia*, pp. 94-98.
37 *Argus* (Melbourne), 13 June 1902.

Legally, their status vis-à-vis the commonwealth was more satisfactory. Sawer has pointed out, correctly, that in this period (1901-13), while the political trend was to the left and favoured the extension of commonwealth powers, the judicial trend in the High Court favoured federal balance.[38] The Court's twin doctrines of "immunity of instrumentalities" and "implied prohibitions" undoubtedly gave the states a better position than they could have hoped for from the strict application of sections 109 and 114 of the constitution, as we have seen above. But its failure to insist on the same principle with regard to customs duties on state imports, as well as its peculiar interpretation of section 114 as applied to this matter, was a bitter pill and one which damaged the states' conception of their status considerably. It was undoubtedly true that they remained better off than they were to be after 1920 when the decision in the *Engineer's Case*[39] swept away reciprocity in immunity from interference, except as provided for by section 114. But when the states contemplated the actual losses sustained in the customs duty cases, and the fact that in the income tax cases they had avoided loss only as a result of commonwealth action and not as of right, they were inclined to forget the counterbalancing gains and to feel that they had been compelled to accept a legal status inferior to that of the commonwealth.

We have also seen that the interim financial settlement under the Surplus Revenue Act 1910 left the states subject to commonwealth power, and that while this was in accord with the decision of the 1899 premiers' conference, which had limited the operation of section 87 to ten years, it was not with the original intentions of the conventions of 1897-98. If the final position had not then been determined, it was at least clear that the growing needs of the commonwealth, and the total lack of real bargaining power held by the states, would ensure that it would not change to their benefit.

To some extent, the states had initially regarded the commonwealth as their agent. This was most clearly expressed in a memorandum written in 1906 by Thomas Price, Labor Premier of South Australia. He wrote that "the Commonwealth Government is practically an agency for the management, under a united control, of three departments... (Customs, Post Office and Defense) of all the six States."[40]

This was, admittedly, an extreme statement, but the underlying idea was widely held. The same attitude was clearly implicit in the action of the premiers in arranging conferences annually and inviting

38 Sawer, *Australian Federalism in the Courts*, p. 89. See also his *Australian Federal Politics and Law 1901-1929* (Melbourne, 1956), p. 58.
39 See note 20 above.
40 Memo., Premier S.A. to Governor S.A. (for Secretary of State for Colonies), 12 December 12 December 1906, SAA, GRG, 24/6, 06/519.

the prime minister to attend to discuss certain matters with them and in forwarding to him for action such resolutions as concerned the commonwealth . The states retained the major constitutional functions and expected that they, not the commonwealth, which lacked both prestige and administrative resources, would provide political leadership.[41]

By the war, they were certainly not prepared to regard the commonwealth as their master, but they did have to acknowledge its power. Most of them would probably have agreed by then with words written by Deakin in 1903, that they were becoming aware of "their incapacity to assail the infant Federation even in its cradle, and of the weakness of their defenses against its future aggressions."[42] They would certainly have denied that it had ever been intended that the federal government should work in as wide a sphere as it had assumed by then.

But the commonwealth government had advantages in the attempt to extend its power, simply because it was the national government which represented, and controlled, all the people—this is Sawer's qualitative difference between central and regional governments. The ability of the state governments to resist was necessarily inhibited by the occasional conflict of their own interests and their natural tendency to concern themselves primarily with those pieces of supposed aggression which affected them individually, while paying little heed to those which did not. In Australia at least, the commonwealth did not have to divide to conquer. It only had to exploit the preexisting divisions.

As well as having these natural advantages, the commonwealth always displayed considerable eagerness to increase its own power and to enlarge its sphere of action. As early as May 1902, the Governor General, Lord Hopetoun, expressed the opinion to one of the state governors that it was too inclined to centralize and grab power.[43] It must be remembered that at this time Edmund Barton, architect and chief apostle of the coordinate "balance," was still Prime Minister, and in many senses the government was still feeling its way. In 1908, the retiring Governor of Victoria, Sir Reginald Talbot, publicly if politely, expressed a similar view and pointed out that the nature of the continent and population of Australia made too great a degree of centralization undesirable at the time.[44]

Alfred Deakin was ready to stretch commonwealth power to the furthest extent of its constitutional limits, but not beyond. In 1902, commenting anonymously in the *Morning Post* on his own political activity, he noted that he was taking "the largest views of the powers and immunities of the Commonwealth." Writing in the same medium

41 Davis, "Co-operative Federalism in Retrospect," p. 219.
42 *Morning Post* 26 June 1903; Deakin Papers, NLA, MS. 1540.
43 Entry for 11 May 1902 in Lord Tennyson's diary, Tennyson Papers, NLA, MS 479/2.
44 *Advertiser* (Adelaide), 3 July 1908.

in 1906, he pointed out that those who looked for the time when every truly national function would be in the hands of the commonwealth and the states would be restricted to purely local matters had "no more zealous and consistent ally than the present Prime Minister."[45] Also in 1906, the *West Australian* commented, a little sourly, that "[t]here is no more ardent advocate of the extension of the Federal domain than the Prime Minister."[46]

This is not to suggest that Deakin was in any sense a unificationist. He was not. He believed sincerely that the states had a definite sphere of action in which they might operate legitimately and independently of the commonwealth. He further believed that when differences of interest arose between the two spheres of government they should be settled by discussion rather than by the commonwealth acting unilaterally to force its views upon the states. This was illustrated clearly in the negotiations about revenue transfers. But he always remained the ardent apostle of Australian nationalism that he had been during the nineties when he had spoken and worked for federation to the full extent of his powers. Thus it was hardly surprising that he favoured a strong central government and resisted whatever seemed to encroach on its legitimate area of operations, either actual or potential. This general outlook also helps to explain why he was not prepared to agree to the changes sought by Hughes in 1911.

Some thought that until 1908 Deakin was largely under the thumb of the Labor party, which held the balance of power in the commonwealth parliament, and that it was that which inclined him to take so large a view of commonwealth power.[47] It is true that he did show a greater inclination to consider the interests of the states over the financial settlement in 1909, when he was allied to the conservative forces in parliament, than he had on other matters in 1906-07, when he was dependent on Labor support. But many other factors were involved, and in any case there is no evidence that Deakin, the nationalist, ever needed to be pressured into taking a large view of commonwealth power. His biographer, J. A. LaNauze, was unable to detect any undue influence on him, while L. F. Fitzhardinge commented concerning the programme which Deakin implemented in these years that it "represented the ideals common to both parties," (that is, liberal protectionists and Labor).[48] In the context of commonwealth-state relations at

45 *Morning Post* 12 March 1902; Alfred Deakin Papers, NLA, MS. 1540; ibid., 18 September 1906, Deakin, *Federated Australia*, pp. 187-88.

46 *West Australian* (Perth), 23 April 1906.

47 See, for example, Sir Samuel Way to Bishop of Bath and Wells, 29 June 1908, SAA, PRG 30/5, Vol. 12, p. 135; Way to Lord Tennyson, 9 January 1906, Tennyson Papers, NLA, MS. 479/5/181. In 1907 Sir John Forrest, a conservative protectionist, resigned from Deakin's cabinet over the question of Labor dominance. See also *Hobart Mercury*, 10 June 1908.

48 J. A. LaNauze, *Alfred Deakin* 2 vols. (Melbourne, 1965), II: 409-10; Fitzhardinge, *Hughes*, I: 169.

least, it may be better to see the role of the Labor party not as one of
dominance, but as one of "supporting the Commonwealth against the
particularists of the States."[49]

Deakin was not the only man to work for the extension of the
commonwealth sphere. Among his own subordinates, Sir William
Lyne, a radical liberal, and at various times Minister for Home Affairs,
Trade and Customs and Treasurer, held similar views. It was Lyne who
was primarily responsible for the way in which the Surplus Revenue
Act 1908 was implemented to the consternation of the states. At other
times he was responsible for some very heavy-handed diplomacy with
the premiers. On a different level, the third Governor General, Lord
Northcote, has also been shown above to have done his best to ensure
the subordination of the states.

Until 1910 Labor members had little opportunity to implement
their views directly, though they had, as we have seen, supported
Deakin in every move to extend commonwealth influence. In March
1909 Andrew Fisher, briefly Prime Minister, attended a premiers'
conference called to discuss financial relations, but he refused to be
drawn into discussion with the premiers, though his own ideas on the
subject were firmly settled. (Labor policy on the question had been laid
down at a conference in 1907). Quite obviously he was telling the
premiers that they should mind their own business—he was not prepared to discuss with representatives of the states a matter which he
believed the constitution committed to the commonwealth parliament,
and to that alone, for settlement.

When Deakin, again Prime Minister, proposed to attend the premiers' conference of August 1909, a number of Labor members,
among them W. M. Hughes, protested that at least the government
should first receive instructions from parliament as to the attitude
which it should take at the conference. They appeared to fear that
these discussions would mask an attempt to coerce the federal parliament or to take its proper work out of its hands.[50]

Hughes' attitude was to become more important after Labor's
electoral victory in April 1910. We have already seen what it was. He
wanted a strong central government, with ample powers to carry out
the social reform legislation which was the core of its policy. It is
improbable that he was in any sense a doctrinaire unificationist. For
him, government was a means to an end, and if the existing constitution stood in the way of achieving those ends then it must be changed.
Notions of "federal balance," "co-ordinate jurisdiction," and "state
rights" could not be allowed to impede social progress. More particularly, he saw a strong centre as the best means to achieve that progress

49 B. R. Wise to J. H. Catts, 5 January 1907, Catts Papers, NLA, MS. 658/I/1/6.
50 *CPP*, 50 (11 August 1909): 2323, 2335; 51 (31 August 1909): 2793.

because it promised a way round the notoriously conservative upper houses then existing in every state parliament.

Commonwealth ministers, naturally, did not always see themselves as seeking to extend the limits of federal power. Rather, they felt that they were resisting the last assaults of parochialism. Barton's comment on a despatch written in 1902 by the Lieutenant Governor of Queensland, Sir Samuel Griffith, would have seemed to them to have had more general application: "Provincialism dies a slow death, and all that is possible for a Federal Government, which must not nurse it, is to ease the pangs of its passing."[51]

It is certainly true that in the early years of the federation, the regional governments were more concerned than the central government about their rights and privileges. Adoption of the federal system implied willingness to surrender only a limited range of powers. The regions knew that any power that they let go by default would never be recovered. But, even allowing for this, the Australian states did at times go beyond the point where the defense of legitimate constitutional rights shaded over into parochialism. The action of the New South Wales premier in the wire netting case, discussed above, was a good example of this kind of behaviour. The ultimate in perversity for perversity's sake was probably South Australia's dogged exclusion of the commonwealth for well over a decade from certain rooms in a building legally transferred to the commonwealth with the Postal Department.[52]

The most important arguments—those concerning channels of communication, mutual noninterference and finance, which did most to determine the trend of Australian federalism—involved all states, though to varying extents. But there do seem to have been some differences in the attitudes of the states to the commonwealth .

Before World War I, and in sharp contrast with its attitude in the sixties and early seventies, Victoria was clearly the most cooperative, and least likely to indulge in wanton recriminations against the "aggressions," supposed or real, of the commonwealth . There were good reasons for this. It had the substantial advantage of having temporarily "captured" the parliament and government of the commonwealth.[53] No doubt the adoption at the national level of its system of tariff protection also counted for something. Above all, both of these considerations gave it an immense psychological victory over its rival, New South Wales, and there can be no doubt that this added much to the sourness of the latter state.

51 Minute for Governor-General by Prime Minister, 3 April 1902 (with Governor-General to Secretary of State for Colonies, 5 April 1902), NLA, AJCP 2150, CO 418/18, No. 18503.
52 Wright, *Shadow of Dispute*, pp. 103-05.
53 Ibid., chapter 2.

In September 1903, Lord Tennyson, then Governor General, wrote to his successor, Lord Northcote, that "the jealousy between Victoria and New South Wales is stronger than any feeling against the Commonwealth. . . ."[54] Possibly it would be more accurate to suggest that New South Wales tended to identify the commonwealth as a Victorian institution. Over the years, nothing contributed to this feeling more than the failure of the commonwealth to select a site for the federal capital acceptable to New South Wales. Early attempts to place this virtually on the Victorian border, where, though nominally in New South Wales, as required by the constitution, it would have fallen primarily under the influence of Melbourne, created great bitterness in the senior state. Only in 1909, with the passage of the act placing the capital at Canberra, and, therefore, reasonably within the ambit of Sydney, did it feel that justice had been done.[55] All this may go some way to explain the early dissatisfaction felt by New South Wales with the new system.

But this was not all. New South Wales had J. H. Carruthers as its premier for three crucial years (1904-07), and he had always been a provincialist at heart. At the convention he had fought the South Australians bitterly over the Murray waters question.[56] His attitude to the commonwealth was best summed up by T. R. Bavin, who wrote Deakin's column in the *Morning Post* while the Prime Minister was at the Colonial Conference of 1907, and who commented that Carruthers was "a hopeless irreconcilable as far as the Commonwealth is concerned" and that he saw "a Commonwealth assassin behind every political bush."[57]

When Carruthers resigned office he was succeeded first by his Attorney-General, C. G. Wade, who was not much less parochial than he. Later, when the Labor party came to power in 1910, its most powerful minister, the deputy Premier, W. A. Holman, was another strong advocate of state rights.[58]

South Australia was not far behind the "mother" state in recalcitrance. Its high degree of self-consciousness and its arrogant assurance of the rightness of its cause made it particularly sensitive about matters

54 Tennyson to Northcote, 16 September 1903. Tennyson Papers, NLA, MS. 479/3, pp. 73-75. The whole letter is an interesting commentary on the state of the federation at the time.
55 This incident is dealt with at length in Wright, *Shadow of Dispute*, chapter 2. See also G. E. Sherington, "The Selection of Canberra as Australia's National Capital," *JRAHS* 56 (June 1970): 134.
56 J. Quick and R. R. Garran, *The Annotated Constitution of the Australian Commonwealth* (Sydney and Melbourne, 1901), p. 196.
57 *Morning Post*, 4 June 1907, Deakin Papers, NLA, MS. 1540.
58 On Holman's early career as a state righter see D. I. Wright, "W. A. Holman and the Commonwealth, 1898-1911, the Early Career of a Labor State Righter," *Labour History* 18 (May 1970): 40-49. For his later battle with Hughes over the industrial powers referendum see C. Joyner, *Holman v. Hughes* (Gainesville, 1961).

involving status. The Attorney General of South Australia in the early years, J. H. Gordon, was the man who had joined issue most strongly with Carruthers over the question of the Murray waters. He was ably backed up by his Premier, J. G. Jenkins, and by Sir Samuel Way, Chief Justice and Lieutenant Governor of the state, who administered the government during a long and vital period from mid-1902 to mid-1903, between the time when Lord Tennyson was made acting governor general and when his successor as governor arrived in Adelaide.

It is worthwhile considering briefly the means by which the states sought to defend their interests and "rights." The constitution created a body specifically as a "states" house: the federal Senate. It is not appropriate to consider this body in any detail here, but it may be said that throughout its entire history it has only fitfully and intermittently fulfilled this function. The reasons for this are complex. It has always been directly elected by the people, and senators have thus felt themselves responsible to their immediate electorate rather than to the reigning government or parliament of their state. More important, it quickly divided on party lines, as did the House of Representatives, and loyalty to party has overshadowed loyalty to state on most occasions.

Before the first World War there was yet another reason why it could not become the vehicle used by the states to defend their interests. The Senate is essentially a legislative body, while most of the issues over which the question of supremacy was fought out were primarily administrative. The one exception was the industrial powers referendum which had a strong legislative component, but this was raised at a time when the Labor government was backed by an overwhelming Labor majority in the Senate. Given the nature of Labor discipline, there was no likelihood of trouble for the government from that quarter.

The state governments soon felt the need for another, more direct, means of putting their views before the commonwealth, and of exerting pressure on it. None was provided in the constitution and there was no reason why any should have been, since the plan was for coordinate federalism. The theory was that neither commonwealth nor state governments would impinge on each other's sphere of action so no method of dealing with such incursions was necessary. (Even the Senate was seen rather as a means by which the less populous states could defend themselves against the more populous, which would dominate the House of Representatives, than as one by which the states generally defended themselves against the commonwealth.)

But in prefederal days, the premiers had met from time to time in conference to discuss matters of common interest and this tendency had been strengthened by the movement towards federation. There was no reason why they should not continue to do so, except that it might be presumed that the important matters of common concern had been surrendered to the commonwealth. In fact, in the years before 1914, the chief matters of common interest were commonwealth-state relations.

Conferences were held annually, on the average, and, with the exception of the first, in November 1901, were called by the states.[59] Indeed, they became something of an antifederal caucus. Usually only state ministers were "members," though commonwealth ministers were invited to attend some sessions to discuss questions on which the former had already tried to reach a measure of agreement. As far as possible (and too often it was not possible) the states sought to present a common front to the enemy. Before 1908, once the conference was over, individual states approached the commonwealth about resolutions which interested them. From that year, the New South Wales premier was appointed executive officer and he approached the commonwealth on behalf of all states and reported back to the next conference.

There is no doubt that, except in 1901, these meetings represented a state initiative for state purposes and that one of the main purposes was to develop a joint attitude in their negotiations with the commonwealth, or in opposition to its proposals. Even in 1901, when the prime minister called and chaired the meeting, it was held in response to vigorous state protests against a proposed piece of commonwealth legislation affecting their interests. It was only after many years had passed that the commonwealth captured this conference and made it too a part of the machinery through which it now asserts its superiority over the states.

There was, however, another side to the premiers' conference, one which contrasted strongly with that discussed above. If it was an opportunity for the states to express their opposition to the commonwealth, it was also an occasion which could lead to cooperation with the centre. In Australian federalism there has always existed this same paradox, of vigorous defense of state or commonwealth "rights" on the one hand, and of willing cooperation over a wide range of matters on the other. The premiers' conference has been (and continues to be) a main venue for both.[60]

When the Australian colonies federated on 1 January 1901, most men thought they had created a system of government in which the keynote would be balance. Instead, and as a result of the "open wrestle for mastery"[61] in the years before World War I, involving many matters but especially finance, the states found it increasingly difficult to keep

59 For the conference reports see note 26 above.
60 See also Davis, "Co-operative Federalism," pp. 219-23.
61 *Morning Post*, 12 May 1902; Deakin, *Federated Australia*, p. 94.

pace with the commonwealth . Even before war took a hand and aided the process of centralization, it was becoming clear that they would not be able to maintain the equal and independent status given them by the constitution. Nothing has happened since to reverse the trend established in those early years.

XIII

Race as a Factor in the Strengthening of Central Authority: White Australia and the Establishment of Compulsory Military Training

THOMAS W. TANNER

> "*L'état, c'est moi,*" proclaimed Louis XIV, *Le Roi Soleil*, in words which even the earliest avatar of Atum-Re would have recognized as a factual statement. But it was only with the French Revolution that the state, under a republican mask, actually achieved in its system of universal conscription the powers that Louis XIV did not dare to exercise completely....[1]

Probably the most forceful statement a government can make about its authority is the introduction of military conscription. In the above quotation, Lewis Mumford points out that conscription was first introduced in modern times by republican France; Louis XIV, for all his might and majesty, did not have the power to risk making such a demand.[2]

The central government in Australia enacted compulsory military training just nine years after federation. This was not quite the same as conscription,[3] but nonetheless it was an unambiguous statement of the

---

1 Lewis Mumford, "The City and the Machine," in *Towards the Ideal Society*, ed. James A. Ross (Toronto, 1969), p. 12.

2 Modern conscription dates from the French Revolution and the Conscription Act of 1798 passed by the Directory. See Theodore Ropp, *War in the Modern World* (New York, 1962), pp. 115, 148, 153, 198-99, etc. K. S. Inglis, "Conscription in Peace and War, 1911-1945," *Teaching History* 1, part 2 (October 1967): 6-7.

3 Compulsory military training or "compulsion," such as operated in Australia before the First World War, differed from "conscription" in several respects. The compulsory trainee retained civilian status and continued to work during his period of military obligation. Drill was carried on during weekends, in the evening, and at camps held for a specified number of days each year. The conscript, however, becomes part of the standing army and is a full-time soldier during his two, three, or five years with the forces. Fundamentally, compulsion was a scheme for training

supremacy achieved by the federal power in less than a decade. It was all the more remarkable because Australia was the first English-speaking nation to implement such a measure in peacetime, and because of the Australian's celebrated distaste for authority, regimentation and imposed discipline. A study of the ideas and events which prompted the introduction of compulsory military training thus serves as a theme, and a benchmark, in understanding the balance of power in Australia's federal system.

*   *   *   *   *

Australians welcomed the twentieth century with a bold show of confidence and a newly minted federation. They could boast of "a nation for a continent and a continent for a nation" while also expressing pride in being part of the British Empire—mightiest the world had ever known. Security seemed assured, at least as soon as the new parliament could tidy up the immigration laws and institute a scheme of national defence. But there was no real hurry about the state of defence. Britain ruled the waves, and Australia's island continent was secure behind the Royal Navy.

There was, however, the matter of immigration. Racial feeling had been present in Australia at least since the 1850s. During that decade of gold rush and feverish immigration, Chinese had arrived in Australia by the boatload. By 1857, Victoria had a mixed population in which one adult male in seven was Chinese.[4]

The various colonies soon instituted restrictive laws to reverse the trend to a multiracial Australia. Queensland did some backsliding as the Kanaka trade flourished along with the sugar industry, but by 1901 even tropical Australia seemed convinced that their continent should be reserved for the "white race." Sentiment for immigration restriction may have contributed to the success of the federation movement. By 1901 "white Australia" was settled policy which remained only to be enacted into federal law.[5]

George Reid, leader of the Free Trade party in the new commonwealth parliament, wrote the following comment on the first federal election campaign: "The doctrine of a "white Australia"—a term I invented—would have been a leading question if it had not commanded almost universal assent."[6] All parties, Free Trade, Labor and Protectionist, believed that Australia had to be kept for people of British or European stock.

civilians in the techniques of warfare so that they might defend the homeland; conscription is a method of reinforcing the standing army by obliging young men to forsake civilian life for a period of continuous service with the forces.

4 Russel Ward, *Australia* (Englewood Cliffs, New Jersey, 1965), p. 58.

5 Herbert Ira London, *Non-White Immigration and the "White Australia" Policy* (New York, 1970), p. 12.

6 George Houstoun Reid, *My Reminiscences* (London, 1917), p. 203.

Parliamentarians used three basic arguments in favour of white Australia.[7] Some pointed to the economic threat posed by low-wage coloured labour. Others underlined their belief in racial inequality, while a third group praised Australian society and sounded a warning against the introduction of elements which could not be assimilated into the commonwealth which they were helping to make a reality. Labor Senator J. C. Stewart of Queensland pictured the task facing parliament in an image of permanence and purity: "If we are going to succeed as a nation, we must build upon the foundation of a white Australia. We must lay the foundations of this young country in the purest and whitest of marble without streak or strain."[8] The member for Capricornia, Free Trader Alexander Paterson, was less evocative and more exact. He believed that white Australia was "a question involving the purity of the race—freedom from foreign diseases, contamination, and consequent degradation."[9] J. C. Barrett, a Victorian Labor senator with a great interest in education, stressed the seriousness of the matter. He evoked "the teaching of history" and warned fellow senators "to be very careful to see that we leave no loop-holes for inferior races throughout Australia."[10] Immigration restriction was obviously a matter which had to concern the central government. It was also an issue, and soon a policy with the force of law, which worked to strengthen the central authority in the evolving Australian federation.

Although racist sentiments were usually intended when members used the word "inferior," it also, and more creditably, expressed a resolve that there would be no second-best or lower order in Australian democracy. According to Protectionist J. H. McColl:

> . . . we want to keep Australia for people who will live and think and work under the same conditions as ourselves. We find that, whenever races of a lower type are admitted into a country, they sink down to a condition of slavery and serfdom, and that this condition of things breeds a lazy aristocracy, and demoralizes the whole community, by leading to the physical, moral, and even religious degeneration of the people.[11]

In 1901, an aristocracy was as distasteful as a coolie class to most Australians. Their vision of society had no place for either the very rich

7 A careful study of the sentiments expressed is found in Michael V. Moore, "Unequal and Inferior: The White Australia Policy in the First Commonwealth Parliament" (bachelor's honours thesis, University of New England, 1962).
8 *Commonwealth Parliamentary Debates* (CPD) 1 (1901), 266-67. Stewart had been a coal merchant in Glasgow before immigrating to Australia. He arrived in Rockhampton in 1888 and was an alderman for North Rockhampton by 1892.
9 Ibid., p. 693. Paterson retired from politics in 1903 and died in 1908. His occupation was that of "manager."
10 Ibid., p. 368.
11 Ibid., p. 525. J. H. McColl represented Echuca, Victoria. Formerly a mechanical engineer, he had given that up to become a member of the firm of McColl and Rankin, legal managers.

or the very poor; white Australia was, to a significant degree, an attempt to legislate against social extremes. Barriers of race were not to interfere with the devleopment of an egalitarian society in Australia.

Before the end of 1901, the Immigration Restriction Act and the Pacific Island Labourers Act had secured uniformity of race for Australia. Repatriation arrangements and the lack of nonwhite women assured that coloured people would form a steadily decreasing percentage of the population. The new central government had embarked on a course which would guarantee its increasing predominance as Australia's sense of security was eroded by a series of external events. The white Australia policy was soon to be viewed as a prime reason for increased self-sufficiency in defence. And the federal government inevitably gained significance, importance and power.

Australia could have chosen a variety of ways to strengthen her defence force. The eventual outcome of the discussion, however, was determined to a large extent by the persuasiveness of advocates favouring one particular scheme. They started early; the case for compulsory military training was voiced in both houses of parliament during the first debate on defence. Henry Dobson, a Tasmanian, introduced it into the Senate while W. M. (Billy) Hughes made sure the lower house was conversant with the idea, and the ideal behind it.[12] Hughes saw the meagre volunteer forces proposed by the defence bill as "wretchedly inadequate to repel a foreign invader" but, worse still, they were "sufficiently strong to overawe on some occasions—perhaps on many—the citizen in pursuit of constitutional reform or in the maintenance of civil liberty and right."[13] In order to retain democracy in its true form, citizens must be prepared to fight their battles themselves. Hughes reminded his colleagues that "the responsibility of citizenship carries with it the right of defending one's country."[14]

As the chief exponent of compulsory military training, Billy Hughes saw his scheme as necessary for efficient defence and for the maintainance of democracy. If citizens really did rule, they must be ready, willing and able to defend their power. Knowing human nature, however, Hughes realized that some Australians would have to be prompted to fulfill their sovereign democratic role. Thus he argued for compulsory military training so that all would be properly equipped to be citizens of the commonwealth. He espoused "compulsory democracy" and in doing so, argued for increased centralization as well. Although, in a sense, the ultimate aim of his scheme was the complete dispersal of power to the citizenry, the effect in the short run

12 Henry Dobson (1841-1918) was a lawyer who had been Premier of Tasmania from 17 August 1892 to 14 April 1894.
13 *CPD*, 3 (1901), 3296.
14 Ibid., p. 3297.

(compulsory period) was sure to be an accumulation of authority in federal hands.[15]

In 1901, however, parliament could not muster much enthusiasm for any military scheme, conventional or radical. It is safe to say that, in general, Australians were aware of the increasing activity in their "neighbourhood," but they were not apprehensive for their national security. Alarmists existed, of course, but defence expenditure in the colonies decreased before federation, and the first federal defence bill was withdrawn after a debate which extended over 205 pages of *Hansard*. A feeling of comfortable isolation was still in the air, and Britain's maritime supremacy made worry unnecessary. As the *Sydney Morning Herald* put it in concluding the editorial "New Year's Day 1901," Australia confidently awaited the future.[16]

The first significant diplomatic development in Australia's neighbourhood after federation was the signing of the Anglo-Japanese Alliance in 1902. This was generally received by Australians with satisfaction. Some wondered about its implications with regard to the white Australia policy, as Japanese immigrants were excluded as completely as other non-Europeans, but most were inclined to trust Britain's good intentions. They agreed with the "sweet reasonableness" of the *Sydney Morning Herald* when it said: ". . . though the susceptibilities and interests of our new ally must now receive more consideration, there is little reason to suppose that the Commonwealth will be asked to discriminate in any legislation on behalf of Japan."[17]

Consensus was not achieved, however, and the *Bulletin* put the contrary view most forcefully. Thundering its unalloyed nationalism, the "bushman's bible" proclaimed that "the alliance marks a further move in the process of converting the British Empire into a nigger state."[18] Republican flutterings animated its conclusion: "It is no easy matter to remain white, and yet remain part of an Empire that grows blacker every day."[19]

Such heresy was a long way from the sentiments expressed by members of parliament when they discussed the defence bill of 1903. There was virtually no apprehension that Japan might use her position as Britain's ally to win special privileges for her citizens in white Australia. If anything, parliamentarians felt that Australia was more secure because of the Anglo-Japanese alliance.[20] Enemies seemed few and far away; Australia was safe behind her oceans and the British fleet.

15 *CPD*, 14 (1903), 2269.
16 *Sydney Morning Herald*, 1 January 1901, p. 14.
17 Ibid., 13 February 1902, p. 4.
18 *Bulletin* (Sydney), 22 February 1902, p. 6.
19 Ibid.
20 D. C. S. Sissons, "Attitudes to Japan and Defence 1890-1923" (masters thesis, University of Melbourne, 1956), p. 24.

If any one year can be chosen, 1905 marks the beginning of growing apprehension in Australia. On 27 May of that year, Japanese warships virtually annihilated Russia's Baltic fleet as it was on the last lap of an epic voyage to Vladivostock. The British Admiralty judged the victory as equivalent to Trafalgar.[21] It was apparent that a new power had matured in the East.

Now that Japan was so obviously a power of rank, some Australians began to take a new interest in defence. On 5 September 1905 over fifty men gathered at the Australia Hotel in Sydney to found the Australian National Defence League. This remarkable pressure group was supported by conservatives and Laborites alike.[22] It played a significant role in promoting concern for defence, especially among members of parliament, and had a large part in creating a climate for the enactment of compulsory military training in 1909.

The Defence League was never a mass movement. Its chief organ, *The Call*, was well written, carefully edited by William Morris Hughes, and expensively produced. Members of parliament appear to have received *The Call* free; League propaganda was directed carefully and with effect. The League capitalized on the degree of centralization present in Australia and was rewarded for its efforts. It used and thus promoted the power of the central government.

Within the houses of parliament, Henry Dobson and Billy Hughes functioned as something of a two-part pressure group in support of compulsory training. Both made annual speeches to Senate and Representatives respectively, pointing out the need for increased defence and promoting compulsory training as the best scheme for the Australian situation. As time passed and apprehension grew, their presentations were granted more attention and received increased support. In company with the Defence League, Dobson, and especially Hughes, could take credit for making the idea of compulsion familiar to the members of parliament. When drastic changes in the defence scheme seemed called for, compulsory training had already been presold.

On 10 February 1906, King Edward VII christened the battleship *Dreadnought*. Britain's latest technical triumph was so clearly superior to any previous warship that she became the standard of comparison and provided the generic name for all her imitators. A revolution in naval design, strategy and tactics dates from her launching. Richard Hough has claimed: "The *Dreadnought*'s launching was unquestionably the most important naval event leading up to the First World War."[23] In 1905 British superiority in predreadnought battleships was over-

21 Arthur J. Marder, *The Anatomy of British Sea Power: A History of British Naval Policy in the Pre-Dreadnought Era, 1880-1905* (Hamden, Connecticut, 1964), p. 441.
22 Names of those present at the foundling meeting are preserved in the minutes of the Australian National Defence League, War Memorial, Canberra, pp. 3-4. An account of the meeting will be found in *Sydney Morning Herald*, 6 June 1905, pp. 7-8.
23 Richard Hough, *Dreadnought: A History of the Modern Battleship* (London, 1965), p. 2.

whelming—forty-four to Germany's sixteen.[24] The advent of the *Dreadnought*, however, allowed Germany by quick imitation to compete with Britain on nearly equal terms, and, as L. C. F. Turner has put it, "injected a harsher note into Anglo-German relations."[25]

Besides ordering the construction of *Dreadnought*, Sir John Fisher, Admiral of the Fleet, instituted several other changes designed to increase the effectiveness of the Royal Navy. The reform which probably had the greatest effect on Australia's sense of security involved the redistribution of naval forces. In the days of sailing ships, it had been necessary to distribute squadrons widely in order to protect trade, but steamships, cable communications, and later wireless, lessened the need for many isolated squadrons. The whole system of stationing was rendered obsolete by the Japanese Alliance (1902), the French Entente (1904), and by the growth of the German navy after 1901.[26] In order to meet these changed conditions better, Fisher undertook to concentrate the major portion of the fleet in home waters and reduce the number of squadrons from the 1904 total of nine to the more realistic figure of five.

Taking careful note of geography, Fisher became convinced that "five strategic keys lock up the world!"[27] Britain held all five: Singapore, the Cape of Good Hope, Alexandria, Gibraltar, and Dover. Fisher organized the navy into five great fleets to hold these keys. The new fleets were capable of rapid concentration, and their creation meant the withdrawal of squadrons from the Pacific, South Atlantic and North American stations. Australia was to be protected by the fleet whose strategic centre was Singapore, but it was clear that the antipodes were broadly exposed. For the most part, Britain's strongest ships were stationed near the United Kingdom; the Pacific was virtually abandoned to the United States and Japan. It is little wonder that Australians began to feel increasingly uneasy about defence in general and naval defence in particular. And it was inevitable that this increased interest in national security focussed more attention on the federal authority.

Most Australians did not expect to be abandoned by Britain. A strong national self-image allowed them to combine imperial allegiance with a deep feeling for their own land. These strong bonds with Britain worked to quell fears voiced by some nationalists that the mother country might not always stand by Australia. But even while it lulled some apprehension, the imperial connection worked to nurture Australian *malaise* by insuring that the antipodes were aware of the

24 A. J. P. Taylor, *The Struggle for Mastery in Europe 1848-1918* (Oxford, 1957), p. 426.
25 L. C. F. Turner, *The Coming of the First World War* (Melbourne, 1968), p. 24.
26 Arthur J. Marder, *From the Dreadnought to Scapa Flow: The Royal Navy in the Fisher Era, 1904-1919*, vol. 1: *The Road to War, 1904-1914* (London, 1961), p. 40.
27 Ibid., p. 41.

English perception of threats being hatched in Europe. The view from London was transmitted "down under" in daily news reports and dispatches. Australians could perceive emerging threats in their own Asian neighbourhood, and they could know a fair share of the fear being engendered in Europe by an increasingly powerful Germany.

Even when they were not prompting their uneasiness by viewing the world from London, Australians could find cause for disquiet thanks to a more subtle bequest of empire. Federation occurred at the end of the historical phenomenon called "new imperialism." Great Britain acquired charge of more than double the population and almost forty times the area of the home islands in the course of a single generation (1870-1900).[28] The myth of imperialism permeated British society. Great parades of men from throughout the empire marked festive occasions, and the sense of conscious superiority found voice in authors like G. A. Henty and Rudyard Kipling. In Australia the myth was also potent, but transformed by the new society so that the imperial hero was not an upper class youth, but the average Australian transported to an exotic setting. The imperial myth of white superiority was democratized in Australia so that all Australians could feel its power, and its terror.

"Myth" wrote Ernst Cassirer, "is filled with the most violent emotions and the most frightful visions. But in myth man begins to learn a new and strange art: the art of expressing, and that means of organizing, his most deeply rooted instincts, his hopes and fears."[29] What hopes and fears were embodied in the imperial myth? For Australians, the hope was bound up in their dreams of a free and equal society over the length and breadth of their continent-nation. They would be masters of their own vast land; a nation of superior people enjoying equality and freedom.

Joseph Conrad showed the darker side of the imperial myth in *Lord Jim*. One brief moment of panic made a lie of Jim's superiority, and he was haunted through the far reaches of empire until his suicide-death. Nobility and idealism were deep in Jim's character, but he betrayed his breeding and was doomed to stand before a coloured man for execution. This was the "frightful vision" of the myth, the lapse that meant death.

What consequences would follow a lapse on the part of Australia? England's neighbours were white; Australia's were swarthy or black. To many Australians the threat posed by Asia was very real, and it was reinforced by the imperial myth. Agitation for a white Australia dates from the 1850s, and the deep fear it reveals prompted Australians to concentrate their gaze on the elements of white superiority so basic to British imperialism.

28 J. A. Hobson, *Imperialism: A Study* (London, 1954), p. 20.
29 Ernst Cassirer, *The Myth of the State* (New Haven, Connecticut, 1946), p. 47.

In the antipodes the imperial myth worked in two seemingly contradictory ways. It strengthened confidence, but it also added to uneasiness by magnifying the racial consciousness of Australians. Nonwhites were regarded as far more loathsome than European people, and the thought of serving under a coloured master or ruler was far more horrific to Australians than was the possibility of being ruled by another white nation. Since Australia was a lonely outpost of European settlement in an area populated by the dark and dusky, her fear of conquest was magnified by racial prejudice, and her resolve to keep the commonwealth white was strengthened by fear as much as it was encouraged by a conviction of superiority.

Myth, by definition, is an imaginative expression of belief. It is frequently the codification of "thoughts too deep for words," the end result of the artist's "raid on the inarticulate." A great multitude of ideas and fears intimately bound up with Australia's apprehension of invasion found expression in a novel by Charles H. Kirmess which was first published in the *Lone Hand* beginning 1 October 1908.[30] The story was released in book form as *The Australian Crisis* in April 1909.[31]

It is impossible to estimate the influence of *The Australian Crisis*. Even the size of the edition is unknown as the records of the printer, Butler and Tanner, were destroyed by German bombing during World War II.[32] But in trying to understand the reasons why Australia adopted compulsory military training, Kirmess' book has real importance; it gives expression to the wide-spread and ill-defined fear which existed in Australian society during the years around 1908. Kirmess expressed the myth in fictional form; he examined the disquiet and produced a work bordering on literature which embodied virtually all aspects of Australian anxiety. His tale of invasion cannot be regarded as a powerful and widely influential work which changed the course of history; it is rather one among many significant symptoms of the growing apprehension which infected Australian thought after 1905.[33]

The Australian Crisis emphasized the tyranny of distance which was and is a fact of life in the antipodes. Australia's remoteness from Britain,

---

30 Charles H. Kirmess, "The Commonwealth Crisis," *Lone Hand* (Sydney), 1 October 1908, pp. 683-91. The last instalment was published in August 1909. "Charles H. Kirmess" is a pseudonym. Neville Meaney maintains that Frank Fox was Kirmess. See Neville Meaney, *The Search for Security in the Pacific, 1901-14* (Sydney, 1976).

31 Charles H. Kirmess, *The Australian Crisis* (Melbourne, 1909).

32 Sissons, "Attitudes to Japan and Defence," footnote 3, section IIId, p. 27.

33 *The Australian Crisis* was not the first nor the only piece of invasion literature to circulate in Australia. In 1897, Kenneth Mackay, Member of the Legislative Assembly of New South Wales, published "a romance of the Asiatic invasion of Australia" entitled *The Yellow Wave*. A play by F. R. C. Hopkins, *Reaping the Whirlwind*, was arousing comment at the same time that Kirmess' book was in circulation. Again the theme was invasion, this time in 1915, but the author's viewpoint was consistently anti-Labor whereas Kirmess was staunchly pro-Labor. See Sissons, "Attitudes to Japan and Defence," pp. 68-69 and footnotes; Humphrey McQueen, *A New Britannia* (Ringwood, Victoria, 1970), pp. 59-60.

proximity to Asia, great internal distances, and poor distribution of population seemed to invite an invasion from the north. Kirmess underlined these geographic realities but built his drama around four main themes which reflected the political and social elements in the widespread uneasiness felt throughout Australia. He maintained that: (1) white Australia was the most important policy for Australians; (2) the English did not understand the Australian devotion to white Australia; (3) when the crisis came, Great Britain would not stand by Australia; and (4) Australia was too weak to defend her racial purity on her own.

Kirmess' novel helps to explain why parliament eventually voted for compulsory military training and an Australian navy. Men in public life appreciated at least some of the perils which Kirmess evoked, and they voted for the 1909 defence bill in order to prevent the unthinkable—a powerless and abandoned Australia forced to submit to Asian occupation of at least some of her territory.

Significantly enough, among the reviews of *The Australian Crisis* which have come to light, the papers with an obviously Labor bias spoke well of the book, while those with conservative leanings were much less kind. The *Bulletin* thought that "Australians who are con- cerned about the future of their country and care for something better than mere time-killing sensations will find the book well worth reading."[34] Similarly, the *Worker* judged it "worth attention,"[35] but the *Sydney Morning Herald* and the *Daily Telegraph* balked at having to accept the British abandonment of Australia. The *Herald* commented that "the initial premise of the author, that Great Britain, even in the hands of Little Englanders, would do anything like this, is ridiculous. . . ."[36] Similarly, the *Daily Telegraph* thought that "the author mars the probability, and also the continuity of his narrative by violent anti-British outbursts depicting the Imperial Government as en- couraging the Japanese against the Commonwealth Government, and imagining a situation at last in which the British warships subsidised by the Commonwealth are used to blockade the Australian ports. . . ."[37]

Here was the debate on compulsory training in miniature. The nationalist papers found nothing to criticize in the imagined British abandonment of Australia, while the conservative and imperialist pa- pers regarded such a suggestion as totally impossible. In many respects, the degree of reverence in which an Australian held Britain seemed to determine his attitude to compulsory training. Of course, some im- perialists saw compulsion as a means of offering greater support to the empire, and some nationalists saw no necessity to increase Australia's

34 *Bulletin* (Sydney), 17 June 1909, red page.
35 *Worker* (Sydney), 18 August 1909, p. 21.
36 *Sydney Morning Herald*, 29 May 1909, p. 4.
37 *Daily Telegraph* (Sydney), 5 June 1909, p. 6.

military strength, but on the whole those who put Australia first generally lined up as compulsionists while those who most revered Britain
supported the theory of voluntarism. Either way their views focussed
on the central government and enhanced its power.

Naval defence came first. After negotiations stretching from 1902
until 1907, the British Admiralty conceded Australia her own naval
force. Once naval policy was settled in a manner which would harmonize with nationalist ambitions, the Prime Minister, Alfred Deakin,
was free to focus his attention on land defence. While in London
attending the 1907 Imperial Conference, Deakin came out unequivo-
cally in favour of compulsory military training.[38] Just before the
Christmas recess of that same year, Deakin announced his
government's committment to a defence policy which included compulsory military training.[39] Opinion had evolved to the point where the
Prime Minister could safely introduce compulsion without taking a
grave political risk.

Alfred Deakin was widely respected, eloquent, and a very skillful
politician. More than most who follow his calling, he deserves the
appellation of statesman. At the time when he announced his new
defence policy, he was the leader of the smallest of the three parties in
the House of Representatives; Deakin Protectionists numbered sixteen
members in the seventy-five seat assembly. Given this political situation, Deakin had to take care not to alienate members of the Labor
party who kept him in office through their support. He also had to seek
a widespread consensus, for his position was vulnerable to public
outcry. His defence policy was radical, yet a careful blend of nationalist
and imperial themes. Deakin knew how to harmonize the conflicting
strains of Australian opinion and how to popularize his views in search
of widespread support.

At this time, President Theodore Roosevelt was trying to prove the
worth of America by sending sixteen battleships first to the Pacific and
thence around the world. In order to stimulate interest in defence and
make his government's policy more completely acceptable, Deakin
decided to invite the American fleet to Australia. Diplomatically this
was a touchy business, for the invitation could come formally only
through the British government. The Admiralty viewed the American
world cruise with something much less than enthusiasm and worried
lest the pugnacious President Roosevelt should turn his ships on
Britain's ally, Japan. Relations between the United States and Japan
were not the most cordial, due to disputes centring on California's
discriminatory practices directed against Japanese residents. As the

38 Australian National Defence League Correspondence (Canberra, manuscripts held
    by Australian War Memorial), George F. Shee to Gerald Campbell, 22 May 1907.
    This is a very vivid account of the meeting where Deakin made his declaration.
39 *CPD*, 42 (1907): 7509-36.

American historian Thomas Bailey has put it, the cruise was "not so much a threat to Japan as a demonstration for the benefit of Japan."[40] It was a search after authority, prestige, publicity; it was a collossal display of the "big stick." Deakin had to overcome formidable British objection in order that the invitation for the fleet's visit might come through proper diplomatic channels. He succeeded, however, and in spite of misgivings on the part of such men as Winston Churchill, the invitation was duly issued on 24 January 1908.[41]

As Australian correspondent for the *Morning Post* of London, Deakin wrote anonymously that the invitation had "made a hit."[42] He took great pains to assure his English readers that the Australians had acted in all sincerity:

> The invitation, though hospitable, was given in deadly earnest and is being warmly pressed on other grounds that are not mentioned. For Australia the entrance of a fleet under the Stars and Stripes into the Pacific is an incident of the utmost significance. Whatever the immediate cause of its going there may be the act is popularly associated with the racial disputes which recently became acute in the West of the Dominion and of the great Anglo-Saxon Republic. Nowhere in the Empire, and perhaps nowhere outside the Southern States of the Union, is the importance of the colour question more keenly realized than in the Commonwealth. The ties of kinship are potent, too, and when these happen to be invoked in connection with a visit of the imposing American fleet to an ocean in which the Union Jack has foregone its old supremacy the significance of the invitation given by our Government assumes its true proportions.[43]

The "colour question"—that was the key. On 7 May 1908, anticipating the visit of the American fleet, the *Bulletin* changed its nationalistic slogan, "Australia for the Australians," to the more inclusive but equally blatant cry, "Australia for the White Man." Britain was abandoning the Pacific to Japan, and white Australia felt terribly exposed. Deakin felt, and well understood, this feeling of nakedness. He also realized that a visit by the American fleet, a positive demonstration in its own right, would promote enthusiasm for his defence scheme. The Australian correspondent wrote on 2 March that Deakin's "invitation to President Roosevelt to spare his fleet to us is already directing public attention into channels which must promote a sounder concep-

40 Thomas A. Bailey, *A Diplomatic History of the American People* (New York, 1955), p. 572.

41 Donald C. Gordon, *The Dominion Partnership in Imperial Defense, 1870-1914* (Baltimore, 1965), p. 213. Winston Churchill was Under-Secretary of State for Colonies in 1908.

42 A collection of Deakin's articles, written anonymously for the *Morning Post* (London), is found in the National Library of Australia, Canberra. In reference to these articles the Sydney date is given, not the date of publication. *Morning Post*, 2 March 1908. The story of these remarkable articles is told in J. A. LaNauze, *Alfred Deakin* (Melbourne, 1965), pp. 347-61.

43 Ibid.

tion of our national obligations."[44] Even before Australia's invitation
was accepted, it was having its desired effect.

After the visit was certain, the nation almost quivered with anticipation. By the middle of July the *Methodist* was concerned lest things
might get out of hand: "The coming of the American battleships is
causing a good deal of stir in this city. It is the opinion of some that
there is just a danger of the thing being overdone."[45]

A visit such as this was unprecedented. Australians reacted as if
they were welcoming the Messiah—and, as some saw it, perhaps they
were. C. E. W. Bean, later Australia's official war historian, wrote of
the Anglo-Saxon race as God's chosen people in a poem called "West
and South."[46] The *Lone Hand's* "American Fleet Number" sported a
full-colour cover showing a great white ship flying "old Glory" plough-
ing through blue seas.[47] From the troubled sky a great white hand
opens, offering the ship as a good and wonderful gift. Norman Lindsay
had captured the extravagant sentiment poured out in thousands of
words.

Inside, the leading article was entitled "The Friendly White
Hand." It gushed a torrent of racism and genuine enthusiasm: "As a
friendly hand across the Pacific comes to Australia the Great White
Fleet. In flashing white it comes, as it were a symbol of a racial ideal to
be upheld, and yet of a pacific purpose. And we Australasians can find
no words great enough to express the thought of our welcome."[48]

It seems highly significant that contemporary Americans referred
to the sixteen white ships as the Grand Fleet, the Atlantic Fleet, or the
Battle Fleet.[49] They did not speak of the Great White Fleet—but Australians did! Racial kinship with the Americans and a common distaste
for the Japanese were recurring themes in the Australian press. The
fleet's symbolic colour drew frequent comment, and many levels of
meaning were drawn from the adjective "white."

The *Lone Hand* was more flamboyant than many Australian journals. That is to say, it put oft-repeated arguments into the most expres-
sive language. Expounding history's task for the white race, the *Lone
Hand* drew upon Darwinian concepts to justify its rejoicing about the
American fleet:

> If there is one clear principle amidst the welter of wrongs and reprisals
> and deceits called "international politics", it is that the supremacy of the
> white man must be maintained. "My country, right or wrong", may be
> questioned as a maxim of conduct, but most will affirm without a

44 *Morning Post* (London), 2 March 1908.
45 *Methodist* (Sydney), 18 July 1908, p. 7.
46 *Sydney Morning Herald*, 20 August 1908, p. 3.
47 *Lone Hand* (Sydney), 20 August 1908. This issue also featured a lavishly illustrated
   history of the American fleet which ran for thirty-seven pages.
48 Ibid., p. 351.
49 Robert A. Hart, *The Great White Fleet* (Boston, 1965), p. viii.

moment's doubt, "The White Race, right or wrong". And for this reason: that it is not possible to imagine any abiding civilization, or any system of government, which is not European. Asiatic dynasties have at various times risen to great magnificence and to splendid material prosperity, but have never yet evolved a stable and democratic power, have never produced that type of civilization which has human liberty and human right as its pillars. The interests of the world are bound up with the White Race which stands in the vanguard of evolution. . . . The Caucasian, with his passion for liberty, for individuality, bears the banner in the van of humanity. If we were to stop to dally with races which would enervate or infect with servile submissiveness, the scheme of human evolution would be frustrated.

The American Fleet which now peacefully invades the Pacific we take as an armed assertion that the White Race will not surrender its supremacy on any of the world's seas.[50]

If lavish celebration is a mark of supremacy, Sydney did everything it could to be supreme. Thousands of pounds were expended on decorations; Pitt Street was adorned with a series of arches, and a replica of the Statue of Liberty rose to a height of five stories in front of the *Daily Telegraph* building. People poured into the city, and the *Sydney Morning Herald* commented: "Only one other event in our history has attracted a gathering so representative in character and so united in sentiment. That was the inauguration of the Commonwealth."[51]

Record-breaking crowds overloaded trams and delayed traffic as half a million people jostled their way to a view of the fleet. August 20, 1908, was fine and sunny; Sydney harbour provided "the world's most beautiful theatre" for a pageant of splendid magnitude.[52] A wave of enthusiasm swept round the harbour as the fleet glided slowly to its moorings. Cannon boomed, church bells pealed a greeting, small boats shrieked their whistles in delight, and powerful American guns thundered a salute. Nothing like this had ever been seen in Australia, and it could never be repeated with the same significance. Other fleets might come and go, but Port Jackson would no longer be virgin and the sense of reunion would never be the same.

Short of a war, the Great White Fleet provided the most dramatic and powerful argument for increased defence which could have been arranged. A similar British fleet would have inspired confidence and inaction. A Japanese fleet could not have provided the sense of identification and positive encouragement, although its shock value would have been greater. Deakin's defence policy received an incalculable boost when Australians saw with their own eyes the might of a modern fleet. And as defence awareness increased, the forces promoting centralization gained strength apace.

50 Ibid., p. 352.
51 *Sydney Morning Herald*, 20 August 1908, p. 3.
52 Ibid., p. 9.

The fleet's departure provoked the *Worker* to further reflection. Focussing on the present, the paper pointed out that if the American ships had come in war instead of peace, Sydney's defences and the British warships present would have been powerless to protect the helpless town. Sydney could have done nothing but endure the agony if twelve-inch shells had rained down on rich and poor alike. This had a sombre lesson for those working for a better world. The *Worker* was honest in its reasoning, and concluded, as the Labor party had in July, that compulsory service and an Australian navy were necessary if the paradise they hoped to build was not to exist "on sufferance only."[53]

The first defence bill incorporating compulsory training was introduced in September 1908.[54] By this time the Labor party had bound its members of parliament to vote for compulsion. Labor acted according to the theory which was central to the whole structure of the party; the very theory which caused them to bind their parliamentary representatives to vote in a specific way prompted them to endorse compulsory training.[55] Labor party organization was designed to insure that parliamentarians voted according to the wishes of the majority of party members—their votes were to reflect a real democratic majority—they were to be compelled to act democratically. Similarly, compulsory military training was to compel young Australians to act in a democratic manner as full commonwealth citizenship was conceived as including the obligation of defending one's country. This same theory was to reach its zenith in 1924 with the introduction of compulsory voting in commonwealth elections.

A shrewd grasp of human nature lay behind the conception of "compulsory democracy." According to Ernst Cassirer, "if man were simply to follow his natural instincts he would not strive for freedom; he would rather choose dependence."[56] It is easier to rely on others than to think and decide for oneself. Because freedom requires thought and decision, it is often considered more of a burden than an advantage. Not all men bother to respond to the demands of democracy, and therefore, it was felt, if a state is to be truly democratic, citizens must be compelled to exercise their privileges. "Compulsory democracy" was to insure by means of law that Australians acted out their roles as responsible citizens of the commonwealth.

The Dreadnought scare of 1909 provided a final boost for the acceptance of compulsory military training by the Australian parliament. It became clear to Australians that German naval power could prevent the Royal Navy from coming to Australia's aid in time of war,

53 *Worker* (Sydney), 27 August 1908, p. 16.
54 *CPD*, 47 (1908): 437.
55 *Official Report of the Fourth Commonwealth Political Labour Conference* (Brisbane, 1908), p. 20.
56 Cassirer, *The Myth of the State*, p. 288.

even if there were a strong British desire to aid the embattled commonwealth. Now Australia had to face the possibility of standing alone to fend off whatever invaders might covet her land and resources. Surely all parts of the country would have to stand together in mounting an effective defence. Although authors such as C. H. Kirmess sometimes imagined situations of peaceful invasion by settlement which went unchecked partly because of secessionist action by Western Australia, the cause for centralization gained as the realities of isolation were recognized.

The Defence Act incorporating compulsory military training received royal assent on December 13, 1909. This marked a new high for the power of the central authority. Soon young Australians were engaged in drill, and, rather belatedly, protest began. It focussed on the compulsory aspect of training, but it was unable to accomplish much change before World War One drew Australia into a very different arena.

During the period from federation to war, Australians moved to translate many of their social ideals into effective legislation. The Immigration Restriction Act was designed to insure that all citizens could participate fully in national life, but it also worked to increase the apprehension Australians felt when assessing foreign threats. As this *malaise* grew, it fostered the power of the central government. The theory of compulsory democracy strengthened the central authority as well; the Labor party, chief exponent of compulsory democracy, focussed much of its attention on the commonwealth. Centripetal forces were built into the popular social concerns of the years 1901-1914. From the very beginning, Australians set the course which has placed Canberra in its present lofty position over the states.

XIV

Imperial Sentiment as a Factor in Centralizing Australian Federalism

J. J. EDDY

The Australian colonies federated at a time of great imperial sentiment, as part of a global empire on whose crises the sun never set.
Indeed, the history of European settlement in Australia and the subsequent economic and political development of the separate colonies had
always taken place against a background of imperial policy, administration, demography and feeling. To that extent, Australian history was a
"footnote to British history." Geographically, England and her antipodes were far apart, but in Australia there developed the kind of
community one would expect to find within a "few miles of Land's End
or the Cinque Ports."[1] Yet, in spite of this, each colony had its own
specific character and its own particular problems when Britain, almost
eagerly, granted self-government in the years following 1850. Furthermore, the Australian colonies were able to adapt to their own requirements the experience of their sister colonies in British North
America, in spite of the dramatic differences which existed between
the continents in which they were placed.

Ironically, the "tyranny of distance" worked for a long time in a
centrifugal way within Australia, and rule from London was not always
a centralizing factor. When the first occupation of the continent was
complete, it became obvious to the imperial authorities that the problems of local communication alone made government from Sydney
impractical. It has been fashionable to say that the Australian states had
their origins in arbitrary lines drawn on the map by Colonial Office
clerks, but this does scant justice to the very real dilemmas faced by
nineteenth century administrators. Sometimes, as in Queensland and
Victoria, it was local demand which forced "separation"; sometimes, as
in Van Diemen's Land (Tasmania) and South Australia, the very con-

1 G. Blainey, *The Tyranny of Distance* (Melbourne, 1966), p. 316.

cept behind the original foundation, and the composition of local society—based in the one colony on a rigid convict system and in the other on a free settler vision—differed radically. In the case of Western Australia, the governor of New South Wales was adamant that he did not want the oversight of its government or development. Separation, once it took place, had many social and political effects, some of which were foreseen, some not. So the centrifugal tendency at once strengthened local community, setting up a tension against premature surrender of government to any central authority. Nevertheless. an essential homogeneity assured the existence of parallel institutions and colonial style. For the imperial power there were decided advantages in devolving sovereignty, expense and responsibility on local communities in the developing colonies, provided that the process did not prevent the satisfaction of those aims which had led to imperial involvement and settlement in the area in the first place and also that it made possible the peaceful and progressive expansion of the various new colonial entities.

In Australia, where the colonies had, despite their geographical and economic diversity, an essential unity and common origin, and where there was no strategic or social profit to the imperial power in a strict separation, the British government also saw great advantage in encouraging a shared development at all levels. Hence, paradoxically, no sooner had Earl Grey acknowledged the need for local autonomy than he set about forming links between the locally autonomous colonial societies. Australia's first governor general was Sir Charles Fitzroy, **Governor of New South Wales 1846-55. Elements of this original unsuccessful "union" were maintained in the mental baggage of those** who in subsequent years turned their thoughts to the future federation, confederation or unification of the Australian colonies. Later, a course of natural growth and change in British-Australian relations seemed to impel the Australian colonies to see their local patriotism flower not as a separate loyalty or fully-fledged nationalism but rather as a linking of destinies against a background of resounding imperial achievements.[2] Only for a few, especially during the eighties, was the radical republican alternative offered by the United States attractive. While there were at least two strands in Australian nationalism—one thrusting towards independence and autonomy, the other looking rather towards Britain and interdependence—colonial nationalism turned out in practice to be easily compatible with positive imperial sentiment. But this complex evolving nationalism, whether republican or imperial in tone, was on the whole centripetal or centralizing. It entered into both the planning and the consequences of federal nation-building. In Australia, despite many political divisions and po-

2 *Age* (Melbourne), 21 December 1889, 11 February 1891.

tential conflicts, geographical isolation and national homogeneity were of vital significance as they could not be in Canada. Though the colonial Irish counted as a powerful and differentiated subgroup, somewhat comparable to the French Canadians, and the aboriginal and Indian minorities raised somewhat similar problems, a unified Australia within the Empire was almost universally acceptable. Although there were relatively few enthusiasts for full-blown imperialism as an idea the permanence of the British connection had long been a fact of life. As much as for federalism, supporters of imperialism were middle class. Imperialism helped coordinate that colonial nationalism which went to make up, in its own subtle way, the content of an emergent Australian personality and self-awareness before, during and after the time of federation and nation-building. In turn the structures of federal nationalism in Australia were encouraged by the Imperial authorities who were able to draw on a vast network of world experience. The imperial factor of common dependence on Britain thus proved to be a centralizing one in many ways, whereas in diversified Canada, with its large French-speaking minority, imperial sentiment often worked against centralization and even encouraged provincialism.

In Australia the imperial link could be exploited or exaggerated by some anti-federal imperialists for whom being British came even before being Victorian or South Australian. Most federalists could, however, strike a balance between local loyalties and imperial demands. The economic, political and historical development of Australia inevitably meant that the middle class colonial politicians who were attracted by wider nationhood had to merge in many ways their accrued local patriotisms. In the long run states rights had to be secondary. In depressing their separatist impact a greater imperial feeling proved to be straightforwardly a positive and centralizing element in nation-building. Radical nationalists and republicans, of course, suspected the Imperial power in all its manifestations, for both theoretical and practical reasons; but they, together with the working classes, often had at the same time reservations about the new and federal nation coming into being, yet that nation soon elicited a strong sentimental attachment of its own which cut across state boundaries. Being suspicious of any centralist moves initiated either by the middle class or by the Imperial authorities, rejected imperial sentiment in so far as it ran counter to their immediate interests or the ideas and principles which they thought important to uphold and defend. Yet, for the most part, the wider horizon and vision provided by the imperial dream was acceptable, and by the time of federation had become a habit. In self-governing Australia, where no rebellion had ever been necessary, colonial sentiment was able to embrace three levels: local, federal and imperial. Even anti-imperialism might in theory have united the federating Australian colonies. This three-tiered sentiment coalesced and thereby aided in passing real political power and authority from the local, historically restricted states into the hands of a more centrally ambitious and logically unified continental nation-state.

The stories of the Australian Natives' Association and the Imperial Federation League illustrate the strength and variety of national sentiment in Australia.[3] The ANA cultivated a unified national feeling, fostered national symbols and, while laying itself open to the charge of "little Australianism" at the hands of the Imperial Federationists did much to spread the idea of "One People, One Destiny." It exerted a powerful influence against mere parochialism and in favour of continental federation, and yet it did not exhaust colonial nationalism. Nor, on the other hand, did the Imperial Federation movement enjoy more than a spasmodic interlude in Australia. Logistics as well as psychology rendered imperial federation highly unlikely even in times of general imperial fervour.

Australia was firmly part of the Empire and would continue to be so after federation. Australian foreign policy, if it could be dignified with that name, was heir to the old colonial patterns and long held views concerning the Pacific, New Guinea and Asia. These views had been conceived against the backdrop of empire. In the 1890s imperial self-satisfaction had reached a high point in Australia as elsewhere. Indeed the coming federation seemed only to strengthen the Empire and to add to that satisfaction. Imperial sentiment certainly helped to unify Australian feelings, though it could not be presumed that the Empire would itself become more centralized. Yet events were about to take place in Europe, Asia and Africa which would tend to consolidate and strengthen the centripetal forces influencing both the Empire and the new federation.

That great imperial event, the Boer War, ineluctably directed Australian, as it did English-Canadian nationalism along Imperial lines.[4] With neither Canada nor Australia likely to become involved in the daily administrative burden of empire, the Imperial connection seemed to offer most of the advantages of "imperium" without many of the disadvantages. The zeal and enthusiasm for empire which peaked during the period of the Boer War brought with it the seeds of frustration and future scepticism, as well as giving radical or liberal critics the opportunity to express their dissent. So, once the war had turned sour, it both accelerated and retarded certain aspects of colonial nationalist awareness.[5] At the time, however, in Australia, special reasons existed

3 C. S. Blackton, "Australian Nationality and Nativism: The Australian Natives' Association 1885-1901," *Journal of Modern History* 30 (March 1958): 37ff.
4 R. J. D. Page, "The Canadian Response to the Imperial Idea During the Boer War Years," *Journal of Canadian Studies* 5 (February 1970): 33-49.
5 Barbara Penny, "The Australian Debate on the Boer War," *Historical Studies Australia and New Zealand*, 1971.

for an upsurge of national feeling. These included not only the imminent coming of federation itself, but also the effects of the dissemination of "popular history" (especially in state schools) and the expression of "racial and national virility."[6] There was satisfaction too in Britain's taking the initiative in foreign affairs, because Australians had favoured a forward policy for some time, especially in the Pacific. Vigorous debates in the colonial parliaments illustrated all the complex current attitudes, hopes and fears, sympathies and prejudices. In theory, Australians who supported Britain against the Boers might seem to be endangering many years of respect for the autonomy of colonial self-government. In practice, they found many special reasons to rally to the Uitlander cause, to support Britain's military initiatives, and to pursue their own strategic and financial interests. For most there was a coming together of "colonialism" and "nationalism." Yet when Alfred Deakin was asked in London in 1900 whether Australians would always be ready with money and men to fight Great Britain's battles, he said firmly that no precedent had been established and that Australians would judge each incident as an individual case. The federal parliament proved a cooler forum, more deliberate and mature than the colonial bodies had been, in the discussion of Imperial issues. But in 1902 the nascent Australian commonwealth was as yet neither powerful enough nor self-conscious enough to exert itself over the peace terms, as it would over the peace treaties following the First World War.

At the same time, the Boer War strengthened the genuinely Australian strand of nationalism. Many Australians undoubtedly found the war tedious and considered foreign policy a luxury for a collection of colonies scarcely able to mature into a single domestic entity, but others took great pride in learning that the colonial troops were equal to their part in defence of the Empire. Indeed, the military exploits of the "dreaded" Australians helped exorcise from the Australian mind the attitude that their own achievements were in all respects inferior to things English. In the tradition of the Australian people, the military experience in South Africa became a vivid thread in the scarlet band which would wind nobly but sadly to Gallipoli, Villers Bretonneux, Crete, Tobruk, Kokoda, Korea and Vietnam. A national myth was made on the veldt, as the Australians gathered in arms for the first time beneath the new federal flag. Imperial strategists, anxious to centralize and rationalize the forces of empire, took careful cognizance of a new military development. Yet in retrospect, it could be argued that Australia's blooding could have been in a worthier and more clearly justifiable cause.

6 S. G. Firth, "Social Values in N. S. W. Primary Schools 1880-1914," *Melbourne Studies in Education* (Melbourne, 1970), pp. 123-59.

After federation, only slowly did a separate and distinguishable Australian nationalism emerge. John Foster Fraser, writing in *Australia: The Making of a Nation* (London, 1910), noted that "you drop from imperialism to something like parochialism in Australia with little of the real national spirit intervening."[7] Richard Jebb, in his *Studies in Colonial Nationalism* (London, 1905), brilliantly described the strange relationship that colonial loyalty to empire had to emergent patriotism, and the causal connection between nationalism and imperialism. He detected too that "Australian patriots are predisposed to imperialism, so long as it connotes the defensive cooperation of white nations rather than the exploitation of Australia by the coloured races, notwithstanding the fact of official jingoism and the Japanese alliance." For him nationalism in its maturity had to have an independence in practice, but he perceived that for the Australian colonies at the time of federation the imperialist and nationalist streams coincided and coalesced. The true "colonial" period of expecting assistance in return for no contribution was already past: the time for active separate independent action had yet to come. For the foreseeable future the colonies would continue to experience lively local rivalry, with petty jealousies still dividing the federated states. The story of federation had been partly that of a surrender of parochialism, but full national identity had yet painfully to evolve. The centralizing force of belonging to a great and powerful international community, the Empire, did not automatically mean that the Australian states would hurriedly merge their local identities in favour of the new commonwealth. Though in Australia the symbols of loyalty, the monarchy and much more, were derived from Great Britain, and through the Imperial authorities might exercise a centralizing influence by forcing the pace a little towards what Deakin called "collective" imperialism, imperial sentiment could be used by very different people—in whose hands it could be a weapon to attack either federal nationalism or state provincialism. There was room in the sphere of imperial feeling as elsewhere for an open "struggle for mastery" between states and commonwealth.[8]

Australia's role in the Boer War had affected eebate on the relationship between federation and Empire. When the Constitution of Australia Bill was introduced into the British House of Commons, Chamberlain accepted that "where the Bill touches Empire interests Parliament occupies a position of trust which it is not the desire of the Empire, and which I do not believe for a moment it is the desire of Australia, that we should fulfil in any perfunctory or formal manner."[9] A week later Asquith, in the debate on the second reading, esteemed

7 P. 12.
8 Pp. 85 and 283. Note also Don Wright, "An Open Wrestle for Mastery," chapter 12 above.
9 *Hansard*, 14 May 1900.

the measure as transcending "in interest and magnitude almost any legislative proposal of our time," yet insisted on imperial questions remaining a responsibility of the home parliament. It is clear that federation, at a time when the colonies all had troops in South Africa, brought about a strategic rethinking in which British, local and federal interests and responsibilities had to be sorted out and reinterpreted. This had to be done not in a vacuum of constitutional theorizing but against a background of excited popular opinion and jingoism.[10] The search for national justification was not just a quest for moral rectitude. It was important that at a key period of nation-building the ideas which went towards the formation of patriotic feeling and attitudes be discussed freely and critically. The press, though predictably pro-British and frequently chauvinist, did honestly attempt to comment on the various opinions expressed about issues of Imperial and national concern, and it reported the views of those like H. B. Higgins who were keen that the new commonwealth be truly *Australian* and not just a pale imitation of Europe.[11] Only a strong central government in Australia could either cooperate with Britain as an equal or resist unreasonable Imperial demands.

At the time of constitution-making, the Australians had no doubts of their competence to draw up their own documents and they saw no need for Imperial interference, however well meant. Individually the Australian colonies had achieved more independence by the 1890s than the Canadians had by the 1860s.[12] Yet along every track Imperial precedents existed, and valid Imperial guidelines had to be acknowledged on the road to federal nationhood. Any Australian constitution had essentially to be "under the crown."[13] Federated Australia would have to depend on Britain not only in matters of defence and foreign policy. Some questions, commercial as well as constitutional and legal, vital to Australian sovereignty, proved to be almost intractable in the beginning. The Imperial authorities were of course encouraging and helpful but long experience of the Colonial Office and its denizens had made the colonial politicians wary. In 1897 most of the Australian premiers attended Chamberlain's Colonial Conference and the Diamond Jubilee celebrations, and by this time it was almost inconceivable that federation would not take place. Most of them, as founding fathers of the new commonwealth, had no objection to the Colonial Office making suggestions about such matters as treaty powers and passports, for they realized and accepted that they were not "assuming

10 J. A. Hobson, *Imperialism* (London, 1948), p. 352, and *The Psychology of Jingoism* (London, 1901).
11 H. B. Higgins, "Australian Ideals," *The Austral Light*, January 1902.
12 J. A. LaNauze, *The Making of the Australian Constitution* (Melbourne, 1972), pp. 38ff.
13 B. K. de Garis, "The Colonial Office and the Commonwealth Constitution Bill," in *Essays in Australian Federation*, ed. A. W. Martin (Melbourne, 1969), pp. 94ff.

an independent entity in international law." Indeed, the more reasonable of them welcomed suggestions from all quarters. They were, in their conventions and debates, drawing up, after all, a federal compact which would have to be embodied in an imperial act. Many matters, including such contentious ones as appeal to the Privy Council, had deep roots in the colonial past and would have to be left to the future and history.[14]

The new commonwealth succeeded to a long process of nationalist growth and thought in an imperial setting.[15] By and large the emphasis in legislation and debate in the first years would be devoted to domestic concerns and internal development aimed at embodying the noble aims and ideals which had inspired the federal movement. In imperial and foreign affairs, however, there were also responsibilities to be undertaken eventually as part of the movement towards national maturity and independence, with fresh national values to be forged amid a shifting balance of world power. Imperial authority was still paramount, exercising a controlling role over foreign affairs. This was acceptable to the majority of Australians. Bernhard Wise remarked correctly that "a federated Australia able to protect herself and ready to play her proper part in the protection of the British Empire, by guarding British interests in the East, may be in a position far sooner than anyone had dared to hope to make the alliance with the other free communities of the British Empire which was the political ideal of Sir Henry Parkes."[16] Commercially and financially the relationship of Britain and her Australian colonies had been close and cordial. The interests of Britain and other parts of her empire were not necessarily identical, nor were they always the same as Australia's. Yet few saw the imperial link as a sign of exploitation, and British capital investment continued to be a lynch-pin of Australian federal development. Not even the Labor party saw the British connection as a "Tory plot"; it was only later, under the tensions of war and the conscription conflict, that left-wing anti-imperialism regained a prominent place in its platform. Australia remained closely linked with Britain but not in a servile way, and the commonwealth was capable of showing a good deal of independent initiative concerning social legislation and immigration restrictions. Federal Australia was able to become protectionist in spite of colonial history, and in any case imperial preference seemed to offer clear advantages to Australia when it arose as an issue. In foreign policy formation and defence matters, the commonwealth's importance grew. Under the guidance of such men as Alfred Deakin, Australia's

14 LaNauze, *The Making of the Australian Constitution*, pp. 171, 173, 184, 220, 249 and 264.

15 C. Grimshaw, "Australian Nationalism and the Imperial Connection 1900-1914," *Australian Journal of Politics and History* (1958): 161ff.

16 *Bulletin*, 5 May 1900.

position could never be one of subservience. The Labor party may not have been as experienced nor as enthusiastic as Deakin to reconcile local nationalism, grounded in self-respect, with the formation of a modern British commonwealth of free nations to succeed the old Empire. Yet Andrew Fisher's Labor government was in 1911 neither parochial nor insular, even if it seemed more muted in imperial councils. The Empire had proved flexible enough to contain most of the strains placed upon it by local nationalist demands for new social, economic, political and military arrangements.

The Colonial and Imperial Conferences from 1887 to 1911 became arenas where the growing central power of the federal commonwealth of Australia was reflected.[17] Specifically imperial affairs might not have loomed large in comparison to the engrossing domestic processes which absorbed colonial politicians after federation, but the issues of defence and foreign policy could only be confronted, and suitable new institutions elaborated, in an imperial context. As the new nation forged its military, naval, diplomatic and commercial links, the tensions between Australian and imperial interests were not the only ones to emerge. Colonial premiers, long accustomed to direct communications with the authorities in London, and wishing to maintain existing contacts and influence, continued to assert state rights after federation, or to attempt the creation of institutions which would preserve and consolidate their local power and dignity. As late as the 1897 Colonial Conference Sir Edward Braddon of Tasmania had renewed an old idea of calling an imperial parliament to sit permanently at Westminster. For the 1907 Conference, Joseph Carruthers demanded representation for the state premiers. Proposed innovations such as an imperial council, or a permanent imperial secretariat were carefully analyzed for their potential impact on state rights. As in other spheres the dice was inevitably loaded in favour of the federal government, though the states managed to rescue a number of important areas from the centralizing storm. Carruthers attempted to capture imperial sentiment for his own ends by fostering the celebrations of Empire Day in New South Wales as a state function, but he and his kind were easily enough checkmated. The most interesting confrontation, however, in the Imperial Conferences of the early twentieth century, was that between Alfred Deakin and Sir Wilfrid Laurier. Laurier, having to consider Canadian conditions, balances and domestic politics, was somewhat distrustful of disturbing the *status quo* by encouraging the creation of new institutions which might regularize imperial centralization. The Australians, and especially Deakin, while no more desirous of imperial centralization than they had been before federation for the centralization of political power in Australia, nevertheless were more

17 J. E. Kendle, *The Colonial and Imperial Conferences 1887-1911* (London, 1967).

ready to construct modernized administrative procedures and instruments which they judged would enlarge the freedom and activities of the self-governing colonies and make them more equal to Great Britain. It was perhaps more a difference of methods rather than of aims.

A great new imperial link opened up with the creation of the Australian high commission in London.[18] It gave the already existing and powerful representatives of the states, the agents-general, a considerable federal fillip. It had been intended to have a high commission in London from January 1901. Barton, despite considerable efforts and advice, found the question a thorny one. The very functions of the high commission caused some questioning, though it was recognized that the federal government would need British representation in the diplomatic, financial, social and intelligence fields. The high commission would inevitably become a source of information and a channel through which imperial discussions would flow.

The colonial agents-general in the nineteenth century had had a long record of service, presenting the colonies to the mother country, conducting the business of overseas finance and commerce in the great metropolis of London and performing coordinating functions with respect to migration, propaganda, constitution-making and the daily conduct of administration.[19] When the commonwealth came to establish its own commission, therefore, it was able to call on a great body of precedent, and Barton sought advice also from the Canadians. Laurier replied that Canada had found it necessary to open up agencies in many places—London, Scotland, Ireland, Wales, Paris, Sydney, etc.—to perform useful and necessary representative tasks in the area of trade especially, and the Canadian provinces kept agencies in Britain too, chiefly to assist in immigration programs. The cost of a new building and appointments in London and hesitations about the impact of a new commonwealth institution, as well as personal jockeyings for the prestigious among colonial politicians, brought about a substantial delay; so too did state fears that the new office would simply be another means by which the commonwealth could enlarge its influence by impinging on their spheres of activity in a way which the constitution-makers had never intended. This was an area in which local particularism, commonwealth ambition and the requirements of imperial communication could become intermingled in an almost inextricably complex fashion. Discussions at the time showed that high expectations were held for the new commission both as an imperial agency and as an instrument of the Australian government. George Reid, very prominent in the federal movement, popular and forceful,

18 J. R. Thompson, "The Australian High Commission in London: Its Origins and Early History 1901-16" (master's thesis, A.N.U., 1972).
19 A. R. Hall, *The London Capital Market and Australia 1870-1914* (Canberra, 1963).

finally in 1910 became the high commissioner, and his lively talent for publicity was a considerable asset at a time when the federal government was setting out on an integrated and intelligent immigration drive. The task of preventing apathy or antagonism from overclouding Australia's "image" was vital, especially when it came to attracting loans and conducting delicate negotiations with various private and public authorities in Britain. In 1911-12 the building of Australia House in the Strand symbolized the solid success of a federal body which took up many of the old imperial contacts and adapted them to the needs of the new commonwealth. The work of the high commission as an Australian and imperial institution was of course vital during the testing years of war, 1914-18. Yet the offices and buildings and functions of the agents-general of the states, though overshadowed, would continue.

When Britain had first envisaged Australia as a single entity, Grey established Sir Charles Fitzroy as the first governor general, hoping —out of time—that this would be a first step to federation. Most of his successors, and indeed most of the colonial governors, favoured eventual federation, and their gentle pressure was an encouraging element in the movement whenever the efforts of local politicians flagged. The role of governor was, therefore, important in the evolution of the Australian tradition.[20] Thus it was expected that the governor general of the new commonwealth would be central. He would both play a key role in the safeguarding of the imperial connection as well as perform his strictly Australian constitutional duties. The 1891 draft of the Australasian Constitutional Convention left the matter of the relationship between the governor general and the state governors an open question. Bernhard Wise even argued against the "wasteful . . . absurd . . . separate . . ." Government House and establishment in each colony, and he hoped that the states would form the practice of choosing local men to govern.[21] But it was clear that the Australian representative of the crown would have to be both domestic constitutional monarch and imperial diplomat. Canadian precedent was not quite appropriate. In Australia the constitutional struggles which Durham, Sydenham and Elgin had fought were already far behind when federation came, but the workings of constitutional monarchy in general still had far to go, as Lord Hopetoun was to discover in 1901. Between 1850 and 1901, the powers of governors had diminished, though their social, constitutional, administrative and imperial influence was still important. Governors were often the best connoisseurs of intercolonial jealousies, misunderstandings, failures in communications, hopes and

20 N. I. Graham, "The Role of the Governor of N.S.W. under Responsible Government 1861-1890" (doctoral dissertation, Macquarie University, 1972).
21 C. Cunneen, "The Role of the Governor-General in Australia 1901-27" (doctoral dissertation, A.N.U., 1973).

fears, ambitions and discouragements. Even those governors who played a positive role in the federal movement had not wanted to subordinate the colony they governed to the other colonies, nor to the new commonwealth which they saw rather as a supplementation of existing government. It was to Lord Carrington in 1889, entertaining Sir George Parkin of Canada, that the veteran Parkes boasted that "he could confederate these colonies in twelve months." By the time of federation the imperial function of a governor had undergone deep scrutiny, criticism and adjustment. By 1885 a new interest in empire assured a succession of lively, young, aristocratic governors from Britain who introduced a forceful personal element into already established channels of communication and offered to the colonial communities a local image of monarchy. Various constitutional crises had warned governors to steer clear of local partisan politics, but naturally the course of events brought them, however cautious and well-intentioned, into delicate and often complicated embroglios.[22]

When the federal movement gathered strength it became obvious that the coordinating role of a future governor general had many advantages to offer in strengthening both intercolonial and imperial structures. The new commonwealth was to be, after all, a "federal union under the crown," and it was the desire of the Australian constitution-makers to incorporate into their new arrangements as much of the British constitutional tradition as possible. The governor general was to be an agent of the central British government, but he was not normally to exercise even the strong powers sought for the Queen's representative in the federal executive without the advice of his ministers. More important perhaps were the difficulties raised in sorting out the precise powers and functions of the office and in solving the problems which arose in practice. The governor general was the natural channel of communication with the Imperial government, which had vainly hoped with federation to cut and contract its formal obligations in Australia from six to one. But the states were jealous of any attempt to interfere with their right to communicate with Britain. The governor general did not therefore become the "sole" office of communication. The centralists wanted the governor general in principle to be paramount, while the provincialists wanted state governors to be clearly autonomous. After a number of attempts at change, including an effort by Sir John Forrest of Western Australia in 1898 to have lieutenant governors appointed by the governor general in council, as in Canada, it was decided to retain the state governors, who then made sure for themselves that their constitutional and social position was secure. In time the importance of state governors declined in relationship to that of the governor general, but they always remained

22 B. Penny, "The Blake Case," *Australian Journal of Politics and History* (1960): 176ff.

more significant than the lieutenant governors of the Canadian provinces.[23]

Joseph Chamberlain knew how important it was to select the right man as the first governor general and to consult the Australians. Yet at first there was no central government to consult. He was anxious to capture the new federation for the purpose of extending his imperial vision: to appoint someone such as Curzon, Munro or Milner. There was some question as always of a member of the royal family taking the job, but finally Lord Hopetoun, who had been governor of Victoria, 1889-95, was chosen. His character and experience did much to settle the style of the office, and his disappointments also set a pattern for the future. His career began with a blunder when he chose Sir William Lyne, Premier of the senior state New South Wales, to be the first prime minister, overlooking Barton who had been in the forefront of the federal movement: but this was corrigible. Hopetoun had moments of triumph when the new federation was inaugurated: the tour of the Duke of York in 1901 proved an imperial success, the Boer War and its conclusion provided opportunities for the new commonwealth to show its loyalty and devotion to Empire, and the political life of the nation developed into a rapid maturity. But Hopetoun also experienced difficult relations with jealous state governors, and was forced into endless and expensive rounds of socializing. He suffered the consequences of undiplomatic political moves and the accusation of interference in party matters. He finally resigned amid a strong degree of disillusionment.

Hopetoun's term of office was a difficult transition period in the relationship of Australia to Britain, with the commonwealth evolving towards a modern dominion, and the governor general acting not so much as a supervisor, administrator or even figurehead but as a specially privileged ambassador. Lord Tennyson, his successor, inaugurated a period of "bureaucratic consolidation" (1901-03). His father, the poet, had written of "one life, one flag, one fleet, one throne," and the son was an enthusiastic imperial federalist. His term in South Australia had made him a vigorous states-righter, but he was able in his brief term of office to set up a better working relationship with the commonwealth government and officials than the more ambitious Hopetoun had managed to do. But he, too, encountered inevitable difficulties as he threaded his way to a workable *modus vivendi* in the various roles he was called upon to play. In defence matters and immigration he played the part of the Queen's representative, meddling too much in matters concerning naval policy, and often coming into dangerous involvement in local feuds by his strong and partisan expression of opinion.

23 J. T. Saywell, *The Office of Lieutenant Governor* (Toronto, 1957).

With Chamberlain's departure from the Colonial Office in October 1903 and Tennyson's resignation in January 1904, the early "forward" period of policy formation and implementation was over. Lord Northcote (1904-08) was a stabilizing influence, an experienced public servant, factful, friendly and modest. During his period such fundamental questions as the role of the High Court, arbitration, the dissolution of federal parliament and appeals to the Privy Council had to be faced. He appears on the whole to have encouraged the Australian solution of constitutional and social problems. The question of federal citizenship raised dilemmas which concerned the relationship of the states to the commonwealth, and, in the sphere of honours, of both to the imperial power. In practice both states and commonwealth recommended honours, which were awarded by the monarch. Northcote managed against odds to establish a regular system in this and other matters. He was fundamentally centralist and urged the British government to do all it could "to make Australians realize what federal citizenship means; and to induce them to feel that they are Australians first, and New South Welshmen, Victorians, etc. only in the second place."[24] As federal figurehead, he felt obliged to assist in making federalism work to "promote nationalism as opposed to provincialism." The successors of Northcote, Lords Dudley and Denman (1908-11 and 1911-14), consolidated established practice and deepened the governor general's appreciation of the limits of the office, but it was Sir Ronald Munro-Ferguson (1914-20) who held office during the Great War of 1914-18, thus presiding over an event which highlighted as never before both the continuing strength of the imperial connection and also the centralization of Australian federal nationalism.

At the commencement of that imperial world war, Labor Prime Minister Fisher pledged Australia to fight "to our last man and our last shilling." The war, which Australia entered as part of the Empire, did more than any preceding event to encourage the growth of a vigorous nationalism which would weaken, but not destroy, the particularist state and local loyalties which had traditionally been so prominent a feature of the Australian political scene. The direction of movement towards the Australian centre, however, began long before the guns of August brutally dissipated forever the tyranny of distance.

24 Northcote to Elgin, 28 May 1906, quoted in Cunneen, "The Role of the Governor-General," p. 245; D. I. Wright, *Shadow of Dispute* (Canberra, 1968), pp. 7-13.

XV

Federal Politics and Social Policies

RONALD NORRIS

The period from the foundation of the commonwealth to the outbreak of World War I was an unusually interesting one in the history of Australia. These years saw the introduction of a new form of government and the advent of an additional administrative structure: the birth pangs and growing pains of an infant federal structure have a peculiar fascination. Federalism in this formative stage was guided by men, who, as prominent federationists in the 1890s, had shaped the federal constitution. Alfred Deakin dominated the first decade of federal politics, while George Reid generally led the opposition. Edmund Barton, leader of the Federal Convention of 1897-98 and first Prime Minister, retired from the front bench to the judicial in 1903. Samuel Griffith, chief architect of the draft bill of 1891, became first Chief Justice of the High Court. There Griffith and Barton, together with Justices Higgins, O'Connor, and Isaacs—all Founding Fathers —interpreted their own creation. In these circumstances the doctrine of judicial review, and the adage that the constitution is what the High Court says it is, assume added interest.

The period was one of great transition in the role of government in industrializing societies. The demands and consequences of industrial capitalism, and the advance of mass education, literacy, and communications, led to rising expectations of the state in the late nineteenth century and early twentieth. Thus even as the commonwealth came into existence under the guidance and jurisdiction of its creators, new socioeconomic issues confronted politicians.

The early history of Australian politics may therefore be seen as an era in which former colonial beings, transformed into federal creatures, attempted to adapt to an alien, and changing, social and political environment. These new political animals fought to survive and thrive. They hunted in packs because this proved safer and more effective. The fledgling bands of colonial times evolved rapidly into fully fledged parties. Above all, they sought engagement with pressing issues of the day, notably in the socioindustrial field, because these most concerned their masters in the electorate. In so doing the conflict of ambitions and interests, and heat of battle, riveted attention on the federal area wherein the major campaigns took place.

The federal constitution empowered the commonwealth parliament to do many things, but it provided limited opportunity for direct federal impingement on the social life of Australian citizens. Section 51 listed few such functions in its catalogue of thirty-nine powers (sometimes irreverently called the thirty-nine articles). The commonwealth could provide invalid and old age pensions.[1] It could legislate with regards to conciliations and arbitration to prevent and settle industrial disputes extending beyond one state.[2] It could act with regard to marriage and divorce.[3] Elsewhere the constitution gave the national parliament sole authority to determine the common external tariff.[4] In providing limited access to social and industrial questions, the constitution reflected the negative nature of the federation movement and the positive strength of state rights. Federation was more concerned with destroying barriers to economic recovery than with building a strong national authority to disturb provincial autonomy. Conservatives and liberals agreed that socioindustrial issues in particular were the proper concern of the states, not the commonwealth. Convention delegates incorporated the few overt social powers into the constitution with considerable reluctance. Commonwealth politicians, freed from pre-federation inhibitions but bound by post-federation constraints, responded to changed circumstance.

Federal politicians involved themselves with contemporary social questions in three main ways. They exploited given constitutional powers. They tried to enlarge their area of activity, especially in the socioindustrial field, by amending the constitution. They sought to use and extend existing delegated powers in ways that the makers of the constitution had not envisaged.

The promise of social legislation came shortly after federation as candidates campaigned for election to the foundation commonwealth parliament. Many campaigners, liberal protectionists in particular, included old age pensions and conciliation and arbitration in their platforms. Barton, in his policy speech in January 1901, intimated that a protectionist ministry would introduce pensions as soon as the financial situation was sufficiently clear to provide funds: Kingston would draft early legislation on arbitration as a precautionary measure. While Free Traders sometimes alluded to these subjects, the question of old

---

1   Commonwealth of Australia Constitution Act, section 51 xxii.
2   Ibid., section 51 xxxv.
3   Ibid., section 51 xxi and xxii.
4   Ibid., sections 86, 88.

age pensions placed them in a dilemma. Pensions were desirable but costly, and in practice revenue for at least ten years had to be derived from the commonwealth's share of customs duties. Such schemes therefore meant high tariffs: Barton's plan was "absurd," Reid asserted.[5]

Fulfilment of these promises took considerable time. Federal parliament necessarily gave priority to formulating a common external tariff, a task, which according to the constitution, had to be completed within two years. Though most parliamentarians agreed in principle on a federal system of conciliation and/or arbitration, they disagreed as to its detailed form. Kingston resigned his portfolio when cabinet refused to extend the scope of the bill to seamen in the coastal trade. Labor initially wanted compulsory arbitration but not conciliation. Later it demanded provisions to embrace state public servants, a demand anathema to most protectionists. Deakin resigned. The unexpected but brief spell of the Watson Labor government ended with defeat on the issue of preference to unionists. Eventually, the Reid-McLean administration, a coalition of Free Traders and conservative Protectionists (in theory the combination least likely to pursue the issue) passed a compromise measure in 1904.

Commonwealth legislation on old age pensions, as Reid's criticism of Barton rightly implied, faced formidable obstacles of cost and the Braddon clause.[6] The majority of members approved the notion of a national pension scheme—liberal democrats as a right, conservative paternalists as a privilege. But implementation of one had to await the raising of higher tariffs than the early compromise measures, and the passing of the Surplus Revenue Act 1908, which enabled the commonwealth to build up funds.[7] The Reid-McLean ministry appointed a select committee in 1904 to investigate the problem. A royal commission of 1905-06 made recommendations which the second Deakin government incorporated in its legislation of 1908. Old age pensions became payable throughout the commonwealth in 1909, invalid pensions in 1910.

Attempts to amend the constitution began early in the life of federal parliament and continued, at intervals, throughout the period. Ironically, liberal and conservative members, who had themselves devised the federal blueprint, immediately acted to enlarge commonwealth powers: Labor, supposedly centralist, remained inert. In June 1901 Higgins moved that the commonwealth acquire, subject to agree-

5 *Sydney Morning Herald*, 13 February 1901.
6 Section 87 provided that for the first ten years and thereafter until federation parliament decided otherwise, the commonwealth would get one-quarter of the net customs and excise as revenue. Parliament could introduce direct taxation, but no party dared to advocate this.
7 The main needs for the fund were pensions and defence.

ment of the states, "full power to make laws for Australia as to wages and hours and conditions of labour."[8] Barton, liberal Protectionist Prime Minister, and McMillan, conservative Free Trade opposition leader in the absence of Reid, supported the motion. Both had consistently opposed federal industrial powers at federal conventions. Labor, insecure and divided, sat silent. State premiers, those who considered Barton's subsequent invitation to surrender industrial powers worthy of reply, declined firmly. A. J. Peacock, Premier of Victoria, publicly declared industrial legislation "a domestic affair that belonged to the States."[9]

Thus rebuffed by state premiers, federal politicians of all persuasions, unwilling as yet to seek amendment of the constitution by referendum, sought other means of entering the forbidden field. In 1903 J. C. Neild, Free Trade, tried unsuccessfully to prevent the payment of a bonus on white grown sugar to growers using white women and children as cheap replacements for banished Kanakas. Labor, suspecting a devious plot to undermine white Australia legislation, opposed the suggestion. In 1905 George Pearce, a Labor free trader, had incorporated in the Sugar Bounty Act a section making payment of bounty conditional upon growers meeting commonwealth approved wages and conditions for white workers.[10] New protection sentiments had emerged before federation in Victoria. There, the Anti-Sweating League and the Protectionist Association —organizations with strong employer and employee representation and support—campaigned vigorously for the "social side" of federal protection.[11] W. E. Johnson, Free Trade, in the tariff debate of 1906, suggested that manufacturers in protected industries be forced to pay increased wages to their workers. Labor's Andrew Fisher and E. L. Batchelor proposed a method of relating working conditions to excise rebates and customs duties. Deakin, a new protectionist by inclination, linked fiscal legislation and industrial conditions in his new fiscal measures of 1906. Justices Griffith, Barton, and O'Connor, with Higgins and Isaacs in dissent, declared the method unconstitutional in 1908. New protection was stillborn.

Thus rebuffed by the High Court, federal politicians now attempted amendment of the constitution by referendum to permit commonwealth legislation on industrial questions. In 1911 and 1913 referenda proposals sought to empower the federal government to make

8 *Commonwealth Parliamentary Debates* 2, p. 1819.
9 Cutting from Melbourne *Herald*, July 1901, in Commonwealth Archives Office, Commonwealth Record Series A8, file 01/46/-. The file contains replies from four premiers but none from Queensland and Victoria.
10 Pearce acted on his own initiative.
11 *Minute Book of Protectionist Association of Victoria*, November 1902, in Australian National Library, Mauger Papers, MS 403/13.

laws with respect to terms and conditions of labour, control and regulation of corporations, dealing with combinations and monopolies, and widening the scope of arbitration. By this time, however, the political situation had altered drastically. Labor waxed, Protectionists waned, and Free Traders changed. Labor, which entered federal parliament as the smallest party, gained sufficient strength and confidence to eject Deakin from office in 1908 and triumph in the election of 1910. Protectionists, the major party in 1901, became the minor in 1906. Free Traders, recognizing that federal free trade was a lost cause, campaigned against the alleged socialism of Labor and thereby maintained their strength as antisocialists. An exhausted Deakin, his new liberalism outpaced and overtaken by Labor radicalism, fused his depleted party with his erstwhile Free Trade opponents in 1909. The very flood of reform had drained the liberal well. Similar polarization took place in most states where, the once divisive fiscal issue removed to the federal sphere, non-Labor coalesced to fight the common foe.

The proposed amendments and threatened policies of the federal Labor party, under these fresh circumstances, became focal points for concentrated attacks on "socialism" and "centralism." Opposition came from many quarters, federal and state, anti-Labor and state Labor alike. Former Free Traders posed as champions of home rule. Former Protectionists, now that Labor was in the ascendancy, discovered the need to preserve the original "federal compact." Samuel Mauger, foundation secretary of the Protectionist Association—which earlier demanded federal industrial powers—implored voters in 1913 to defeat the referendum in the interests of a "Free and Federal" Australia.[12] Metropolitan newspapers thundered opposition to Labor's anti-federal, socialist schemes. The Melbourne *Age*, normally preoccupied with the federal tariff, warned of "centralisation."[13] State governments and vested interests, ever watchful of their rights, feared central encroachment. Prominent state Labor politicians, especially in New South Wales where the party secured office in 1910, jealously guarded state interests against aggrandizement by their rival federal colleagues. Anti-Labor campaigners seized remarks of James McGowen and W. A. Holman, respectively Labor Premier and Attorney-General of New South Wales, to discredit federal acquisition of industrial powers: the proposals were "too sweeping"; they "exceeded the bounds" of the Labor platform; they meant the "end of State Labor Parties."[14] The referenda failed.

Explanations for the radical measures of the commonwealth parliament and for the keen regard of its members for social affairs and

12 *Age* (Melbourne), 30 May 1913.
13 Ibid., 24 May 1913.
14 *To Wage Earners, Do Not Be Misled! Read What Labor Leaders Say*, pamphlet in Australian National Library, Symon Papers, MS 1736.

reform have generally centred on the peculiar political situation which existed in the first decade. Labor, a disciplined party united on everything but the fiscal issue, entered parliament determined to right social wrong by means of federal legislation. Labor held the balance of power between Protectionists and Free Traders. This advantageous position, therefore, enabled it to exchange support in return for concessions, a tactic first applied with great effect in the three-party parliaments of New South Wales in the 1890s. As the progressive liberalism of Deakin (chief recipient of support) had much in common with Labor radicalism, the degree of Deakin's compliance (willing or otherwise) with Labor demands and the exact nature and extent of concessions are difficult to gauge. Even so, Labor clearly exerted great influence on Deakin and the character of legislation, particularly progressive socioindustrial measures, until 1908-09 and fusion. Thereafter, in what became the customary alignment of parties, Labor initiative had to overcome anti-Labor resistance to provide social reform: hence, for example, the maternity allowances of 1912.

This interpretation suffers from several shortcomings. Initially, Labor was united on few issues and its federal platform for the election of 1901 had but five planks.[15] Nor were the party's federal members at first convinced that central action on socioindustrial issues would necessarily be preferable to local: hence the failure of Labor in 1901 to support the motion of Higgins to acquire industrial powers. (Many state Labor politicians, particularly in New South Wales, remained unconvinced, and W. M. Hughes and W. A. Holman feuded and debated the proper functions of commonwealth and state). Insufficient attention and credit is given to the role of Free Trade, which, though generally more conservative than other parties, contained liberal elements.

The main weaknesses of the account, however, are that it misunderstands the dynamics of the three-party era and neglects adequate consideration of the objective situation which faced all federal politicians regardless of party. Labor did not possess the vital bargaining position implied in the account. In the first place, Labor's inability to agree on the fiscal question meant that caucus could not command the votes of its members on the tariff:[16] as it happened this was the very issue for which Free Trade and Protectionist parties most wanted support. In the second, Reid and free trade was not a credible alternative to Deakin and protection. Free trade was a minority sentiment within Labor ranks, and Reid and his colleagues soon campaigned

15 Adult suffrage; exclusion of coloured and other undesirable races; old age pensions; amendment of constitution to provide for the initiative and national referenda. In May 1902 caucus dropped the last plank, and added a citizen army and compulsory arbitration.
16 The Labor pledge to abide by caucus decisions applied only to items in the platform.

against socialism. Labor could scarcely barter with a party that adopted an antisocialist stance or trade support in return for concessions with a party terming itself antisocialist. Nor could antisocialists offer socialists concessions in return for support. It would seem more reasonable to conclude that for the most part Deakin held the balance between antisocialism on the right, and socialism on the left. Labor did indeed exert influence, but not in the manner described. Rather, the presence of Labor in the federal parliament (which contrasted sharply with its absence at federal conventions) helped liberalize or radicalize the legislature. This put conservatism on the defensive, made progressive social measures—emanating from whatever source—more likely, and increased the prospects of success.[17]

Moreover, astute politicians realized that they must broaden their appeals for election to early commonwealth parliaments beyond calls for free trade or protection for a number of related reasons. Not all Australians were committed on the tariff. The tariff question was the greatest issue in New South Wales and Victoria, but it assumed less importance elsewhere. In South Australia, for instance, parties had divided since 1893 into Liberal and Conservative: the Liberal cabinet of Kingston, a dedicated protectionist, included prominent free traders such as F. W. Holder. Aspiring federal politicians, therefore, sought to attract the support of electors either uncommitted on the tariff or more committed on other issues: in the case of non-Labor candidates they tried also to enlist the sympathy of some working class voters, who were being wooed by Labor.

Again, the necessity for government intervention into social and industrial matters had become apparent during the 1890s. The turbulent strikes of this decade highlighted the urgent need for effective forms of compulsory arbitration. Trade unions humbled by defeat, and victorious bosses seeking calm conditions conducive to good business, came to recognize the disadvantages of industrial anarchy. The great depression produced mass unemployment, which fell heaviest on weaker sections of the community, such as aged and infirm workers. Voluntary charitable institutions, chiefly church, were unable to cope with the resultant problems. Colonial politicians—protectionist and free trade, Labor and non-Labor, liberal and conservative—responded to the demands of electors. Colonial governments found it expedient to establish machinery to regulate industrial relations. New South Wales and Victoria passed pension legislation, which became operative in 1901.[18] The effects of the depression persisted well into the new

17 See R. Norris, *The Emergent Commonwealth, 1901-10* (Melbourne, 1975), chapter 6, and Peter Loveday, "Support in Return for Concessions," *Historical Studies* 14 (October 1970): 376-405 for fuller discussions of the above.

18 A reported 18,000 applicants, instead of the anticipated 6,000, applied for pensions at the outset of the Victorian scheme: "none are Australian born. So far all are old

century and were most severe in Melbourne, wherein, as it happened, the federal parliament sat. Bad times, defensive unions, and increasing mechanization of industry encouraged unscrupulous employers to impose degrading conditions. Sweat shops proliferated. Slow workers found it difficult or impossible to keep up with the "fire-eater" who set the rate.[19] Federation abolished colonial tariff barriers but left intact unequal state conditions of work and production that had grown up under the protection of these barriers. Employers, who felt disadvantaged by their own "good" conditions, and employees who believed their counterparts better treated in other states, demanded equality throughout the nation. The fact that some states provided pensions and others did not (federation interrupted the movement of some colonies to this end) led to calls for uniformity.

In sum, federal politicians, like their colonial predecessors and state contemporaries, could ill afford to ignore the similar needs and demands of the self-same electors. The criterion was, of course, political advantage (tinged perhaps with humane concern) in electorate and parliament. Therefore, while they soon made use of constitutional provisions for arbitration and pensions, and sought in a variety of ways to acquire industrial powers, they conveniently overlooked the provisions for marriage and divorce, subjects clearly providing no political capital.[20] Federal politicians, once the tariff was determined, had to justify their existence. They could scarcely sit idly by, in splendid isolation, during an era of state innovation and social turmoil. They themselves had frequently been the very instigators of reform in colonial times. In a sense, federal politics was an extension of colonial-cum-state politics, especially Victorian. Social issues became prominent in the federal arena because social issues became prominent in the colonies and states.

The period 1901-14 saw a shift of public interest from state politics to federal. Pageantry and celebration accompanied the inauguration of the commonwealth in Sydney and the opening of its parliament in Melbourne. But citizens of Australia at large displayed no special concern or enthusiasm for federal affairs. Candidates for the foundation parliament numbered most of the major political figures in Australia. Yet a mere 57 per cent of voters troubled to poll in the general election of 1901.[21] Electoral response to the federal election in each

colonists whose arrivals date from the fifties. ..." *Sydney Morning Herald,* 15 January 1901.

19 As late as 1909 one Melbourne bootmaker wrote Higgins to describe the appalling conditions in the sweatshop, where the "fire-eater" set the rate. A. Brown to Higgins, 11 October 1909, National Library of Australia, Higgins Papers, MS 1057/162.

20 In the event federal politicians did not see fit to legislate on marriage and divorce until the 1960s.

21 Voting figures taken from Colin A. Hughes and B. D. Graham, *A Handbook of Australian Government and Politics 1890-1964* (Canberra, 1968).

state fell far short of response to the first post-federation state elections in every instance (in South Australia about 20 per cent short). In Western Australia, where, according to tradition a tide of nationalism on the goldfields swept the colony into federation, little more than a third of the electors voted. Polling in 1903 slumped to barely half the Australian electorate. Interest in national events quickened as the commonwealth concerned itself with pressing problems—mainly, but not solely, social—in the era of consensus policies up to fusion. It accelerated as politics polarized and turmoil erupted in the era of conflict thereafter. The twin spectres of socialism and centralism loomed large as Labor representation increased and its ambition grew. Social reform was one thing, but social revolution and unification were different matters. The power of conservative upper houses in the states could be relied upon to curb the worst excesses of socialism, but no such confidence could be placed in the senate to thwart either socialist or centralist tendencies. The federal arena began to appear the place where crucial events were taking place. The referenda of 1911 and 1913, with the proposals for wider arbitration powers and commonwealth authority to tackle industrial conditions, corporations, and monopolies seemed to threaten federalism and capitalism. The federal arena *was* the place where crucial events were taking place. Electoral response reflected heightened concern. Voting rose from the trough of 50 per cent in 1903 to peaks of 73 per cent in the elections of 1913, with the referenda proposals, and 1914, after double dissolution and outbreak of war.[22] Federal elections now outdrew state. Probably Australians had no greater affection for commonwealth politicians than they had for state. But the days of massive indifference to national affairs evident in the federation referenda of the late 1890s and the general elections of the early 1900s were past.

22 Labor lost the election of 1913 by one seat, but retained the senate. The Labor-controlled senate twice rejected the Liberal's Government Preference Prohibition Bill, and Joseph Cook secured a double dissolution of the house and senate.

XVI

The River Murray: Microcosm of Australian Federal History*

DON WRIGHT

The many facets of the history of Australian federalism, both the movement towards union and development since that time, are reflected almost perfectly in the political history of the continent's only great river, the Murray. Nor is this surprising. The Murray forms the boundary between two large and jealous states, New South Wales and Victoria, and it flows from them into their smaller and suspicious neighbour, South Australia. Being a vital commodity in a dry continent, the waters of the Murray have always appeared well worth struggling over; they have always been the focus of serious tension and of uneasy cooperation between the three riparian governments. At the heart of this confusion stands the River Murray Waters Agreement of 1914, the goal towards which the riparian colonies struggled in earlier days, and their lodestar ever since.

From the early 1850s, trade across and along the Murray drew the three colonies of New South Wales, Victoria and South Australia into contact over the thorny issue of customs duties. Two factors were responsible for this. The extension of settlement in the eastern Riverina (the Riverina may briefly be described as the land between the rivers Murray and Murrumbidgee) and north-eastern Victoria led to increasing trade in that area. Riverina settlers found communication with distant Sydney slow and difficult. It was usually more convenient to trade through Melbourne, the natural outlet of their economic region. But Melbourne was separated from the Riverina by a political boundary and goods imported through that city were subject to double duties. Similarly, when South Australia opened up trade along the river in 1853 it soon became clear that it was the quickest and easiest

---

* The author gratefully acknowledges the assistance of Ellen M. McEwen, graduate student in History, University of Sydney, in drafting this paper.

way to move goods to and from western New South Wales and the gold fields of northern Victoria.[1] But trade, whether along or across the Murray, raised the issue of payment of customs duties. The problem lay in the fact that each colony levied duties at a different rate and that goods dutiable in one colony were not necessarily so in another. There was general agreement with the view of an Adelaide businessman that "To attempt the protection of the Borders of two thousand miles of navigable inland waters by a revenue Guard would be simply absurd."[2] But unless smuggling was to flourish, and colonial revenue to suffer, some solution had to be found.

Initially, the problem of trade upriver was solved in accordance with the South Australian suggestion that it collect duties at its own rate on goods designated for New South Wales and Victoria and distribute them to those colonies, so far as their respective customs laws allowed.[3] In 1855 it was further decided between New South Wales and Victoria to make trade across the river free.[4]

Neither agreement was destined to last. South Australian duties were lower than Victorian, and Melbourne merchants soon realized that this was causing them to lose the gold fields trade to their Adelaide rivals. The Victorian government was likewise losing revenue. Consequently, the colony put pressure on its neighbour to change the system. Eventually, as a compromise, South Australia agreed to collect duty at the New South Wales rate (which was between that of South Australia and Victoria) and distribute this to the eastern colonies.[5] This increased their revenue and reduced (but did not eliminate) the advantage of the Adelaide merchants.

Even worse for intercolonial amity was the fact that in 1860 the expansion of trade across the Murray led New South Wales to end its free trade agreement with Victoria. New South Wales complained that it could no longer afford to bear the "enormous loss" to its revenue.[6] Despite periodic suggestions for total tariff assimilation,[7] it was not

1 G. D. Patterson, "The Murray River Border Customs Dispute, 1853-1880," *Business Archives and History* (August 1962): 122ff.
2 South Australia Archives (SAA), GRG 24/6, 1854/418, memo, W. Younghusband to Colonial Secretary (Col. Sec.) S.A., 13 February 1854.
3 For a summary of the early correspondence, see memo dated 5 October 1855 by J. N. Blackmore, in SAA, GRG 24/6, 1855/2141. See also unsigned and undated addendum (in Blackmore's handwriting) accompanying same.
4 The correspondence between the Col. Secs. of the respective colonies (12 and 13 September 1855) is in Victoria, *Votes and Proceedings of the Legislative Council (V&P,LC)*, 1855-56, vol. 1, no. 87, pp. 8-10.
5 See SAA, GRG 24/6, 1856/2730, 3460; 1857/249; ibid., 24/4, vol. 29, pp. 660-64; Victoria, State Archives (VSA), CSO, outletters 1857, E1, pp. 16-18; N.S.W., *V&P,LA*, 1857, vol. 2, pp. 404-05, 408, 412-18.
6 Victoria, *Parliamentary Papers (VPP)*, 1859-60, vol. 4, no. 70, p. 6, Col. Sec. N.S.W. to Chief Sec. Vic., 30 May 1860.
7 See, for example, N.S.W. Archives, C.S.O., special bundle 4/748.2, "Border Customs," Chief Sec. S.A. to Col. Sec. N.S.W., 18 March 1862.

until seven years later, in 1867, that the two colonies reached an agreement, to operate for five years, whereby there was free trade across the river, but under which Victoria paid New South Wales a lump sum in lieu of the duties which the latter might have collected.[8] When the treaty expired in 1872 a year was taken to renew it and to bring South Australia in under the same arrangement.[9] Seven months later (January 1874), Victoria abrogated the treaty amidst accusations from New South Wales of "fickleness of policy and instability of purpose."[10] Thereafter no further agreement could be made on the subject between the two eastern colonies. However, the agreement between South Australia and New South Wales continued uneasily and unsteadily until January 1884 when New South Wales, seeing no further advantage for itself, refused renewal.[11]

From this time, no one saw any point in raising the border customs issue again. There could be no new prefederal solution. But a new issue arose over the Murray which was to cause equal difficulty and frustration.

From 1885, Victoria began to show interest in using the Murray waters for irrigation.[12] The mere mention of this word was anathema to South Australia, which continued to see the river as a great arterial highway, the "Gateway of the Interior."[13]

Both Victoria and New South Wales appointed royal commissions to study the use of the Murray waters. These conferred informally and recommended to their governments the division of the waters between the two colonies (with an unspecified allowance for South Australia) and the administration of the river above the South Australian border by a joint commission.[14]

This only made matters worse because it seemed to threaten South Australian interests. That colony believed that it had been slighted by being deliberately left out of the negotiations and that the agreement disregarded its needs. It was not prepared to depend on the charity of its more powerful neighbours for its water supply—even if it did intend to use that water mainly to sustain the already diminishing river trade. (The gradual extension of inland railways in both Victoria and New South Wales had already begun to damage the river traffic noticeably).

8 Patterson, "Murray River Border Customs Dispute," pp. 129-30.
9 Ibid., p. 133.
10 N.S.W., V&P,LA, 1873-74, vol. 2, pp. 899-900, Col. Sec. N.S.W. to Chief Sec. Vic., 21 January 1874.
11 See SAA, GRG 24/28, vol. 2, pp. 308-09; vol. 3, pp. 24, 178-79; ibid., 24/6, 1884/28, 86, 1731.
12 S.A. *Parliamentary Papers (SAPP)*, 1886, vol. 3, no. 59, p. 1.
13 This was the title of a pamphlet about the River Murray written by S.A. publicist D. J. Gordon in 1902.
14 "Royal Commission—Conservation of Water. Second Report. 23 June 1886" (Sydney, 1886).

It preferred to take its stand on the British common law doctrine of riparian rights, a doctrine of dubious applicability in a continent like Australia.[15]

The Murray ought to have been, as the Melbourne *Argus* held, "a great agent of federation,"[16] but the two upstream colonies seemed bent on ensuring that it would not be. Victoria pushed on actively with irrigation proposals, and New South Wales, while it did little, adopted a dog-in-the-manger attitude. The New South Wales Constitution Act of 1855[17] had put the whole course of the Murray within the senior colony, and Sir Henry Parkes was prepared to assert that all the waters of the river belonged to it. He refused to attend a conference on the issue lest this should seem to involve an admission that the other colonies had an equal right with New South Wales to deal with the question. Victoria had no more right to the Murray waters than to the streets of Sydney, and, while South Australia might use the waters within its own boundaries, it must not do so to an extent which would unduly reduce their level in New South Wales.[18]

Strangely, Parkes pushed this belligerent, legalistic line at the very time when he was involved in federal negotiations with the other colonies. The *Argus* laid the contradiction bare when it wrote: "He has come with union in one hand and separation in the other, and we are not even to have a choice, for we are expected to take both."[19]

For ten years Victoria pushed on with irrigation and New South Wales refused to discuss the Murray question. Although any practical threat to South Australian interests at the time came from Victoria, it was the cavalier disregard of its position by New South Wales which most angered the smaller colony. Because the senior colony totally refused to recognize South Australia's rights, the latter determined to force debate on the issue at the federal conventions of 1897-98. The issue would then be settled as part of the overall federal compact.

The tedious and often bitter debate occupied many days at both the Adelaide and Melbourne sessions.[20] Basically, South Australia sought to establish federal control over the whole Murray system, while New South Wales refused to surrender control over the tributaries at

15 S. D. Clark and I. A. Renard, "The Riparian Doctrine and Australian Legislation," *Law Review* 7 (September 1970): 475-506.

16 *Argus* (Melbourne), 31 May 1889.

17 18-19 Vic., c. 54, section 5.

18 *SAPP*, 1890, vol. 3, no. 34, appendix J, Col. Sec. N.S.W. to Premier S.A., 6 March 1890; V.S.A., Premier's Dept. inletters, P94/2210, Col. Sec. N.S.W. to Premier Vic., 6 March 1890; interviews with Parkes in *Argus* (Melbourne), 31 March, 12 April 1890. Parkes was so arrogant about this that when the Murray flooded Echuca (Vic.) a little later, the mayor telegraphed him to come and take his N.S.W. water out of the Victorian town!

19 *Argus* (Melbourne), 12 April 1890 (editorial).

20 For the debates, see *National Australian Convention Debates* (Adelaide, 1897, Melbourne, 1898), passim.

all and sought to maintain the supremacy of irrigation over navigation on the Murray itself. New South Wales was not, as its Premier, G. H. Reid, put it, prepared to reduce itself to the status of catchment area for South Australia.[21]

No really satisfactory constitutional solution was found. South Australia's navigation rights were left dependent on the general trade and commerce power given to the commonwealth under section 51(i) of the constitution, with the limitation that these powers should not "abridge the right of a state or its citizens to the reasonable use of the water of the rivers for water conservation or irrigation" (section 100).

The summer of 1901-02 brought the culmination of a long and damaging drought of unprecedented severity. As a result, the River Murray Main Canal League, a body composed predominantly of New South Welsh graziers, called a conference of representatives of the river districts of New South Wales and Victoria at Corowa in April 1902. The Prime Minister and Premiers of the three riparian states were also invited to attend. Most of the delegates were practical farmers who understood little of the working of federation and cared nothing for constitutional niceties. All they wanted was that some government—any government—should provide them with an assured water supply. Their earnestness, and the gravity of the circumstances in which they met, enabled them to persuade the tardy states to establish an interstate royal commission to report on the allotment of the waters of the Murray to the states, and the best methods of conservation and distribution, both for irrigation and navigation.[22]

Even before the royal commission reported, in December 1902, New South Wales and South Australia had found it necessary to charge Victoria with bad faith for proceeding with diversion schemes on certain tributaries of the Murray while the whole question was *sub judice*.[23]

Predictably, the report of the commission showed a sharp division between the New South Welsh and Victorian commissioners on the one hand and, on the other, their South Australian colleague. The former emphasized the primacy of irrigation and conservation, while the latter persisted in the view long taken by his political masters that these must be subordinate to navigation. At least it established two points clearly and forever: the waters of the Murray must be divided proportionately among the riparian states, and the whole river system must be treated as a unit under the joint management of the three states.[24]

21 Ibid.
22 *Official Report of the Corowa Water Conference*, 2-4 April 1902 (Corowa, 1902).
23 See, for example, SAA, GRG 24/28, vol. 21, pp. 269a, 286, 294.
24 "Interstate Royal Commission on the River Murray, representing the States of N.S.W., Victoria and South Australia. Report of the Commissioners, 9 December 1902," N.S.W., *V&P,LA*, 1902, vol. 4, pp. 637-96.

The riparian premiers held a series of conferences from 1903 to 1914.[25] At these the attempt was made to work out a detailed agreement satisfactory to all parties. The urgent need for a solution to a problem which was both political and technical impressed itself ever more closely on those involved, but the apparent conflict of economic interests between South Australia and the upstream states remained a barrier to settlement.

Gradually it was realized that canalization of the river could give an adequate supply of water for irrigation in New South Wales, Victoria and South Australia without unduly restricting navigation, but negotiations always bogged down over the fairness of any particular proposed division of the water. Victoria, especially, was constantly applying pressure for better terms and was anxious to reduce as far as possible the volume reserved for South Australia.[26]

The problem occasionally came under discussion in the commonwealth parliament, but it was generally felt that it was an issue which was best dealt with by the states concerned. Briefly, in 1904, the Watson Labor government suggested that the whole question be referred to the commonwealth, but there was no response from the states.[27] During this early period of federal history, relations between the commonwealth and the states were so strained that there was no likelihood that the latter would seek the assistance of the former to resolve conflict between themselves lest this should allow the commonwealth an opportunity to extend its sphere of action.

As time passed, however, some people realized that only federal intervention, but of the right kind, could bring the states to their senses. A South Australian member of Joseph Cook's Fusion (Liberal) government of 1913-14, P. McMahon, who had been interested in the question since the 1880s, persuaded the commonwealth to participate in negotiations and to provide the catalyst of a £1 million contribution towards the cost of river works (weirs, locks and storages) expected to cost about £4,463,000. A formal agreement was completed in September 1914. It provided for a reasonable division of Murray waters and allowed for permanent navigability of the Murray, along with more than enough water for the irrigation needs of all states in the then foreseeable future. Finally, it established a River Murray Commission, with a member representing each of the three states and the federal government, to administer the river.[28]

25 See especially ibid., 1903, vol. 2, pp. 877-79; *SAPP*, 1905, vol. 2, no. 59; N.S.W., *V&P,LA*, 1906, vol. 5, pp. 223-25; "Report of the Proceedings of the Interstate Conference on theMurray River Waters," N.S.W., *Parliamentary Papers*, 1911, vol. 1.

26 See above, and also "Report of the Royal Commission on the Murray Waters" (14 March 1910), *VPP*, 1910, vol. 3, no. 7.

27 Commonwealth Archives Office (CAO), CRS A1, 16/126.

28 "River Murray and Lake Victoria Agreement," *NSWPP*, 1914-15, vol. 6.

The 1914 agreement was a beginning as well as an ending. The new agreement, truly federal in nature, had to be made to work. There would be difficulties with the water federation as with the political. In a sense, neither New South Wales nor Victoria really made much attempt to keep to the original terms of the agreement. They were prepared to push ahead with works for conservation and irrigation, but delayed endlessly over those for navigation, in which South Australia alone was still, rather pathetically, interested. In 1922-23 they tried to have navigation works removed from the programme, but the commonwealth stood fairly and firmly by South Australia and refused to allow any departure from the original agreement. When the commonwealth tried to give the River Murray Commission greater control over the initiation and construction of works (the 1914 agreement had left this largely with the states) Victoria and New South Wales resisted, fearing, correctly, that this was a device for forcing a construction of all works at the fastest possible pace. The whole incident showed the wisdom of the commonwealth being partner to this great joint project.[29] In 1933, the upstream states did finally obtain consent for the deletion of the still uncompleted locks (the economic depression was playing havoc with all government works), but only at the price of agreeing to the construction of barrages at the Murray mouth to prevent the influx of salt water, which South Australia now regarded as more urgent.[30]

Since 1933 the pattern has not changed: a debate on the control of the catchment areas for the Hume Dam in the late 1940s, one over the distribution of waters diverted from the Snowy River to the Murray in the late 1950s and another over the placement of a new major storage in the late 1960s tell the same story: the attainment and operation of federal arrangements in Australia is never easy.

The paradox of the Murray—and it was this which caused the trouble—was that it did not only divide. It also united. On the one hand, it was a political boundary and the bearer of a commodity in short supply which might be fought over. On the other, it "tended to unite the affairs of the people dwelling on both sides of the river"[31] and even, to some extent, to link them to those who lived downstream in South Australia.

The three colonies of New South Wales, Victoria and South Australia developed rival economies based on Sydney, Melbourne and Adelaide. The divergent interests of the capitals made it likely that they would struggle to draw the trade of the Murray area to themselves.

29 See SAA, GRG 24/6, 22/928; V.S.A., Premier's Dept. outletters, P22/1202, P26/3131.
30 CAO, CRS A461, B423/1/2; MP 608, box 10, file 1588, part 1.
31 G. S. Habgood, "Organized Separatist Movements in N.S.W. in the Nineteenth Century: A Comparative Analysis" (master's thesis, University of Newcastle, N.S.W., 1970), p. 93.

Moreover, the determination of the governments of New South Wales and Victoria to preserve their colonial revenues intact increased the probability of conflict.

In the 1880s, when the question of the use and division of the waters arose, the situation was similar but not identical. New South Wales and Victoria both believed in the primacy of irrigation and conservation, though they were not always at one over the actual division of the water, but South Australia still believed that the river's first use should be a highway for trade. If South Australia mistook its real interest, and it did, that did not lessen the conflict at the time. In any case, however it saw its interests, South Australia would still have felt the need to fight for a fair share of the water and to see that those interests were not neglected by its upstream sisters.

No one ever actively disputed the social and cultural homogeneity of the settlers across and along the river. In 1855, C. D. Riddell, Colonial Secretary of New South Wales, seeking the free trade agreement with Victoria, stressed this very fact, arguing that it made tariff barriers in the area totally inappropriate.[32] By 1860 the exigencies of the colonial treasury had caused his pragmatic successors in office to become unsympathetic to the essential truth of his position. By 1867 Sir Henry Parkes had swung back to the original line (at least for oratorical purposes) and claimed, in a statement marked by that hyperbole which flowed naturally at nineteenth century political banquets, that tariff divisions between people of common origins and habits "would be a perpetual annoyance, goading on men to desperation and rebellion."[33] Probably he had in mind the discontent of the Riverina settlers. The inconvenience to which the border tariff dispute subjected them for the sake of the merchants and administrators in distant Sydney was an important element in their sporadic attempts to establish a separate colony for themselves.[34] But on less convivial occasions, as we have noted, Parkes could make very divisive statements about the Murray waters. His most dogmatic statement (in March 1890) was made, ironically, only a few weeks after he had proclaimed, at the Melbourne premiers' conference of February 1890 called to discuss federation, that "the crimson thread of kinship runs through us all."[35]

In the 1850s, at the inception of the tariff question, and again in the 1880s, when the use of waters question first arose, the men closely involved realized that the problems associated with the Murray could

32 Victoria V&P,LC, 1855-56, vol. 1, no. 87, pp. 9-10, Col. Sec. N.S.W. to Col. Sec. Vic. 12 September 1855.
33 Parkes at a banquet at Scott's Hotel, Melbourne, 16 May 1867. Quoted in U. R. Ellis, New Australian States (Sydney, 1933), p. 80.
34 Habgood, "Separatist Movements in N.S.W.," chapter 3.
35 The metaphor was developed from the red strand put in Royal Navy ropes for identification purposes. D. Cole, " 'The Crimson Thread of Kinship': Ethnic Ideas in Australia, 1870-1914," Historical Studies 15 (April 1971): 511n.

only be solved permanently by federation. But in the 1850s they were far too concerned with obtaining self-government at the hands of Britain to be able to adopt this solution, though they sometimes recognized that, in the long term, there was a certain inevitability about its coming. The men who were involved in the struggle to gain full control over their own local affairs from the "mother" country were not psychologically prepared to surrender even a measure of that control for the sake of easier relations with "sister" colonies. Rivalry was a more natural condition for them. It needed a later, more mature, more confident and self-assured generation of politicians to make such a surrender.

Meanwhile, inland contacts among the colonies grew with the passage of time. These threw into relief both the centrifugal and centripetal forces which operated, but it was the former which continued, for the time, to be emphasized by politicians and merchants. Even by the mid-1880s, the federal spirit had not developed sufficiently to allow of an easy solution to the new range of problems which arose. Given all this, it was no wonder that, in the next decade, when the federal movement took root and grew to maturity, the people of the river districts often proved to be the most federally minded on the continent. Throughout the 1890s it was in the Riverina that the Australasian Federation League was strongest, and it was there, and in the river ports of Victoria and South Australia, that the vote for federation was particularly high in 1898. In a real sense, the problems of this area and the reaction of people to them are an apt illustration of the argument that economic causes were vital in the attainment of Australian federation.[36]

Federation solved the customs issue by committing tariff policy entirely to the central government—it had to unless the union was to be a complete sham—but it did not at once resolve the question of the Murray waters. Not until 1914 did men realize that only a national policy could lead to the proper development and utilization of a vital natural resource. The achievement of that settlement reflected yet another constant feature of Australian federalism: it was brought about only by the injection of commonwealth funds. In turn, this gave the commonwealth a continuing role in the River Murray commission.

36 See R. Norris, "Towards a Federal Union" (chapter 10 above) and "Economic Influence on the South Australian Federation Referendum," in *Essays in Australian Federation*, ed. A. W. Martin (Melbourne, 1969), pp. 137-66. See also the following articles in J. J. Eastwood and F. B. Smith, eds., *Historical Studies, Selected Articles* (Melbourne, 1964): (1) R. S. Parker, "Australian Federation: The Influence of Economic Interests and Political Pressures"; (2) G. Blainey, "The Role of Economic Interests in Australian Federation"; (3) R. S. Parker, "Some Comments on the Role of Economic Interests in Australian Federation." See also D. I. Wright, "The Australasian Federation League in N.S.W., 1893-1899," *Journal of the Royal Australian Historical Society* 57 (March 1971): 58-73.

The reality of dependence by the states on federal funds has been the principal and obvious means by which the commonwealth has expanded its sphere of action in the political life of Australia.

The passage of time has gradually brought the three riparian states to a realization of the great interests which they have in common. This has led to an increasing emphasis on cooperation and centralized planning and control, without entirely overcoming the rivalries and jealousies which can still burst out at times in all their old animosity.[37] In this, as in so many other ways, the political history of the Murray has proved itself to be a microcosm of Australian federal history.

37 See the author's article, "Politics, Psychology and Water: Chowilla," *Australian Journal of Politics and History* 20 (December 1974): 370-79.

Epilogue

XVII

Canada and Australia: Continuing but Changing Federations

BRUCE W. HODGINS and DON WRIGHT

Within fourteen years of their creations, both the Canadian and Australian federations had actually moved significantly away in practice from the apportioning of powers and responsibilities between the centre and the units that had been arranged by the countries' respective Fathers. Yet in neither case had the formal constitutions of the two sister federations been markedly altered. Most of the Canadian Fathers, certainly Macdonald, Brown, Galt and Tupper, had wanted a strong, centralized union, a union in which politics at the centre and progressive commerce throughout the soon-to-be broad dominion would bind the new nationality together and mitigate against both geographic distance and diversity and linguistic, social, cultural and economic cleavage and conflict. Most of the Australian fathers, certainly Deakin, Barton, and Griffith, had clearly wanted a union, but a very limited union which, while establishing an Australian common market, would preserve the broad autonomy of the states. Social realities overcame the intentions of the Fathers. Territorially-based diversity and genuine sense of local and regional community made Macdonald's subordinate federalism impractical for Canada, though economic development and population concentration helped to give ascendancy to the Toronto-Montreal axis. The territorially-based, relative homogeneity and the general sense of being Australian, made limited and strictly coordinate federalism ephemeral for Australia, though the states continued to be viable and their growing capital cities continued to assert metropolitan status. Canada in 1880 and Australia in 1914 were certainly genuine federations, Canada in fact more so than it had been in 1867, but each union was moving unevenly in opposite directions along a federal line away from its point of origin. Movement along this line would continue. Enduring federalism is not static and merely constitutional. It is dynamic, often unstable. It is highly political and is ultimately rooted in territorially-oriented, social and cultural diversity.

By 1880 Canadian federalism had moved decisively away from the system of provincial subordination projected by most of the Fathers. The original plan, while noble, grand, even generous, in conception, was short on realism. The Canada of 1880 was composed of scattered and culturally diverse regions, all but one of which, the North-West, already had political viability. Three regions each had a single provincial regime to govern them, and one region, the Maritimes, had three provincial regimes. Canada had territorially-based social diversity which showed no signs of weakening. With a free, restless and open "federal society," it rested uncomfortably under a constitution which emphasized central direction. Yet all its regions were not of equal strength or extent, and all did not have equal access to the exercise of power at the central level.

The economic and social leaders in the metropolitan centres of the two strongest regions were themselves ambivalent about the direction the new polity should take. They were committed to development and expansion. They were committed to constructing provincial systems. But they were interested in nation-building as well as province-building. Although the central regime was often inappropriate as a vehicle and too insensitive to their local or provincial aspirations, that regime was, nevertheless, vital to their national aspirations. So the imperial, even mercantile, aspects of Canadian federalism continued, but these aspects continued unevenly in their impact on the various regions. In Toronto-led "Empire Ontario" the ambivalence was the greatest. Ontarians, while seeing themselves possessed of a Canadian national sense, led the battle for provincial rights and advanced the alien doctrines of classical federalism and, later, the compact theory of Confederation.[1] Yet Torontonians gradually gained greater influence over decision-making in Ottawa, especially decision-making in the economic sphere. Until at least 1900, Montreal had the edge on that economic influence, but in the long run Montreal had many disadvantages. It was farther east, while the country was developing northwestwardly, and for various reasons few of the sons and daughters of Quebec joined the western migration.[2] Furthermore, Montreal's economic leadership was in the hands of members of the English-speaking minority, while politics was almost exclusively in the hands of members of the French-speaking majority.

1 Ramsay Cook, *Provincial Autonomy, Minority Rights and the Compact Theory 1867-1921* (Ottawa, 1969); and Allan Smith, "Old Ontario and the Emergence of a National Frame of Mind," in *Aspects of Nineteenth Century Ontario*, ed. F. H. Armstrong et al. (Toronto, 1974), pp. 194-217, especially footnote 101.
2 A. I. Silver, "French Canada and the Prairie Frontier, 1870-1890," *CHR* 50 (March 1969): 11-36.

Although change away from the aims of the Fathers was evident by 1880, it became more obvious by 1896. Premier Oliver Mowat won most of his classic battles against Prime Minister Sir John A. Macdonald during the 1880s. By 1896 significant provincial victories had been upheld by the Judicial Committee of the Privy Council. In 1891, Macdonald had died, and with him went both the soul of subordinate federalism[3] and the national strength of its already faltering vehicle, the national Conservative party. That party tried but was unable to use the Canadian imperial power to reestablish tax-supported schools for the Catholics of Manitoba and to preserve the status there of the French language. Furthermore, the Conservatives of Ontario, especially the Orange Conservatives who had rejoiced in Louis Riel's hanging in 1885, refused or would have refused to back that kind of imperial thrust.[4]

In 1896 Canada under Wilfrid Laurier began its long and still continuing period of Liberal ascendancy, an ascendancy based on preponderance in Quebec and great Grit strength in Ontario. Like his *Rouge* predecessor A. A. Dorion (but minus Dorion's radicalism) and like his own first Justice Minister Sir Oliver Mowat, Laurier believed in coordinate, and not subordinate, federalism. The Laurier-Mowat entente was not the Macdonald-Cartier entente. Nevertheless the struggling Conservatives were soon accepting the main outlines of that new entente. Certainly the Conservatives who, under James Whitney, won Ontario in 1905 (and have held it ever since, with two relatively short interruptions) accepted the main outlines of both Mowat's developmental policies and his federalism. For both Ontario parties, the assumed wealth of Northern Ontario became crucial to the vision of the province's future; a centralizing Ontario manifest its own imperial thrust over a huge region which had neither provincial status nor federal territorial status.[5] Yet Laurier continued and expanded the broad features of Macdonald's national policy and showed little reluctance in exercising an imperial role over the West and the Maritimes. Under Interior Minister Clifford Sifton and his successors, immigration from Britain, the United States and, most significantly, from continental Europe was promoted, and the West was settled. Two more transcontinental railways, one partly government-owned and both publicly promoted, joined Macdonald's CPR in striking off from Central Canada to the Pacific.

3 W. L. Morton, "Confederation, 1870-1896: The End of the Macdonaldian Constitution and the Return to Duality," in *Canadian History Since Confederation*, eds. Bruce Hodgins and Robert Page (Georgetown, 1972), pp. 189-208.
4 Lovell C. Clark, "The Conservative Party in the 1890's," in *Canadian History Since Confederation*, pp. 261-79.
5 H. V. Nelles, *The Politics of Development: Forests, Mines and Hydro-Electric Power in Ontario, 1849-1941* (Toronto, 1974). For British Columbian parallels note Martin Robin, *The Rush for Spoils: the Company Province, 1871-1933* (Toronto, 1972).

When Laurier took power well over half of the real estate of Canada was not part of any province. Laurier delayed creating new provinces in the North-West until 1905. He then followed Macdonald's example with tiny Manitoba in not giving the new Saskatchewan and Alberta control over their natural resources, including land. Until 1930, the prairie provinces had special status in reverse. Although Laurier tried, he was unable, mainly because of Ontario objections,[6] to guarantee most of the traditional linguistic rights of the French-speaking minority or the educational rights of the Catholic minority in the two new provinces.

By 1910 the North-West, now the Prairie Provinces, had articulated a set of grievances which were henceforth to be a continuing part of Canadian federalism. This low tariff region derived its wealth from the exploitation of agriculture. Its people comprised a mixed lot of colonists from eastern Canada and abroad. It had formulated an identity different from other regions. Now it objected to some of the basic tenets of Canadian national policy which it saw as a "new feudalism."[7] The region, diverse within itself, was frustrated by its collective weakness in Ottawa.

World War I had similar effects on federalism in both Australia and Canada. The war centralized power. But whereas this moved Australia further from the aims of its founders, the war briefly and unevenly moved Canada back toward the aims of its founders. Prime Minister Sir Robert Borden, as leader first of his Conservative regime and then as leader of the Unionist forces, exercised the kind of control over manpower and the economy which Sir John A. would have relished. But just before the war began, he extended northward the boundary of Manitoba to give it equality with the other western provinces; he also extended Ontario and Quebec northward to the shores of James Bay, Hudson Bay and Hudson Straits where they heretofore had had no influence. This further unbalanced an already unbalanced federalism and encouraged the provincial aspects of the imperialism of Central Canada.[8] Two fundamental aspects of the Macdonaldian constitution had been the central protection of minority rights and the continued viability of the French fact. This had severely limited majoritarianism. War-time conscription, over French-Canadian objections, was heavy-handed majoritarianism and hence

---

6 Edward McCartney, "The Interests of the Central Canadian Press, Particularly the Toronto Press, in the Autonomy Bills, 1905," in *Canadian History Since Confederation*, pp. 317-33.

7 Paul Rutherford, "The Western Press and Regionalism, 1870-1896," *CHR* 52 (September 1971): 287-304; W. L. Morton, *The Progressive Party in Canada* (Toronto, 1950); Vernon C. Fowke, *The National Policy and the Wheat Economy* (Toronto, 1957); Edward Porritt, *The Revolt in Canada Against the New Feudalism* (London, 1911), and his *Sixty Years of Protection in Canada* (Winnipeg, 1913).

8 Bruce W. Hodgins, *Maritime Claims Relative to the Prairie Provinces "Land" Subsidy and to the Northern Lands Question* (Charlottetown, 1957).

not Macdonaldian. Borden's Unionist government was made up of Conservatives and English-speaking Liberals. This alliance was not the Macdonald-Cartier entente. As in 1759-63 and 1837-41, Quebec was contained by superior force. In the end it all passed over. The Conservatives were reduced, briefly, to third party status, thanks to the total alienation of French Canada and English-speaking Montreal and to the political rebellion of the West and the farmers of Ontario.

In the 1920s and 1930s the prewar trends reasserted themselves, and, if anything , Canada became even more decentralized. This was what most Canadians seemed to want, and the trends were generally reinforced by the courts.[9] As the sphere of governmental activities expanded in general, the areas of social welfare, education, resource management and highways, areas which fell into provincial jurisdiction, expanded the more dramatically. The financial resources of most of the provinces other than Ontario proved inadequate to the task. Nevertheless, during the Depression, political dynamism was more in evidence in the provinces, with Mitchell Hepburn, Maurice Duplessis, William Aberhart, Duff Pattullo and Angus Macdonald, than in the centre, with R. B. Bennett and W. L. M. King. When in 1935 Bennett finally tried to move, his interventionist New Deal was thrown out by the courts. The Depression was not, apparently, to be confused with a national emergency such as the war—or alcoholism during the 1870s.

Meanwhile, much of Canadian labour and the intelligentsia was becoming increasingly centralist. It was the dawn of the age of planning and of expanding bureaucracy. Social democrats came together in the party which they called the CCF, backed by the highly centralist and Fabian-like League for Social Reconstruction.[10] King—"Do nothing by halves which can be done by quarters"[11]—established a royal commission, the Rowell-Sirois Commission, to investigate Canadian federalism.[12] In many provincial quarters, especially in Ontario, Quebec and Alberta, it met with noncooperation. When, during the Battle of Britain in 1940, it finally reported on problems of federalism during the Depression, it advocated continued and renewed coordinate federalism. Fiscal resources were to be somewhat redefined to help the provinces, the provinces were to give up their responsibility for unemployment insurance, and poorer provinces were to receive statutory national adjustment grants. Both levels were to become

9 Alan C. Cairns, "The Judicial Committee and its Critics," *Canadian Journal of Political Science* 4 (September 1971): 32-41.
10 Michiel Horn, "The League for Social Reconstruction and the Development of a Canadian Socialism, 1932-1936," *Journal of Canadian Studies* 7 (November 1972): 3-17.
11 From the poem, "W.L.M.K.," by Frank Scott, in *The Blasted Pine* (Toronto, 1963), pp. 27-28.
12 Donald V. Smiley, ed., *The Rowell-Sirois Report* (Toronto, 1963), and his *The Canadian Political Nationality* (Toronto, 1967).

stronger and more indepednent of one another. The provincial-rights provinces rejected the report.

Nevertheless, 1940 to 1960 could be called the great period of Canadian centralism. The Second World War proved even more conducive to federal initiative than had the First. Provincial rights, except for part of the time in Quebec, became unpatriotic. The centralist academic planners entered the senior ranks of the federal civil service. From 1943 to 1945, the CCF seriously threatened King on his left and helped move him into a dynamic late-war and post-war activist phase with regard to social security and fiscal policy. After the war, fear of another depression (and therefore possible social revolt) continued the centralist intervention.[13] In the cabinet, C. D. Howe managed the post-war reconstruction, expansion and fantastic boom—with the almost full support of the central Canadian business communities. In Canada, the Liberal party seemed itself alone to be fulfilling the functions which in Australia were bitterly divided between the Labor party and the Liberal party. A.R.M. Lower, the great whig historian, suggested in 1948—as Gough Whitlam did in 1971 for Australia—that what Canada needed were more and smaller provinces. Ontario should be split into five provinces based logically on socioeconomic interests. All this would facilitate national development, just as a multitude of states had facilitated American development.[14] J. A. Corry, one of the country's leading political scientists, argued that provincial rights were outdated, that federalism should continue to exist mainly to mitigate against the curse of bigness; the future lay with the centre.[15] Despite the negative attitudes of the reactionary Duplessis in Quebec, English Canadians under Prime Minister St. Laurent seemed to believe that national problems caused by English-French differences were fast being solved; Canadians, during these years, relished telling lesser breeds round the world how to solve their own divisive domestic problems. The Canadian Broadcasting Corporation expanded, and the Massey Commission successfully recommended major federal contributions to national (but bilingual) culture and post-secondary education. A Canadian identity, at least a general English-Canadian identity to match the French-Canadian identity which already existed, was being discovered. Furthermore, the victory of John Diefenbaker in 1957 was not in any major way directed against the Liberals' centralism; it was more against their arrogance, elitism, and neglect of the Atlantic Provinces and the West (politically evident in 1958).

Then in the 1960s came the Quiet Revolution in Quebec. The great movement for social and intellectual change coincided with the

---

13 *Canadian Economic Policy and the War* (Canadian Trade Committee, Ottawa, 1966).
14 *Maclean's*, 15 October 1948, reprinted in *History and Myth: Arthur Lower and the Making of Canadian Nationalism*, ed. Welf H. Heick (Vancouver, 1975), pp. 175-84.
15 J. A. Corry, *Democratic Government and Politics* (Toronto, 1946).

North American revolt against bigness, world-wide political turbulence, the world-wide revival of the intellectual respectability of decentralism,[16] diversity and separatism, and finally the profound alienation of Western Canada. These currents made the previous twenty years into a mere interlude in Canada's trend toward uneven decentralism within a lasting federal framework—lasting probably even if Quebec ultimately separated. Without Quebec's "*épanouissement*" and its new-found commitment to secular change, would Canada instead have followed Australia's trend toward increasing centralism? Perhaps. But, more likely, probably not. The various regions of Canada had remained diverse and had grown in sophistication and in the diversity of their political cultures. The single English Canada seemed more elusive than ever.[17] In Ottawa, the later Diefenbaker years and the Pearson years seemed like ones of drift.

P. E. Trudeau entered federal Liberal politics and became prime minister, allegedly to stop Quebec separatism and to restore true coordinate federalism based solidly on bilingualism, biculturalism and individual rights. Yet in the West and in the Atlantic Provinces, Trudeau, the *Reports* of the Royal Commission on Bilingualism and Biculturalism, and the Official Languages Act (1969) all seemed to be concerning themselves, typically, with a Central Canadian problem. As in 1864, Central Canada was using the rest of British North America to solve a domestic dilemma. The continuation in Ottawa of policies which seemed more imperial than truly national only served to strengthen that conviction. The myriad number of federal-provincial conferences—which were both elitist and wholly executive and appeared unreal to so many people—led to the Victoria Charter of 1971.[18] It and other reports proposed a revised constitution, finally with its own amending formula, based on flexible and rather decentralized coordinate federalism, recognizing wide regional diversity and complexity, and allowing for delegation of power each way. But, mainly because of Quebec, it came all again to naught, at least officially.

In the 1970s new elements were added which gave added depth to continued but uneven decentralism. First and most importantly, the West, both Prairie and Pacific, with increased population and wealth, secured more leverage. A Vancouver-Edmonton axis (despite its in-

16 George Woodcock, *The Rejection of Politics and Other Essays on Canada, Canadians, Anarchism and the World* (Toronto, 1972); *Nationalism or Local Control: Responses to George Woodcock*, eds. Viv Nelles and Abraham Rotstein (Toronto, 1973): J. M. S. Careless, "Limited Identities in Canada," *CHR* 50 (March 1969): 1-10; and Allan Smith, "Metaphor and Nationality in North America," *CHR* 51 (September 1970): 247-75.

17 Ramsay Cook, *Canada and the French-Canadian Question* (Toronto, 1966).

18 Canada, *Constitutional Conference Proceedings: Victoria, British Columbia, June 14, 1971* (Ottawa, 1971). Note also Canada, *The Special Joint Committee of the Senate and of the House of Commons on the Constitution of Canada: Final Report* (Ottawa, 1972).

ternal rivalries and contradictions) might yet challenge the old Toronto-Montreal axis (with its old internal rivalries). Alberta had oil and natural gas, and both cities were strategically located to exploit the alleged resource wealth of the far North. The West had its own image of Canada. This image had previously involved a one-Canada emphasis, a melting pot dominated by the rather bland Anglo-Celtic taste. As its diverse European population had grown to political maturity, this had finally given way to the concept of the mosaic or multiculturalism under the continued ascendancy of the English language. In this mosaic, the French were only one group among many, and far from the most numerous or significant. Trudeau adjusted his official description of the country to bilingualism and multiculturalism. This was welcomed in the West and in the new cosmopolitan Toronto, but it was not nearly enough, and it was rejected forthrightly in French Quebec. For the West, the answer was either much more meaningful autonomy or a radical redirection of national policies, or, typically, probably both. When, during the energy crisis, Alberta's Premier seemed to some to be holding Central Canada to ransom like an Arab sheik, his fellow Conservative Premier of Ontario called for strong federal initiative and denounced the Alberta version of provincial rights. Ottawa and Edmonton engaged in the bilateral feuds and decisive talks which had once been so common between Ottawa and Toronto or Ottawa and Quebec City.

But continued decentralism in the mid-seventies had other supports. Some of the big cities, especially Toronto, and other municipal bodies and voluntary community organizations elected reformers to office who seriously resisted even provincial centralism and development; they harkened back to old community-centred local initiative and decision-making. Meanwhile, the moderate left in the New Democratic Party, having discarded the centralist solution, gained power in three out of four of the western provinces and held the official opposition in Ontario. Although by the end of 1977 it had lost power in all but Saskatchewan and slipped back to strong third place in Ontario, this limited success for social democracy indicated that the decentralized Canadian federation could sustain, despite its regional diversity, a system of creative politics based at least in part, as in Australia, on ideological and class differences.[19]

Canada's central government, meanwhile, had not lost all its capacity to act decisively. Late in 1975, when Trudeau launched his major anti-inflationary programme, he was initiating a system of economic controls unprecedented in peacetime. Its basic legislation was

19 John Porter, *The Vertical Mosaic* (Toronto, 1965), pp. 373-85; and Bruce W. Hodgins, "The Bankruptcy of Consensus Politics in Canada," *South Atlantic Quarterly* 65 (Summer 1966): 325-44.

defended (as was the implementation in 1970 against the FLQ of the War Measures Act) under the "peace, order, and good government" (POGG) clause of section 91 of the BNA Act. Unlike Bennett's initiative in 1935, Trudeau's was basically upheld by the centrally-appointed Supreme Court of Canada. It was also supported by the politically and economically beleaguered Conservative Premier of Ontario, who even placed Ontario civil servants and teachers under the severe wage restraints of the federal act.

Then, on 15 November 1976, the nationalist *Parti québécois* under René Levesque won a decisive victory at the Quebec polls. Dedicated as its *raison d'être* to the peaceful achievement of sovereign independence for Quebec, the party had promised to promote good, reform government and not to move to secession before receiving democratic approval from the people, in a plebescite or referendum to be held before the next provincial election. Made up of social democrats, economic liberals (even continentalists) and old-line nationalists, the *Parti québécois* enacted legislation making Quebec officially unilingually French, with a recognition of the historic educational rights of the established, nonimmigrant English-speaking minority. While promoting its dependent relationship with the New York money market, the new regime emphasized its commitment to a common market type of association between an independent Quebec and the rest of Canada. The future Quebec would be a unitary state associated outside and beyond the confines of even decentralized federation, with the continuing Canada which, presumably, would remain a federation. While surveys indicated that a majority of even the French-speaking citizens of Quebec were not yet prepared to accept full independence, the percentage so-prepared was rapidly growing, and a majority clearly favoured more power for Quebec.[20] While the central government, with francophone ministers in an unprecedented number of crucial portfolios, continued to stress official bilingualism, but with less emphasis on personal bilingualism, it basically stood for "national unity" and continued flexible, functional federalism without a special constitutional position for Quebec. The vague and diffused response in English-speaking Canada revealed, however, that entity's still tenuous nature.[21] But the advocacy, in response to the *Parti québécois* victory, of reform in the direction of more decentralism, of more power to provinces, was on the increase.[22]

20 *Toronto Star*, 24 September 1977 and the next few subsequent issues.
21 Committee for a New Constitution, "Canada and Quebec: A Proposal for a New Constitution," *Canadian Forum* 67 (June-July 1977): 4-5; Ralph Heintzman, "A Future as Well as a Past" [the editorial], and "Thinking About Separation: les conséquences de l'élection du 15 novembre 1976," *Journal of Canadian Studies* 12 (special issue, July 1977): 1-2, 128-35; and Bruce W. Hodgins and Denis Smith, "Canada and Quebec: Facing the Reality," ibid., pp. 124-26.
22 *Toronto Star*, 24 September 1977 and subsequent issues; "Power to the Provinces"

At the same time, the West and the Maritimes hardly appear less alienated from the centre than before the *Parti québécois* victory, though clearly for the Maritimes a major new devolution of power from the centre and the concomitant decline in available equalization payments and programmes for the disadvantaged but relatively static provincial regimes would hardly advance genuine democratic decentralization.[23] Furthermore, many of the nonfrancophone thrusts for meaningful local self-determination in Canada do not fit provincial boundaries. This is particularly true with regard to the assertions of the Dene nation in the Mackenzie Valley of the Northwest Territories,[24] the anti-French Inuit "rising" in the Ungava area of far northern Quebec, and the growing alienation of northern Ontarians from their far off imperial centre of Toronto.

The relatively poor performance of the Canadian economy in recent years, coupled with the increasing interlocking of much of the Canadian corporate elite with the American-dominated branch plant manufacturing and resource-extracting industries, may, moreover, be in the process of destroying the Macdonaldian east-west basis of the union.[25] If this process were to continue, the new continental economic system might be more important than the traditional vitality of regional cultural diversity in promoting political decentralization. Then it would be sensible for Quebec and Alberta each to prefer to deal with the centres of real powers south of the border rather than with the derivative, bureaucratic centre in Ottawa.

On the other hand, the relative calm with which the country debates its possible reorganization or dismemberment, the relative lack of verbal abuse and physical violence and the widespread rejection of military force as an element in any solution, may be an indication of great social and political maturity and sophistication. It may indicate that the Canadian federation in one form or another, with Quebec a part of it or associated some way with it, may long endure. Certainly, for the moment, Canada remains clearly within the federal spectrum[26]

[editorial], *Globe and Mail*, 2 February 1977; and Northrop Frye, "Lively Culture the Answer to Canadian Unity," *Globe and Mail*, 18 October 1977.

23 George A. Rawlyk, "Quebec's Separation and the Atlantic Provinces," in *Must Canada Fail?* ed. Richard Simeon (Montreal, 1977). Note also the essays by Richard Simeon, John Archer, John Trent and Edwin R. Black in the same volume. Note also Gary Geddes, ed., *Divided We Stand* (Toronto, 1977).

24 Mr. Justice Thomas R. Berger, *Northern Frontier: Northern Homeland: The Report of the Mackenzie Valley Pipeline Inquiry*, vol. 1 (Ottawa, 1977), and Mel Watkins, ed., *The Dene Nation: The Colony Within* (Toronto, 1977).

25 Wallace Clement, *Continental Corporate Power: Economic Linkages Between Canada and the United States* (Toronto, 1977).

26 Note Edwin R. Black, *Divided Loyalties: Canadian Concepts of Federalism* (Montreal, 1975); and Michael Stern, "Federal Political Systems and Federal Societies," in *Canadian Federalism: Myth or Reality*, ed. J. Peter Meekison (2nd ed., Toronto, 1971), pp. 30-42.

though at the opposite end from that envisioned by the Canadian
Fathers.

* * * * *

If, in the period 1901-14, Australian federalism began to show a
tendency to move away from the coordinate structure envisaged by the
founders towards a more centralized position—towards something
more like the subordinate federalism enacted thirty years earlier by
their Canadian cousins—that trend did not then cease.[27] The fundamental truth of this thesis may be quickly illustrated.

The struggles of the states and the commonwealth in the 1920s to
find an adequate solution to the perennial dilemma of financial relations; the inability of the commonwealth to solve the problem of divided control of industrial arbitration, and the activities of the "new
staters" in New South Wales, all led to or indicated growing dissatisfaction with the operation of the constitution. In 1927, the Bruce-Page
(Nationalist) government appointed a royal commission to investigate
the whole problem.

The report of this commission, issued in 1929,[28] acknowledged the
inconvenience of the federal system for ministers and parliaments, but
came down heavily in favour of its retention. Federalism allowed the
development of public spirit and local patriotism in the states further
removed from the seat of central government; it provided the best
means of supervising development; it was the best safeguard against
some dangerous legislative experiment. Greater cooperation was
needed, and, in the light of experience, readjustment of the division of
powers was warranted; but the concentration of all legislative and
executive functions in the hands of one authority was likely to produce
"paralysis at the centre and anaemia at the circumference."

No action was taken as a result of the report.

At much the same time, W. K. Hancock wrote that the average
citizen still looked more frequently to his state government rather than
the commonwealth government. "It is," he said, "this closer, more
intimate Government which protects him from the wicked, educates
him, watches over his health . . . performs, in short, all those functions
which seem to affect most nearly his economic and social well-being."
Even the radicals, who preached unification and clearly preferred to
"stake everything on the issue of one struggle for the control of one
Government," had to accept the facts which gave meaning to Australian
federalism and use them to whatever advantage they could. But,

27 It was the financial problem of the post-World War One years which led eventually to
    the abortive W.A. secession movement of the 1930s.
28 "Report of the Royal Commission on the Constitution," *CPP*, 1929-1931, vol. 2.

"[c]ontrol of the Federal Government [was], nevertheless, the great prize of political struggle."[29]

Twenty years later, at a seminar at the Australian National University (the very existence of which was a monument to change), P. H. Partridge felt able to argue a different, less complex, line. Contrary to the views of the founders, there were no "distinct and decisive" state interests which could be represented separately. The federal system continued only by its own momentum. There was no popular loyalty towards the states as such, no "lively conviction that . . . the people of the State ought to be free to govern themselves, ought not to be subject to the remote and alien government in Canberra. . . ." There were no longer any "solid social or economic foundations for political divisions within the federal structure."[30]

Another commentator, J. D. B. Miller, pointed out that while this view was acceptable for the large states, Victoria and New South Wales, which were both economic microcosms of the whole country and had a balance of rural and industrial wealth, it was not wholly so for the smaller states. True, there were no great social cleavages, but there was, he held, a strong sense of loyalty to the political unit in those areas, possibly "a sense of locality nourished upon resentment" of the larger states and the commonwealth. There was, too, a degree of economic separateness which was significant.[31]

Another twenty years on, in 1970, social difference was even less evident. True, only New South Wales had poker machines; true, the Murray (or, perhaps, the Murrumbidgee) was still the great divide between rival football codes; and men might argue over the relative merits of the products of the Swan, Carlton and West End breweries. But there was little other differentiation in social mores or in culture, whether "high" or "popular."

In 1970 political and administrative federalism still persisted. It was in difficulties, but seemed likely to continue to persist.

On 6 October 1970, the Victorian Attorney General moved a resolution in the Victorian House of Assembly calling for an all-states convention to discuss potential amendments to the constitution. Supporting his motion, he argued that "[w]e [the states] are in grave danger of becoming colonial dependencies of Canberra."[32]

The root cause of Victorian dissatisfaction was finance—the fact that the commonwealth controlled all the major sources of revenue (especially those with a capability for growth) and that it did not return

29 W. K. Hancock, *Australia* (London, 1945 [first published in 1930]), pp. 64-65.
30 P. H. Partridge, "The Politics of Federalism," in *Federalism, An Australian Jubilee Study*, ed. G. Sawer (Melbourne, 1952), especially pp. 175, 192-95. Partridge was Professor of Social Philosophy at the Australian National University.
31 J. D. B. Miller, *Australian Government and Politics* (London, 1954), especially pp. 121-43.
32 *Victorian Parliamentary Debates*, 6 October 1970, p. 715.

adequate funds to the states for them to perform their constitutional functions. A few days before Reid's motion, the Liberal Premier of Victoria, Sir Henry Bolte, had argued in his budget speech that autonomous budgeting by state governments was becoming a myth in view of federal control of funds, and he lamented that "the trend is quickening for more and more of the purposes of government to be determined in Canberra."[33]

Other state governments were no happier with the working of the federal relationship than the Victorian, and for the same reason, because the division of the financial cake was causing "anaemia at the circumference," though not "paralysis at the centre." As Don Dunstan, Labor Premier of South Australia, had said a little earlier, "The states have the responsibility for an enormous area of public activity and yet no effective revenue powers to cover their responsibility."[34]

The long-sought convention was finally held in September 1973. By this time, Sir Henry Bolte had passed from the political scene and the federal Liberal government had been replaced by Labor.

The new Prime Minister, E. G. Whitlam, had for some time been the apostle of what he called "new federalism." According to him, this concept involved "not domination but consultation, not centralisation but co-ordination." However, this consultation and coordination would, if Whitlam had his way, take place not with the "anachronistic" states whose meaningless boundaries had been devised more than a century ago, but with a larger number of regional councils possessing more limited powers. There would be what he called "a delegated but supervised system of local government." Power would be returned to the people (and here his political radicalism shows out) because the new federalism would "rest on a national framework for the establishment of investment priorities and a regional framework for participation in all those decisions which most directly determine the quality of our lives."[35]

He clearly recognized the difficulty of achieving this in the face of opposition from the states, even those governed by Labor. Indeed, his party had proved willing to include only a modified version of his proposal in its platform. The relevant plank now sought amendment of the constitution "to balance the functions and finances of the Commonwealth, State and local Government to ensure adequate services and development of resources."[36] Apparently state Labor men had forced a measure of compromise from him.

33 Ibid., 29 September 1970, pp. 405-23. For Dunstan's remark, see extract from *Lot's Wife*, 27 July 1967, quoted in *Australian Politics, A Second Reader*, ed. H. Mayer (Melbourne, 1967), p. 85.
34 *Sydney Morning Herald*, 8 October 1970.
35 E. G. Whitlam, "A New Federalism," *Australian Quarterly* 43 (September 1971): 3-17, especially 11, 17.
36 Ibid., p. 6.

Even this, however, was anathema to a Country party Premier, like Bjelke Petersen of Queensland, who feared that the growth of central power would encourage sinister practices. For him, it was likely to lead, in our children's time at least, he argued, to "a system of government involving fear and the midnight doorknock."[37] Probably few outside Queensland, however, were able to take him seriously.

Like the 1929 commission, the convention gave every appearance of achieving nothing. The only aspect of the debate at the opening session which caught the public ear was the squabble over whether the states should surrender to the commonwealth the right (which most did not exercise to any great extent) to control prices, and the question of what added financial security the commonwealth might give to the states as a *quid pro quo* for the surrender of additional powers which would enable it to control the national economy better. The new Liberal Premier of Victoria, Dick Hamer, sought the implementation of what he deliberately called the "Canadian system," whereby the federal government returns to each province a substantial percentage of the income tax collected in it. Whitlam rejected this outright, closely echoing his centralist Liberal predecessor, John Gorton, who, three years earlier, had rejected a similar proposal from Sir Henry Bolte.[38] The passage of another three years and another election saw a modified version of this scheme thrust upon the states by the highly conservative Liberal-National Country party government of Malcolm Fraser, though it was then linked with a programme of tax indexing which ensured that the state revenue still would not grow as freely as the premiers hoped.

A second session of the convention met under the shadow of the 1975 dismissal of the Whitlam government by the Governor General, Sir John Kerr, and achieved little. It is clear that no carefully planned updating of the constitution will emanate from it and that it will not become a memorable landmark in Australian history. Indeed, it is irrelevant. In May 1977 four proposals for constitutional change were put to the electorate. The most important, one for simultaneous elections to the Senate and House of Representatives, which had the support of the major national parties, was opposed by a few dissident Liberal senators and by sections of the Liberal and/or National Country party in some states on the ground that it would infringe the rights of the Senate and the states, and failed to secure the double majority of electors and states necessary for it to become law.

37 *Australian*, 12 May 1973.
38 Ibid., 5 September 1973. For Gorton's earlier rejection of the similar proposal, see ibid., 27 February 1970. For a detailed assessment of the 1973 convention see J. E. Richardson, "The Australian Constitutional Convention, Sydney 1973," *Australian Quarterly* 45 (December 1973): 90-113.

Politically and administratively Australia will retain a federal structure for the indefinite future. When a federal Labor government is in office the threat to the states will appear marginally greater than under the Liberal-National Country party alternative, but the difference will be one of rhetoric rather than reality. Under no foreseeable government will the trend established before 1914 be reversed. Because Australian federalism is based not on genuine social divisions (for, as one writer of the federation period proclaimed, "Our country, by the law of God, is one and indivisible"),[39] but rather on political and administrative convenience, it cannot be the federalism envisaged by the founders, whose plans have long since been frustrated.

*   *   *   *   *

Just as each generation must rewrite its history, so each generation in a complex society must reexamine and reinterpret its federalism. Indeed federalism itself is an essentially contested concept.[40] Some observers would emphasize its aspects of unity while others would emphasize its aspects of diversity and disunity. Some liberal traditionalists would stress the value in limiting the power of government through division of that power; others would extoll the benefit of cooperation and integration amid a continuing dispersal of implementation and administration. But if a dynamic society continues to operate meaningfully within some variant of the federal context, that federalism itself will remain unstable and contested. In 1867 and 1901, British North Americans and Australians formed federal unions. The nature of these unions so formed flowed logically out of the colonial experiences as perceived by the respective dominant progenitors of those unions. The dynamic nature of the two societies, one more "federal" or territorially diverse than the other, affected the direction and thrust of their respective federalism.

The small group of Anglo-Canadian politicians who with their Franco-Canadian colleagues met in Charlottetown and Quebec with their Maritime counterparts, wanted to expand their political economic influence northwestward over half a continent in the face of strong American competition, British retrenchment and a restless native population. They were troubled by their apparent inability to keep their officially unitary but actually dualistic province functioning satisfactorily while promoting that ambitious design. One or two of their French-speaking colleagues shared this vision and frustration, but all

39 R. Thompson, *Australian Nationalism* (Burwood, 1888), p. 35.
40 See Edgar M. Arundell's forthcoming master's thesis for the University of Western Australia in which this Canadian scholar argues that federalism fits the category of being "an essentially contested concept," a category developed by William F. Connelly in his *The Terms of Political Discourse* (Lexington, 1974). Note also J. Holmes and C. Sharman, *The Australian Federal System* (Sydney, 1977).

of them, less troubled by the status quo, were concerned lest the restless majoritarianism of relatively recent English-speaking arrivals threatened *la survivance* of *le petit nation.* Accommodation was essential. Maritime unionists convinced themselves that the economy of their region would expand with better inland markets and transportation links and that they themselves would have a more appropriate national stage for their legitimate political ambitions. And south of all the scattered borders lay an expansive, rather unsympathetic neighbour whose recent civil war showed the dangers of decentralization and states rights and whose new-found greater centralization and therefore strength posed a seemingly greater threat than ever. Deep social division, great ambition coupled with great distances and exposure to immediate outside danger all convinced the conservative and predemocratic liberal leadership that a highly centralized union was desirable. The very enduring centrifugal forces which the union was supposed to overcome helped to ensure that the centralized nature of the union would not long endure.

The Australian leaders, from five of the six colonies, who met in Adelaide, Sydney and Melbourne, had limited objectives. An Australian society was already emerging. The dry interior of the island continent was clearly Australian. Away from this interior were not foreign borders but the common seas, apparently still dominated by the Royal Navy. Although isolated and exposed, far from mother Britain, the Australians did not perceive the Asian threat as imminent nor did they then regard union as decisive to its containment. But democratic union would enhance a logical mutual destiny, and the establishment of a common market would, they anticipated, promote economic expansion and prosperity. Only a limited union was necessary. Only a relatively decentralized federation could secure the ratification of the deeply democratic but rather constitutionally lethargic populace. The very enduring but soft centripetal tendencies which the union movement expressed, helped ensure that the decentralized nature of that union would be ephemeral.

Appendices

Appendix A

I. Chronology: The Achievement of Canadian Federal Union

1864 – (March) Province of Canada: fall of the John Sandfield Macdonald Reform government. Attempt at coalition fails.

– (June) Canada: fall of Taché-John A. Macdonald Conservative government. Report of constitutional committee in favour of using the federal system applied either to the Province of Canada alone or all of the British North American provinces. Political reconciliation of George Brown (Grit Reformer) and John A. Macdonald (Conservative). Coalition formed (Taché, Macdonald, Cartier, Brown, Galt) to work for the federal principle in Canada "coupled" with provisions for admission of other British North American provinces. Canadian cabinet works out basic plan.

– (September) Charlottetown Conference called ostensibly to consider Maritime union of Nova Scotia, New Brunswick and Prince Edward Island. Canadians ask and are allowed to attend and present broader idea. Preliminary plan drawn up.

– (October) Quebec Conference: delegates from all eastern provinces draw up 72 Quebec Resolutions on basic plan for union.

– Brown goes to London. Colonial Office enthusiastic about union.

1865 – (February-March) Canadian legislature in Quebec City debates and approves Quebec Resolutions by a "double majority."

– (March) New Brunswick electorate defeats pro-union Tilley government; Prince Edward Island legislature rejects union.

1866 – New Brunswick constitutional crisis leads to another election; pro-unionist forces win, and new government is authorized to carry on discussions about union; Nova Scotia legislature authorizes Tupper government merely to carry on further discussions about union.

- (July-August)   Canada: legislature meeting in Ottawa adopts constitutional structure for Ontario and Quebec.

- (December)   Westminster Palace Conference in London on union.

1867 - (January)   London Conference draws up resolutions which are a modified version of the Quebec Resolutions.

- (March)   BNA Act passes British parliament.

- (July 1)   Canada (now divided into Ontario and Quebec), Nova Scotia and New Brunswick united in federal union.

1870 - Rupert's Land and North-Western Territory transferred to the Canadian union; tiny Manitoba on the Red River created by federal parliament; the remainder of the land transferred is called the Northwest Territories.

1871 - British Columbia joins Canada.

1873 - Prince Edward Island joins Canada.

II. Chronology: The Achievement of Australian Federal Union

1890 - (February)   Conference in Melbourne decides it is feasible to frame a constitution for a federalist Australia.

1891 - (March)   Constitution drafted at first federal convention in Sydney, presided over by Sir Henry Parkes. It does not pass the colonial parliaments.

1893 - (June-July)   Formation in New South Wales of the Australian Federation League which presses the federal cause there.

- (August)   Meeting of the New South Wales and Victorian Branches of the Australian Federation League and other pro-federation groups at Corowa, New South Wales, to discuss all means of promoting their cause.

1895 - (January)   Conference of colonial premiers at Hobart, where they pledge themselves to secure acts authorizing elected delegates to a federal convention to frame a constitution and submit the results of it to the people.

1896 - (November)   People's Federation Convention held at Bathurst, N.S.W., in support of Australian union.

1897 – (March)   Second federal convention held in Adelaide where 1891 constitution revised. Queensland does not attend.

   – (September)   Convention continues in Sydney, main business being consideration of amendments proposed by the colonial parliaments to the Adelaide draft.

1898 – (March)   Convention continues in Melbourne until problems solved.

   – (June)   First referendum on federation fails in New South Wales and passes in Victoria, South Australia and Tasmania.

1899 – (January)   Conference in Melbourne of the various premiers, including that of Queensland, considers such constitutional amendments as would secure the approval of the federation bill by New South Wales.

   – (June)   Bill enabling federation approved by referendum in all colonies except Western Australia.

1900 – (March)   Conference in London where Colonial Office slightly alters draft bill.

   – (July)   Federation Act passes British parliament and approved by the Queen.

   – (September)   Western Australia approves by referendum the draft of the Commonwealth of Australia Act as worded by the London Conference.

1901 – (January 1)   Inauguration of the Commonwealth of Australia.

Appendix B

Prime Ministers of Canada: 1867-91

1867-73 – Sir John A. Macdonald, Conservative, leading a Conservative-dominated coalition of Conservatives (including *Bleus*) and anti-Grit Reformers.

1873-78 – Alexander Mackenzie, Liberal (or Reform).

1878-91 – Sir John A. Macdonald, Conservative.

Prime Ministers of Australia: 1901-15

1901-03 – Edmund Barton, Liberal Protectionist

1903-04 – Alfred Deakin, Liberal Protectionist.

1904   – (April-August) J. C. Watson, Labor, heading Labor government supported by radical liberals.

1904-05 – (July) George Reid, Free Trade, heading Free Trade-Protectionist coalition.

1905-08 – Alfred Deakin, Liberal Protectionist, heading a Liberal government supported by Labor.

1908-09 – Andrew Fisher, Labor.

1909-10 – Alfred Deakin, Liberal Protectionist, heading Liberal-Conservative coalition, the first effective union of non-Labor forces.

1910-13 – Andrew Fisher, Labor.

1913-14 – Joseph Cook, Liberal.

1914-15 – Andrew Fisher, Labor.

Index